Symbol	Meaning	Pages
‖	Lack of **parallelism**	91–93
PV	**Point of view** vague or shifted	13–14
Red	**Redundant** (wordy)	67–68, 98–100
Ref	Faulty **reference** of pronouns	290–292
Rep	Weakening **repetition**	67–68, 98–100
S, SS, or St	Faulty **sentence structure**	76–109
Shift	**Shifted** construction	92, 296
sp	Wrong **spelling**	340–357
Sub	Faulty **subordination** or coordination	82–86
T	Wrong **tense**	295–296
tr	**Transpose** words, phrases, or letters	
Trans	Faulty **transition**	53–54, 69
Vag	**Vague**	8–9
Var	Lack of sentence **variety**	101–102
Wdy	**Wordy**	67–68, 98–100
WW	**Wrong word**	131–132
⊙	Insert period	316–317
?/	Insert question mark	317
!/	Insert exclamation point	317–318
⌃	Insert comma	318–327
;/	Insert semicolon	327–328
:/	Insert colon	328–329
᪾/᪾	Insert quotation marks	330–333
᪾	Insert single quotation mark or apostrophe	332, 347–348
$\frac{1}{M}$	Insert dash (two hyphens on typewriter)	333–334
=	Insert hyphen	348–349
(/)	Insert parentheses	335
[/]	Insert square brackets	335–336
⌃	Caret designating omission	42
ꝏ	Delete (throw out)	
⌒	Close up (*double‿speak*)	
#	Separate; leave a space	
?	Do you mean this? Is it correct? or clear?	
X	Obvious error	

An
American
Rhetoric

FIFTH EDITION

An American Rhetoric

William W. Watt
Lafayette College

Holt, Rinehart and Winston, Inc.
Fort Worth   Chicago   San Francisco   Philadelphia
Montreal   Toronto   London   Sydney   Tokyo

Library of Congress Cataloging in Publication Data

Watt, William W
  An American rhetoric.

  Includes index.
  1. English language—Rhetoric. I. Title.
PE1408.W443   1980   808'.042   79–19764

ISBN 0–03–044166–8

Printed in the United States of America

9 0 1 2   059   5 4 3

Acknowledgments

ROGER ANGELL. Excerpt from *Five Seasons*. Copyright © 1972, 1973, 1974, 1975 by Roger
Angell. Reprinted by permission of Simon & Schuster, a Division of Gulf & Western
Corporation. Also by permission of International Creative Management. First published in
The New Yorker. Copyright © 1977 by Roger Angell.

WINSTON CHURCHILL. Excerpt from *Blood, Sweat, and Tears*. Copyright 1941 by Winston S.
Churchill. Reprinted by permission of G. P. Putnam's Sons.

WINSTON CHURCHILL. Excerpt from *A Roving Commission: My Early Life*. Reprinted by
permission of Charles Scribner's Sons. Copyright 1930 Charles Scribner's Sons; renewal
copyright © 1958 Winston Churchill.

T. S. ELIOT. Three lines from "Little Gidding," *Four Quartets*. Copyright 1943 by T. S.
Eliot; renewed 1971 by Esme Valerie Eliot. Reprinted by permission of Harcourt Brace
Jovanovich, Inc. Also by permission of Faber and Faber, Ltd.

CHARLES FRANKEL. Excerpts from *The Case for Modern Man*, 1956; pp. 156–157,
188–189. Reprinted by permission of Harper & Row, Publishers, Inc.

LEARNED HAND. Excerpt from *The Spirit of Liberty*. Published 1952 by Alfred A. Knopf, Inc.
Reprinted by permission of the publisher.

ERNEST HEMINGWAY. Excerpt from *A Farewell to Arms*, p. 259. Reprinted by permission of
Charles Scribner's Sons. Copyright 1929 Charles Scribner's Sons; renewal copyright ©
1957 Ernest Hemingway.

ALDOUS HUXLEY. "Time and the Machine" from *The Olive Tree*. Copyright 1937 by Aldous
Huxley. Reprinted by permission of Harper & Row, Publishers. Also by permission of Mrs.
Laura Huxley and Chatto & Windus, Ltd.

Preface

For this new edition I have made the following changes, most of them in direct response to instructors and students who have used the book in classroom and study:

1. I have added numerous new illustrations and exercises.
2. I have clarified and, in some places, simplified the language to make it accessible to a wider range of readers.
3. I have made regular changes in the point of view to address the undergraduate reader directly as a presence called "you" and avoid, wherever possible, references to that absent third person called "the student."
4. Without resorting to simplistic streamlining, I have shortened some chapters to make the discussion less discursive and the key points more clear.
5. In Chapters 4, 5, 6, 10, and 11—where it seemed most feasible—I have distributed the exercises so that each follows immediately after the discussion to which it applies. This provides periodic pauses for immediate testing instead of sending the reader on a search at the end of the chapter.
6. For the specimen research paper I have included a modernized version of "Martians and Mass Hysteria," which some of my older readers may remember from the first two editions. Several friendly critics suggested that it would be hard to find a suitable subject of more general interest to undergraduates in this age of star wars.

7. I have significantly expanded the book in the following places:
   Chapter 2—to include more emphasis on pre-writing.
   Chapter 9—to enlarge the number of sample entries for footnotes and bibliography, all in strict accordance with the *MLA Handbook.*
   "A Glossary of Grammatical and Rhetorical Terms." This is a completely new supplement, included on the assumption that readers, especially the many students who come to college with little previous knowledge of grammar and rhetoric, will welcome a handy alphabetical guide to the standard nomenclature used throughout the text. This Glossary, taken together with the "Glossary of Usage" and an unusually extensive general index, should greatly increase the value of the book as a ready reference and encourage students to consult it regularly without benefit of classroom assignments.

Finally, the book has been completely redesigned and reset with larger, clearer type to make it much easier to read, study, and teach than the fourth edition.

Despite all these changes, I have not abandoned my convictions— apparently shared by thousands of other users—about what a college composition text should be: readable as well as teachable; serious but lively—never solemn or stuffy; accurate but not pedantic; complete, without trivial details; generously supplied with a variety of examples of good and bad writing, both professional and amateur; equipped with a mixed bag of practical exercises; full of useful advice based on the living language, not cluttered with awful warnings from dead rulebooks; designed to develop lively, adaptable, versatile writers, not limited specialists in "the college essay" or "the five-paragraph expository theme."

With the encouragement of my critics I have kept the basic organization of the fourth edition. "A Guide to Good Writing" (the "Rhetoric") is followed by "A Guide to Correctness" (the "Handbook") and the two Glossaries. The order of the chapters, though far from arbitrary, is not compulsory. The instructor, or whoever prescribes the local ground rules, is encouraged to take them up in whatever sequence best fits the course requirements and student needs. Whether the instructor begins with Grammar, Punctuation, or Spelling, or uses them merely for reference; or assigns Words before Sentences and Paragraphs; or postpones the introductory chapter till a final review; or entirely finesses the formal study of the Dictionary or the Research Paper; or regularly prescribes the Exercises or studiously ignores them—the book is flexible enough to allow such freedom.

I have prepared an *Instructor's Manual* that contains a detailed analysis of the exercises. It may be obtained through a local Holt representative or by writing to English Editor, College Department, Holt, Rinehart and Winston, 383 Madison Avenue, New York, N.Y. 10017.

My gratitude for extensive quotations is expressed in the proper place and form. I hereby acknowledge all debts to other sources, including the dictionaries listed in Chapter 5, the rhetorics and handbooks by my competitors, and the colleagues and students at Lafayette who have taught me more than I ever taught them. I am grateful to the following critics around the country whose useful comments first set me on the road to revision or helped to improve the final manuscript; Joanne Cockelreas, East Texas State University; Loren C. Gruber, Simpson College; Jule Kaufman, University of Cincinnati; Clemens H. Neuhaus, San Bernardino Valley College; Jim Raymond, University of Alabama; Liz Rosenberg, State University of New York at Binghamton; Robert S. Rudolph, University of Toledo; Joseph P. Sperry, Capital University; Joyce S. Steward, University of Wisconsin; Richard Tuerk, East Texas State University; William Wiley, Riverside City College.

More particularly, I want to thank two friends at Holt, Rinehart and Winston, Kenney Withers, for hospitality and encouragement, and Pamela Forcey, whose conscientious efficiency as an editor is matched only by her good judgment and cheerful patience; Richard S. Beal of Boston University, whose good-natured criticism has been consistently sensitive and sensible; Marilyn Kastenhuber, a superior departmental secretary, who interrupted her summer vacation to type the *Instructor's Manual;* and my favorite collaborator, Sidney Watt, who, as always, pulled a strong and steady oar in the galleys.

W.W.W.
Easton, Pennsylvania
November 1979

Contents

Preface   vii

I A Guide to Good Writing   1

1 Good Writing and Correct English 3
Content 5 / Originality 6 / Honesty 7 / Sincerity 8 /
Clarity 8 / Economy 9 / Correctness 10 /
Appropriateness 13 / Consistency 20 / Naturalness: Writing and
Speech 20 / Exercises 22

2 Getting Under Way 26
Something to Write About 26 / Selecting a Subject 30 / Staking
Out a Claim 31 / The First Draft 33 / Beginnings 35 /
Endings 39 / Revision 40 / The Final Draft 42 / The
Title 43 / Exercises 44

3 Organizing and Developing 46
Form and Content 46 / Four General Principles 47 /
Paragraphs 49 / The Parts and the Whole 68 /
A Summary 69 / Exercises 70

4 Sentences 76

Complete Sentences 77 / Incomplete Sentences 78 / Exercise A 79 / Exercise B 81 / Two Related Errors 81 / Exercise C 82 / Coordination and Subordination 82 / Exercise D 86 / Modifiers 87 / Exercise E 90 / Required Parallelism 91 / Faulty Comparisons 93 / Exercise F 94 / Length 94 / Exercise G 97 / Wordiness and Economy 98 / Exercise H 101 / Variety 101 / Emphasis 102 / Exercise I 106 / Summary 107 / Exercises J, K (General Review) 107

5 What's in a Word? 110

Building a Vocabulary 110 / Exercise A 111 / Choosing a Dictionary 111 / What Words to Look Up 112 / How to Look Up a Word 113 / Pronunciation 115 / Exercise B 116 / Grammar and Idioms 116 / Exercise C 117 / Etymology 117 / Exercise D 118 / Definitions 119 / Exercise E 120 / Exercise F 121 / Exercise G 126 / Synonyms and Antonyms 126 / Denotation and Connotation 127 / Exercise H 128 / The Limitations of a Dictionary 129 / Exercise I (Review) 129

6 Words in Action 131

Right and Wrong Words 131 / Exercise A 132 / Fresh and Tired Words 133 / Exercise B 135 / Exercise C 139 / Long and Short Words 140 / Concrete and Abstract Words 141 / Exercises D, E 145 / Exercise F 147 / Charged and Neutral Words 147 / Exercise G 151 / The Sound of Words 152 / Exercise H 156 / Simile and Metaphor 156 / Exercise I 161 / Summary 163 / Exercise J (Review) 163

7 Style and Tone 166

What Is Style? 166 / What Is Tone? 178 / Exercises 186

8 Clear and Cloudy Thinking 196

Prejudice vs. Opinion 196 / Definition Again 197 / Ignoring the Question 199 / Deduction vs. Induction 200 / Errors in Deductive Argument 202 / Problems of Inductive Argument 204 / Exercises 211

9 The Library Research Paper 217

What Research Is 217 / What a Research Paper Is Not 218 / Choosing and Limiting a Subject 218 / Finding Material 219 / The Preliminary Bibliography 226 / Discriminating Among Souces 229 / Note-Taking 231 / The Outline 231 / Writing the Paper 233 / Footnotes and Endnotes 237 / The Final Bibliography 243 / Reminders 244 / A Specimen Research Paper 245

II A Guide to Correctness 277

10 Grammar 279

The Importance of Terms 280 / The Parts of Speech 281 / Exercises A, B 284 / Exercise C 290 / Exercise D 292 / Exercise E 296 / Exercise F 299 / Exercise G 300 / Exercise H 303 / Agreement 304 / Exercise I 310 / Phrases and Clauses 311 / Exercises J, K 313

11 Punctuation 315

Rules and Reasons 316 / The Period 316 / The Question Mark 317 / The Exclamation Point 317 / The Comma 318 / Exercise A 320 / Exercise B 324 / The Semicolon 327 / The Colon 328 / Exercise C 330 / Quotation Marks 330 / The Dash 333 / Parentheses 335 / Square Brackets 335 / Dots (Ellipsis Points) 336 / Underlining (Italicizing) 336 / A Last Word 338 / Exercise D (General Review) 338

12 Spelling 340

Good and Bad Spellers 340 / Reading Aloud 341 / Using the Dictionary 342 / Spelling Conventions 343 / Spelling Lists 350

A Glossary of Usage 358

A Glossary of Grammatical and Rhetorical Terms 374

Index 391

Symbols for Correction and Revision   inside front cover
A Quick Questionnaire for the Writer   inside back cover
Common Mechanical Errors   inside back cover
Common Problems in Usage   inside back cover

An
American
Rhetoric

part

I

A Guide to Good Writing

1 Good Writing and Correct English

How can I tell what I think till I see what I say?

E. M. Forster

In language, as in life, it is possible to be perfectly correct—and yet perfectly tedious, or odious.

F. L. Lucas

A cartoon in a magazine depicts a disheveled scrubwoman knocking at a door labeled "Professor of the English Language" and saying timidly: "It is I." Although the professor is not in the picture, he or she is obviously an eccentric pedant who is obsessed by dangling participles and split infinitives. It is handy to have this authority around to settle occasional moot points of usage ("My friend and I have been having an argument. What is it, *ice* tea or *iced* tea?"). But the rest of the time such a professor is about as useful to society as the harmless hobbyist who gets his picture in the papers by spending seven years building a miniature Statue of Liberty with 7496 pieces of burnt toast.

Of course, all grown-up students know that this species of academic monster is actually almost extinct on the college campus. But the monster continues to haunt the classroom. Many students still enter college under the illusion that the whole duty of the English instructor is to teach "correct English" rather than good writing. Correct English consists entirely of observing a forbidding list of thou-shalt-nots; literary skill is in indirect ratio to the expenditure of red pencil in the margins; the unmarked page is perfection. "Only one measly spelling error and he gives me a C minus!" The familiar campus war cry betrays the illusion.

Another illusion follows from the first: that there is a yawning gap between writing "themes" or "compositions" for the English department and writing under any other circumstances. The English instructor is a hawk-eyed detective eager to mistake a flyspeck for a misplaced comma, but easily soothed by a fancy phrase. The biology instructor—

so goes the undergraduate myth—doesn't care how you say it as long as you get it all down somehow. One wants embroidery; the other wants facts.

The English instructor may explain patiently that English is a language, not merely a technique for passing a six-credit course in composition scheduled Monday—Wednesday—Friday at eleven; that theme-writing is simply a practical method of developing a student's powers of expression—which are related not only to writing but to speaking, reading, thinking, and listening as well; that though a student may use different strategies in writing a short "creative" composition for English, a long term paper for biology, and an essay answer in a history examination, common standards should govern them all. The biology instructor may turn out to be a highly literate purist who insists that students who can't explain the amoeba clearly haven't proved that they know an amoeba when they see one. But the illusion persists. Writing for an English course, especially writing themes, is done in a lonely, unreal world of its own.

Closely related to the other two is a third illusion: that the student in English composition must always adjust, not only to a rigid departmental code, but also to the peculiar eccentricities of the instructor drawn in the registration lottery. This notion is often revealed in the very first class of the semester when a hand pops up and a well-meaning voice says, "Professor, can you give us some idea of what kind of writing you want on these themes?" The instructor might answer something like this: "I admit I have my idiosyncrasies. I don't want you to label irony with question marks in parentheses (?) or call all persons *individuals* or write *due to the fact that* instead of *because*. Although I don't know any logical reason why we shouldn't have such a verb, I am uncomfortable whenever somebody gets *enthused* about something. And I am tired of seeing *contact* used, in the loose commercial fashion, as a verb meaning anything from waving a dotted line under a business prospect's nose to making a transatlantic phone call. These things I don't want. But in the last analysis I hope I want the same kind of writing that anybody wants if he knows good writing when he sees it."

Intelligent, educated people may differ about the particular problems of "correct English" or argue about the virtues of an experimental novel or an original play. But they do not disagree widely about the fundamentals of good writing.

There is even closer agreement about the importance of learning to write well. Students who do not regard the elementary composition course in college merely as a final dose of "English"—something to "take" like medicine or survive like measles—will find that any improvement in their writing and language sense will help them to talk more effectively, read and listen more perceptively, and think more clearly. These goals still have priority in a genuine education.

More tangible dividends will come both before and after graduation.

In many college courses, students are required to write literate reports and essay answers for instructors who do not or cannot take the time to teach composition. "Intermediate" and "advanced" courses in writing itself are merely specialized applications of the fundamental skills that must be learned first. After graduation, the ability to write may be a prerequisite to success in business or professional life or in the fulfillment of community obligations. In a lecture or sermon, a business letter or sales directive or house-organ recital, an engineering report or legal brief, a political speech or a talk to the county medical society or PTA—the basic requirements of good writing are the same. The general public, optimistically perhaps, still expects the college graduate to be able to write with a respectable degree of correctness and clarity. Whoever can write also with force and flavor, whose prose is lively and readable—not merely tolerable—is in a minority that may be growing more select as the mechanized years tick by. This is not an academic sermon; it is the testament of thousands of college graduates, many of whom have awakened too late to a full awareness of the value of a discipline they neglected in college.

The fundamentals of good writing will be discussed in detail in various places throughout this book. But students cannot postpone writing a complete theme until they have traveled over every inch of the ground. The rest of this chapter, therefore, is a preliminary survey of the land, with some of the main signposts tentatively illuminated.

CONTENT

"Are we graded for what we say or for how well we say it?" The inevitable classroom question can be quickly answered. Content and form are inseparable. On any piece of writing, whatever the subject, you will be judged for what you say, not for what you seem to be trying to say—and the difference between the two is measured by how well you say it. You should not get a high grade in an English course for neatly saying nothing or in any other kind of course for clumsily saying much. The old adage—"If you have nothing to say, don't say it"—may seem severe to a writer with a regular deadline to meet, but if you try to say nothing for 500 words, you will quickly betray yourself with empty generalities and repetitious double-talk.

In most kinds of writing it is not enough to have something substantial to say: you must be especially careful to *get the facts straight*. Though the novelist and the scientist may look at life through different lenses, accurate observation and meticulous recording are equally important to them both. Consider Ernest Hemingway's confession that during his apprenticeship he was obsessed by the difficulty of trying "to put down what really happened in action; what the actual things were which produced the emotion that you experienced. . . . The real thing, the sequence of motion and fact which made the emotion and which would be as valid in a year or in ten years or, with luck and if you stated it purely enough, always, was beyond me and I was working very hard to get it."

The less dedicated theme writer may alter the facts of a personal experience and get away with it. But in reporting a familiar campus incident, supporting an opinion, explaining a technical process, analyzing a reading assignment, or summarizing historical events, the smallest factual error may unpin a point or betray a profound ignorance of a subject on which the English instructor may be embarrassingly well-informed. The most eloquent paper—flawless in organization, sentence structure, diction, punctuation, spelling, and grammar—may be failed because the writer has ignored or falsified essential facts. In good writing the "what" is as important as the "how."

ORIGINALITY

Originality—in the highest sense of the word, *creativeness*—is not a quality that can be acquired from a textbook or an instructor. A gifted undergraduate may turn out a distinctly original short story. A patient investigator in an advanced course in literature may produce a good piece of original research. But such students are rare. Most freshman instructors are not looking for genuinely creative writing—though they are delighted to discover it—but only for the clear, intelligent, lively writing that should be expected of high-school graduates but is far too seldom found.

If you cannot be strikingly original, you can at least avoid being annoyingly unoriginal. You can evade the hardy perennials that have flourished for years: the theme on how hard it is to write a theme; the description of a beautiful woman that turns out in the end to be a portrait of a favorite Pekingese; the short-short-story with the "then-I woke-up" snapper ending. You can also try to avoid trite phrases (clichés) and obvious statements. In writing an autobiography, for example, you do not have to start with "In the beginning, of course, I was born" and go on to record that when you "first saw the light of day," your "proud parents" were delighted with their "blessed event."

But the absence of triteness is only a negative virtue. *You can take a positive step toward originality by drawing freely on your own experiences, accurately recording your own observations, and doing your own thinking.* If you stereotype yourself as an "average" undergraduate, you may conclude that neither your life nor your view of life is any different from those of thousands of your contemporaries. But this is a surrender of individuality. Strictly speaking, your experience is as unique as your fingerprints, and you are the world's leading authority on it. Draw on that experience for fresh, authentic illustrations regularly, not merely when the instructor assigns an exercise in autobiography. Record what you see, in your own words. Do your own thinking instead of letting columnists and commentators and instructors and fellow students do it for you. Then you may surprise yourself by writing interesting, original themes.

"Originality," wrote James Stephen, "does not consist in saying what no one has ever said before, but in saying exactly what you think yourself."

HONESTY

Whether or not you succeed in being original, you must learn to give due credit to the originality of others by honestly paying your literary debts. The details of proper scholarly acknowledgment are discussed in Chapter 9. The general principles can be summarized briefly. Acknowledge indebtedness

1. whenever you quote another persons's actual words;
2. whenever you use another person's idea, opinion, or theory, *even if it is completely paraphrased in your own words*; and
3. whenever you borrow facts, statistics, or other illustrative material—unless the information is common knowledge.

Plagiarism is a formal word for literary stealing or, to use the campus equivalent, cribbing. It is as immoral to steal from other people's writing as from their wardrobes or their wallets. Even when the crime appears to pay, the instructor, unwilling to act without clinching evidence, may quietly file the suspect's name away for future reference. The severe penalties on conviction include expulsion from college. Finally, cribbing is the worst possible way of learning to write. Honesty is the only policy.

You can hardly compose a whole semester's themes entirely out of your own head. Sooner or later, an assignment will send you to a newspaper, a magazine, or a book, whether or not the instructor has explicitly required a "source theme," a "library report," or a "research paper." You cannot, of course, borrow without acknowledgment until the fatal week of the research paper arrives, at which time you are suddenly compelled by law to steal honestly. Though incidental debts in informal papers are not usually acknowledged by footnotes, bibliography, and all the other paraphernalia of modern scholarship, all borrowings should be clearly identified in the text of the theme or at least in an accompanying headnote.

SINCERITY

Insincerity is another, more intangible sort of literary dishonesty. How often have you said, not what you actually think about a subject, but what you think the instructor thinks you ought to think? A natural desire to make a good impression may cause you to strain beyond the limits of your vocabulary and strike a whole series of false notes. When the grade is sacred and the teacher is judge, jury, and executioner rolled into one, few students are entirely free from this temptation. But when students consciously set out to impress the reader by conjuring up emotions they do not feel and concocting opinions they do not hold, they are as intellectually dishonest as the plagiarist.

The tongue-in-cheek is, of course a conventional pose for the ironist or humorist, who may be falsely assuming a tone of sincerity to serve legitimate literary ends. It would be naïve to deny that insincerity or mock sincerity often helps to oil the joints of a business letter, political speech, or funeral eulogy. And the most genuine sincerity can be deadly when a writer solemnly flaunts it on his sleeve. But the undergraduate author would still do well to resist the temptations of hypocrisy.

Sincerity is more than an ethical virtue in writing. In Stephen Leacock's phrase, "it implies . . . a sort of inevitable relation as between the words used and the things narrated." In an insincere writer this relation breaks down. Phony writing is fuzzy writing; insincerity, as George Orwell says, is "the great enemy of clear language." More than that, unless you clearly intend irony or humorous exaggeration, the slightest suspicion that you don't honestly mean what you say helps to destroy the bond of sympathy that must exist between writer and reader.

CLARITY

Above all, good writing is clear. In some kinds of writing—for example, the directions for assembling a toy—clarity may be all that really matters. In all kinds, it is important. It isn't enough to "get the general idea across." An experienced reader is willing to meet a writer halfway, but it is too much to expect any reader to be trained in mental telepathy. In page after page of bad writing, vagueness is the villain.

You must not, of course confuse clarity with oversimplification. Some writing is clear because a puzzling thought has never beclouded the author's limited horizon. The intuitions of a poet or the profundities of a philosopher can't always be reduced to "plain talk" for "the common reader." Paradoxes, riddles, or intentional ambiguities—including puns—may be essential to a writer's purpose. But the college writer would do well to remember Anthony Hope's terse warning: "Unless one is a genius, it is best to aim at being intelligible."

It has already been said or implied that a writer who has nothing to say, or who squints at the subject through the fog of indifferent observation or insincerity, cannot write clearly. Clumsy sentence structure, faulty punctuation, careless choice of words, cloudy thinking—all are enemies of clarity that will be discussed later in detail. But two broad aspects of the problem deserve preliminary emphasis here:

1. Much undergraduate writing is unclear because it is not specific A number of topics expanded elsewhere—the use of details in building paragraphs, illustrations to bolster generalities, concrete instead of abstract words—all add up to one commandment: *Be specific.* This is a time-honored classroom watchword. "I think you understand the point, but I'm not quite sure," says the instructor. "Can't you be more specific?" "Be specific," reads the warning at the head of the examination paper; "support your answers with detailed references to your reading in the course." "Use more specific detail!" reads the comment on the corrected theme. Yet some students retain their affection for lonely, unsupported generalities. The writer who has learned to support generalities with concrete details and illustrations has won half the battle for clarity.

2. Many student papers are vague because they are badly organized The reader is confused because the writer's train of thought has wandered from the track. At any given point in a well-organized expository theme, the readers should know exactly where they are and how they got there, and have some notion of where the writer is taking them. In a story, mystery and suspense should result from conscious craft, not from careless construction. A good writer who doesn't have a clear plan in mind at the start will bring order out of chaos during the revision of the first draft. In the final draft the parts must be arranged in a reasonable order, their size must be proportionate to their importance, and the whole must be the sum of all its parts. A composition should be *composed*—literally *put together*. A theme that is merely made up of disconnected tidbits, like the random jottings of a private diary, is not a composition.

ECONOMY

"An army of words escorting a corporal of thought." Ambrose Bierce's definition of *pleonasm* fits many entire student themes. *Pleonasm, tautology, verbosity, prolixity, diffuseness, redundancy, circumlocution, periphrasis*—these words differ slightly in dictionary definition, but they have a common core of meaning. All are kinds of wordiness. And the variety of terms suggests the prevalence of the disease.

Good writing is economical. Good writers use no more words than are needed to express thoughts and feelings adequately. This does not mean, of course, that you should be stingy with details, forsaking all adjectives, illustrations, and effective repetition, and paring your style to the barest bone. Wordiness and length are not synonymous: a one-page memo may be wordier than a detailed report of 20 pages. Though brevity may be the soul of wit, it may also be the product of laziness or busyness. But as a general rule, you should not use three words when one will serve. When the instructor prescribes a minimum word limit, words acquire a statistical value that has little relation to their meaning. Instead of trying to compress phrases—an indispensable process in revision—students are tempted to inflate them like balloons. No word limit is meant to be taken literally at the expense of economy. The good writer is concerned, not with counting words, but with making every word count.

CORRECTNESS

Now that it is evident that correcting themes does not consist entirely of searching for errors, it is time to admit that good writing does involve *correct English*. What does the expression mean?

Trained modern linguists recognize no absolute standard of right and wrong in the use of language. Equipped with the latest electronic devices and aiming at scientific detachment, they record the language as it is used—the facts of *usage*—with special emphasis on the spoken tongue. Though careful to note variations due to time, place, and the social and educational levels of the speakers, they are not concerned with drawing distinctions between "good" English and "bad" or with laying down laws for correctness. Whatever is, is right if it is current in the dialect they are recording.

The compilers of general dictionaries take a similar tack, with more emphasis on the written language than on the spoken. Though most people approach the dictionary as the linguistic law of the land, modern lexicographers try only to describe usage, not prescribe it. If they do not succeed in eliminating prescription entirely, it is because the final decisions on what words to include and how to define them are still made by human beings, not computers.

The modern composition instructor doesn't devise private rules that are unrelated to usage or cling to dead laws that no longer reflect the living language—if these laws ever did. The conventions of correctness are not chiseled for eternity in stone, but are subject to erosion. Yesterday's polite expression may be today's social error, today's "nonstandard usage" may be acceptable English tomorrow; no dictionary or rhetoric is ever right up to date. Moreover, *correctness* is a relative term. An expression may be apt in one context and inept in another, and, even on the same level of language, usage may be so divided between two words or spellings or grammatical constructions that neither can be safely designated as "preferred." On the map of correctness, there is always an area of gray between the black and the white.

But the composition instructor cannot hope to achieve the same degree of detachment as the full-time linguist or lexicographer. Expected not only to describe the written language but to help students to write better, the instructor must sooner or later confront them with a more or less specific set of "rules" for their guidance. These will vary to some extent with the instructor and the handbook. The rules in this book are intended to conform as nearly as possible to the usage of careful, educated writers in the second half of the twentieth century. They are meant as aids to good writing, not as a penal code for correcting themes. The strictness of their enforcement will depend, of course, on the individual instructor.

Before considering any rules in detail, ponder these general suggestions:

1. Some violations of the conventions of correct English are obviously more serious than others   A word that completely misrepresents a writer's meaning is a more serious offense than a neglected apostrophe; a badly misplaced modifier is more misleading than the weak phrase ending an unemphatic sentence. The student who wrote *physialocial* for *psychological* was doing more damage to meaning than the author of this book when he scrawled on the outside of a theme: "Your spelling is *attrocious*." Generally speaking, clumsy sentence structure and careless choice of words are more serious crimes than slipshod punctuation and spelling.

But in spite of some undergraduate opinion to the contrary, even a slight typographical error is not a completely pardonable sin. The reader cannot be expected to distinguish carefully between bad typing and bad spelling or to supply the missing phrase in a hastily copied final draft. A student once wrote, for example, "What may begin as a causal relationship may quickly grow into a serious involvement." Was the reader to assume merely that a careless finger transposed the *s* and the *u* in *casual*? Or was the student actually ignorant of the difference between *casual* and *causal*? Was the error in typing, spelling, or diction?

2. The rules are not always logical   The reasons for some rules can be easily explained. Obviously the omission of an *m* in the word *comma* could lead to a misunderstanding. But you must not expect an equally satisfying explanation of the teacher's refusal to accept the contraction *ain't I* for *am I not* or to permit the spelling *alright* by a logical analogy with *already* and *altogether*. There are conventions in the language as unreasonable as the etiquette of dress: despite the long struggles of reformers, English-speaking people continue to retain their illogical spellings for somewhat the same reason that men insist on torturing

11

themselves with neckties. You must not blame the English instructor for warning you not to conduct a private revolution against the linguistic traditions of several hundred million people. You must resign yourself continually to the argument that this or that expression is questionable or incorrect simply because careful, educated twentieth-century writers do not ordinarily use it.

3. You cannot learn to write by rules alone   The handbook and the English instructor are inadequate substitutes for discriminating reading and careful listening to observe the language in action. You must be a word-watcher. You must train yourself—as Otto Jespersen put it—"to hear the linguistic grass grow"; but, remembering that not all growth is progress, you must choose your models with care. Although thousands of presumably educated people no longer distinguish between *imply* and *infer* or between *uninterested* and *disinterested*, these distinctions are worth keeping. Though college graduates are spawning combinations ending in *-wise* (*usage-wise, correctness-wise*) and *-ize* (*opportunize, concretize, slenderize, functionalize*), no usage poll can prove that such monstrous births add either precision or grace to the English language.

Nor are the most celebrated modern writers always the best models for undergraduate writing. There are answers for students who defend their own errors by arguing that Gertrude Stein, E. E. Cummings, and James Joyce often ignored conventional grammar and punctuation. One rather condescending answer is that most instructors would gladly lend any potential Shakespeare in the class a more generous amount of rope if he would promise to produce another *Hamlet* instead of hanging himself. Another is that print is not sacred, nor any mortal writer infallible. But perhaps the best answer is that many contemporary writers are ceaselessly experimenting with language; that when they take liberties with the rules, they usually know what they are doing and why; and that this can seldom be said of the apprentice. A tennis player should learn the fundamentals of orthodox footwork before trying to bring off a shot with both feet facing the net. By the same logic, the college writer is expected to display an understanding of accepted conventions before experimenting with the unconventional.

4. Finally, you must not expect to be supplied with a handbook rule, complete with name and number, to support every objection the instructor makes   Will Rogers' wisecrack about the pedestrian traffic laws—"If you get hit outside of the white lines, it doesn't count"—is not applicable here. Any writer can create clumsy expressions that the most imaginative rhetorician could not encompass in a thousand rules. That is why one of the most useful correction symbols in the instructor's arsenal is a large *K* or a raucous *awk*—meaning, not incorrect, but just plain awkward.

APPROPRIATENESS

"One time," wrote E. B. White, "a newspaper sent us to a morgue to get a story on a woman whose body was being held for identification. A man believed to be her husband was brought in. Somebody pulled the sheet back; the man took one agonizing look and cried, "My God, it's her!' When we reported this grim incident, the editor diligently changed it to 'My God, it's she!' "

In the final reckoning, the key question is not whether a word or phrase is correct according to a textbook rule, but whether—like "My God, it's her!"—it is *appropriate* in its context. In judging appropriateness, you must be constantly aware of (1) the point of view from which you are writing, (2) the reader for whom you are writing, and (3) the purpose you want to accomplish.

1. Point of View

As any experienced reader knows, writers of fiction or plays or parodies will often assume a point of view—a way of seeing and talking about life—that is vastly different from their own. This is not Mark Twain's grammar but Huck Finn's: "You don't know about me without you have read a book by the name of *The Adventures of Tom Sawyer*; but that ain't no matter." And this is not J. D. Salinger's sentence structure or literary criticism but those of the precocious adolescent from Pency Prep who narrates *The Catcher in the Rye*: "What really knocks me out is a book that, when you're all done reading it, you wish the author that wrote it was a terrific friend of yours and you could call him up on the phone whenever you felt like it."

If you adopt such a technique, or attempt dialogue, your paper will be judged partly for your skill in portraying the mind and language of somebody else. Most of the time, however, you will be required to express your own opinions in your own words. The problem of point of view will focus on two questions: How impersonal should you be? If you bring yourself into the picture, what should you call yourself?

In some kinds of writing—a formal report, for example—you may want to preserve an attitude of detachment by staying out of the picture entirely. In other kinds—an autobiographical narrative or an informal critical essay—you will be naturally subjective. Consider some of the choices:

You may choose to write about yourself in the third person, a common convention in story-telling. But do not be misled by a quaint custom or false modesty into dubbing yourself "the writer," "the present writer," "your scribe," or "our hero(ine)."

The "editorial *we*" is a defensible convention in newspapers and magazines, where one writer presumably reflects the sentiments of the entire staff; but in other contexts it usually gives off an unnatural air of importance, like the "royal *we*" of monarchy.

You may sometimes adopt the "pedagogical *we*" ("Now *we* become aware of the importance of point of view") as long as it clearly refers to the writer and the reader, and not at the same time to *we-the-editors*, *we-meaning-I*, or *we-the-people-in-general*. It is better in most expository writing than the completely impersonal approach because it helps to avoid the clumsy passive voice. Roundabout expressions such as "now it can be observed that" are guaranteed to increase the density of any piece of writing.

Most of the time, the easiest way out of the dilemma of point of view is to call yourself what you naturally call yourself every day of your life—*I*. If you are afraid this will make you look egotistical, remember that all writing is partly autobiographical and that a genuine egotist cannot hide behind grammar. It is monotonous to repeat *I* too often at the beginning of a sentence, or to overwork such expressions as "I believe" and "in my opinion" when the reader hasn't the slightest doubt about whose opinion is being expressed. But repetition, like egotism, cannot be cured by merely borrowing a new set of pronouns. "We commonly do not remember," wrote Thoreau, "that it is, after all, always the first person that is speaking."

2. The Reader

Who is the reader going to be? A professional writer discussing the dangers of atomic fallout may be preparing a *technical* paper for a select group of Ph.D.s in physics; a *semitechnical* article for a larger audience of educated laymen, who require some definition but resent too much sugar-coating on the scientific pill; or a *popular* explanation for "the man in the street"—whoever that may be.

As a college student you will be tempted to adjust your style and ideas to the supposed tastes and prejudices of the only regular member of your audience—to write what the instructor presumably wants. In a sense this is good, for any audience is better than none. On the whole, however, you will do well to forget, as far as is humanly possible, that you are writing a "theme" for an English instructor. If you can, you will avoid the offensive "Dear Teacher" familiarity of some undergraduate writing ("As you said in class last Friday, Prof"), and you will escape the evils springing from the illusion that there is a unique species of jargon appropriate only to English themes. You can hardly adapt every asignment to a different audience (atomic energy for a group of Rotarians; how to bunt a baseball as explained to the members of an English cricket team). The difficulty of addressing only your classmates is that you may never rise far above the level of campus conversation. A reasonable compromise, on most assignments, is to aim at a hypothetical well-educated adult.

3. Purpose

The appropriate kind of writing for this hypothetical reader will depend, of course, on your purpose. "What am I trying to do in this paper?" Although the question seems inevitable, many students can't answer it and some never think of asking it. Are you telling a story *(narration)?* or describing a scene *(description)?* or explaining a process or mechanism or idea *(exposition)?* or taking a position in a controversy *(argumentation)?* These old-fashioned categories overlap in practice, but theoretically each type requires a separate technique. And the questions don't stop here. If you are telling a story, do you have a point or theme or moral, or is it just an interesting tale? If you are explaining somebody else's idea, will you be content with merely summarizing it, or do you propose to analyze and evaluate it? Do you intend to move your readers to tears or laughter, tease them with irony, arouse them with an angry shout, or soothe them with a quiet meditation? And—a most important question in a composition course—what is the relation between your purpose and the implied or expressed aim of the assignment? Your purpose may be explicitly stated—as at the beginning of a technical report—or it may be artfully concealed for the reader to detect. But you should see it clearly from the start.

The following introductory note shows how the three aspects of appropriateness—point of view, the intended reader, and the writer's purpose—are naturally connected in an author's mind:

This book is not intended for the scholar. I have tried to write with a man's pen, so that he who runs may read. Even so, I fear, an attempt to read these chapters on the run will prove to be quite an obstacle race. I could not level the hills and valleys and make all the rough places plain without giving up my main purpose in writing, which was to give a fairly definite idea of what the Dead Sea Scrolls are, why there has been so much excitement over them, and how they are important.—Millar Burrows, *The Dead Sea Scrolls*

Levels of Usage

A brief consideration of *levels of usage* can serve as a general guide to appropriateness, especially for students who tend to think of the language as a running fight between "good" English and "bad." The English language can be roughly divided according to three levels: (1) formal, (2) informal, and (3) nonstandard.

1. Formal
Though far less common than it once was, formal English is still in evidence, especially when the occasion calls for a dignified or exact treatment of a serious subject. It is common in scholarly books on all subjects, research papers, technical reports, essays in criticism,

textbooks, legal briefs, business letters, and addresses for such ceremonial occasions as commencements and inaugurations. Formal writing avoids colloquialisms and slang and tends to use technical or learned terms, many of them abstract. The sentences and paragraphs are often long and carefully contrived; and the grammar conforms closely to the rules of the traditional schoolroom. The style and tone vary with the purpose, depending, for example, on whether the writer aims to move the reader or only to inform; but formal writing seldom has the flavor of natural conversation.

Here is an example:

But it is when we come to Mr. Toynbee's idea that human societies (unless they are dying) are integrated wholes that we touch the ultimate idea on which Mr. Toynbee's entire philosophy of history rests. For Mr. Toynbee, a healthy civilization is all of a piece. Its economic activities are not separate from its moral standards, its moral standards are warmed by a religious vision. No one part can be treated independently of the rest without throwing everything off balance. Nothing happens at random or serves no purpose; everything harmonizes with everything else and serves the unity of the whole.

Here is the ultimate choice with which Mr. Toynbee's philosophy of history confronts us. It is a choice between the partial piecemeal reform of social institutions and waiting for a miraculous spiritual vision; between empirical social analysis and dependence on the superior insights of intuition and feeling; between a pluralistic society, containing many visions of man and God, and a monolithic society in which everything is part of the same chorus singing the same song. It is more: it is a choice between a view of human destiny in which chance and accident play a part, but in which human beings are free to give history the direction they choose, and a view of human destiny from which chance and accident disappear, but in which the freedom of human beings means only their perfect obedience to a course that has been laid down for them in advance. It puts before us ultimate questions about the nature of our troubles, the powers we have at our disposal for dealing with them, and the ideals at which we should aim.—Charles Frankel, *The Case for Modern Man*

In a serious analysis of contemporary ideas, a professor of philosophy is summarizing a central assumption of Arnold Toynbee's *A Study of History*. The passage contains one or two informal touches (*all of a piece, part of the same chorus singing the same song*), but the vocabulary is essentially abstract (*spiritual vision, empirical social analysis, pluralistic, monolithic, human destiny*)— fitting language for a thoughtful consideration of ultimate questions. The sentence structure is marked by the writer's consistent use of the formal inversion placing the preposition before the end of the clause or sentence (*on which Mr. Toynbee's entire philosophy . . . rests* instead of *which Mr. Toynbee's entire philosophy . . . rests on*). The pattern is repeated six more times in the passage. The calculated balance of the sentences is evident. In Professor Frankel's first paragraph the two pertinent examples are short (*Its economic activities are not separate from its moral standards, its moral standards are warmed by a religious vision. . . . Nothing happens at random or serves no purpose; everything harmonizes with everything else and serves the unity of the whole*). In the second paragraph he develops his comparison intricately by sustaining the balance for longer flights. A reader of the second and third sentences in the second paragraph might object that, by knitting together so many uniform clauses with *between, and,* or *which,* Frankel is creating a formal rhetorical effect at the cost of redundancy and monotony. But most English instructors would probably agree that his formal language is appropriate for its purpose, though less useful as a model for the inexperienced writer.

2. Informal

The informal level is represented by a great deal of writing among educated Americans today—in friendly letters and many business letters, newspaper columns, magazine articles, talks, and many serious books, including this one. Though good informal writing avoids obscenities, it has a good many colloquialisms—or expressions common in conversation but not in formal writing—and a limited amount of slang, handled with care but not with gloves. The writer sticks reasonably close to the conventions of correct English, but doesn't reveal excessive concern over worn-out warnings about the split infinitive, the preposition at the end of the sentence, or the difference between *shall* and *will, farther* and *further,* or *till* and *until.* He or she prefers familiar, concrete words to technical and abstract words, likes short sentences in natural word order, and is suspicious of rhetorical tricks that may call too much attention to the style. The informal writer doesn't mind taking a few shortcuts: omitting unnecessary connectives and using occasional contractions. Informal writing has a clear echo of the everyday talk of educated men and women.

Here is an example (the reference to synthetic milk repeats a note struck earlier in the essay):

It seems to me that the beginning of man's artificial, synthetic world lies back in the early Stone Age. It is perhaps natural enough for a monkey or ape to pick up a rock and throw it or use it to pound with. But hundreds of thousands of years ago some manlike animal started shaping his stones so that they were better adapted to his particular purposes.

The action of shaping stones, or bone, or wood, for a particular purpose was something new in the world of nature—and as such, unnatural. I suppose there were a lot of grumpy elders around who maintained that natural stones were good enough for them, and that this deliberate reshaping of things could only lead to a bad end. Sometimes now, when we look at the tremendous powers of destruction we have acquired, it seems as though they may have been right.

Synthetic milk—there is nothing really very odd about it when you look at the rest of human environment. We live in synthetic caves—great improvements, I think, over the natural ones. We don't find our natural skin an adequate protection, so we cover it with clothing.

Clothes, of course, are for looks as well as for comfort—which gets us into odd situations. In the days when I commuted from Connecticut to New York, I

17

was particularly impressed by the summer behavior of my friends (and myself). We could take our coats off as soon as we got on the train, put them on again for the New York streets, and take them off as soon as we got to our offices. The only reason for this I can think of would be to impress strangers with our respectable status. But why bother to impress strangers?—Marston Bates, "It's a Big, Big, Synthetic World," *New York Times Magazine*

Although that passage was written by a distinguished professor of zoology, everything about it, including the rather folksy title, suggests the relaxed informality of a "popular" magazine article. The vocabulary belongs to a human being talking—easily but not at random—a literate, civilized man, but not necessarily an expert here on anything but his own reactions. The first-person point of view is kept throughout (*It seems to me, I suppose, I think, the days when I commuted*). Phrase after phrase has the ring of an unrehearsed speech (*a lot of grumpy elders around, good enough for them, lead to a bad end, nothing really very odd about it, take our coats off, put them on again*). Neither the sentences nor the paragraphs—both shorter than in most formal writing—suggest any sort of contrivance for rhetorical effect. In a number of places the writer pays no attention to traditional handbook warnings that might prick the conscience of a more formal writer: he ends the second sentence with a preposition; uses the natural *so* as a subordinating conjunction; permits himself an equally natural indulgence in "broad reference" (*Clothes, of course, are for looks as well as for comfort—which gets us into odd situations*); and uses *myself* as the object of a preposition (*of my friends and myself*) instead of the more formal *me*. He ends with two shortcuts: he does not write "The only reason for this *which* I can think of" (or "of which I can think"), or "But why *should one* bother to impress strangers?"

Professor Bates's manner would be inappropriate for a more formal essay, including many undergraduate assignments. But he does succeed in throwing a lively light into one corner of an old controversy. The passage shows that writing on the informal level can be illuminating, not merely entertaining.

3. Nonstandard

Though written on different levels, the passages illustrating formal and informal usage are both in *Standard English*. The term applies to writing and speech that are generally accepted by educated people. *Nonstandard* is a general term for a level of language that is little touched by formal education. In print it is most frequently represented by the speech of characters in literature with limited schooling. This level does not represent a tragic degeneration of the language from high to low estate; many nonstandard expressions are not careless or ignorant lapses from Standard English but hardy survivors of a day when they were thoroughly respectable.

Nonstandard usage has distinctive features. The sentences tend to be short (though some are the interminable concoctions of speakers with no clear notion of what a sentence is); the vocabulary is limited (though the range of obscenities is wide); and the grammar reveals a surprisingly uniform pattern of constructions that would be "errors" on a higher level. Such expressions as these occur with remarkable consistency: I *seen* it; I *done* it; we have *came;* you *was* there; I *ain't* saying so; *us* people *is* going; he played *good;* it *don't* make *no* difference; *that there* car; *this here* woman; *my sister, she* is beautiful; *youse.*

Of course, these generalities and illustrations simplify a complex picture. The usage level of any piece of writing is determined not only by vocabulary, grammar, and sentence structure but by punctuation and intangibles such as rhythm. A discussion of usage eventually broadens out into a consideration of style and tone. Obviously there is considerable overlapping from level to level, and other levels or sublevels could be added. The writer's goal is not to memorize three pat formulas but, by wide reading and careful listening, to develop an awareness of what is appropriate when and where. When the use of a word or construction or mark of punctuation is common in informal writing, but not in formal, this book will make that distinction. The question of the appropriate use of words will be discussed at length in Chapters 5 and 6. Particular problems of usage are treated in the Glossary of Usage at the back of the book. Dictionaries use status labels *(nonstandard, substandard, vulgar)* to identify some words as less widely accepted than the Standard English comprising the great bulk of the vocabulary. But a well-developed awareness of usage levels cannot be acquired from any single book, or instructor, or course in composition.

Effective and ineffective expression are possible on all levels. "What is past is prologue" is effective formal English; "You ain't seen nothing yet" is effective nonstandard. Formal writing can be dignified or stuffy, eloquent or flowery, precise or clouded by vague abstractions, intellectually detached or frigidly impersonal. Informal writing can be simple and relaxed and close to the sound of human speech, but it is too familiar, imprecise, or undignified for some occasions and may slip into self-conscious breeziness. Nonstandard English can be direct, lively, or even beautiful, but it is often merely crude or dull. Though in some areas of expression it is notoriously versatile, as a flexible tool for written thought it is inaccurate and inadequate because of its impoverished vocabulary and limited sentence patterns.

Though college graduates may use nonstandard expressions, consciously or unconsciously, when talking to friends or assuming a particular point of view in writing, they are usually required by the demands of their subject and the conventions of their social group to speak and write on one of the other two levels. It was once fashionable in freshman English texts to stress formal writing, but in recent years the pendulum has swung to the middle of the scale. The informality of contemporary America is reflected in its prose: the modern businessman is more likely to dictate, "Dear Mr. Jones" and "Sincerely" or "Very truly yours" than "Dear Sir" and "I remain, yours respectfully"; the old academic distinction between the formal and informal essay is now largely confined to courses in the history of literature.

As an undergraduate, you should learn to read formal English and to write it, on the proper occasion, with precision, not prissiness. You should appreciate the special values of formal rhetoric and know the conventions of formal grammar. But because most of the writing expected of the college graduate is informal, it is especially important for you to practice writing accurately and naturally on the informal level.

CONSISTENCY

After choosing the appropriate point of view and level of usage, follow them consistently unless you have good reason to change; and do not change without carefully preparing the reader. A careless shift in point of view is common: "In preparing *my* new book, 'Above All Nations,'. . . *the present writer* was confronted with the question. . . ." (George Catlin, "T. S. Eliot and the Moral Issue," *Saturday Review*). A sudden switch from one level of usage to another, or an unmotivated change in tone, can be equally disconcerting. Sir Arthur Quiller-Couch quoted the well-meaning native of India who wrote of his mother's death: "Regret to inform you, the hand that rocked the cradle has kicked the bucket." This line is not only a mixture of usage levels—a ridiculously sudden switch from formal English to nonstandard; it is a bewildering mixture of tones: the impersonal austerity of official jargon ("Regret to inform you"), the sentimentality of a Mother's Day cliché ("the hand that rocked the cradle"), and then, capping the anticlimax, the bluntness of street-corner slang ("has kicked the bucket"). Not only are the two figures of speech on different levels of usage—clear proof that figurative language is not necessarily formal language; they collide to form a bizarre mixed metaphor—inconsistency number three.

The general requirement of consistency also applies to spelling, to punctuation, and to grammar and sentence structure: you must avoid violations of parallellism and confusing shifts in tense or in the number of pronouns. More fundamental are flaws in the logic of the paper as a whole. Obviously a writer must be particularly careful not to undermine point one by saying something under point two that completely contradicts it.

NATURALNESS: WRITING AND SPEECH

The resemblance between informal writing and speech, already mentioned, must not be pushed too far. Obviously writing is not speech but an ingenious way of representing language—the spoken tongue—on paper. Because they can clarify and amplify meaning with facial expressions, gestures, and tones of voice, even highly educated talkers—in casual conversation—are allowed to take liberties with grammar, sentence structure, and diction that would not be permitted in writing. With no audience present to react and question, writers must plan and revise, molding their meaning with conscious craft, always aware that they may be misunderstood. They can't grope for meaning while the reader waits; they can't, like many spontaneous talkers, scatter words at random in the hope that one will hit the bull's-eye; they can't leave sentences dangling in mid-air with a wave of the hand or a "you-know-what-I-mean." Readable prose is not conversation spilled on paper.

But despite these obvious differences, good writing—especially on the informal level—always comes close to creating the illusion of natural speech. When you are stuck for a word or conscious of an awkward phrase, ask yourself not "How shall I write it?" but "How would I say it?" If you have had ample opportunity to listen to the speech of educated people, you should be suspicious of any expression in your writing that doesn't *sound* natural.

The early crop of college compositions often produces hothouse blooms like this:

It was with some mental confusion that I set foot on the tossing deck of college education because I had not regained the all-conquering drive of inspiration that leads to lasting intellectual satisfaction. I had, however, a sufficiently inflated ego, which was the balloon tires to cushion my ride in the mental carriage of pseudo-self-sufficiency, so that I believe myself capable of mastering any educational course.

The reader winces, throws a large red lariat around it, and in the adjoining margin scrawls "vague," "forced," "mixed," or just a large red question mark. In a conference he hopefully asks the student:

"What do you mean by that?"

"Why," answers the author with little hesitation, "I meant that when I first came to college, I was confused because I had lost the desire to study. But I had enough self-confidence to know that I would come through all right."

"If you meant just that, why didn't you say just that?"

"I thought that in an English course—"

The wheel has come full circle and the monster portrayed at the beginning of the chapter is looming up again.

But there is hope for this student, more hope than for a writer with a smaller vocabulary, a more limited imagination, a less vivid sense of metaphor. This student can be taught that good informal writing is spontaneous speech sharpened by reflection and revision. Like the famous character in Molière who woke up in middle age to discover he had been talking prose for forty years, students may learn at eighteen that they have been talking English not far removed from the writing that is appropriate for an English theme.

EXERCISES

A. Write a 500-word summary of your experience in learning to write before coming to college. Give frank answers to the following questions: To what extent have your English courses in school been concerned with teaching you how to write? How much and what kind of writing was required of you in courses not labeled "English"? How much and what kind of writing have you done outside of school?

B. Considering books, magazines, and newspapers, write a 500-word analysis of your reading habits. Discuss the relation between your reading and your ability to express yourself in writing. If you have acquired the bad habit of not reading anything, explain how you propose to cure it.

C. With direct references to this chapter and to your previous instruction in English, write a 500-word diagnosis of your shortcomings as a writer.

D. In no less than 500 words discuss the extent to which the doctrine of this chapter differs from your view of "good writing and correct English" before coming to college.

E. Characterize the level of usage in each of the following passages, citing specific evidence to support your conclusion. Regardless of usage level, to what extent is the writer successful in expressing his apparent purpose?

1. Given the universal character of its ethical standpoint, classicism draws a marked distinction between centrality and diversity, between man's unified rational grasp of his ideal nature, and his peripheral and independent development, as a particular, of the impulses and reactions which comprise what is occasionally called his personality. Indeed, classicism assumes that only through the former can genuine individual fulfillment be found. For it regards man's feelings as by themselves helpless, blind, and eminently susceptible to dictation of some sort. They are not, that is, free to determine themselves, but are inevitably led by something else: they are subject to whatever is in closest or most vital proximity to them—whether it be a rationally determined end which is vividly and firmly held in the mind, or whether, if this end be lacking, it be merely whatever external environment chance may offer. It is in this respect that Dr. Johnson could state, with complete practicality: "Whatever withdraws us from the power of our senses, whatever makes the past, the distant, or the future predominate over the present, advances us in the dignity of thinking beings." True individual freedom accrues in the channeling of man's responses towards an end which reason conceives to transcend the local and temporary; its opposite exists when such a formative and determining conception is lacking and habit is established through chance, fashion, local custom, or individual caprice.—Walter Jackson Bate, *From Classic to Romantic*

2. It was the raft, and mighty glad was we to get aboard of it again. We seen a light now away down to the right, on shore. So I said I would go for it. The skiff was half full of plunder which that gang had stole there on the wreck. We hustled it into the raft in a pile, and I told Jim to float along down, and show a light when he judged he had gone about two mile, and keep it burning till I come; then I manned my oars and shoved for the light. As I got down towards it three or four more showed—up on a hillside. It was a village. I closed in above the shore light, and laid on my oars and floated. As I went by I see it was a lantern hanging on the jackstaff of a double-hull ferryboat. I skimmed around for the watchman, a-wondering whereabouts he slept; and by and by I found him roosting on the bitts forward, with his head down between his knees. I gave his shoulder two or three little shoves, and begun to cry.—Mark Twain. *The Adventures of Huckleberry Finn*

3. Historians looking back on this particular age will have to have some handy label for it. They may, of course, call it the age that destroyed civilization; but we have a suspicion they might call it the age that destroyed the adjective. Since the adjective is of ancient lineage and is a basic tool in our trade, its decline fills us with a certain sense of sadness. We understand how an old-fashioned woodworker must feel these days, with all the machine-made plastic stuff around. You know how it is with many of these glamorous-looking plastic things—they get busted and nobody can repair them. That is what is happening with adjectives today—they're getting busted all over the place. The only difference is that people go on using them, not realizing that they are busted.

If civilization busts in our time, the Russian Communists get our personal blame for it; but it's a different story with the adjectives. We Americans think we are totally unlike the Russian Communists in every respect, but the unhappy truth is that we and the Politburo are just alike in respect to adjectives. Both have arrested, tortured, imprisoned, poisoned, and thereby destroyed more adjectives than any other people in any other time. Of course, we bust different kinds of adjectives. We are a private-enterprise system, so we bust private-enterprise adjectives. What the advertising business, especially in the movies, has done to such noble adjectives as *colossal, stupendous,* and *earth-shaking* hardly bears thinking about. Those adjectives have simply been used up, they have lost their meaning; and an adjective without meaning is a dead adjective. They give forth an odor now because nobody has thought to bury them.—Eric Sevareid, *In One Ear*

4. Harry, you been jacking me up about how I been neglecting Rotary here lately, so I'm just going to break down and tell you something. Now I don't want you to take this personal, Harry, because it's not meant personal at all. No siree! Not a-tall! But, just between you and I, Harry, I'm not going to be coming out to Rotary lunches any more. I mean I'm quitting Rotary! . . .

Now whoa there! Whoa! Whoa just a minute and let me get a word in edge-ways. Just let me finish my little say.

Don't you never take it into your head that I haven't been wrestling with this thing plenty. I mean I've argued it all out with myself. Now I'm going to tell you the whyfor and the whereof and the howcome about this, Harry, but kindly don't let what I say go no further. Please keep it strictly on the Q.T. Because I guess the rest of the boys would suspicion that I was turning highbrow on them. But you've always been a buddy to me, Harry, you mangy old son of a hoss thief, you, so what I'm telling you is the straight dope.—George Milburn, "The Apostate"

5. So far only a few people have had the nerve to come out flatly against the independent researcher, but the whole tenor of organization thinking is unmistakably in that direction. Among Americans there is today a widespread conviction that science has evolved to a point where the lone man engaged in fundamental inquiry is anachronistic, if not fundamental inquiry itself. Look, we are told, how the atom bomb was brought into being by the teamwork of huge corporations of scientists and technicians.

Occasionally somebody mentions in passing that what an eccentric old man with a head of white hair did back in his study forty years ago had something to do with it. But people who concede this point are likely to say that this merely proves that basic ideas aren't the problem any more. It's nice to have ideas and all that, sure, but it's American know-how that does something with them, and anyway there are plenty of ideas lying fallow. We don't really need any more ivory-tower theorizing; what we need is more funds, more laboratory facilities, more organization.—William H. Whyte, Jr., *The Organization Man*

6. These are the main features of the tragic spirit. It lifts us above self-pity and reconciles us to suffering by showing that evil is a necessary part of the intelligible and just order of our experience. It lifts us above the divisive spirit of melodrama by showing that men are neither naturally good nor inherently evil. It saves us from the pitfalls of utopianism and fatalism. It teaches moderation by showing that the way of the extremist is short, but at the same time it shows the man of principle that an uncompromising stand is not without its just compensations. And most important, it teaches us that all men are united in the kinship of a common fate, that all are destined to suffer and enjoy, each according to his capacity.—Henry Alonzo Myers, *Tragedy: A View of Life*

7. It is our inclination almost always to wait until there is a crisis before we come to grips with situations which grow increasingly aggravating. We can put up with the most annoying pains in the neck almost indefinitely, and it is not until a neck gets broken that we stop sighing and start thumping the table. And even then we are likely to think that our thumping falls on the deaf ears of "the Interests," that vague bunch of faceless "villains" on whom we blame the ills of civilization. Like the Establishment, the Interests are an ill-defined, ill-identified concept of powerful machinators who somehow control our destinies, the wheeler-dealers of public policy and private money. It is not as easy as that. Very often the problem is to draw a distinction between "the people" and "the Interests," because they are all too often the same. Are the people who insist on air travel to meet every whim also the Interests? Are the businessmen who want their offices where they have the greatest "visibility" the people or the Interests? The Interests, like "pressure groups," are usually the people we happen to disagree with and who want to get their own way, in opposition to our way. Since our polity is based on the reconciliation of the differences among pressure groups we are likely to move from crisis to crisis, patching rather than solving as we go.—Russell Lynes, "Stacked-Up," *Harper's*

8. Lintzie was a thin man with a Charlie Chaplin moustache and hollow cheeks that were made hollower still by his habit of leaving out his upper plate. He was young to have false teeth; in his late twenties. He had been in the Marine Corps, although he had not gone overseas, and all the worldliness, all his travels, were by benefit of his having been a Gott damn chyrene. He was a Pennsylvania Dutch farm boy, from somewhere east of Reading, and it wondered me, as the Dutch say, how he had ever heard of the marines. So, being in my teens and curious, I asked him. "How I heart abaht the Marine Corps? I didn't never hear about them till once I seen one of them there posters in the post office. I seen a picture of a marine, all dressed up in his plues, his rifle at right shoulder arms, his bayonet in a white scabbard. He looked handsome to me, so I went home and said to my old man I was going to enlist. I won't tell you what the old man said. He said to go ahead, only he said other things besides. Glad to get rid of me. Him and my brother could run the farm without me. My brother was glad

to get rid of me too. That way the old man would leave him the farm and me nothing. So I went to where it said on the poster and signed the papers. By Jesus if I knew what it was like them first three months I would of never enlisted. Son of a bitch sergeant with a swagger stick. Drill. Bivouac. Snakes. By Jesus nights I was too tired to cut my throat. That's no joke. But I guess it all done me good. I come out stronger than I went in, but minus the most of my teeth."—John O'Hara, "Fatimas and Kisses," *Waiting for Winter*

9. Now it may be possible to lessen the gap between the real and the ideal by bringing the ideal a long way back toward reality, by setting small, modest goals all along the line—not "temperance" but less criminal alcoholism; not perfect sexual freedom on earth but fewer divorces; not the elimination of "soap operas" but better-balanced radio and television programs; not complete economic security but less disastrous depressions with widespread unemployment; not a world government that will forever guarantee peace, but a United Nations that will help us stave off war and perhaps make it less barbarous when it comes. The list could be prolonged indefinitely. The moderate realist asks that democracy give up some of Its eighteenth-century optimism about the natural goodness and reasonableness of man, about the magic effect of a readily changeable social and political environment (laws, constitutions, treaties, new educational institutions and curricula), about the nearness of the approaching millennium. He asks that democracy accept some of the pessimism of traditional Christianity as embodied in the doctrine of original sin, some of the tragic sense of human limitations that has inspired great literature, some of the doubts about the universal capacity of all men to think straight that come out of modern psychology, some of the practical, common-sense awareness of the impossibility of perfection that most of us have in those fields of activity where we act under the burden of responsibility.—Crane Brinton, *Ideas and Men*

10. All groups talk a particular language. That statement is not open to question and I think it is not a matter to be regretted either. It is the natural way of things. You say something one way which the lawyer says another way. If you used the lawyer's language you would sound (if you were myself) a pretentious fool parading learning that you were without, and the lawyer using your language might sound as though he were trying to be more "human," more of a terribly decent chap about it all than it is likely he can be. The lawyer and you understand this and lose no respect for each other. Same with doctors, same with sailors, same with all other craftsmen. We recognize each other's groups and do not necessarily assume that one group is superior to other groups. But there is a point where professional language turns into professional jargon. Here usage is very much open to objection if it is ever used except within the group. It is reasonable to insist that all members of all professional groups must be intelligible to people outside. A doctor who can only talk like a text book may leave you in serious doubt as to your state of health. A clergyman who can only address his congregation in the difficult terms which theologians use among themselves might not succeed in his professional duty of saving souls. Some art historians and literary critics would not appear to agree with this, to judge from their public play with professional slang, but the great and unforgotten experts and critics have understood the point and obeyed the rules it implies.—Christopher Sykes, "What U-Future?" *Noblesse Oblige*

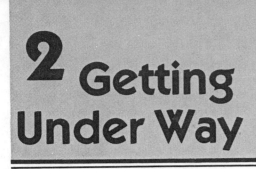

2 Getting Under Way

What we call the beginning is often the end
And to make an end is to make a beginning.
The end is where we start from.
 T. S. Eliot, "Little Gidding," Four Quartets

Revision is mostly compression—frying the
fat out of it.
 Peter De Vries

Undergraduate opinion traditionally divides student writers into two classes: those who can dash off a passing theme in an hour and those who have to sit down for hour after frenzied hour, enduring an agony that can best be described as "sweating it out." The ranks of the facile performers are probably thinner than their envious classmates assume. Whatever their temperaments or talents, most writers, including experienced professionals, agree that *writing well is hard work.* The general rule has a corollary in the words of Richard Brinsley Sheridan: *Easy writing's curst hard reading.* The manufacturers of mass-production fiction may have their formulas; the magicians of the how-do-you-know-you-can't write ads may peddle "tested" recipes; but serious professional writers testify, both in their confessions and their countless revisions, that there is no shortcut to creation. Some of them still spend as much time typing idle doodles and chewing pencils as the average undergraduate. Most of them are still learning their craft through ink, sweat, and tears.

   This chapter promises no magic solutions, only suggestions to ease the hard work, with special emphasis on the common problem of getting under way.

SOMETHING TO WRITE ABOUT

Whether or not the instructor gives a specific assignment, you may belong to the large number of students who habitually protest that they have "nothing to write about." Taken at its face value, this familiar complaint reveals symptoms that go deeper than the inability to write readable English. The obvious advice is this: Open your eyes and ears to what's going on around you, including the larger world beyond the campus walls. Be a regular reader of a good newspaper and one or two serious magazines. Read some of the books that are not required in your courses, and, if the books belong to you, pencil comments in the margins. Approach the TV and movie screens with a critical eye and ear. If out of all that you have seen and heard and probably read, you are consistently unable to accumulate 500 words' worth of coherent reactions, you are sleepwalking through life. Wake up.

Confronted with such a stern prescription, you may concede that what you really meant is that you seldom have a "good idea" for an English theme. Or you may insist that, despite the variety of your experience, your memory can't retain the specific details that make writing come alive. There is a time-tested solution to these problems:

Keep a journal   A good journal should be kept in a large notebook (eventually a series) separate from any that you might use for notes on the class discussion and required reading. You may make journal entries on your reading, required and elective, but not systematically to prepare for an examination or a research paper (see pp. 231–232). Nor is a good journal to be confused with a methodical diary in which a conscientious drudge makes a routine record of daily events with no reader in mind but the secret self. Whether or not your instructor requires you to submit a journal at regular intervals, the entries should be not only useful to you, but potentially interesting to a reader who doesn't know you.

A genuine writer can create a readable journal even if—like Samuel Pepys's *Diary*—it is intended only for private consumption. When he was in high school and college during World War I, E. B. White kept a journal of which he later wrote: "The entries are disappointingly lacking in solid facts. Much of the stuff is sickening to read. . . ." But even the shortest entries sometimes go beyond the facts to reveal a young writer's awareness of the ironic contrasts of life:

February 18, 1918. The talk is of Universal Peace after the war—everlasting peace through the medium of an international council. Nations will be ruled by brotherly love and divine principle, arms will be laid down forever and man will return to the ploughshare. Bosh!

. . .

September 21, 1918. My serial number is 3751 and I don't understand what it means, except that I can remember the days when I didn't have a number. The harvest moon is full tonight . . . and looking through the window 3751 enjoys the splendor.—"First World War," *One Man's Meat*

Other celebrated writers have kept journals (sometimes labeled "Diary" or "Notebook") as indispensable aids to literary creation: James Boswell, Henry David Thoreau, Arnold Bennett, Virginia Woolf,

Thomas Wolfe, F. Scott Fitzgerald, Theodore Roethke, to name only a few. Entries range from random jottings—a curious word or phrase, invented or overheard; an unfamiliar quotation; a glimpse of a face or detail or scene; a trifling notion that might germinate into an idea; a clipping from a magazine or newspaper; a comment on a news event or book or play or person—all the way to an extended essay or story or description that lacks only structure and polish to make a finished composition.

As illustrations of the variety of entries, consider two from the journals of famous novelists. Here is Arnold Bennett's record of a football weekend at Princeton:

Saturday, November 4th [1911]   Waldorf
7:45. Business men—the humanity beneath. A man said, "I'm just going to get a bromo-seltzer." Thus giving the whole show away. Postal Telegraph. Girl coming behind her counter in hat and cloak, and turning on her counter lights and opening up her shop. Luggage men sitting in a group under stairs and discussing their affairs. Princeton. Man conducting the "official yell." Quarterback calling numbers. Adams said there was a Glee Club concert last night that was delightful. Contortions of enthusiasts. Artistic amenity in contrast to this bloody barbarity. Reserve men waiting in pairs under red rugs. Whole crowd rising up and sitting down at points of play. Nassau Club. Confusion. Princeton Inn. Confusion. After freshman game met Booth Tarkington at Nassau Club. Drink in dining-room. He said he had been drinking beer with undergraduates late, and then couldn't sleep owing to men singing Chinese songs all night in corridor. Auto back to club and then to field. Coloured effect of hats on stands, heaps of violet colour. Harvard opposite to us. Cheer-leaders with megaphones. Standing up and sitting down. At high moments standing on seats. Accident at start. Man led off amid cheers. Several minor accidents. Naïve and barbaric! Merely an outlet for enthusiasm. Touch and goal scored. Left at half time.—*The Journal of Arnold Bennett*

These are random jottings in sentence fragments, scrappy and inconsecutive, with little of the careful structure of an orderly description. But the passage was obviously written by an alert observer whose eyes and ears were open; and in the emphasis on confusion and barbarity—anticipating the final note—it clearly reveals his attitude toward the experience. If Bennett had decided to convert this raw material into a finished product—say an essay on "The Confusion of a Football Weekend" or "The Barbarity of College Football"—he would have had an authentic collection of specific details to supplement his memory.

Here is Virginia Woolf, commenting on a more significant event:

Saturday, March 28th [1931]
Arnold Bennett died last night; which leaves me sadder than I should have supposed. A lovable genuine man; impeded, somehow a little awkward in life; well meaning; ponderous; kindly; coarse; knowing he was coarse; dimly floundering and feeling for something else; glutted with success; wounded in his feelings; avid; thicklipped; prosaic intolerably; rather dignified; set upon writing; yet always taken in; deluded by splendour and success; but naive; an old

bore; an egotist; much at the mercy of life for all his competence; a shopkeeper's view of literature; yet with the rudiments, covered over with fat and prosperity and the desire for hideous Empire furniture; of sensibility. Some real understanding power, as well as gigantic absorbing power. These are the sort of things that I think by fits and starts this morning, as I sit journalising; I remember his determination to write 1,000 words daily; and how he trotted off to do it that night, and feel some sorrow that now he will never sit down and begin methodically covering his regulation number of pages in his workmanlike beautiful but dull hand. Queer how one regrets the dispersal of anybody who seemed—as I say—genuine: who had direct contact with life—for he abused me; and I yet rather wished him to go on abusing me; and me abusing him. An element in life—even in mine that was so remote—taken away. This is what one minds.—*A Writer's Diary*

As in the Bennett entry, the sentence structure is incomplete: mostly a series of fragments separated by semicolons and jotted down with no consistent pattern of organization. But Woolf is not merely recording what she has seen and heard; she is dipping into her own thoughts to examine her sincere feelings about Bennett. Though the thinking has come in fits and starts, she *is* thinking. In phrase after phrase the words seem carefully weighed: "dimly floundering and feeling for something else," "glutted with success," "deluded by splendour and success," "covered over with fat and prosperity and the desire for hideous Empire furniture." What emerges is a sharp sketch for a finished portrait, complete with contradictions, evolving into a moving comment on the loss of a fellow writer.

In commenting on the value of keeping a journal (she called it a diary), Woolf notes one advantage of writing at a "rapid haphazard gallop":

Still if it were not written rather faster than the fastest type-writing, if I stopped and took thought, it would never be written at all; and the advantage of the method is that it sweeps up accidentally several stray matters which I should exclude if I hesitated, but which are the diamonds of the dustheap.

You may be reluctant to concede your ability to strew diamonds in a diary dustheap. But consider Woolf's further comment on the value of journal-keeping:

It loosens the ligaments. Never mind the misses and the stumbles. Going at such a pace as I do I must make the most direct and instant shots at my object, and thus have to lay hands on words, choose them and shoot them with no more pause than is needed to put my pen in the ink.

The entry contains a lesson for the student whose mind is supposedly a "total blank" when confronted with a writing assignment:

Try free writing   If you do not keep a journal, reach for the nearest piece of blank paper and start writing. Try to set your mind free, for the time being, from the pressures of academic achievement and the particulars of the course or assignment. Write for ten minutes without stopping, saying whatever is on your mind or comes into your head en route. Let one thought lead to another, however trivial or absurd, even if you write in egocentric circles. Don't wait for inspiration, whatever that is, or pause for the appropriate word, correct spelling, acceptable grammar or punctuation. There are quick minds and slow minds, original minds and commonplace minds, excited minds and bored minds—but there is no such thing as a blank mind. The human mind works spontaneously night and day in a continuous reverie or "free association of ideas." For only ten minutes transfer your reverie to paper. The result, or part of it, might look something like this:

Free writing—that's what the instructor calls it. About as free as that guy who isn't free to cry fire in a crowded theater. A few minutes ago my roommate asked if I was free to go to the movies. Said I wasn't because I had to write an English theme. If I were really free to choose my thoughts in free writing I wouldn't be sitting here doing free writing while she's downtown or thinking that when she comes back I'm going to tell her not to turn on the record player the way she does every night. So who's free even to do free writing? Even if you are, you're just putting off the evil hour when you have to pick a gimmick for a paper. May be some good though in doing settingup exercises on the typewriter like this. Even if it's just flexing your fingers by typing the top line of letters over and over. QWERTYUIOP QWERTYUIOP QWERTYUIOP. Sounds like some sort of exotic bird. The qwertyuiop, ladies and gentlemen, is a native of Tahiti that nests in high trees. Recognized by its call—Qwertyuiop. Protected from predatory animals by its natural coloring of cranberry red. Predatory—where did I get that word? Maybe my vocabulary is not so small after all. Maybe I'm warming up. Like football players before a game. Or basketball players tossing practice baskets. Or tennis players rallying before a match. My roommate always says volleying. But she's a free spirit. Free to play records when I'm trying to study.

This ramble could not be dignified, of course, as a composition, or even a first draft. It is not composed—put together—with even a semblance of form. But it could conceivably give the writer a clue to an organized paper: one, for example, on the limits of freedom or conflicts with a roommate or exotic words or the value of warming up before game time. Failing that, it could at least relax the inhibitions that often paralyze the inexperienced writer. Such scribbling, like the "journalising" of Virginia Woolf, "loosens the ligaments." That is why free writing has proved useful in composition courses, especially in the early weeks of the freshman year.

SELECTING A SUBJECT

Eventually, of course, you must confront a more restricted writing assignment. You may be allowed complete freedom in selecting your subject, requested to choose from a varied menu the item that comes closest to tempting your palate, or required to write on one assigned subject, perhaps using a particular technique. Whatever the assignment, you will be no longer free to record your thoughts at random.

If you are given freedom of choice or requested to choose from a varied menu, keep three principles in mind:

1. Select a subject that interests you   Enthusiasm and boredom quickly infect the reader. If you are uninterested in the subject, how can your writing be interesting? If the assignment strikes no sparks, propose a subject that does. The instructor may give you permission to write on it.

2. Select a subject that you are competent to handle adequately at the required length

3. Stay close to your own experience, especially at the beginning of the course   You can probably write a better story about an insurance agent next door than about a secret foreign agent in Moldavia, a better description of a dormitory room at 7 A.M. than of a tropical sunrise, a better explanation of fraternity combines than of international cartels. This does not mean, however, that you should confine yourself to those limited areas of experience in which you presume to be an authority. Don't permit yourself to be silenced by false humility ("Who am I, a poor freshman, to be writing on a subject like 'World Peace'?"). The phrase "a subject you are competent to handle" must not be taken too literally. The most rewarding assignment is not the one that lets you explain a hobby you have understood backward and forward for years but the one that makes you dig around and learn something you haven't known before.

STAKING OUT A CLAIM

The main trouble is not that students insist on writing about "World Peace" when they ought to stick to "Peace in My Family," but that they often try singlehanded to solve in 500 words a problem that the peoples of the world have not been able to solve in millions. *You cannot solve a big problem in a short theme.* You must divide the vast area and sub-divide it and resubdivide it until you have staked out a small, unambitious claim. If you don't do this, you can only scratch the surface with dull generalities; and the instructor can fairly object both to the vagueness of what you say and to the absence of what you might have said. Nothing will more quickly reveal your limitations than your failure to limit a broad subject.

Some theme assignments come in neat little packages that can be unwrapped, explored, and wrapped up again in 500 words. But even "simple" subjects may conceal complexities of which the instructor is more aware than you are. Few topics are so narrow that further limiting is unnecessary. The process can be illustrated in this way:

**INSTRUCTOR'S ASSIGNMENT OR
STUDENT'S GENERAL "IDEA"**   Television (500 words)

Steps in limiting: 1. General aspects of television (discovery, early technical developments, recent improvements, influence on American society, ratings and mediocrity, programs)
2. Types of programs (giveaway shows, game shows, talk shows, situation comedies, soaps, police and detective serials, imported British dramas, sports, newscasts, old movies, children's programs)
3. Children's programs (artistic value, entertainment, educational value, commercial impact)

Final topic: 4. The harmful effect of TV programs on children's diets

Title: How to Sell Breakfast Food

Though the steps in limiting may not always be so systematic, the illustration shows that the writer, by eliminating numerous choices, has cut down a *general subject*—an impossibly vast area for a short paper—to a more or less *specific topic*.

Though the words are often interchanged, it is useful to think of a *subject* as a broad map and a *topic* as a precise location. In an expository or argumentative essay, a well-chosen topic can be expressed as a *topic sentence* or *thesis statement* (see pp. 34, 50) in which the writer makes a clear-cut assertion. Example: "TV programs have a harmful effect on children's diets." Whether it is specifically stated in the paper or merely implied, such an assertion can be a guide to *unity* throughout (see pp. 47, 50–53).

Consider another example:

SUBJECT   An Opinion on College Education (Exposition, 500 words)

Steps in limiting: 1. General subject areas (admissions policies, administrative rules, teaching standards and methods, student discipline, student government, social life, extracurricular activities, curriculum)
2. Curriculum (degrees awarded, divisions and departments, elective courses, required courses)

*Final topic
(stated
as a thesis):*   3. Required courses (Freshman English? science? social science? mathematics? literature? a foreign language?)
4. A foreign language should be required of all students.

Title: The Gift of Tongues

The limiting process varies, of course, with the assignment. If the instructor, for example, should require "An Autobiographical Narrative"—a common assignment early in the term—your story might not be readily expressed in a topic sentence or thesis statement. But here too limiting would be compulsory. In Lytton Strachey's metaphor, you should "lower the little bucket" instead of trying to swallow the vast ocean of material. The development of a special interest; the influence of a particular person, book, or event; the growth of a dominant character trait; a segment of time (life in the fifth grade); or a pivotal point (high school commencement)—possible approaches are numberless. The lives of few students are so sensational that a mere summary of the-story-thus-far is exciting, or so dull that all the flavor can be concentrated in a general biographical sketch.

THE FIRST DRAFT

Having cut the subject down to size, how do you go about writing on it? There are as many answers to that as there are writers. In the absence of foolproof formulas, these suggestions may help:

1. Use your subconscious Don't fool yourself into supposing that the writing process consists entirely of putting words on paper. That is the final stage. Most experienced writers do a vast amount of thinking and planning before the paper goes into the typewriter. You will naturally set aside a period, perhaps the same evening each week, to write your theme. But there is no law forbidding preliminary rumination. Shortly after the subject is chosen, turn it over in your mind a few times. Then, if inspiration is going to strike at all—a fresh approach, an arresting beginning, a well-turned phrase—it may pop suddenly into your head while you are strolling idly across the campus dreaming about a weekend date; and, without much conscious labor, your mind may nourish the first fleeting impression into a full-grown plan. If, on the other hand, you assiduously avoid all thought about English until 7:45 the night before the deadline, and then, starting behind scratch, try desperately to decoy inspiration from a glaring sheet of virgin paper—you will probably have to settle past midnight for a handful of empty generalities.

2. Make a few rough notes Whether or not you keep a journal, you can use the same technique of random jotting that is illustrated in Arnold Bennett's account of the football weekend (see p. 28). Brainstorm yourself to see how much raw material accumulates in your mind as you reflect on the assignment—words, phrases, notions, all summoned up by an "association of ideas" with a sharper focus than the reverie in free writing. Do not concern yourself about order or relevance; this is not a process of systematic note-taking. Some of these jottings will turn out to be useless. But it is easier to hang a composition on visible pegs than to visualize it in the mind's wavering eye.

3. Choose at least one main point   The traditional handbook rule that every theme should have a "guiding" or "controlling" purpose is based on two assumptions: (1) that unless students keep one aim clearly in mind, they are in grave danger of ending up nowhere, of writing a theme without a theme; and (2) that one main point (or *thesis*) is all that can be adequately developed in a short paper. The second assumption is open to some question: a purpose may be broader than a point; a 500-word paper may have two points or even three. But the danger of aimlessness increases with the number of points. Many students are confused at the outset because, having no clear goal in mind at the start—no "angle," as a journalist might say—they are busily riding off in all directions at once, like the gifted horseman in a story by Stephen Leacock. There is, of course, the discursive familiar essay, which begins anywhere, goes everywhere, and ends nowhere, and the "stream-of-consciousness" narrative, which wanders with the whims of the rudderless mind. But even these methods have a subtle unity that the undergraduate does not always perceive.

Again you are reminded that an exercise in free writing is not a composition. If you merely open a door in your forehead and pour the miscellaneous contents of your brain onto the paper, you are headed for trouble. At least in the beginning of the course, you would do well to stick to a single thesis in every short theme.

4. Make an informal outline   After the preliminary jottings and the choice of an angle, you may find yourself still pen-tied until you have tentatively determined the order of the parts. Try listing your main details or illustrations or points (if you have more than one) in several different arrangements until a logical sequence emerges. This may differ from the rough notes only because it is more selective and more orderly; unless the instructor requires you to submit one, it doesn't need to be a detailed formal outline complete with main points, subpoints, and sub-subpoints. A formal outline can be indispensable, however, in planning a long paper (see pp. 231–233, 247). By clarifying the relation between the parts and the relative importance of each part to the whole, it can guard against overlapping, contradictions, illogical subordination, and the common error of burying a main point beneath a stack of trivialities. But only the unusually weak organizer or the exceedingly methodical writer needs a complete blueprint for an informal paper of 500 words. Detailed outlines can be a nuisance, curbing natural expression and producing firstly-secondly-thirdly themes with the bare bones of the skeleton glaring through the transparent flesh.

5. Begin your first draft wherever you like   The first sentence you write doesn't have to be the first sentence of the final product. If you assume that it does, you may be so worried about getting off on the right foot that you will never get started. Begin with the part that comes easiest to you—it may eventually turn out to be somewhere in the middle of the third paragraph—and get that much down. After you have written that, you can write the rest of your paper around it. The preface to most books is fashioned on the home stretch. Richard Wright said of his first novel: "The book was one-half finished, with the opening and closing scenes unwritten. . . . The entire guilt theme that runs through *Native Son* was woven in after the first draft was written."

6. Write your first draft any way you please The first draft is no place to worry about the instructor and the textbook. Don't interrupt yourself at this stage to juggle phrases, quibble over grammar, track down the inevitable word. Revision will come later, and it is easier to twist a poor sentence on paper into a good one than to pluck a good one out of the air. The white heat of your creation may be only lukewarm to begin with. Don't let it cool off completely by stopping for revisions en route.

BEGINNINGS

How should the theme eventually begin? If you are a slave to the formula that every piece of writing must have Beginning, Middle, and End (or Introduction, Body, and Conclusion), free yourself from bondage now. This is a convenient pedagogical pattern based partly on a misunderstanding of Aristotle, partly on the natural fear of abrupt beginnings and dangling, inconclusive conclusions, partly on the intelligent assumption that any organization, however rigid, is better than none. It may be useful in composing formal arguments or long reports. But in 500 words of informal writing, the I-am-about-to-make-this-point, I-am-making-this-point, I-have-made-this-point structure implies a weakness in your reader's perception and memory that you probably have no right to assume.

Poor Beginnings

Four kinds of beginnings, to name only a few, are likely to elicit an automatic protest from any experienced instructor:

1. The truism
Sometimes a self-evident truth is disguised in pretentious rhetoric. This, for example:

Throughout the history of the world men have had affairs with women. Adam and Eve, Antony and Cleopatra, Napoleon and his Austrian princess, and so throughout the centuries. This ancient tradition is more common in the modern era than ever.

35

Or this:

Down through history, from Eve to Joan of Arc, from Cleopatra to Eleanor Roosevelt, we find that women have provided inspiration for men and molded their lives, their efforts, and their destinies. For the love of women men have robbed, murdered, pillaged, gained riches, and gained greatness.

After opening cannonades like those, no short theme could be anything but an anticlimactic sputter of birdshot.

More often the writer settles for an undecorated banality:

There exists a necessity for everyone to explain himself.

There can be no doubt that studying requires concentration.

As a general rule of writing, anything that goes without saying should not be said.

2. The complaint about the difficulties of writing on the assigned subject

Who am I? This question is quite a difficult problem to analyze, even though it looks quite simple at a glance. To give a complete analysis of yourself takes quite a considerable length of time, even though you have lived with yourself all your life. Not many students take this viewpoint that I take, so I shall try to give an analysis of myself.

The author of this windup is like the public-speaking nuisance who spends the first five minutes complaining that he can't possibly begin to cover his subject in the fifteen minutes allowed.

3. The personal apology to the instructor

After searching vainly for a subject on which to write which would be related to the assignment, I came to the conclusion that everything I considered as a possible theme had already been well "hashed over" in class. Therefore, I gave up and succumbed to a desire I've had since very early in this course—to write about my experience with pinball machines.

The personal apology belongs, if anywhere, in a headnote or a memo clipped to the outside of the theme.

4. The dictionary definition

Before entering into a discussion of the wit of Oscar Wilde as displayed in *The Importance of Being Earnest*, it is first necessary to ask ourselves: What do we mean by *wit*? *Webster's New Collegiate Dictionary* defines *wit*. . . .

This kind of beginning is less objectionable than the others. It is based on the plausible assumption that sooner or later key terms should be defined. The student is to be commended for naming the source instead of vaguely writing: "The dictionary says. . . ." But regardless of the importance of definition, the dictionary definition beginning has become thoroughly hackneyed.

If you have to warm up to your subject in your first draft, one obvious solution is to cross out the first paragraph and begin the final draft with the second. There is some truth to the stories about novelists who regularly jettison the first hundred pages of every book they write. George Meredith tossed away three of the first four chapters of *The Ordeal of Richard Feverel*. Keats threw out the entire first stanza of his first draft of the "Ode on Melancholy." Thomas Wolfe, notoriously unable to dam his own wordflow, had to submit when Maxwell Perkins "relentlessly kicked out" the entire first chapter of *Of Time and the River*—even though the editor agreed it was as good a piece of writing as he had ever done. The trouble, Wolfe admitted, was that "it was really not a true beginning for the book but merely something which led up to the true beginning; therefore it had to go." In many opening passages a writer is tediously beginning to begin.

The old rule—Begin at the beginning—is sound in principle but not too helpful. Here are a few more tangible suggestions:

Useful beginnings

1. A direct statement of fact

I underwent, during the summer that I became fourteen, a prolonged religious crisis.—James Baldwin, "Letter from a Region in My Mind," *New Yorker*

Bryan woke up on the icy side of a hill with a buffalo licking his face.—John Sayles, "Breed," *Atlantic*

2. A simple announcement of the subject

This is a book about social character and about the differences in social character between men of different regions, eras, and groups.—David Riesman, Nathan Glazer, and Reuel Denney, *The Lonely Crowd*

The aim of this article is to consider the highest temperatures suspected to occur in the universe—the temperatures in the interior of the stars. The discussion will, we hope, throw light on the formation of the universe as we know it and on its future evolution.—Fred Hoyle, "Ultrahigh Temperature," *Scientific American*

3. A statement intended to startle the reader with its bluntness or frankness

I do not believe in Belief.—E. M. Forster, "What I Believe," *Two Cheers for Democracy*

Lie detectors lie.—Jonathan Kwitney, "The Dirty Little Secret of Lie Detectors," *Esquire*

4. A question or series of questions

How does the mind work? To answer that question we must look at some of

the work performed by the mind—Noam Chomsky, "Language and the Mind,"
Psychology Today

What is race? A myth, as some popular writers would have us believe, or a
rigid division of mankind into superior and inferior groups? A reverse freedom
rider northward bound? America's greatest and most divisive unsolved problem? The white, black, yellow, red, and brown races pictured in the school
geography books? Or a relatively recent and superficial division of mankind?
No. Examined in the light of science and history, race is not exactly any of
these.—Carleton S. Coon, "New Findings on the Origin of Races," *Harper's*

In those two passages the answer, which takes the entire article, is
only begun in the sentences quoted. In this one the opening sentence
implies its own answer; it is an ironic tone-setter couched in question
form:

Has it been duly remarked by historians that the late William Jennings
Bryan's last secular act on this globe of sin was to catch flies?—H. L. Mencken,
"In Memoriam: W. J. B.," *Prejudices*

Beware, however, of beginning with the empty rhetorical question
that goes without asking:

Which of us has not at one time or another wanted to do something that he
shouldn't do?

5. A quotation that is short, fresh, and pertinent

"My boy is something of a genius," said the Scarsdale commuter to his seat
companion on the 5:26 P.M. train. He wasn't speaking metaphorically, he wasn't
joking and he wasn't consciously boasting. He said it in a matter-of-fact way, as
he might have said, "My boy has a pet hamster." After pausing long enough to
let his companion express a decent interest, he went on to report the basis for his
judgment—the very high scores his youngster had made on a scholastic aptitude
test.—John W. Gardner, chapter beginning in *Excellence*

"The lad has good manners," said the Earl. "He will be in no one's way.
Children are usually idiots or bores—but he can answer when he's spoken to and
be silent when he is not." Modern readers will be quick to detect the flavor of
anachronism in these remarks, and those whose temples are brushed with gray
will have no trouble identifying the exemplary youngster to whom the Earl
refers. It is, of course, Frances Hodgson Burnett's blue-eyed hero, Little Lord
Fauntleroy.—Janet Agle, "Come Back, Little Lord Fauntleroy," *Harper's Bazaar*

6. An authentic illustrative anecdote

Someone said recently to an old black lady from Mississippi, whose legs had
been badly mangled by local police who arrested her for "disturbing the peace,"
that the civil rights movement was dead, and asked, since it was dead, what she
thought about it. The old lady replied, hobbling out of his presence on her cane,
that the civil rights movement was like herself, "if it's dead, it shore ain't ready
to lay down!"—Alice Walker, "The Civil Rights Movement: What Good Was It?"
American Scholar

The adjectives *authentic* and *illustrative* have been carefully chosen to warn against the favorite recipe of the after-dinner speaker: the synthetic appetizer that bears no noticeable relation to the main course. The effective opening story will have the simple directness of once-upon-a-time, not the artificial flavor of have-you-heard-the-one-about.

7. A significant dramatic incident, followed by the steps leading up to it

A shiver went through Lonnie. He drew his hand away from his sharp chin, remembering what Clem had said. It made him feel now as if he were committing a crime by standing in Arch Gunnard's presence and allowing his face to be seen.

He and Clem had been walking up the road together that afternoon on their way to the filling station when he told Clem how much he needed rations. Clem stopped a moment to kick a rock out of the road, and said that if you worked for Arch Gunnard long enough, your face would be sharp enough to split the boards for your own coffin.—Erskine Caldwell, *Kneel to the Rising Sun*

The beginnings recommended vary considerably because of their context. A dramatic opening such as Erskine Caldwell's is common in fiction and biographical narrative but would be out of place in a scholarly report. The sober announcement of the subject is more fitting at the beginning of a serious piece of exposition, such as a technical paper, than in an informal personal confession, in which a snappy quip such as Forster's would be more appropriate. But all these beginnings have one trait in common: they are simple and direct. In each one the writer not only gets off to a fast start but takes the reader right along.

ENDINGS

Ending is easier than beginning. *When you have finished what you have to say, stop.* Summaries are for long papers, not short ones. The danger of leaving a reader "up in the air" has been overrated. In a story an inconclusive ending may be a conscious device. In exposition or argument, a point left up in the air is one that has never really been put across in the first place, and no stylish epilogue will save it. Actually more students botch endings by saying, not too little, but too much:

So ends the analysis of myself and the question of who am I has been answered in a brief form.

This ending, by the same student who contributed the beginning under (2) on page 36, is about as unnecessary as the old-fashioned *Finis*. It is as if the writer were signing off like a radio announcer to clarify matters for a reader who has tuned in in the middle of the fourth paragraph.

The temptation to indulge in truisms and clichés is at least as common in endings as in beginnings:

In conclusion let me say.

We arrived home tired but happy.

As for the future, only time will tell.

The most objectionable ending is that of students who, having no clear-cut plan from the start, wander along until they hit a blind alley, count words hopefully, and find they are still below the minimum, and then, gathering forces for one last struggle, either append an unnecessary summary of what has just been said, or shoot off bravely on a brand new course that they haven't the slightest notion of pursuing to a logical conclusion.

Even good writers have made the mistake of going a step too far. Joseph Conrad admitted in a letter to H. G. Wells that he should have ended "Youth" with the men sleeping in the boats, exhausted after the exasperating voyage to the East, instead of permitting Marlow to launch once more into a rapture on the courage of youthful hearts. It is a common student error to begin discussing a point and abruptly drop it. It is equally common for students to make a point and then mar it by pointing out the point they have just made.

REVISION

When your first draft is ended, you are ready to revise. Revision is not the simple act of giving the first draft a once-over-lightly for missing commas and occasional misspellings. It is a major step in composing. It demands not only painstaking proofreading for mechanical errors in grammar, punctuation, and spelling, but recasting awkward sentences, rearranging passages for more effective order, adding details and subtracting others, substituting sharp, concrete words for fuzzy abstractions. For every trained writer who has never blotted a line in revision, there are hundreds whose first copies are almost illegible mazes of insertions and deletions, cobwebs of carets and circles and meandering arrows. Honest revision is often so complete as to require at least one intermediate draft before the final copy.

Here are some general aids to meaningful revision:

1. Put your first draft aside for some time before attacking it again After a reasonable interval—the longer the better—you should be able to approach it with some detachment. The memory of what you meant to write will be dulled, and you will have a clearer perspective on what you actually have written. More than once you will ask yourself: "Did I really write that?" This advice assumes, of course, that you haven't postponed the whole project until the last minute.

2. Persuade another student to read it—preferably a better writer
Obviously, if someone makes extensive alterations for you, you will learn little; the final product should be yours, not a collaboration. There is no reason, however, moral or otherwise, why you should not invite suggestions from another critic. An ambiguity which has never occurred to you may strike someone else at once (on this point, ask any teacher who has tried to make out a set of examination questions that will convey the same meaning to a whole roomful of undergraduates). Few trained writers would think of writing without inflicting an early draft on one or more previewers.

3. Read it aloud   Unless you are a trained proofreader, your eyes will play tricks on you—ignoring words and pretending to your brain that you have seen them. The ear will catch many errors—clumsy, unemphatic sentences, awkward phrases, weakening repetition, careless omissions—that the eye will never see.

4. Read it at least three times   A sound plan, if somewhat arbitrary, is to read once for such broad aspects as logical organization (including intelligent paragraphing); a second time for your favorite errors (you should know after two or three themes are returned whether spelling, punctuation, grammar, or sentence structure is your special weakness and lay your emphasis accordingly); and the third time as a sort of final check for good measure. If this ambitious plan seems to assume that you have nothing to do but write English compositions, remember that you can read five hundred words slowly in less than five minutes and can afford fifteen or twenty minutes to save yourself a lot of woe. Remember also that perhaps half of all errors are due to sheer carelessness. Moreover, the ideal final copy should be nothing but a clean duplicate of your rough draft—with no last-ditch rewriting.

5. Use reference books freely   It doesn't take much longer to consult a dictionary for a correct spelling than to consult your roommate, who may not know how to spell either. Moreover, the book you are now reading is intended to be more than a series of consecutive lessons to be approached only when "pages 100–118" are "assigned for next time." You may not "study" punctuation formally until two months from now, but that is no reason why you should blissfully misuse the semicolon until you get there. Use the Index, Glossary of Usage, and Glossary of Grammatical and Rhetorical Terms freely.
   This advice applies also to the content of your theme. Get direct quotations straight. Replace generalities with specific facts. Don't try to get by with a rough guess about a historical event when five minutes in the library will put the record straight.

41

THE FINAL DRAFT

After you finish revising, make a neat, final draft in strict accordance with all the local ground rules. These will probably require the following:

1. Write legibly in blue or black ink or type double-spaced on one side of medium-weight white paper (8½ by 11 inches). Do not use erasable paper or onionskin.
2. Use lined paper for handwriting, unlined for typing.
3. If the theme is handwritten, center the title on the top line of the first page and leave a space between title and text. For a typed theme, center the title about two inches from the top of the first page and leave about an inch before beginning the text. Do not underline the title or enclose it in quotation marks.
4. Leave good-sized but not excessive margins (1¼ inches at the left and one inch at top, right, and bottom). Indent each paragraph five typewriter spaces (or about ½ inch).
5. After the first page, number the pages in the upper right-hand corner with Arabic numerals, not Roman.
6. Arrange the pages carefully in the proper order and fasten them with a paper clip.
7. Put your name, the course and section, and the date in the upper left-hand corner of the first page. (If you are asked to fold the pages lengthwise so that they open like a book—not a Japanese book—enter this information at the top of the outside sheet to the right of the fold. For a long paper, you may use a separate title page—see p. 246.)

The rules may not require that you type, but you are unfortunate if you can't and foolish if you don't learn at the first opportunity. Try as they might to be strictly objective, most instructors can't help preferring a neat, double-spaced manuscript in clean black type to even the most beautiful specimen of penmanship. They may suspect immaturity in an "immature" hand, assume misspelling of an illegible word, and refuse to pore over sprawling, slanting hieroglyphics or "cultivated" backhand. Another advantage of typing is the ease of making an accurate carbon of the final draft. Whether or not you type, never hand in a paper without keeping at least one copy to insure against loss.

After you have made your final draft, *give it at least one farewell reading,* scouting particularly for the common errors of copying: the omission of words and punctuation marks. Make all final corrections, preferably few, neatly in ink or with correction fluid. If you delete a word or phrase with ink, use a single horizontal line ~~like this~~. Do not indicate
                                                              thus
omissions with parentheses (like this). Make additions ∧ with a caret.

42

This final reading is important. There is only one answer to the student who says, "I had it right in my first draft." The instructor doesn't see your first draft.

THE TITLE

You may have hit on a suitable title long before this stage, but you don't have to. For every book written to conform to a bright, prefabricated title, there are a hundred whose labels are not chosen until the last minute just before the manuscript goes to press.

1. Remember that the subject, whether yours or the instructor's, is not a title   "An Autobiographical Sketch" or "Exposition of a Process" is a pointless label for a theme.

2. In much expository writing the best title is often a sober, factual statement of the ground covered   This is true, for example, in research papers, where readers want only to know whether the article touches on their field of interest: "The Bearing of Science on the Thought of Arthur Hugh Clough." Yet even in this kind of writing, compression and imagination may help. "Martians and Mass Hysteria" is a more intriguing title than "A Study of the Orson Welles Broadcast of 'The War of the Worlds.'"

3. In most kinds of writing, a good title may suggest mood and tone without being explicit about content   *Arsenic and Old Lace* evokes the quality of a popular play more subtly than the original title, *Bodies in Our Cellar*. In *My Life and Hard Times* the simple insertion of an adjective, *hard*, changes a conventional, matter-of-fact title into one that suggests some of the comic desperation of James Thurber's modern classic.

4. A matter-of-fact title is better than one that is too cryptic or clever   An apt quotation may make an excellent title, but the modern tradition under which the author chooses a favorite obscure quotation from a favorite obscure poet and challenges the reader to guess its connection with the story is wearing thin. It is a more natural strategy merely to lift a key phrase from the theme you have just completed. If you are original, an original title may come to you. If you are not, be explicit and concise, and let who will be clever. "Cyrano: Ham, Heel, or Hero?" is on the borderline of good taste. The student who entitled the account of a visit to the mental hospital "A Pound of Mixed Nuts" crossed over the border. In writing, as in golf, it is a good rule not to press too hard.

EXERCISES

A. Write rapidly for ten minutes without stopping, recording, as far as possible, whatever comes into your mind. Then identify in what you have written a number of subjects that might be appropriate for a short theme.

B. (1) Make a list of five subjects that you consider too broad for adequate treatment in 500 words. (2) Subdivide one of the subjects into five topics, each of which you consider appropriate for a 500-word theme. (3) Suggest an effective title for a theme on each of the five topics under (2). (4) Write two drafts of a 500-word theme with one of the titles listed under (3). (5) Hand in both drafts along with a written explanation of each of the essential changes in revision.

C. Which of the following beginnings are effective and which are ineffective? Why? (The unidentified passages are from student themes.)

1. According to the Book of Genesis, God first created man. Woman was not only an afterthought, but an amenity. For close on two thousand years this holy scripture was believed to justify her subordination and explain her inferiority; for even as a copy she was not a very good copy. There were differences. She was not one of His best efforts.—Elaine Morgan, *The Descent of Woman*

2. Biologists all agree that living matter never arises under the influence of pre-existing matter. I generously conformed to their beliefs and popped into being like a firecracker on July 4, 1961. My birth only partly conforms to Wordsworth's poetic rule that "our birth is but a sleep and a forgetting"; for, though I have certainly forgotten the experience, I have been told that I was very much awake at the time.

3. Sleeping is a fundamental process which the body of every person must experience quite frequently to remain in a healthy state and alive.

4. Everyone who cares about the use of language is faced sooner or later with this problem: When the person you are talking to makes a mistake in grammar, or pronounces a word mistakenly, do you interrupt with a correction? Or would such a correction be seen as a put-down, the action of a wiseguy? Or would a failure to correct be taken as agreement with the mistake?—William Safire, "The Wiseguy Problem," *New York Times Magazine*

5. When I reach the shades at last it will no doubt astonish Satan to discover, on thumbing my dossier, that I was once a member of the Y.M.C.A. Yet a fact is a fact. What is more remarkable, I was not recruited by a missionary to the heathen, but joined at the suggestion of my father, who enjoyed and deserved the name of infidel.—H. L. Mencken, "Adventures of a Y.M.C.A. Lad," *The Vintage Mencken*

6. When *The Grass Harp* came to life as a play in 1952, its critical reception was surprisingly lukewarm. Despite Capote's careful adaptation—graced by Cecil Beaton settings and performed by a fine cast—the production proved disappointing; somehow the magic was gone from what had once been a poignant and delicate prose original.

Many books have resisted translation into working drama; but Capote's failure to make lightning strike twice succeeds at least in being instructive; for it provides a point of departure as we try to define precisely what makes the novel unique—that special quality that prompts a critic to choose the word "mesmerizing" in praising its particular brand of whimsical reminiscence.

7. Here I am in the college of my choice. It is still too early to know if I was right. But the process of choosing—a baffling mixture of reason and roulette—may be worth explaining, if only as a guide to future undergraduates.

8. On the 29th of July, in 1943, my father died. On the same day, a few hours later, his last child was born. Over a month before this, while all our energies were concentrated in waiting for these events, there had been, in Detroit, one of the bloodiest race riots of the century. A few hours after my father's funeral, while he lay in state in the undertaker's chapel, a race riot broke out in Harlem. On the morning of the 3rd of August, we drove my father to the graveyard through a wilderness of smashed plate glass.—James Baldwin, "Notes of a Native Son"

9. When it was suggested to Walt Whitman that one of his works should be bound in vellum, he was outraged—"Pshaw!" he snorted, "—hangings, curtains, finger bowls, chinaware, Matthew Arnold!" And he might have been equally irritated by talk of style; for he boasted of "my barbaric yawp"—he would not be literary; his readers should touch not a book but a man. Yet Whitman took the pains to rewrite *Leaves of Grass* four times, and his style is unmistakable.—F. L. Lucas, "On the Fascination of Style," *Holiday*

10. Reading is all around. Books, books, books; wherever you go, you can't get away from them. In the library, in the home, in every shape and form there is some type of reading material. Books and all other literature are very important to everyone. From them much knowledge can be obtained and many things can be told that otherwise would never reach the outside world.

11. In Rhodesia a white truck driver passed a group of idle natives and muttered, "They're lazy brutes." A few hours later he saw natives heaving two hundred pound sacks of grain onto a truck, singing in rhythm to their work. "Savages," he grumbled. "What do you expect?"—Gordon W. Allport, *The Nature of Prejudice*

12. You may have seen my mother waltzing on ice skates in Rockefeller Center. She's seventy-eight years old now but very wiry, and she wears a red velvet costume with a short skirt.—John Cheever, "The Angel of the Bridge," *The Stories of John Cheever*

D. Write three different beginnings of at least fifty words each on some aspect of the following subject: "My Home Town."

3 Organizing and Developing

The paragraph is a device of punctuation
Herbert Read

If the paragraph did not exist, we would
have to invent it.
E. D. Hirsch, Jr.

FORM AND CONTENT

In some writing, organization is not a major problem; the writer has an accepted form to follow. For example, in presenting instructions for operating a simple machine, the natural form is a series of numbered steps, each providing a single clear direction for the reader. The business-letter writer has a conventional mold to fill: heading, inside address, greeting, body, close, and signature. The writer of the standard news story will begin with a short summary of the event—a "lead"—before moving first to significant details and then to items of less importance.

Of course, the existence of standard molds for such writing doesn't mean that the problem of organization is as easy as pouring Jello: the form of any extended piece of prose is fixed not only by the broad outline but by the shape of the words selected and by the shaping of words into sentences, sentences into paragraphs, and paragraphs into the work as a whole. But often the general pattern is clearly dictated by logic or convention.

Though the organization of any idea is inseparable from the idea itself, form is not always so clearly related to content. On many assignments the instructor will not supply a prefabricated mold. You, the writer, must mold the material to suit your purpose. An idea may "take shape" in your mind and fit neatly into an outline before you begin to write. Or it may be "whipped into shape" during the process of writing and rewriting. In either event, organization is supremely important. The final product must not be formless.

FOUR GENERAL PRINCIPLES

Though every assignment is a separate challenge, four general principles of organization can serve as useful guides: (1) unity, (2) coherence,
(3) completeness, and (4) emphasis.

Unity

Any well-organized piece of writing has unity or "oneness." Each
part—sentence or paragraph—should have its own unity, and all the
parts should be related to a single whole. The easiest way to achieve this
is to stick to one point. If you choose to make three points, they should
be so related as to produce a *total impression.* Suppose you decide to
write on some aspect of intercollegiate athletics. You may achieve unity
by developing the thesis that athletic scholarships should be abolished
(or increased). Or you may elect to stake out a larger claim and develop,
in less detail, three "suggestions for improving athletics": (1) the abolition (or increase) of athletic scholarships, (2) the abolition (or revival) of
spring football practice, (3) the scheduling of fewer (or more) games
with national pigskin powers. But if you wander from citing the case of
a "typical" athlete who couldn't afford to join a fraternity to a consideration of fraternity rushing tactics—if only within a single paragraph—you are violating unity.

Coherence

The parts of any piece of good writing *cohere,* or stick together. It
doesn't necessarily follow that because you have carefully selected the
parts to form a single impression (unity), you will weave them together
(coherence) into a well-knit whole. Or, to put it another way, even
though you are moving steadily ahead toward a single goal—via one
path or more—you can still lose the reader en route unless you supply
adequate signs and bridges.

Obviously the problem of coherence is closely related to the problem
of order. If you are telling a story in strict chronological order, setting
down events as they occurred; if you are describing a scene in a simple
spatial sequence; or if you are explaining a process in an order that is
inevitably decreed by the nature of the process itself, the chain will
grow more or less automatically without special attention to the links.
But if, for example, you are explaining something as intangible as an
idea, you must impose a logical order on the parts, and you must hang
them together—or they will all hang separately.

Completeness

In the references to "a single whole" (unity) and "a well-knit whole"
(coherence), the stress is on the adjectives. But the noun *whole* cannot be

taken for granted. Though *completeness* is a relative term (when is a whole a whole?), it is a fundamental principle of organization. A writer may consciously aim to produce the effect of incompleteness: to compose an intentional fragment or leave a situation or an issue hanging. The storyteller may do this for dramatic effect or simply because the lives of the characters go on past the period—of time or punctuation—at the end of the story. But even in narrative, the reader has a right to a sense of something accomplished, something developed, something "finished."

Completeness in expository writing is easier to define. Whatever its length, any piece of exposition is incomplete if the writer has not accomplished what he or she ostensibly set out to do. If, whether in title or text, you make clear your intention of taking an informal look at something—merely making a try or, in the literal sense of the word, an "essay"—you cannot be fairly blamed for failing to exhaust every aspect of the subject. In a more formal piece of writing, if you have clearly staked out a limited claim at the start, you cannot be expected to explore the whole field. But if, on the other hand, your title or opening sentences promise a thorough excavation, and the final product is only a series of surface scratchings; if you have obviously ignored a central issue entirely; if you have announced three points and covered only two—the reader has a right to fault you for incompleteness. Oversimplified in a formula, completeness can be defined as the quotient of promise divided by performance.

More common than the omission of the material expected is the *inadequate development* of the material included. Inexperienced writers often produce mechanical exercises in composition that are "correct," unified, coherent—and underdeveloped. Such papers may make "perfectly good sense"—as most banalities do—but they are too thin to make good reading. This problem will be considered in more detail in the discussion of paragraphing.

Emphasis

In organizing your material, consider not only the relation of the parts but their relative importance. Decide what to stress and how to stress it. *Emphasis* as a principle of sentence structure is discussed in later chapters. Emphasis within the paragraph and in the composition as a whole can be achieved in four ways: (1) isolation, (2) position, (3) repetition, and (4) proportion.

1. Isolation   An obvious way of emphasizing a point is to isolate it in a short paragraph. This is often done in a single bald sentence unencumbered by details (see p. 56). The details are usually supplied in one or more preceding or following paragraphs.

2. Position A main point is more likely to stand out if made near the beginning or near the end of a paper. Undergraduate writers often make the mistake of burying their most precious gold deep in the middle of a theme. Or, enslaved by the tradition of "putting first things first," they overlook the danger of writing a paper that begins with a bang and ends with a whimper. Many ideas can be best expressed by using the climactic order, which leads by gradual stages to the main point at the end.

3. Repetition Important points can be reinforced by stating them more than once, either in the same words or in different words. This is often done by making an assertion at the beginning of a paragraph or a composition and restating it at the end. But all forms of repetition should be administered in moderate doses (see pp. 65–68).

4. Proportion Though the correlation is not strictly mathematical, there is an obvious proportion between the importance of a point and the amount of space devoted to it. If three parts of a paper deserve equal emphasis, it is logical to develop them at approximately the same length. An undergraduate writing a short narrative often starts too far behind the dramatic crisis, devotes too much space to the preliminaries leading up to it, and then underplays the main event. In a poorly proportioned argument a student will sometimes devote a page and a half of a two-page theme to developing a trivial quibble and crowd two significant points into the final half-page. A well-written paper is a well-balanced paper.

So much for the general principles of good organization. The rest of this chapter will contain a discussion of how these principles operate in practice—first in the paragraph, then in the composition as a whole.

PARAGRAPHS

The Purposes of Paragraphing

"If the paragraph did not exist, we would have to invent it." Why? Consider three main purposes of paragraphing; (1) to *divide* the whole into parts; (2) to *combine* the smaller units into larger; (3) to *relieve* the reader.

1. To divide A paragraph indention is a mark of punctuation, a sign for the reader. Just as a period signals the end of one sentence and the beginning of another, a paragraph break signals the end and beginning of main divisions. Inexperienced students will sometimes submit an entire composition of, say, 500 words without a single paragraph indention after the opening sentence. Almost certainly such writers have not divided their thought into parts, arranged in an orderly sequence. Even if the division is clear in their minds, they have imposed on the reader by not supplying visual evidence.

2. To combine   At the other extreme from students who fail to divide the subject—or to identify those divisions with indentions—are writers who make no effort to *combine* the particles of their thought into solid segments. They make no significant distinction between sentences and paragraphs. Instead of asking the reader to swallow the meaning in a single gulp, they serve it up in tiny nibbles. Instead of limiting the paper to a single indention, they may have a random dozen; instead of helping the reader, these merely interrupt. The result is not a composition because nothing is composed—put together.

3. To relieve   Expecting paragraph breaks because they are conventional, the experienced reader also *needs* them because human attention focuses on meaning one segment at a time. The mind requires the relief of putting one point aside, at least for the time being, and moving on to the next. Paragraph indentions also spell relief for the eyes. Blocks of solid print, however exciting the text, can weary the keenest vision if they are not periodically varied with empty white spaces. If this were not so, we would still designate paragraph breaks like the ancient Greeks, merely by using the symbol ¶.

Organizing Paragraphs

In a sense there is no such animal as *the* paragraph. Any experienced writer with an orderly mind can arrange material in dozens of different paragraph patterns of all sizes and shapes. But most of these, at least in serious exposition, will conform closely to the basic principles of good organization. Three principles—unity, coherence, and completeness—require further discussion in turn. The fourth, emphasis, will be considered in passing as it relates to the others.

Unity: the topic sentence
The sentences of the standard expository paragraph relate to a single point represented by a *topic sentence*. The topic sentence may come anywhere in the paragraph—beginning or end or in between—depending on the nature of the subject and the emphasis the writer wants to achieve. The writer may echo the keynote by repeating the topic sentence more than once, either in the same words or in different words. Or, leaving the point to be inferred by the reader, the writer may not express it in a topic sentence at all. *The standard test for unity is whether the whole point can be summarized in one good sentence.*

Each of the following paragraphs is unified in a different way (the topic sentences are italicized for the purposes of this book):

1. In this example the topic sentence comes first, and the other sentences accumulate supporting evidence:

From the founding of Jamestown on, the history of the United States has been the story of growth. The most influential textbook of our history, by Samuel Eliot Morison and Henry Commager, bears the title *Growth of the American Republic.* It was always the manifest destiny of the dynamic American people to expand across their empty continent, and their unquestioned conviction as they won their way West was that they must lay their hands freely upon its riches to do so. For by the authority of their Puritan Bible, man was lord of the nature he subdued. Americans could do with nature what they pleased. They were justified in the exploitation of its bounty. In the freebooting exercise of such beliefs, they leveled its seemingly endless forests, gouged out its seemingly bottomless mineral mountains, and drained its seemingly limitless underseas of oil. Going on to triumph in two great twentieth-century wars, they proceeded to add to their prosperity by expanding overseas for yet more economic growth. American military-industrial power, founded ultimately upon energy derived from the nation's stocks of oil, spread-eagled the world.—Carl Solberg, *Oil Power*

2. In this paragraph the student writer reverses the order, using a single illustration to lead up to a simple and arresting topic sentence at the end:

There's a sixty-mile auto trip that I take about a dozen times a year. About twenty miles from the college campus along that route is an utterly indefensible small-town traffic light. In order to avoid it, I make a hairpin turn about two blocks from the intersection and desert the smooth highway for a miserable little alley, which meanders aimlessly in and out of people's cabbage patches and finally rejoins the main road a half a block beyond the light. The alley is a garage man's Shangri-La, pitted with large pocks and generously sprinkled with broken bottles and tenpenny nails. I know it doesn't save me money, and I'm not sure it saves me time. But when I am directing a friend over that highway, I say to him with a knowing glint in my eye: "Now when I get here, I always take a little shortcut I discovered. It isn't on the map"; and I beam all over as if I'd just planted the Stars and Stripes on an uncharted iceberg in the Antarctic. There's only one reason why I take that shortcut: I'm an American. *And we Americans are a nation of incurable shortcutters.*

3. In this opening paragraph the topic sentence comes in the middle, serving as a transition between two halves of a comparison: a "false" picture and a "true" one:

Everyone knows the popular conception of Florence Nightingale. The saintly, self-sacrificing woman, the delicate maiden of high degree who threw aside the pleasures of a life of ease to succour the afflicted, the Lady with the Lamp, gliding through the horrors of the hospital at Scutari, and consecrating with the radiance of her goodness the dying soldier's couch—the vision is familiar to all. But the truth was different. *The Miss Nightingale of fact was not as facile fancy painted her.* She worked in another fashion and towards another end; she moved under the stress of an impetus which finds no place in the popular imagination. A Demon possessed her. Now demons, whatever else they may be, are full of interest. And so it happens that in the real Miss Nightingale there was more that was interesting than in the legendary; there was also less that was agreeable.—Lytton Strachey, "Florence Nightingale," *Eminent Victorians*

4. Though Arnold Bennett, in this paragraph, does not supply a ready-made topic sentence, the reader can easily devise one: *Many people are short-sighted observers, staring at trivialities and overlooking essentials.*

A man went to Paris for the first time, and observed right off that the carriages of suburban trains had seats on the roof like a tram-car. He was so thrilled by the remarkable discovery that he observed almost nothing else. This enormous fact occupied the whole foreground of his perspective. He returned home and announced that Paris was a place where people rode on the tops of trains. A French-woman came to London for the first time—and no English person would ever guess the phenomenon which vanquished all others in her mind on the opening day. She saw a cat walking across a street. The vision excited her. For in Paris cats do not roam in thoroughfares, because there are practically no houses with gardens or "areas"; the flat system is unfavorable to the enlargement of cats. I remember once, in the days when observation had first presented itself to me as a beautiful pastime, getting up very early and making the circuit of inner London before summer dawn in quest of interesting material. And the one note I gathered was that the ground in front of the all-night coffee-stalls was white with eggshells! What I needed then was an operation for cataract. I also remember taking a man to the opera who had never seen an opera. The work was *Lohengrin*. When we came out he said: "That swan's neck was rather stiff." And it was all he did say. We went and had a drink. He was not mistaken. His observation was most just; but his perspective was that of those literary critics who give ten lines to pointing out three slips of syntax, and three lines to an ungrammatical admission that the novel under survey is not wholly tedious.—Arnold Bennett, *The Author's Craft*

To sum up, in each of the first three paragraphs the topic sentence is *expressed* in a different position: (1) at the beginning; (2) at the end; (3) in the middle. In the fourth example a topic sentence is only *implied*. But each paragraph is built around a single point, and not one sentence is irrelevant. They are all models of unity.

For contrast, look at these two:

During my senior year I had a very nice time in high school. My marks came up a little and I graduated with an average of about eighty-two. About last December my Dad bought me a Pinto. I have had a great time with this little car even though I could not always afford to buy gasoline. I have worked for my Dad on weekends and during vacations for some years now. My Dad is a funeral director and I have been of some help to him most of the time. Dad has a good business built up and I would like to follow in his footsteps. My grandfather was an undertaker and my mother was the first woman in the county to obtain her undertaker's license. Therefore it seems only natural that I try to get into the business.

I have liked to read ever since I was quite small. This is not unusual. Most children are fond of reading. In the earlier grades of school, there was always anticipation and eagerness for the time when you could "read the story." It is like having a constant companion, and I am never lonely when I have something to read. Reading can consume a good deal of your time, but it can never be counted as time wasted, regardless of what you may be reading. A great deal of pleasure can be had from reading a current best-seller, but this is by no means its only asset. For almost any kind of work you may want to do, there are numerous books to read on how to do it. I cannot imagine a lawyer or a doctor without shelves filled with reading material. For myself historical reading has always been able to hold my interest. This is strictly reading for pleasure. I cannot, like some people, read well in an atmosphere of confusion and noise. I like a quiet spot without interruptions. This is especially true when reading is part of my studies.

Try to distill each of those paragraphs into a good sentence and what do you get? (1) I had a good time during my senior year in high school, and for years I have helped my father in the family undertaking business, which I expect to inherit myself some day. That is a "Siamese Twin" sentence: separate assertions unnaturally joined. (2) I have enjoyed reading since childhood, and most children enjoy it, and it keeps me from getting lonely, and it is a useful way to spend time, and it brings pleasure, and lots of books are full of know-how, which is useful for professionals, but I prefer reading history for pleasure, and I have to have it quiet when I read, especially when I'm studying. The student obviously has no unifying assertion clearly in mind, but is merely strewing the page with flotsam and jetsam about "Reading in General," a subject broad enough for a book.

Coherence: transitions

A paragraph may be unified without being clearly organized. The sentences should be not only related to a single point but arranged in a clear order and connected so that the reader can cross from one to another without danger of falling into the chasm between. The most common *transitions* are

1. Conjunctions (*and, but, for,* etc.), conjunctive adverbs (*also, however, therefore,* etc.), and directive phrases (*in other words, on the other hand,* etc.)
2. Pronouns
3. Repeated words
4. Synonyms and other substitutes

Here is a short paragraph with the key transitions italicized:

Most undergraduates are under the illusion that they take satisfactory lecture notes. *But* very few know the first principles. Good *note-taking* does not consist of cryptic scrawls among the doodles in the textbook margin. *It* is a minor literary skill, the art of intelligent digesting. Even if students can read

53

marginal hieroglyphics six weeks later, they seldom have the vaguest notion of their meaning. The professor's pearls on Henry the Eighth, *for example,* are melted down—as in Christopher Morley's epigrammatic example—to: "H 8, self-made widower." Can *this little splinter of knowledge* serve as the foundation for an intelligent discussion on an examination? *Yet* students insist that they have "taken notes on the lecture."

The transitions are obvious. The conjunction *but* links the second sentence with the first. *Note-taking* in the third repeats *take* and *note* in the first. The pronoun *it* in the fourth sentence refers to *note-taking*. *Marginal hieroglyphics* in the fifth is substituted for *cryptic scrawls* in the third. *For example* bridges the gulf between sentences five and six. *This little splinter of knowledge* stands for *H 8, self-made widower. Yet,* another conjunction, ties in the final sentence.

But transitions are not always so obvious within the paragraph. As a matter of fact, a formal paragraph cluttered with *moreovers, furthermores,* and *accordinglys* is like a highway bristling with signboards at every turn. Despite the longstanding prejudice against beginning sentences with *and, but, or,* and *nor,* these simple conjunctions make smoother transitions than their more obtrusive formal cousins among the conjunctive adverbs. Moreover, explicit transitions are sometimes redundant. For example, *as a matter of fact* in sentence two of this paragraph, *moreover* in the fourth sentence, and *for example* at the beginning of this one could all be eliminated without sacrificing clarity. And one of the commonest kinds of wordiness is the *inch-worm transition* that unnecessarily repeats half the previous sentence (see p. 68).

Because incoherence is a greater evil than occasional wordiness, you can afford to err in the direction of overworking *visible* transitions. But to write with economy as well as clarity, you must eventually learn that in closely knit paragraphs transitions are often *invisible*. When you start with a general assertion, you don't have to begin every subsequent illustration with *firstly, secondly,* or *thirdly*. When you build a statement in parallel construction with a previous one (as in this sentence), the parallelism is mortar enough (see pp. 105–106). If your argument is firmly constructed—if your logic is coherent—the transitions will often take care of themselves.

Completeness: length and development

A complete paragraph is exactly as long as the writer needs to make it to serve its purpose. The minimum limit is one word and there is no maximum. A single paragraph in Aldous Huxley's essay "Wordsworth in the Tropics" runs to 1,257 words, and that is probably no record. Averages by statisticians reveal about what trained readers would expect: that paragraphs, like sentences, have shrunk in the last century; that they are shorter in informal than in formal writing, shorter in narrative than in exposition, shorter in newspapers than in books; and that there is a disturbing tendency in mass-production journalism and advertising to "bomb the paragraph" into glittering bits, perhaps eventually into oblivion. Authorities have urged students to think twice about any expository paragraph of more than 300 words or less than 100, and to cast a suspicious eye on any page of double-spaced typing without a single indention. These are useful formulas if one allows for the common exceptions.

Short paragraphs—often of a single short sentence—are commonly used:

1. In recording dialogue   Ordinarily each new speaker opens a new paragraph:

"Anatole," I said. "It's Gary Harkness, your new roommate. Let's shake hands and be friends."

"We're roommates," he said. "Why do we have to be friends?"

"It's just an expression. I didn't mean undying comrades. Just friends as opposed to enemies. I'm sorry I woke you up."

"I wasn't asleep."

"You were snoring," I said.

"That's the way I breathe when I'm on my stomach. What happened to my original roommate?"—Don DeLillo, *End Zone*

2. For transitions   Notice how Walter Kerr uses a short isolated sentence as a bridge between his comments on Shakespeare's method and that of the modern realistic playwright:

Shakespeare can write "Enter Romeo" and let Romeo be challenged at once. He is under no obligation to say where Romeo has been, how long it has taken him to get there, or, for that matter, just where he is now. If an exciting scene ensues, that is enough justification for his presence.

The realist must work otherwise.

A doorbell must ring. It must ring long enough for someone in another part of the house to hear it, drop whatever he or she is doing, and take a few steps before appearing in the living room. Greater haste would seem implausible and suggest contrivance. The maid, answering the door, must cross the stage at normal speed; if she is a comedy maid, she may cross it at subnormal speed. The door must be opened. Romeo must identify himself, say who he has come for. . . .—Walter Kerr, *How Not to Write a Play*

3. For listing—usually with numbers

Boys and girls may be born alike with respect to math, but certain sex differences in performance emerge early according to several respected studies, and these differences remain through adulthood. They are:

1. Girls compute better than boys (elementary school and on).

2. Boys solve word problems better than girls (from age thirteen on).

3. Boys take more math than girls (from age sixteen on).

4. Girls learn to hate math sooner and possibly for different reasons.—Sheila Tobias, "Who's Afraid of Math?" *Atlantic*

4. For emphasis Notice what a distinguished economist emphasizes by making a paragraph of one sentence:

The first question we might ask is: what can you learn in college that will help you in being an employee? The schools teach a great many things of value to the future accountant, the future doctor, the future electrician. Do they also teach anything of value to the future employee? The answer is: "Yes—they teach the one thing that is perhaps most valuable for the future employee to know. But very few students bother to learn it."

This one basic skill is the ability to organize and express ideas in writing and speaking.—Peter F. Drucker, "How to Be an Employee," *Fortune*

The freedom to write brief paragraphs should be carefully weighed against the risk. If many sentences are splendidly isolated for emphasis, as in some editorials and advertisements, nothing is emphasized—or organized. *Completeness*, at least in exposition, requires that most paragraphs be developed beyond simple statement or assertion. In some undergraduate writing, the "paragraphs" are not merely short; they suffer from anemia.

Anemic paragraphing is common, for example, in answering discussion or essay questions on examinations. It isn't that many of the answers are wrong; a good discussion question cannot be answered right-or-wrong or true-or-false by drawing a thin dark line with a graphite pencil. The trouble is simply that many of the answers are deficient in flesh and blood. Three or four thin sentences on a half-hour discussion of the causes of World War I! Asked to explain the inadequacy of such an "essay," the student often reveals an assumption unrelated to ignorance of the material: "I can't sling it on these discussion questions like my roommate, who's going to be an English major. Me, I just stick to the hard, cold facts." The implication is that there is no happy medium between the "hard, cold facts" unqualified by reasoning and a voluminous fiction unsupported by fact. There is, of course: a well-developed discussion based securely on the evidence.

The chances are, moreover, that the student's hard, cold facts are not facts at all but generalities—half-truths at best. In the hands of a philosopher, an unsupported generality may be an original truth; turned by a wit, it may be a classic epigram; to an ordinary mortal it is merely a blunt tool with which to scratch the surface of an idea. A preacher doesn't get up in the pulpit, announce the text, and promptly sit down again. An experienced writer seldom lets a generality stand alone and impotent. A well-developed paragraph is a well-supported generality.

Ways of Developing Paragraphs

In the long run, of course, the best way to learn how paragraphs are developed is to examine the paragraphs of those who know how to develop them. Here are some samples grouped to illustrate seven com-

56

mon methods of expansion. Read each group first and see what you can discover about the organization before turning to the analysis that follows.

Details

Imagine Banyan Street first, because Banyan is where it happened. The way to Banyan is to drive west from San Bernardino out Foothill Boulevard, Route 66: Past the Sante Fe switching yards, the Forty Winks Motel. Past the motel that is nineteen stucco tepees: "SLEEP IN A WIGWAM—GET MORE FOR YOUR WAMPUM." Past Fontana Drag City and the Fontana Church of the Nazarene and the Pit Stop A Go-Go; past Kaiser Steel, through Cucamonga, out to the Kapu Kai Restaurant-Bar and Coffee Shop, at the corner of Route 66 and Carnelian Avenue. Up Carnelian Avenue from the Kapu Kai, which means "Forbidden Seas," the subdivision flags whip in the harsh wind. "HALF-ACRE RANCHES! SNACK BARS! TRAVERTINE ENTRIES! $95 DOWN." It is the trail of an intention gone haywire, the flotsam of the New California. But after a while the signs thin out on Carnelian Avenue, and the houses are no longer the bright pastels of the Springtime Home owners but the faded bungalows of the people who grow a few grapes and keep a few chickens out here, and then the hill gets steeper and the road climbs and even the bungalows are few, and here—desolate, roughly surfaced, lined with eucalyptus and lemon trees—is Banyan Street.—Joan Didion, "Some Dreamers of the Golden Dream," *Slouching Towards Bethlehem*

The photograph shows a perfectly arrested moment of joy. On one side—the left, as you look at the picture—the catcher is running toward the camera at full speed, with his upraised arms spread wide. His body is tilting toward the center of the picture, his mask is held in his right hand, his big glove is still on his left hand, and his mouth is open in a gigantic shout of pleasure. Over on the right, another player, the pitcher, is just past the apex of an astonishing leap that has brought his knees up to his chest and his feet well up off the ground. His hunched, airborne posture makes him look like a man who just made a running jump over a sizeable object—a kitchen table, say. By luck, two of the outreaching hands have overlapped exactly in the middle of the photograph, so that the pitcher's bare right palm and fingers are silhouetted against the catcher's glove, and as a result the two men are linked and seem to be executing a figure in a manic and difficult dance. There is a further marvel—a touch of pure fortune—in the background, where a spectator in dark glasses, wearing a dark suit, has risen from his seat in the grandstand and is lifting his arms in triumph. This, the third and central Y in the picture, is immobile. It is directly behind the overlapping hand and glove of the dancers, and it binds and recapitulates the lines of force and the movements and the theme of the work, creating a composition as serene and well ordered as a Giotto. The subject of the picture, of course, is classical—the celebration of the last out of the seventh game of the World Series.—Roger Angell, *Five Seasons*

Each paragraph is a carefully designed introduction: Didion sets the scene for a story of sordid murder in Southern California; Angell describes a news photograph of the climactic moment in the career of a pitcher (Steve Blass of the Pittsburgh Pirates) whose profile he is writing. To *realize*, not merely set, the scene, both writers use a technique that is especially common in description: *the accumulation of details*.

It is not a random accumulation. In both paragraphs the details are (1) *specific*, (2) *selected* to serve a purpose, and (3) *organized* to form a pattern.

1. Didion, for example, names the Forty Winks Motel, notes that it has *nineteen stucco tepees*, and quotes the come-on slogan word-for-word—the whole picture suggesting a phony, commercial, palefaced imitation of Indian culture. In Angell's description, the catcher's "body is *tilting toward the center* of the picture, his mask is *held in his right hand*, his big glove is *still on his left hand*, and his mouth is *open* in a *gigantic shout of pleasure*."

2. Didion selects details to create an atmosphere that fades from a lively, if tacky, world of commercial enterprise (with a few ominous hints—"Forbidden Seas," "the harsh wind," "intention gone haywire") to a desolate, struggling neighborhood where the "golden dream" is tarnished. Angell chooses details to portray both the excitement of a high moment of action and the aesthetic appeal of a "classic" photograph which fixes that moment in art.

3. Didion arranges the details in a simple but effective order—a map with one trail clearly inked so that the "traveling" reader can identify each landmark as it appears along the route. Angell composes a word picture to represent his perception of the symmetrical, if accidental, art of the photograph: the catcher running toward the center from the left; the pitcher leaping from the right; both forming "Y's" with outstretched arms and "linked" by their outreaching hands; and in the background, the anonymous spectator in the grandstand forming the third and central Y. The confusion of the moment is focused in an orderly composition.

Illustration

It was an old black man in Atlanta who looked into my eyes and directed me into my first segregated bus. I have spent a long time thinking about that man. I never saw him again. I cannot describe the look which passed between us, as I asked him for directions, but it made me think, at once, of Shakespeare's "the oldest have borne most." It made me think of the blues: *Now, when a woman gets the blues, Lord, she hangs her head and cries. But when a man gets the blues, Lord, he grabs a train and rides.* It was borne in on me, suddenly, just why these men had so often been grabbing freight trains as the evening sun went down. And it was, perhaps, because I was getting on a segregated bus, and wondering how Negroes had borne this and other indignities for so long, that this man so struck me. He seemed to know what I was feeling. His eyes seemed to say that what I was feeling he had been feeling, at much higher pressure, all his life. But my eyes would never see the hell his eyes had seen. And this hell was, simply, that he had never in his life owned anything, not his wife, not his house, not his child, which could not, at any instant be taken from him by the power of white people. This is what paternalism means. And for the rest of the time that I was in the South I watched the eyes of old black men.—James Baldwin, *Nobody Knows My Name*

When I registered again for German this semester, I was possessed by both hope and fear. My adviser had held out the hope. She said I should learn at least one other language besides my native English, and she kept insisting that, after four years of study in school, I should now have reached a "threshold." Scientists, she explained patiently, have identified the threshold as the critical point at which effective learning begins to take root in any discipline. She painted a pleasant picture of a sill in a doorway with the welcome mat out. If I turned back now, my four-year struggle with inflectional endings and irregular verbs would have been in vain; if I crossed over the threshold, I would soon find myself at home in the language. But she did not dispel my fear. As I learned later from my dictionary, the first syllable of *threshold* derives from the Old English verb *threscan*, meaning to *thresh* or *thrash* grain to separate the wheat from the chaff. How long will I thrash at the threshold, treading or flailing to separate the wheat of intelligible meaning from the chaff of grammar? Will I ever enter the door?

Both paragraphs are autobiographical narrative, developed by the familiar method of *illustration*.

Baldwin's purpose is to make the reader aware of the power of white domination and the pathos of black subjugation—to make us feel their persistence as a way of life for generations in the past. An abstract general argument against racism, a detached definition of prejudice, or a selection of facts from the historical record would not serve his purpose. Instead he focuses on a single personal experience, a brief meeting with an aged black man in whose face and through whose eyes the reader is asked to see the oppression of the writer's people. The apt allusion to Shakespeare's tragedy of *King Lear*, the quotation from one blues song and the echo of another ("I hate to see that evening sun go down"), the repetition of the word *feeling*, the unsparing glimpse of the old man's hell—all deepen the emotional dimensions of the picture. A passing encounter with a stranger becomes a haunting memory; one illustration symbolizes the suffering of a race.

Although the second paragraph has a much lighter tone, reflecting a less profound experience, it reveals the same method of paragraph development. The student writer's aim, like Baldwin's, is to persuade the reader to share the writer's feelings—in this instance, the conflicting emotions of hope and fear. The student might have settled for the bald statement in the sentence at the beginning. But this would *tell* the readers something, *show* them nothing. Instead, the writer develops the point by focusing, like Baldwin, on a central illustration—an encounter with the adviser—and relating each emotion to one word: *threshold*. Though the approach may be somewhat whimsical, the paragraph provides a fresh look at a familiar dilemma.

Definition

What then is scientific method? Stated in the fewest possible words, it is a way of investigation which relies, and relies solely, on disciplined empirical observation and rigorously exact proof. Its aim is objective verification. And by objective verification is meant, first, that the investigator's wishes and wants, his aesthetic, moral, or religious predilections, his faith in or desire for a particular conclusion, have been carefully eliminated as determining factors; and second, that proof extends beyond inner or personal conviction, to outer or public demonstration. The extent to which this can be done depends upon the matter to be investigated. But whatever the problem may be, it is possible to devise a technique which assures the highest attainable degree of objectivity as just defined; and whenever this is honestly attempted the investigation is scientific in the comprehensive meaning of the term. The significance of objectivity sought in terms of method instead of subject matter is obviously far-reaching. Its relevancy to the problem of a socially responsive and a socially responsible science need not be pointed out.—Max C. Otto, *The Human Enterprise*

When I speak of *chauvinism*, I do not mean militaristic patriotism, the simple-minded loyalty of Napoleon's soldier, Nicolas Chauvin, who unwittingly fathered the word. Nor am I concerned with the broader meaning: "undue partiality or attachment to a group or place to which one belongs or has belonged" (*Webster's New Collegiate*). When I write the word *chauvinist*, I shall mean "male chauvinist" and drop the adjective. I shall have in mind a male who takes for granted man's superiority over woman. Whether he flaunts his masculinity with flexed muscles and wolf whistles or exhibits a condescending gallantry toward "the ladies" or "the fair sex," he assumes that, by the Creator's endowment, her place is in the home and his in the marketplace—and he intends to be master of both worlds. He may be superpatriotic, like the simple-minded Chauvin, or fanatically partial to his college or his fraternity. But his first loyalty is to his gender—with all the rights and privileges thereunto appertaining.

Both writers are concerned with *definition*, an inevitable requirement in expository writing and argument. Definition is a complex riddle that will be discussed further in later chapters (see pp. 119–126, 197–199). An inexperienced writer, if aware that defining terms is necessary, inevitably will go to the dictionary and quote it directly, often without further consideration. If the term can be scientifically defined, a good dictionary can supply the essential facts: the *genus* or class in which the object belongs and the *differentiae* or features that distinguish it from other objects in the same class. But dictionary definitions are inadequate to explain many terms, especially abstractions such as *beauty, democracy, freedom, loyalty,* and *nature.* The widespread illusion that they can be easily encapsulated is a dangerous enemy to clear thinking. All a thinking writer can do is suggest some limits to their elusive meaning. It can be done not in a scientific definition, but only by what is sometimes called *literary definition*. This kind may be reduced to an epigram: *celebrity*, "someone who is famous for being well known" (Daniel Boorstin); *sentimentality*, "the emotional promiscuity of those who have no sentiment" (Norman Mailer). But a serious attempt to limit an abstraction usually requires at least a paragraph.

Professor Otto is obviously aware that the much-abused term "scientific method" cannot be tightly canned in a scientific definition. The answer in his second sentence is accurate only as far as it goes. When he asserts in sentence three that the goal of scientific method is "objective verification," he has merely replaced a broad abstraction with a narrower abstraction, and this in turn must be defined in more concrete terms. In moving from the abstract to the concrete, from the general to the particular, he observes a fundamental principle of good definition.

The student writer of the second paragraph has consulted the dictionary but has not stopped there. Two dictionary definitions, one quoted directly, are used only as contrast with a third definition—one that is more subjective, more informal, and more extensive than a standard dictionary entry. This is a common technique, especially at the beginning of an essay: explaining what the writer or the term does *not* mean in order to clear the decks for the particular meaning to follow. The student is not, of course, creating a personal sense unrelated to current usage, but intends to make sure that, when *chauvinism* is mentioned again, there will be no doubt about the intended meaning.

Division

The familiar arguments for and against capital punishment can be arbitrarily divided into two categories: moral and practical.

People whose approach to the problem is essentially moral commonly argue that anyone who has taken the life of another (to use murder as an example) has sacrificed his right to his own life. Implicit in this view may be a memory of God's commands to Moses: "He that smiteth a man, so that he die, shall surely be put to death. . . . Life for life, eye for eye, tooth for tooth. . . ." But a different moral argument comes from those who maintain that no human being has the right to take the life of another regardless of his crime; they may argue that only God, who commanded to Moses, "Thou shalt not kill," can give life and take it away.

Those who lean towards a practical view of the issue often insist that capital punishment is the only penalty for some kinds of murder because even killers sentenced for life are commonly paroled or escape to roam the streets and kill again. Moreover, the threat of capital punishment might have deterred them from murder in the first place. On the other hand, those who argue from practical premises *against* capital punishment ask for evidence that the extreme penalty prevents the crime; and, considering the fallibility of juries and judges, they express horror at the "judicial killing" of innocent defendants.

There are three kinds of book owners. The first has all the standard sets and best sellers—unread, untouched. (This deluded individual owns woodpulp and ink, not books.) The second has a great many books—a few of them read through, most of them dipped into, but all of them as clean and shiny as the day they were bought. (This person would probably like to make books his own, but is restrained by a false respect for their physical appearance.) The third has a few books or many—every one of them dogeared and dilapidated, shaken and loosened by continual use, marked and scribbled in from front to back. (This man owns books.)—Mortimer J. Adler, "How to Mark a Book," *Saturday Review*

Development by *division* is especially useful in introducing a subject. A formal introduction is usually unnecessary in a 500-word theme. But in a longer expository paper it helps the reader to have a preliminary map showing the main divisions of the territory to be covered. If this is done clearly in advance, the writer is spared the nuisance of adding long transitions later. If you give a preview of the key points, you don't have to reintroduce each one at length when the time comes to expand it.

The student writer on capital punishment has divided a large subject formally before launching into an extended discussion, in which the student's own conclusions will eventually be made clear. The writer uses three paragraphs. Notice that in paragraph one—a single sentence for emphasis—the main division into "moral" and "practical" arguments is introduced. In the second paragraph the moral arguments are further divided into those for and against capital punishment. In paragraph three the student makes a similar division of the practical arguments. The method is inevitably arbitrary, as the writer admits, but it provides a map for the reader to follow.

The specimen from Mortimer Adler's essay represents a somewhat different use of division. His reason for introducing the reader to the first two book owners is not that he is going to discuss them in detail later; he uses them merely as foils for book owner number three, the more deserving subject of the rest of the essay. He uses the device of division to eliminate subjects that do not concern him, thus clearing the decks for action on the one that does. (A similar technique occurs in the second definition on page 60.) Like all introductory devices, however, division should be handled with care. There is always the danger that writers, like exhausting after-dinner speakers, will talk too long about the matters they are not going to talk about. The subject of a short paper should be whittled down to size before the opening paragraph.

Comparison and contrast

A comparison of Galileo and Newton provides an interesting study in contrasts. Galileo's worldliness and arrogance could hardly be more remote from Newton's polite and almost mystical reserve. Galileo thought on his feet and was fond of public controversy; Newton was moody and introspective and left his friends to fight most of his battles for him. Where the former could hide his skepticism behind a formal capitulation to the Inquisition without unduly burdening his conscience, the latter remained throughout his life a convinced, if not fanatical, Christian. Galileo's family hoped his studies would restore him to the elevated rank they regarded as the proper family station in life, while it seems likely that Newton's parents would have been content to see him succeed them as a simple dirt farmer.—Robert H. March, *Physics for Poets*

The natural sciences are primarily concerned with the material world (including living organisms insofar as they are parts of the material world), and their aim is to disclose the structure and behavior of material things in generalized terms (in terms of mathematics so far as possible) which will be true irrespective of variable conditions of time and place. In dealing with his subject matter the work of the natural scientist is greatly facilitated by the fact that he is not emotionally entangled with it: he does not care how his subject matter behaves, his subject matter is indifferent to what he does to it, and ignorant of what he has learned about it. Fortunately for the physicist, the atom cannot acquire a knowledge of physics. The physicist can, therefore, proceed on the assumption that any knowledge he may acquire about the behavior of the atom will not modify its behavior and thereby invalidate conclusions based upon its behavior up to date. The social scientist cannot make this assumption, at least not without important qualifications. For his subject matter is the behavior of men in the world of human relations; and men are not, like the atom, indifferent to what is done to them or ignorant of what is learned about them. On the contrary, the subject matter of the social scientist can find out what he has learned about its behavior in the past, and as a result of that knowledge behave differently in the future. This is the fundamental difference between the natural sciences and the social sciences; whereas the behavior of material things remains the same whatever men learn about it, the behavior of men is always conditioned by what they know about themselves and the world in which they live.—Carl L. Becker, "The Function of the Social Sciences," *Science and Man*, ed. by Ruth N. Anshen

Both paragraphs are developed by *comparison and contrast. Comparison* would be label enough, for, in its broadest sense, *to compare* is to set two or more things side by side in order to bring out either resemblances or differences between them. But the familiar academic formula is "compare and contrast the following." Why is this sort of question so common on essay examinations? The reason is not that it is a handy way to ferret out ignorance but that it tests a student's powers of thought. Try thinking for long on any subject without making comparisons. One mark of education is the power to weave disconnected shreds of knowledge into an intelligible pattern, and this requires the ability to see resemblances between them. Another is the power to evaluate—to assess the relative worth of ideas, or works of art, or other human beings; and this demands the capacity to see differences more subtle than that between black and white. "Comparison and contrast" is more than a textbook formula for developing paragraphs.

As the selections from March and Becker show, there are two common ways of achieving this development. After his opening statement, March makes the comparison between the two scientific geniuses point by point en route, carefully balancing his sentences in parallel structure (see pp. 105–106)—half a sentence for Galileo, half a sentence for Newton in regular alternation. By contrast with this dovetail technique, Becker first explains the method of the natural scientist in some detail before turning to the social scientist; then he ties up the contrast in a neat package with a summarizing topic sentence.

Both methods can be effective. The careful dovetail technique of March's paragraph is more useful in making subtle detailed comparisons, but it is not easy for the inexperienced writer. Sustaining the

63

balance of both ideas and clauses requires an acute power of analysis and a sense of rhetorical symmetry, and it can lead to verbal hairsplitting that is more clever than accurate. The method used by Becker is adequate when the comparison is organized around a single main point. Notice that, though his paragraph is long, he focuses the comparison on one fundamental difference.

It is possible, of course, to suggest comparisons without explicitly making them. But this device, though common in narration and description, is often ineffective in exposition. The student writer, when asked to compare and contrast A and B, as on an examination, too often discusses them consecutively at great length without either implying or expressing the resemblances or differences between them. This is evading the question.

Cause and effect

In sum, we can trace the origin of the environmental crisis through the following sequence. Environmental degradation largely results from the introduction of new industrial and agricultural production technologies. These technologies are ecologically faulty because they are designed to solve singular, separate problems and fail to take into account the inevitable "side-effects" that arise because, in nature, no part is isolated from the whole ecological fabric. In turn, the fragmented design of technology reflects its scientific foundation, for science is divided into disciplines that are largely governed by the notion that complex systems can be understood only if they are first broken into their separate component parts. This reductionist bias has also tended to shield basic science from a concern for real-life problems, such as environmental degradation.—Barry Commoner, *The Closing Circle*

Meanwhile, the Army and Navy's victorious inoculation of the anti-linguistic American boy [during World War II] is not hard to account for. It was not a secret; it was mainly Concentration. The men were segregated, put in charge of foreign instructors, drilled morning, noon, and night under conditions of prison-like rigidity. Standards were high and failures from laziness or incapacity were weeded out as fast as they showed up. A competitive game was set going, which keyed up the good minds to outdo themselves. Outside the class hours, the men would quiz each other, talk, joke, and write in the language they were learning. Two powerful motives were at work: the negative fear of not keeping up and therefore being returned to the ranks, and the positive wish for a commission and the pay that goes with it.—Jacques Barzun, *Teacher in America*

Both paragraphs are developed by showing the relation between *cause and effect*, a method common in exposition and argument. In an opening sentence, each writer announces his intention. Commoner will "trace the origin of the environmental crisis"; Barzun will "account for" the success of the Army and Navy language programs during World War II. In a formal summary of points expanded earlier in his chapter, Commoner traces the *causes* of the crisis in a step-by-step "sequence," beginning with the new technologies and then relating them "in turn' (transition) to the reductionist bias of science and the resulting lack of concern for the environment. In Barzun's paragraph the language is less formal and abstract and the order less sequential. But in each sentence he singles out a *cause* of the victory. Concentration, segregation under strict discipline, high standards, competition, continuation after class hours, and strong motivation—each contributes to the victorious *effect* announced in the first sentence.

A combination of methods

Clubs, fraternities, nations—these are the beloved barriers in the way of a workable world, these will have to surrender some of their rights and some of their ribs. A "fraternity" is the antithesis of *fraternity*. The first (that is the order or organization) is predicated on the idea of exclusion; the second (that is, the abstract thing) is based on a feeling of total equality. Anyone who remembers back to his fraternity days at college recalls the enthusiasts in his group, the rabid members, both old and young, who were obsessed with the mystical charm of membership in their particular order. They were usually men who were incapable of genuine brotherhood or at least unaware of its implications. Fraternity begins when the exclusion formula is found to be distasteful. The effect of any organization of a social and brotherly nature is to strengthen rather than to diminish the lines which divide people into classes; the effect of states and nations is the same, and eventually these lines will have to be softened, these powers will have to be generalized. It is written on the wall that this is so. I'm not inventing it, I'm just copying it off the wall.—E. B. White, *One Man's Meat*

This specimen is included to show what may have been evident in other examples: that the techniques of paragraph development are not mutually exclusive. A writer may use a *combination of methods*. Thus E. B. White's penetrating comment includes *division* of the material, *definition* of two terms, *comparison and contrast* between them, the use of a familiar *illustration* from the fraternity house, and a *cause-and-effect* analysis of the influence of the "exclusion formula"—the whole encased in a sweeping comparison of clubs and nations. It isn't that White—or any experienced writer—lays out an intricate blueprint of interlocking techniques in advance. His purpose and the nature of his material lead him naturally to combine several methods.

Repetition—Device and Vice

There is no magic answer to the problem of when and how to repeat. But a look at the following paragraphs may suggest some guiding principles. First, consider three examples of effective repetition:

It has become something of a convenience to refer to the whole endeavor as the "Health Industry." This provides the illusion that it is in a general way all one thing, and that it turns out, on demand, a single, unambiguous product, which is health. Thus, health care has become the new name for medicine.

65

Health-care delivery is what doctors now do, along with hospitals and other professionals who work with doctors, now known collectively as the health providers. The patients have become health consumers. Once you start on this line, there's no stopping. Just recently, to correct some of the various flaws, inequities, logistic defects, and near-bankrupticies in today's health-care delivery system, the government has officially invented new institutions called Health Maintenance Organizations, already known familiarly as HMO's, spreading out across the country like post offices, ready to distribute in neat packages, as though from a huge, newly stocked inventory, health.—Lewis Thomas, *The Lives of a Cell*

The writer uses the word *health*—alone or in combination—nine times in six sentences, not through carelessness but to ridicule its proliferation in the new medical bureaucracy. The paragraph is developed by repeating a single word for emphasis.

By a strange perversity in the cosmic plan, the biologically good die young. Species are not destroyed for their shortcomings but for their achievements. The tribes that slumber in the graveyards of the past were not the most simple and undistinguished of their day, but the most complicated and conspicuous. The magnificent sharks of the Devonian period passed with the passing of the period, but certain contemporaneous genera of primitive shellfish are still on earth. Similarly, the lizards of the Mesozoic era have long outlived the dinosaurs, which were immeasurably their biologic betters. Illustrations such as these could be endlessly increased. The price of distinction is death.—John Hodgdon Bradley, *Patterns of Survival*

In Bradley's paragraph the first three sentences and the last all say essentially the same thing, each in different words. By repeating his idea rather than his words, the author has emphasized a main point with less risk of tiring the reader.

We did sleep that night, but we woke up at six A.M. We lay in our beds and debated through the open doors whether to obey till, say, halfpast six. Then we bolted. I don't know who started it, but there was a rush. We all disobeyed; we raced to disobey and get first to the fireplace in the front room downstairs. And there they were, the gifts, all sorts of wonderful things, mixed-up piles of presents; only, as I disentangled the mess, I saw that my stocking was empty; it hung limp; not a thing in it; and under and around it—nothing. My sisters had knelt down, each by her pile of gifts; they were squealing with delight, till they looked up and saw me standing there in my nightgown with nothing. They left their piles to come to me and look with me at my empty place. Nothing. They felt my stocking: nothing.—Lincoln Steffens, *Autobiography*

The third paragraph shows how the calculated repetition of a single motif can be extremely effective in telling a story. In one sentence Steffens restates the theme of emptiness four different ways: "I saw that my stocking was empty; it hung limp; not a thing in it; and under and around it—nothing." And then to sustain the pathos of the scene, he echoes the word *nothing* three times more, building up the boy's emotion to a climax of disappointment.

Though they have different aims and values, all three paragraphs illustrate repetition as an effective *device* to serve a legitimate purpose. But repetition can also be a *vice*, as the following examples show:

It is indeed true, as the quotation says, that there are marked differences between William Congreve's play *The Way of the World*, and Sheridan's drama *The School for Scandal*. In the first place, the two were writing at different times in the history of the English drama. William Congreve's play, *The Way of the World*, was composed many years before Sheridan's *School for Scandal*. The reader would naturally expect that two plays written by different playwrights in different periods would reveal marked differences in style, and this is certainly the case. *The Way of the World* reflects the dramatic tradition of Congreve's time, and *The School for Scandal* "holds up the mirror" to society in its author's period. This is the first important difference between the two plays.

Like Bradley, the student examination writer is restating the same point several times in several ways. But the point does not require restating because it is already clearly implied in the question ("Congreve's *Way of the World* and Sheridan's *School for Scandal* are representative examples of two different periods in English literature. Discuss.") The writer is repeating not for clarity or for emphasis but out of desperation, concealing ignorance by trying to play an entire symphony on one string. The result is a bluff. The use of repetition to conceal ignorance is not restricted to undergraduates; it is the first refuge of spell-binding politicians and other assorted windbags.

I tried to get my whole family interested in snakes, but I couldn't get them to come close enough to see what a snake really looked like. Finally, however, I was given a room in which to keep my snakes. I then began to start a collection of snakes, catching some local species and buying some other species of snakes not so readily obtainable locally until I had a collection of some twenty-two snakes with nine different species of snakes, all harmless.

Unlike the more ingenious contemporary quoted above, this student snake-fancier is probably unaware of the paragraph's reptilian redundancy. A quick revision can eliminate much of the unnecessary wordiness:

I tried to interest my whole family in snakes but couldn't get them to come close enough to see what a snake really looked like. Finally, however, I was given a room in which to keep my pets. I then began a collection, catching some local species and buying others not so readily obtainable until I had twenty-two snakes of nine different varieties, all harmless.

Unconscious repetition is one of the most irritating habits of inexperienced writers. There are several simple ways of curing it:

1. Read the paper aloud This practice, already recommended in Chapter 2, is especially important for students with the repetition habit. Wordiness is often heard, not seen.

2. Omit references to things already referred to However obvious, this is a step many students are reluctant to take. Intelligent readers, unlike the nuisance in the row behind at the movies, do not have to be *told* everything; they can get the point that the student is writing about snakes without being reminded by continual references to snakes that the theme is about snakes.

3. Use synonyms   For reasons discussed in detail in Chapter 5, this cure should be used with caution. It would be absurd for the pet-lover to open Roget's *Thesaurus* and substitute a synonym for every *snake* after the first. The word *serpent*, for example, conjures up legions of historical and mythological beasts a world away from the writer's modest collection. Moreover, "elegant variation" can become an offensive trick of style. The sports writer who cannot *kick the ball* more than once in a story, who after that must *boot the pigskin, toe the ovate spheroid, propel the leather pellet*, and so on until the reader yearns for the simple statement of a simple fact, is not the ideal model for college writing. On the other hand, there is no reason why the student writer could not have referred once or twice to *pets*.

4. Use pronouns   After all, they were devised to take the place of nouns—as does the *they* in this sentence. They too should be used with caution: faulty reference is always lurking around the corner (see pp. 290–292). But pronouns are handier words than most repeaters know. Their use as transitions, already mentioned, is one of the best ways of achieving economy. Notice, for example, how the author of the following passage rephrases half of the first sentence merely to make a transition at the beginning of the second:

WORDY   Eventually the adults tend to become suspicious of the nature of the affair. Benét illustrates *how the feelings of the adults tend to change during the affair* when Chuck and Helen are seen driving home from the cottage by Miss Eagles, a highly imaginative old schoolteacher, who obviously thinks the children have been making love out in the country.

REWRITTEN   Eventually the adults become suspicious. Benét illustrates *this* when Chuck and Helen are seen driving home from the cottage by Miss Eagles, a highly imaginative old schoolteacher, who obviously thinks the children have been making love out in the country.

The substitution of the single pronoun *this* makes the transition neatly and clearly; eleven unnecessary words are eliminated. A writer can pass smoothly from sentence to sentence within a coherent paragraph without regularly doubling back like a laboring inchworm.

THE PARTS AND THE WHOLE

By merely expanding the recipe, you can apply the principles of good paragraphing to the organization of a short theme. The fundamental principle of *unity* is the same: you may restrict yourself to a single point in a 500-word paper, but if you make more than one, they should be closely related. You may announce your main purpose—or thesis—in a generality at the beginning, as in a topic sentence; you may postpone it until later, perhaps in a concluding summary; or you may, as in a paragraph, lead the reader to infer it from the evidence.

Coherence in the whole theme is as important as it is in the paragraph. Transitions between paragraphs may be longer than a single word or phrase: an entire sentence is sometimes used and occasionally a transitional paragraph. But visible bridges are no more sacred than those between sentences: if the thought of the theme is closely knit and the order logical, you don't have to begin each new paragraph with a transition as obvious as "I proceed now to my second point."

The *completeness* of the whole depends on the development of the parts; anemic paragraphing makes an anemic theme. Entire compositions may be developed by use of details, illustration, definition, division, comparison and contrast, cause and effect—or, more probably, by a combination of methods. Each of these methods requires you to *be specific*, to develop the thought by selecting and arranging *particulars* Strong paragraphs and themes cannot be made of empty generalities.

Nor do the devices of *emphasis* change to fit the larger unit. Repetition, for example, can be both a useful device and a useless vice on the larger scale of the whole theme. You may intentionally repeat in a final summary an important point made at the beginning—though this kind of repeating is usually unnecessary in a short paper; or you may make the mistake of unconsciously returning in paragraph four to a point you already developed completely in paragraph two. If you can organize a unified, coherent, well-developed paragraph, you should have no serious trouble organizing a short theme.

A SUMMARY

For emphasis—and because this chapter has been long and detailed—the essential doctrine is summarized here:

1. Every piece of writing should be organized to present a recognizable form.
2. The general principles of organization are unity, coherence, completeness, and emphasis.
3. The easiest way to achieve unity in expository writing is to stick to a single point within each paragraph and try to create a single impression—though it may be broader than one "point"—in the theme as a whole. The point of a well-built expository paragraph can usually be expressed in a unified sentence, whether or not the writer has supplied a topic sentence.
4. Coherence is achieved, with both explicit and implicit transitions, through the conscious effort to make the parts—the sentences

within the paragraph, the paragraphs in the whole theme—hang together.

5. A complete piece of writing is one in which the writer succeeds in doing what he or she has apparently set out to do. An incomplete paper may suffer from notable omissions or inadequate development. Most underdeveloped papers can be quickly diagnosed as cases of anemic paragraphing. Except when a paragraph is short for a good reason, it should be fully developed by one or a combination of several methods. The most common of these are details, illustration, definition, division, comparison and contrast, and cause and effect. Each method, in its way, compels the writer to be specific, to avoid empty generalities.

6. Emphasis can be achieved by isolation, position, repetiton, and proportion. Repetition, which is both a device and a vice, should be used with particular care.

7. This doctrine, with its inevitable abstractions, should be not memorized but understood. The best way to understand it is to study the prose of good writers, such as those quoted in this chapter and in the exercises that follow.

EXERCISES

A. Analyze each of the following paragraphs to determine (1) the main point or points; (2) the topic sentence, if any; (3) the transitions, both expressed and implied; and (4) the method or methods of development.

1. Paranoids live in a state of perpetual crisis. They are always ready for catastrophe. A psychiatrist has recalled an incident that occurred when he was attached to the staff of a large mental hospital. A gas main had broken, and the poisonous fumes were seeping into the wards. It was vital that the hospital be evacuated, and the staff was undermanned. The expected chaos and panic did not materialize, however, because a group of paranoid schizophrenics, once released from their cells, immediately took charge of the evacuation, organized it, and carried it out quickly and efficiently. These paranoids saw nothing unusual in the fact that the hospital was about to be engulfed by an invisible, deadly, malevolent force.—Hendrik Hertzberg and David C. K. McClelland, "Paranoia Land," *Harper's*

2. And then in simple justice to the undecorated men of the *Reluctant* it should also be pointed out that heroism—physical heroism—is very much a matter of opportunity. On the physical level heroism is not so much an act, implying volition, as it is a reflex. Apply the rubber hammer to the patella tendon and, commonly, you produce the knee jerk. Apply the situation permitting bravery to one hundred young males with actively functioning adrenal glands and, reasonably, you produce seventy-five instances of clear-cut heroism. Would, that is, but for one thing: that after the fifty-first the word would dissolve into meaninglessness. Like the knee jerk, physical courage is perhaps latent and even implicit in the individual, needing only the application of situation, of opportunity, to reveal it. A case in point: Ensign Pulver.—Thomas Heggen, *Mister Roberts*

3. So we might pause to consider the familiar term *nature*, which is as ambiguous and confusing as any in the language. His mentors have often told man to live "in accordance with Nature," finding in Nature the source of his duties and more recently of his rights. So capitalized, the word means something like God and enjoins some ethical code, but it only veils the mystery of the nature and the will of God; what code it enjoins will depend upon the speaker and his culture. Another common meaning of *nature*, the unbaptized universe and everything in it, is no more helpful; in this sense nothing can be contrary to nature, whatever man chooses to do is a natural event in the universal show. In the more common sense of the external world, everything in the universe apart from man, *nature* becomes more misleading. It may now mean a bountiful provider, a haven from care, a playfield, a bloody battleground, a constant menace, an enemy of all man's works—a spectacle beautiful or grim, serene or wild, majestic or awful; but if the familiar counsel to "follow nature" means to follow instincts, live like other animals, it is positively inhuman so far as it is feasible at all. At best, the simple idea of going back to nature simply obscures the real problem, the ultimate concern of all philosophy and religion—the problem of what is the good life for man, a creature for whom all kinds of behavior, from loving to killing, are on the face of it "natural."—Herbert J. Muller, *Issues of Freedom*

4. What Dr. King promised was not a ranch-style house and an acre of manicured lawn for every black man, but jail and finally freedom. He did not promise two cars for every family, but the courage one day for all families everywhere to walk without shame and unafraid on their own feet. He did not say that one day it will be us chasing prospective buyers out of our prosperous well-kept neighborhoods, or in other ways exhibiting our snobbery and ignorance as all other ethnic groups before us have done; what he said was that we had a right to live anywhere in this country we chose, and a right to a meaningful well-paying job to provide us with the upkeep of our homes. He did not say we had to become carbon copies of the white American middle-class; but he did say we had the right to become whatever we wanted to become.—Alice Walker, "The Civil Rights Movement: What Good Was It?" *American Scholar*

B. Select three well-organized paragraphs from your reading and analyze them as in Exercise A.

C. Analyze the paragraphs of one of your own themes as in Exercise A.

D. Each of the following paragraphs lacks unity and coherence. Analyze the flaws in organization.

1. There has been little change in the physical appearance of my neighborhood in the last seventy-five years. Not fifty years ago a woman working as a butcher had her head removed by the Mafia for refusing to pay protection. Three of her six children died of starvation. The buildings are the same, the dress of many of the old people is still the same as it was when they came over on the boat. The control of the section is still the same. As the old men sit upstairs talking of the old days, there is $60,000 on a card table in the basement. A man walked into a barber shop last summer, opened the closet door, and fired six shots just to let the people in the section know who he was. There is a constant influx of new men to take the place of the old and sickly leaders. The buildings have not changed. The people, their jobs, their goals have not changed. The people whose jobs must be done at night have only changed their style of dress.

2. I went out for soccer to get to know people. In a new school you can make friends in a dormitory, but the strongest friendships are based on common interests. Soccer isn't a glory sport, so the players aren't interested in personal gain. They must work together or be beaten. The desire to win is the strongest unifying factor. Winning is the highest objective of any sport. Some people try to degrade winning by saying that a good loser is just as good. If you feel that it's acceptable to be a good loser, you'll never have the ambition to win. In life you must win to survive. In striving for a win each man subordinates his own desires for the team. Like a well-disciplined soldier a player must think of the team before himself. School spirit, no matter how square it may sound, is also a strong binding force. The spirit can be seen in the last minutes of a game when a team fights as hard as in the first period. Our freshman soccer team beat State not because we were that much better but because we had a reason to play harder. Last year's football team worked in reverse. There State was the underdog and we were overconfident. Our spirit fell through, and they won. For me there were twenty-two reasons for playing soccer, one for each man on the team.

3. We have spent billions of dollars on the space program in order to land a man on the moon. At the same time we have shamefully neglected our obligations to men on the earth. Unemployment, poverty, and disease are rampant not only in foreign countries but in our own presumably affluent society. The progress of science and technology should not be halted. The spirit of discovery which led Columbus to our shores has led us to even greater achievements in space. But we do not have to keep a score card in the space race just to beat the Russians. Space flights should not be regarded as so many events in the Olympic Games. In the Olympic Games it should be the individual achievements that count, not the national box score. Nationalism can lead us only to disaster.

E. Rewrite the following paragraphs, eliminating all unnecessary repetition.

1. The main problem of student writers is that they do not work from an organized plan. Often writers when confronted with a writing assignment will start writing before they have even thought about what they are going to write or how they are going to write it. If a piece of writing is incoherent and skips around from one place to another, it is often because of a lack of the preliminary planning referred to above. To compose a good piece of writing, writers must be able to anticipate what they are getting into. If they leap blindly into writing an essay, they may often pass by the important facts, and all their writing will be useless because of lack of planning.

2. One thing that makes my engineering classes so interesting is the people who teach them. From the first day in the classroom it was evident that Professor Best is a man who has had a good deal of practical experience and knows how to explain his knowledge in such a way that it is made interesting to his students. His teaching methods are such that all his classes are enjoyed by his students. He is in close contact with the students at the college and knows what is going on in his students' minds. This, I believe, is very important if a teacher is really going to communicate with his students. Professor Best keeps the channels of communication open through his joking. He keeps the students receptive. Therefore they are always ready to receive any bit of information that he has to offer in the classroom.

3. Although "Little Herr Friedemann" and "A Hunger Artist" may not seem to have many similarities, there are a few. The first similarity is the use of a common ending in which the protagonist commits suicide because he can no longer continue to bear the burden of life. The second of the similarities in the two stories is the characteristic of an ironic theme. This theme appears to be that the men are both happy and success-

ful, but actually they are neither happy nor successful. The last of the similarities between the two stories is the author's use of foreshadowing. In both of the stories key phrases are used early in the story which give the reader warning as to something that will happen later in the story.

F. Compose a topic sentence of your own and develop three different paragraphs, in each of which you use it in a different position: (1) at the beginning; (2) in the middle; and (3) at the end. Then develop a fourth paragraph in which the same sentence is merely implied.

G. Using any one of the methods of development discussed on pages 57–65, or a combination of methods, expand one of the following "anemic" paragraphs to at least 150 words.

1. Although it is common to call all undergraduates students, many of them are only pupils. A student, by any reasonable definition, is somebody who studies—who thinks things through independently, whether in class or library; a pupil just sits in a seat and expects, or even defies, the professor to provide education.

2. As soon as Tom crossed the threshold he knew that the occupant of the room was a slovenly person. The place was the most disorderly mess he had ever seen.

3. Television is unlikely to improve much as long as the medium is in the control of large corporations whose executives are convinced that the only way to make money is to appeal to their conception of the twelve-year-old mind. But it would help if fewer intellectual snobs would stop talking as if the tube had been devised only to sabotage the book.

4. There is a difference between gossip and scandal. Gossip is just the idle chatter of busy-tongues who enjoy the human pastime of talking about other people; scandal implies a sense of outrage over the violation of some moral standard.

5. One of the main reasons for both the progress and the chaos in higher education today is simply the new fashion for getting educated by degrees. Thousands of candidates whose counterparts would never have gone beyond high school in the 1920s are now taking the college degree for granted.

H. Develop any one of the following in a single paragraph of at least 150 words.

1. a description of a student hangout

2. a narrative of a campus or classroom incident

3. an argument in which you use one or more illustrations to support a general assertion

4. a definition of an abstract term (examples: *democracy, liberty, school spirit, amateur, automation, treason, capitalism*)

6. an explanation of the design and purpose of some implement, instrument, or appliance

7. an explanation of a technical process

8. a summary in which you divide a subject into several parts

9. a comparison between two types of teachers or students

10. an argument in which you relate one or more causes to one or more effects

I. Build a well-developed paragraph of at least 150 words on one of these "topic sentences."

1. Learning [is] the kind of ignorance distinguishing the studious.—Ambrose Bierce

2. Man has developed an obvious capacity of surviving the pompous reiteration of the commonplace.—John Kenneth Galbraith

3. Between the belly laugh and the chuckle lies the whole range of primate evolution.—John Ciardi

4. Public opinion's always in advance of the law.—John Galsworthy

5. Hell is full of musical amateurs.—Bernard Shaw

6. A constitutional statesman is in general a man of common opinions and uncommon abilities.—Walter Bagehot

7. All free governments are party governments.—James A. Garfield

8. Science is the topography of ignorance.—Oliver Wendell Holmes

9. The man in the street does not know a star in the sky.—Ralph Waldo Emerson

10. It is the dull man who is always sure, and the sure man who is always dull.—H. L. Mencken

J. With specific references to this chapter, analyze the organization of the following essay. Discuss in detail the ways by which the writer achieves unity, coherence, completeness, and emphasis both within the paragraph and in the essay as a whole.

Time and the Machine

Time, as we know it, is a very recent invention. The modern time-sense is hardly older than the United States. It is a by-product of industrialism—a sort of psychological analogue of synthetic perfumes and aniline dyes.

Time is our tyrant. We are chronically aware of the moving minute hand, even of the moving second hand. We have to be. There are trains to be caught, clocks to be punched, tasks to be done in specified periods, records to be broken by fractions of a second, machines that set the pace and have to be kept up with. Our consciousness of the smallest units of time is now acute. To us, for example, the moment 8.17 A.M. means something—something very important, if it happens to be the starting time of our daily train. To our ancestors, such an odd eccentric instant was without significance—did not even exist. In inventing the locomotive, Watt and Stevenson were part inventors of time.

Another time-emphasizing entity is the factory and its dependent, the office. Factories exist for the purpose of getting certain quantities of goods made in a certain time. The old artisan worked as it suited him with the result that consumers generally had to wait for the goods they had ordered from him. The factory is a device for making workmen hurry. The machine revolves so often each minute; so many movements have to be made, so many pieces produced each hour. Result: the factory worker (and the same is true, *mutatis mutandis,* of the office worker) is compelled to know time in its smallest fractions. In the handwork age there was no such compulsion to be aware of minutes and seconds.

Our awareness of time has reached such a pitch of intensity that we suffer acutely whenever our travels take us into some corner of the world where people are not interested in minutes and seconds. The unpunctuality of the Orient, for example, is appalling to those who come freshly from a land of fixed mealtimes and regular train services. For a modern American or Englishman, waiting is a psychological torture. An Indian accepts the blank hours with resignation, even with satisfaction. He has not lost the fine art of doing nothing. Our notion of time as a collection of minutes, each of which must be filled with some business or amusement, is wholly alien to the Oriental, just as it was wholly alien to the Greek. For the man who lives in a pre-industrial world, time moves at a slow and easy pace; he does not care about each minute, for the good reason that he has not been made conscious of the existence of minutes.

This brings us to a seeming paradox. Acutely aware of the smallest constitutent particles of time—of time as measured by clock-work and train arrivals and the revolutions of machines—industrialized man has to a great extent lost the old awareness of time in its larger divisions. The time of which we have knowledge is artificial, machine-made time. Of natural, cosmic time, as it is measured out by sun and moon, we are for the most part almost wholly unconscious. Pre-industrial people know time in its daily, monthly and seasonal rhythms. They are aware of sunrise, noon and sunset; of the full moon and the new; of equinox and solstice; of spring and summer, autumn and winter. All the old religions, including Catholic Christianity, have insisted on this daily and seasonal rhythm. Pre-industrial man was never allowed to forget the majestic movement of cosmic time.

Industrialism and urbanism have changed all this. One can live and work in a town without being aware of the daily march of the sun across the sky; without ever seeing the moon and stars. Broadway and Piccadilly are our Milky Way; our constellations are outlined in neon tubes. Even changes of season affect the townsman very little. He is the inhabitant of an artificial universe that is, to a great extent, walled off from the world of nature. Outside the walls, time is cosmic and moves with the motion of sun and stars. Within, it is an affair of revolving wheels and is measured in seconds and minutes—at its longest, in eight-hour days and six-day weeks. We have a new consciousness; but it has been purchased at the expense of the old consciousness.— Aldous Huxley, *The Olive Tree*

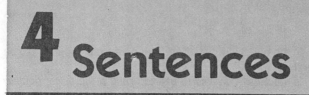

4 Sentences

> You may string words together without a
> sentence-sound to string them on just as you
> may tie clothes together by the sleeve and
> stretch them without a clothes line between
> two trees, but—it is bad for the clothes.
>
> *Robert Frost*

> There is the first satisfaction of arranging it
> on a bit of paper; after many, many false
> tries, false moves, finally you have the
> sentence that you recognize as the one you
> are looking for, the one you have lost
> somewhere, sometime.
>
> *Vladimir Nabokov*

"A sentence," wrote George O. Curme, "is an expression of a thought or feeling by means of a word or words used in such form and manner as to convey the meaning intended." According to this comprehensive definition, when the baby in the play pen says, "Up," when the wild fan at the football game yells, "Yowie," when anyone says, "Me too" or "No can do," all are speaking sentences, for all are clearly conveying the meaning intended. To be sure, the test of meaning is fundamental. Many of the bad sentences discussed later in this chapter fail because, for one reason or another, they don't convey the intended meaning. But many others, even if they get the point across clearly enough, are unsatisfactory for a different reason: they disregard conventions of sentence structure that careful, educated writers normally follow.

A telegram may convey its meaning with clarity and economy: ARRIVE SEVEN THIRTY. DINNER ON PLANE. WILL TAKE CAB FROM AIRPORT. LOVE ALBERT. But the conventions of etiquette require a letter writer to address a weekend hostess in a more finished fashion. A telegrammatical examination answer may contain clear, accurate, information: *The Way of the World*—Congreve's last play—comedy of manners marking highest achievement of type in Restoration—famous for witty dialogue between Mirabell, Millamant." But the conventions in answering discussion questions demand that students unburden their brains more systematically. "Sighted sub sank same" was an admirable dispatch, custom-tailored for the headlines; but the reader of an official report on the incident would naturally expect subjects for the verbs, articles with the nouns, and conjunctions to connect the clauses. The fragmentary sentences that characterize spontaneous conversation may convey the speaker's meaning adequately, even eloquently. But in most written contexts, readers expect sentences that are *grammatically complete*. What is a grammatically complete sentence?

COMPLETE SENTENCES

Reduced to its lowest terms, a complete sentence consists of a *subject* and a *predicate:* Students study. In this example the subject is a single noun (underlined once), the predicate a single verb (underlined twice). The statement may be expanded in numerous ways:

By making the subject compound

Students and teachers study.

By making the predicate compound

Students study and play.

By giving the verb a complement

Students study books.

By adding modifiers to either subject or predicate

Good students study books for general enlightenment.

But whatever is added, the solid foundation of subject and predicate remains. This is true if the *declarative sentence* is changed to an *interrogative sentence* (Do students study?); an *exclamatory sentence* (How seldom students study!); or an *imperative sentence* (Study, students!—in which the subject is *you* understood).

If, on the other hand, the basic sentence is changed in either of the following ways, it becomes incomplete:

Students studying.
Although students study.

The first example does not contain a *finite verb*, one limited in number (singular or plural) and person (first, second, or third). Instead, *studying* is a *verbal*. A verbal may be a participle—like *studying*—a gerund, or an infinitive; it may function as an adjective, a noun, or an adverb; but it cannot be the verb in a complete sentence. To complete the sentence, the writer must add a finite verb (Students studying groan.).

The second example, introduced by a *subordinating conjunction (Although)*, is a *subordinate* or *dependent clause*. To complete the sentence,

77

the writer must either drop the conjunction or supply an *independent clause* (Although students study, <u>they</u> sometimes <u>fail</u>.).

To summarize, *a complete sentence must contain a subject and a finite verb, and every dependent clause must be supported by an independent clause.*

INCOMPLETE SENTENCES

Unacceptable Incomplete Sentences

The incomplete sentences written by some undergraduates are the accidents of ignorance and indifference. Usually they serve no purpose that could not be better served by completing them. This error is commonly known as the *sentence fragment* or *period fault*. Notice how the following student specimens are improved by either completing fragments or incorporating them into complete sentences:

PASSAGE WITH FRAGMENT   The second week the coach called the squad together and broke them into two groups. *The linemen comprising one group and the backfield the other.* (*comprising* is a participle, not a finite verb)
IMPROVED   The second week the coach called the squad together and broke them into two groups, linemen and backfield men.

PASSAGE WITH FRAGMENT   I came to college not only to study English but to get a broad liberal education. *In order to prepare myself for life. (to prepare* is an infinitive, not a finite verb)
IMPROVED   I came to college not only to study English but to get a broad liberal education in order to prepare myself for life.

PASSAGE WITH FRAGMENT   I am glad this college is not in a big city. *Although I miss the theatre and the disco clubs.* (subordinate clause separated from main clause)
IMPROVED   Although I miss the theatre and the disco clubs, I am glad this college is not in a big city.

PASSAGE WITH FRAGMENT   I was born in Jersey City. *Lived in Weehawken until the age of eight, then moved to Newark, where I still live. Started school in Weehawken.* Then I went to Newark to complete my schooling. (omission of subjects—"telegrammar")
IMPROVED   I was born in Jersey City and lived in Weehawken until the age of eight. Then I moved to Newark, where I am still living. I started school in Weehawken and finished in Newark.

PASSAGE WITH FRAGMENT   Thus ended the tragic life of Julius Caesar. *The greatest man that Rome ever produced.* (a phrase in apposition with Caesar, an appositive)
IMPROVED   Thus ended the tragic life of Julius Caesar, the greatest man Rome ever produced.

EXERCISE A

Rewrite all incomplete sentences in the following passages:

1. A college dean once wrote that students come to college for three reasons. These being culture, contacts, and careers. The student who comes for culture not knowing exactly what the word means. Although his conscience tells him that, whatever it is, it is a good thing to get.

2. The student who comes to college for contacts has a clearer aim. Which is to meet the fellow students who may be useful after graduation.

3. Although she never went to college because her father was unemployed, having suffered a crippling injury at the plant, and her mother was unable to find a job with an adequate salary, the result being that she was largely self-educated.

4. Whatever people write reflects their personalities. Even though they try to be completely impersonal.

5. It was clear that because the thief entered the room and rummaged through every drawer and closet without anyone's having seen him, whoever is responsible for security in the dormitories having a lot of explaining to do.

6. Having learned the lesson by observing my father, I am always careful to count all the parts before beginning to put anything together. The picture of my father sitting on the floor on Christmas Eve fuming over a missing screw being one of my keenest memories of childhood.

7. Of several possible arguments for student representation on the Appointments Committee, the Council mentioned two. Neither, however, being convincing to the Faculty.

8. Her coach said that she should keep her eye on the ball. Draw back her racquet head. And follow through with a full swing.

9. Since he had never seen her before in his life, it was unlikely that he would recognize her. When she hurried past without even nodding.

10. Because I hadn't listened carefully to the lecture, I didn't hear the professor's comment. That the Holy Roman Empire was neither Holy, nor Roman, nor an Empire. While assuming that I ought to laugh along with the other students.

Acceptable Incomplete Sentences

Of course, many incomplete sentences in mature writing are intentional and effective. They may simply represent the widespread tendency of contemporary informal prose to carry over into writing the natural shortcuts of speech. For example:

> The third day was the day of spectacular climax: Pickett's charge. *Not really Pickett's, to be technical.*—Bruce Catton, "Gettysburg: Great Turning Point," *New York Times Magazine*

In the second sentence the reader is expected to take the missing subject and verb *(It was)* as much for granted as the unrepeated word *charge.*

An incomplete sentence may be used effectively in one of the following ways:

1. In dialogue

"Haven't seen much of you lately, Sy. Don't you drink tea any more?"
"Once in a while," said Levin.
"You aren't sore about anything in particular?"
"Not me."
"About the Birdless boy?"
"Not any more."
"Good. I didn't think you'd carry a grudge."
"Can't stand them."
"I'll try to remember to get that window fixed," Gilley said absently.
"No hurry."—Bernard Malamud, *A New Life*

2. In description

The city closes in on him now, and in his strange perspective it becomes the antithesis of what he believes. *The citadel not of Quality, the citadel of form and substance. Substance in the form of steel sheets and girders, substance in the form of concrete piers and roads, in the form of brick, of asphalt, of auto parts, old radios, and rails, dead carcasses of animals that once grazed the prairies. Form and substance without Quality.*—Robert Pirsig, *Zen and the Art of Motorcycle Maintenance*

3. For transitions

So much for the origin of war. Now a few words about the way we fought it and particularly about the taking of the Philippines.—George Kennan, *American Diplomacy*

4. As exclamations, questions, and answers

There he remained for two amazingly productive years during which he discovered the binomial theorem in mathematics, invented differential and integral calculus, produced a correct theory of colors, and laid the groundwork for his theory of gravitation. *All this before he was 24 years old!*—R. F. Humphreys and R. Beringer, *First Principles of Atomic Physics*

What price glory? The exorbitant price of war, the price of death and devastation.

5. For emphasis

The high-school period, in America anyway, is surely the worst period in a man's life—the most awkward, uncomfortable, inept and embarrassing of all times. *And the most fruitless.*—Eric Sevareid, *Not So Wild a Dream*

These examples of acceptable incomplete sentences illustrate a fundamental rule of composition: the importance of context. The question of whether an incomplete sentence or any sentence is acceptable or effective cannot be certainly answered without considering its role in the movement of the paragraph.

As a general rule, you should be wary of all incomplete sentences unless you are representing the shortcuts of actual speech. In formal exposition, your instructor may expect you to avoid all incomplete sentences. But you must not overlook their value in other kinds of writing.

EXERCISE B

The writers of the following passages probably had good reasons for using incomplete sentences. Identify all such sentences and explain what the reasons might have been.

1. I wish I could tell you about the South Pacific. The way it actually was. The infinite specks of coral we called islands. Coconut palms nodding gracefully toward the ocean. Reefs upon which waves broke into spray, and inner lagoons, lovely beyond description. I wish I could tell you about the sweating jungle, the full moon rising behind the volcanoes, and the waiting. The waiting. The timeless, repetitive waiting.—James Michener, *Tales of the South Pacific*

2. This trial has been going on since the days of Prometheus. Since before that. Since the days of the Archangel Michael.—Henry Miller, "Defense of the Freedom to Read," *The Henry Miller Reader*

3. Now for the third reason. The career-minded student talks like this: "What price culture in a materialistic society conceived in competition and dedicated to the proposition that success is measured in dollars and cents? Can Shakespeare get you a job? A job teaching Shakespeare. Can poetry pay you a salary? Not unless you write singing commercials. Culture indeed!"

4. Then suddenly, in the Sixties, like a series of underground nuclear explosions, experiments began rumbling throughout the country that presaged perhaps the greatest medical discoveries of all time. In the frantic research activity that has followed, it has become clear that man may, after all, have a mind resource to control his own being down to the most minute fragments of his physical structure. Including his brain.—Barbara Brown, "Biofeedback: An Exercise in 'Self-Control,'" *Saturday Review*

5. The teacher thought I was stupid. Couldn't spell, couldn't read, couldn't do arithmetic. Just stupid. Teachers were never interested in finding out that you couldn't concentrate because you were so hungry.—Dick Gregory, *Nigger: An Autobiography*

TWO RELATED ERRORS

Two common elementary errors in punctuation raise the question of whether the writer can recognize a complete sentence.

1. The Run-on Sentence or Fused Sentence

I was frightened during my first driving lesson the instructor did not increase my confidence.

The writer has let one sentence run on into the next (fused two sentences together) with no punctuation to separate them. That the first sentence ends with *lesson* should be indicated either by a semicolon (;) or by a period followed by a capital letter. (See pp. 317, 327.)

2. The Comma Fault

I was frightened during my first driving lesson, the instructor did not increase my confidence.

A comma is not normally acceptable in separating two independent clauses unless they are joined by a coordinating conjunction (*and, but, for, or, nor,* and *yet*). In this example, the writer could substitute a semicolon or period or add *and,* not *moreover.* Because the comma fault is extremely common in undergraduate writing, it is discussed in greater detail on pp. 319–320.

EXERCISE C

Rewrite the following passages, correcting run-on sentences and comma faults:

1. Though she was fascinated by politics, she was not loyal to any political party her spirit was too independent.

2. As the trees began to turn, Herman took long walks in the woods, however, his interest in leaves declined when he had to stay home and rake them.

3. Though they had much in common, she did not share his passion for detective stories she had no curiosity about how the body appeared mysteriously on the chaise longue.

4. Many voters argued that government spending should be drastically reduced, some were in favor of abolishing all federal programs that did not directly help them.

5. In my neighborhood, jogging has become an obsession, in fact, anyone who doesn't put on a warm-up suit and do at least three miles a day in and out of the traffic is considered an enemy to public health.

COORDINATION AND SUBORDINATION

By the age of three· or four, the normal child is lisping in complete sentences. But they are usually *simple sentences;* that is, sentences with only a single clause: "We went to the zoo. We saw three tigers. They were big ones too. One of them made a great big noise. I was scared. Mommy bought me an ice-cream cone." Before long children begin tying clauses together with a few common conjunctions, not because they have been taught any formal grammar, but because they are unconsciously aware of connections between them. Partly through juvenile breathlessness and partly because they cannot distinguish clearly among these relationships, children are likely to pour out an indiscriminate torrent like this: "We went to the zoo and we saw three tigers and they were big ones too but one of them made a great big noise so I was scared and Mommy bought me an ice-cream cone." From the standpoint of sentence structure, this eager prattle is little different from what comes out of the mouths of some adults: the nonstop talker whose tiresome anecdotes fall into marathon sentences thinly cemented together with "and I says to her . . . and she says to me . . . so I says to her, I says"; the after-dinner speaker who ties clauses together with *and-er* and *so-er* like endless strings of sausages. Children have no monopoly on immature sentence patterns.

You cannot achieve maturity as a writer until you have learned to avoid the infinite monotony of simple sentences. You must not abolish them all: the simple sentence is the backbone of twentieth-century prose. Nor should you string clauses together indiscriminately like a breathless child merely for the sake of making short sentences longer. You must learn to apply two simple and logical rules of sentence organization:

1. If two or more related elements are of equal importance, put them in a *coordinate* construction.
2. If one element is more important than the others, put it in an independent clause and *subordinate* the others.

Since in talking few people have the foresight to distinguish important elements from unimportant, these rules may not be strictly followed in informal writing that intentionally reflects the loose structure of conversation. But all trained writers tend to follow them. That is why mature writing naturally contains, in addition to simple sentences, three other kinds.

Types of Sentences Determined by Clauses

1. Compound sentences contain two or more coordinate independent clauses but no dependent clause:

Frank threw the winning pass and Kelley caught it.

Sometimes the comma and conjunction are replaced by a semicolon:

Frank threw the winning pass, Kelley caught it.

83

2. Complex sentences contain one independent clause and one or more dependent clauses:

Although Frank's <u>pass</u> <u>was</u> high, <u>Kelley</u> <u>caught</u> it.

3. Compound-complex sentences contain two or more independent clauses and one or more dependent clauses:

Although Frank's <u>pass</u> <u>was</u> high, <u>Kelley</u> <u>caught</u> it, and <u>Jones</u> <u>erased</u> the safety man.

Faults of Coordination and Subordination

Failure to understand coordination and subordination results in the following common faults:

1. Primer prose (inadequate coordination and subordination) (A primer—rhyming with *swimmer*—is an elementary textbook, especially for children.)

FAULTY I was seized by a wanderlust every summer. I also wanted to see what the rest of the country was like. Several summers were occupied in this. I hitchhiked from place to place. I usually had no plan. I just went the same place the driver was going. I went across the country and back this way three times. Now I won't be able to do it any more. I'll have to work summers to get through college.

IMPROVED Every summer I was seized by a wanderlust and a desire to see what the rest of the country was like. During several vacations I hitchhiked aimlessly from place to place. Wandering without an itinerary, going wherever the driver was heading, I went across the country and back three times. Now that I shall have to work in the summer to get through college, my hitchhiking days are over.

FAULTY The section I live in is centered around a lake. The lake is oblong and is about three-quarters of a mile in length. At one end of the lake is a small beach. It is private for families who live on the lake. Not far from the beach are a small dam and an old wooden dock. The dam has an old floodgate. This floodgate dates back to the last century. The dock serves as a parking lot.

IMPROVED The section I live in is centered around an oblong lake about three-quarters of a mile in length. At one end is a private beach for families who live on the lake. Not far from the beach are a small dam, whose floodgate dates back to the last century, and an old wooden dock that serves as a parking lot.

Notice that in primer prose the childish monotony of simple sentence patterns is often accompanied by the unnecessary repetition of words.

2. False coordination ("Siamese twin sentences," in which elements are illogically joined)

FAULTY Mildred was an adopted child, and she was having her teeth straightened with shining braces.

IMPROVED   An adopted child whose real parents had neglected her teeth, Mildred was having them straightened with shining braces.

FAULTY   The class of which I was a member had four exciting dances, and we were rewarded at the end of the school term by receiving diplomas. (here it is implied that the diplomas were awards for social activity)
IMPROVED   Although the members of my class had four exciting dances, not a single student failed to study hard enough to get his diploma.

3. Excessive coordination (in which all clauses are made equal with and, but, so, emphasizing everything—and nothing)

FAULTY   The trip was very interesting, but I sometimes wonder about its value, for it practically set me back a year scholastically, for in the Florida schools I could not finish German and chemistry, so upon graduation from high school I had to attend prep school.
IMPROVED   Although the trip was very interesting, I sometimes wonder about its value, for it practically set me back a year scholastically. Because I could not finish German and chemistry in Florida, I had to attend prep school on my graduation from high school.

FAULTY   In my freshman year I came out for goalie on the soccer team, and for my efforts I received a regular position on the first team, but because of my dislike of the goalie position, I tried out for a halfback position, but because of the fact that these positions were held by juniors and seniors I could not avail myself of a position on the soccer team here.
IMPROVED   In my freshman year I came out for goalie in soccer and earned a regular position on the first team. Because I disliked playing goalie, I later tried out for halfback. Since the halfback positions were held by juniors and seniors, I could not make the grade.

4. Upside-down subordination (in which the main idea is put in the subordinate clause or phrase)

FAULTY   He was strolling calmly on the deck when a large wave washed him overboard.
IMPROVED   As he was strolling calmly on the deck, a large wave washed him overboard.

FAULTY   He fell seven stories and broke eight ribs, puncturing a lung and living to tell the tale.
IMPROVED   Although a fall of seven stories gave him eight broken ribs and a punctured lung, he lived to tell the tale.

This fault cannot always be identified in a sentence separated from its context. For acceptable reasons—understatement, anticlimax, rhythm—a writer may intentionally subordinate a main point. The question of emphasis may be more subtle than an arbitrary choice between kinds of clauses (see pp. 102–106).

5. Careless use of connectives

FAULTY   Although these people have a point, but I feel that mine is better. (the writer starts with a subordinate clause, then carelessly makes the main clause coordinate by inserting *but*)
IMPROVED   Although these people have a point, I feel that mine is better.

FAULTY   Politics is a strenuous game and which often corrupts honest men. (by inserting *and*, the writer makes the second clause into an impossible coordinate-subordinate hybrid)
IMPROVED   Politics is a strenuous game which often corrupts honest men.

FAULTY   He tried five times to be elected, and he never succeeded. (the wrong connective expresses an inaccurate relationship between the clauses)
IMPROVED   He tried five times to be elected, but he never succeeded.

For other connectives that are sometimes weak or ambiguous, see *as, that,* and *while* in the Glossary of Usage.

EXERCISE D

The following passages contain examples of primer prose, false coordination, excessive coordination, upside-down subordination, and careless use of connectives. Rewrite the passages in accordance with the principles for effectively combining clauses.

1. After that trip I began my senior year, and I immediately became interested in politics, but I never spent much time at it, for I devoted most of my time to the basketball team, and we nearly became the Class B champions of Pennsylvania, losing only in the final round of the annual tournament.

2. James Fenimore Cooper does a great deal of writing about one character in *The Prairie.* This character is the old trapper or Leatherstocking or Deerslayer or Natty Bumppo. He was called the last two names in his younger years. He spent most of his life in the woods, even though he was born on the seashore. He lived in the woods of a province known as York for nearly seventy years of his life. He fought under Anthony Wayne against the Indians. The old trapper's past adventure with the Delaware Indians is told by a soldier named Middleton. He was a relative of the whites the old trapper helped. Cooper brings in the past in order to tie together the whole of *The Leatherstocking Tales.*

3. My father was an unsuccessful vacuum-cleaner salesman, and his picture shows that in his youth he had an intelligent face and a fine head of wavy hair.

4. Although his subjects and his technique were different from those of the poets who were still popular in the '20s, but he quickly made a name for himself as an exciting new talent.

5. The dampness of spring was in the air that morning, and she got there just in time to see them enter an old trapper's cabin.

6. The magazine never prints long articles, and this is very good if a person wants to get just a few pertinent facts about a subject, but on something like modern whaling you just can't tell what it is all about with only one page of prose, in spite of all the pictures, and in the recent past almost every subject has expanded and become so broad that it takes a fairly good-sized book to tell all about the subject.

7. He was lying quietly in his bunk one morning when the prow of another ship crashed through the bulkhead crippling him for life.

8. Many of the TV movies are not worth watching. Television is very monotonous. Western programs are a good example. After you have seen one Western, you have seen them all. The plots are trivial. The same man is always the hero. Some of them are called *adult* Westerns. American adults are supposed to be watching them. I don't see how the Western movies can appeal to anyone seeking entertainment. They must appeal only to the immature American adult. The shows are uninteresting, simple, and very similar to each other. Yet Westerns are always top favorites with the American public. It is a discouraging fact.

9. I tried to improve my study habits by going to the library every night, and I did not succeed.

10. She was sitting in the front room reading the evening paper when the door opened and her son burst into the room, announcing that Mary had fallen off a cliff to her death.

MODIFIERS

Once you have learned to write complete sentences and to combine clauses intelligently, you have gone a long way toward writing acceptable sentences. But careless use of modifiers may still spell your downfall.

Importance of Position

Adjectives usually come immediately before the noun they modify (He wore an *old, battered* hat on his head). Sometimes they follow immediately after (He wore a hat, *old* and *battered,* on his head). But if you place them anywhere else, you may be in trouble. If you write, "He wore a hat on his head, *old* and *battered,*" the meaning is ambiguous. Is it clear that the hat, not the head, is old and battered? If you write, "*Old* and *battered*, he wore a hat on his head," the meaning is radically changed. In many other languages nouns and adjectives are linked by "inflectional endings" that specify their number and gender. In English, without such links, the position of modifiers is particularly important.

With adverbs there is much more leeway, though position can still be important:

Slowly he slouched down the street with his hands in his pockets.
He *slowly* slouched down the street with his hands in his pockets.
He slouched *slowly* down the street with his hands in his pockets.
He slouched down the street *slowly* with his hands in his pockets.

All these mean essentially the same, though the placing of the adverb makes differences in emphasis and rhythm. But a misplaced adverb can sometimes cause confusion:

He studied the woman who sat in his chair *secretly*.

The adverb *secretly* apparently modifies the verb *sat*. Does the writer really mean that there was something secret about the way the woman sat in the chair? Probably not.

He *secretly* studied the woman who sat in his chair.

The adverb clearly modifies *studied*.

Except with special nuisances such as *only*, few students have real trouble with one-word modifiers. But when adjectives and adverbs are expanded into phrases and clauses, the trouble begins. Whether a modifier has one word or twenty, the same elementary principle applies: A good sentence leaves no doubt about the words to which the modifiers refer. Although it oversimplifies the problem, this is a useful rule: *Place every modifier as near as possible to the word it modifies.*

Misrelated Modifiers

Because they present different problems in revision, it is convenient to summarize the various kinds of misrelated modifiers under two main classes: (1) *dangling modifiers*, which usually have nothing in the sentence that they can logically modify and often require reworking the sentence; and (2) *misplaced modifiers*, which can be corrected in a first draft by merely changing their position with a loop and an arrow.

1. Dangling modifiers

FAULTY *Being rushed* through the registrar's office on the way to the dean, the well-kept records impressed me. (dangling participle)
IMPROVED As I was rushed through the registrar's office on the way to the dean, the well-kept records impressed me.
Or: Being rushed through the registrar's office . . . I was impressed by the well-kept records.

FAULTY My ego was further boosted by *being elected* to the student council. (dangling gerund)
IMPROVED My ego was further boosted when I was elected to the student council.
Or: . . . by my being elected to the student council.

FAULTY *To be* really literate, books should be read thoroughly. (dangling infinitive)
IMPROVED To be really literate, a student should read books thoroughly.

88

FAULTY   When *only one year old*, my family moved to Ashtabula. (dangling elliptical clause—that is, a clause with words omitted)
IMPROVED   When I was only one year old, my family moved to Ashtabula.
Or: When only one year old, I moved with my family to Ashtabula.

FAULTY   *At the age of six* my parents sent me to a private school in York. (dangling phrase)
IMPROVED   At the age of six I was sent to a private school in York.
Or: When I was six, my parents sent me to a private school in York.

As the examples show, the best argument against dangling modifiers is that they are often either (1) *ambiguous* or (2) *unintentionally humorous.* The first sentence is ambiguous: What is being rushed through the registrar's office, the student or the records? Though the actual meaning of the other sentences may be clear, they run the risk of provoking unsolicited laughter. The reader knows that the student's ego did not appear on the ballot, that "To be literate" is not intended to modify *books*, that the family is not one year old or the parents six—but such bizarre conceptions can still be distracting.

Though unambiguous dangling modifiers are common in professional writing, it is safer to eliminate all danglers and to be particularly wary of the attachments of verbals ending in *-ing*.

The dangling modifier should not be confused with the *absolute construction*, which is commonly accepted as modifying the whole sentence rather than any part of it. Some words, for example, though in the form of participles, do not have the force of an adjective seeking an attachment to a noun or pronoun:

Confidentially *speaking*, the participle in this sentence is innocent of dangling.

His homework *finished*, he wandered down to the late movie.

2. Misplaced modifiers

AMBIGUOUS OR HUMOROUS   Judith Henry was killed while lying in bed *by a bullet* which entered her house. (here the phrase *by a bullet* appears to modify *lying*)
CLEAR   Judith Henry was killed by a bullet which entered her house while she was lying in bed.

AMBIGUOUS OR HUMOROUS   J. Alfred Prufrock is walking along a beach, where mermaids are going out to sea, *with rolled up pantlegs*. (the italicized phrase, despite the comma, appears to give the mermaids an unclassical garb)
CLEAR   With rolled up pantlegs, J. Alfred Prufrock is walking along a beach where mermaids are going out to sea.

AMBIGUOUS OR HUMOROUS   I asked him *after the year was over* to lend me the book. (this squinting modifier could modify either *asked* or *lend*)
CLEAR   After the year was over I asked him to lend me the book.
Or: I asked him to lend me the book after the year was over. (depending on the writer's meaning)

AMBIGUOUS OR HUMOROUS   God can *only* make a tree. (the omnipotent Creator is demoted to a specialist)
CLEAR   Only God can make a tree.

When a misplaced *only* leads to absurdity, as in the last illustration, it should be put in its place. The same is true of *almost, also, even*, and *merely*.

Some misplaced modifiers, though they may not result in ambiguity, are awkward because they interrupt the flow of the sentence by splitting parts that normally come close together:

AWKWARD   Professor Thorndike, *always eager to keep his students awake regardless of their obvious lack of interest in either the subject or the course*, puts on a three-ring circus. (long interrupter between subject and verb)
IMPROVED   Always eager to keep his students awake regardless of their obvious lack of interest in either the subject or the course, Professor Thorndike puts on a three-ring circus.

AWKWARD   I did not know, *in spite of the hours I spent in reviewing*, the answers to more than half the questions. (interrupter between verb and object)
IMPROVED   In spite of the hours I spent in reviewing, I did not know the answers to more than half the questions.

AWKWARD   I stood in lonely isolation where I had, *only four short years before*, participated in the greatest invasion in history. (interrupter between parts of the verb)
IMPROVED   I stood in lonely isolation where, only four short years before, I had participated in the greatest invasion in history.

AWKWARD   Smithfield Cobb, played by Melvyn Douglas, is able to, *through the mind of Janet Ames, played by Rosalind Russell*, show her the reasons why five people should be alive and not her husband.
IMPROVED   Through the mind of Janet Ames (Rosalind Russell), Smithfield Cobb (Melvyn Douglas) is able to show the reasons why five people should be alive and not her husband.

Used sparingly, such split constructions can be a conscious trick of style for the sake of suspense and variety.

The last illustration is awkward because it splits two parts of a verbal (*to . . . show*) with a ten-word modifier. It happens to be a *split infinitive*, but reasonable students of the language don't consider all split infinitives as crimes or even awkward expressions. Further discussion of this construction appears in the Glossary of Usage.

EXERCISE E

Rewrite the following sentences, eliminating all dangling and misplaced modifiers:

1. I kept thinking about how religious my parents were for the rest of the night.

2. He would shout like an auctioneer, waving his arms wildly about, usually resulting in curious looks from the customers in the store.

3. As a youngster he and his brother would memorize a poem a week.—Thomas Lask, *New York Times*

4. Numbed and forgetful and frost-blackened, the hum of the spring hive still resounded faintly in their sodden tissues.—Loren Eiseley, *The Night Country*

5. He asked her when the semester was over where she intended to spend the summer.

6. I saw Bobby only once or twice in the city, just nodding to each other in public places.—James Dickey, *Deliverance*

7. Regarded as the biggest hurdle of the season, the coaches warned us not to get overconfident all week.

8. Although unambitious and at times downright lazy, I have never known him to break a promise no matter what the consequences might be.

9. Trying to duck away, his left arm and his head became tangled on the wrong side of the top rope.—Norman Mailer, *The Presidential Papers*

10. In order to facilitate reimbursement for sub-frosh meals, each fraternity is requested to turn in a report of the number of men who were fed to Bruce Locklin at the Sigma Chi House.

REQUIRED PARALLELISM

Importance of Balance

"The world will little note, nor long remember, what we say here, but what was done by them can never be forgotten." This misquotation should jar even the most insensitive American ear. For it does violence not only to history but also to the prose style of a great writer. A glance at the original should quickly reveal the difference: "The world will little note, nor long remember, what we say here, but it can never forget what they did here." The basic meaning is the same in the misquoted version. Nothing really new has been added. Two verbs have been changed from active to passive voice, and that is all. But the whole sentence is tilted off balance and falls flat. Notice the difference in a diagram:

The world will	‖ little note,	‖ nor
	‖ long remember	‖ what we say here,
but it can	‖ never forget	‖ what they did here

| The world will | ‖ little note, | nor |
| | ‖ long remember | what we say here, |

but what was done by them can never be forgotten.

Violations of Parallelism

The awkward paraphrase of Lincoln's famous sentence disregards an important principle of sentence structure: *Put parallel elements in parallel form.* Two common violations of this principle are (1) *shifted constructions* and (2) *careless use of correlatives.*

1. Shifted constructions

NOT PARALLEL   I felt that the activities were dull, and the pampering of the pupils annoyed me. (shift of subject)
PARALLEL   I found the activities dull and the pampering of the pupils annoying.

NOT PARALLEL   If he has a plain gray suit, then a tie should be bought that will match it. (shift of subject and voice)
PARALLEL   If he has a plain gray suit, then he should buy a matching tie.

NOT PARALLEL   He is honest, hard-working, patriotic, and he has a firm nature. (from adjectives to a clause)
PARALLEL   He is honest, hard-working, patriotic, and firm.

NOT PARALLEL   One summer I found a job that seemed to be different and an easy way of making money. (from adjective to a phrase)
PARALLEL   One summer I found a job that seemed to be different and lucrative.
Or: One summer I found a job that seemed to be a different and easy way of making money.

NOT PARALLEL   During five years in the laboratory I advanced from bottle-washing to a chemist. (from job to jobholder)
PARALLEL   During five years in the laboratory I advanced from bottle-washer to chemist.
Or: . . . from bottle washing to chemistry.

For other illustrations of the same principle, shifts in tense and in the number and person of pronouns, see pp. 296, 309.

2. Careless use of correlatives

According to strict usage, such *correlative conjunctions* as *both . . . and, either . . . or, neither . . . nor,* and *not only . . . but also* require parallel construction. The construction is like a simple lever: a misplaced correlative or changed construction on either side of the fulcrum upsets the balance.

NOT PARALLEL   He failed *either* to come to class *or* came unprepared. (*either* verbal or verb)
PARALLEL   He *either* failed to come to class *or* came unprepared. (*either* verb *or* verb)
Either he failed to come to class *or* he came unprepared. (*either* pronoun *or* pronoun)

NOT PARALLEL   I voted for Jones *both* because he was honest *and* intelligent. (*both* conjunction *and* adjective)

PARALLEL I voted for Jones because he was *both* honest *and* intelligent. (*both* adjective *and* adjective)

NOT PARALLEL Miss Brill *not only* feels that she is a member of the audience *but also* an actress on stage. (*not only* verb *but also* noun)

PARALLEL Miss Brill feels that she is *not only* a member of the audience *but also* an actress on stage. (*not only* noun *but also* noun)

NOT PARALLEL Clarence Day's father *not only* was eccentric *but also* lovable. (*not only* verb *but also* adjective)

PARALLEL Clarence Day's father was *not only* eccentric *but also* lovable. (*not only* adjective *but also* adjective)

In formal writing, prepositions, articles, auxiliary verbs, and conjunctions are commonly repeated before parallel elements. This repetition is unnecessary unless the sentence is ambiguous without it:

FORMAL He asked for permission to call the doctor, to visit the hospital, and to bring food to the patient.

LESS FORMAL He asked for permission to call the doctor, visit the hospital, and bring food to the patient.

AMBIGUOUS The critics praised him for having the courage of his convictions and his honesty in presenting the material.

CLEAR The critics praised him for having the courage of his convictions and for his honesty in presenting the material.

FAULTY COMPARISONS

In making comparisons, be sure that (1) the meaning is complete and (2) the terms are comparable.

1. Incomplete comparisons

FAULTY More young women are smoking now.
REVISED More young women are smoking now than ten years ago.

FAULTY Mabel gave Marion more than Cynthia.
REVISED Mabel gave Marion more than she gave Cynthia.
Or: Mabel gave Marion more than Cynthia did.

2. Incomparable terms

FAULTY Rock music brings me as much personal enjoyment as those people who enjoy reading Byron, Shelley, and Keats. (*Rock music* is compared with *people*, implying that the people bring enjoyment.)
REVISED Rock music brings me as much personal enjoyment as the poems of Byron, Shelley, and Keats bring to others.

FAULTY She studies less than any member of the class. (*She* is compared with *any member*, including herself.)
REVISED She studies less than any other member of the class.

EXERCISE F

Rewrite the following sentences, correcting all violations of parallelism and examples of faulty comparison:

1. For many people, life in the suburbs is an endless round of running here and there, a PTA meeting, pick up the kids at school, shopping, play golf at the country club, or an afternoon of cards.

2. He had a paint brush and bucket in his hand, his sweatshirt was torn at the sides, no sleeves, shorts that were formerly dungarees, and gaping holes in his sneakers.

3. The men hired for the town's various sanitary departments such as the dump, street cleaners, and garbage collectors are all underpaid.

4. Modern football is not only a game of brawn but also of intelligence.

5. Until I came to college my attitudes were like other people in my home community: conservative, always conform, and not caring about the plight of the poor.

6. It has developed neither a systematic program for eliminating the growing vacuum between the individual and centralized authority, nor does it have a full-fledged theory of social power at its disposal.—Charles Frankel, *The Case for Modern Man*

7. The play was fascinating both because it entertained the audience while making a significant point about the hypocrisy in our society.

8. My mother not only embarrassed me by showing my grades all around the neighborhood but the newspapers were regularly informed that I had a better record than anyone in my class.

9. My interest in collecting records is as important to me as the books in my room-mate's growing library.

10. The traditional Zen method can be summarized as follows: (1) restrain senses; (2) avoid sleep; (3) moderation in eating; (4) isolation; (5) awareness of the past; (6) practice meditation.

LENGTH

Thomas De Quincey once complained that the German philosopher Kant wrote sentences which had been measured by a carpenter and that some of them ran to two feet six inches. Many readers of Kant will sympathize with his English critic's point of view. But De Quincey must have known that even a three-foot sentence may be a good sentence if it does its job, for he wrote some remarkable three-foot sentences himself. Theoretically it is meaningless to say only that a sentence is too long. When critics add a qualifying phrase—too long for a loosely constructed compound sentence; too long for the concluding sentence of a chapter; too long for readers with twelve-year-old minds; too long considering all the long sentences in the same paragraph—they are measuring sentence length with a more accurate instrument than a carpenter's rule. A good sentence, like a good paragraph, should be exactly as long as the writer needs to make it to serve the purpose. "We try harder" is a complete and compelling sentence in Avis ads. The famous shortest sentence in the Bible is only two words long: "Jesus wept." But another successful sentence, equally effective in a different way, might run to 202 words.

The short and the long of it can be illustrated by two passages from fiction:

She was an old woman and lived on a farm near the town in which I lived. All country and small-town people have seen such old women, but no one knows much about them. Such an old woman comes into town driving an old worn-out horse or she comes afoot carrying a basket. She may own a few hens and have eggs to sell. She brings them in a basket and takes them to a grocer. There she trades them in. She gets some salt pork and some beans. Then she gets a pound or two of sugar and some flour.

Afterwards she goes to the butcher's and asks for some dog-meat. She may spend ten or fifteen cents, but when she does she asks for something. Formerly, the butchers gave liver to anyone who wanted to carry it away. In our family we were always having it. Once one of my brothers got a whole cow's liver at the slaughter-house near the fairgrounds in our town. We had it until we were sick of it. It never cost a cent. I have hated the thought of it ever since.

The old woman got some liver and a soupbone. She never visited with anyone, and as soon as she got what she wanted she lit out for home. It made quite a load for such an old body. No one gave her a lift. People drive right down a road and never notice an old woman like that.—Sherwood Anderson, *Death in the Woods*

Just with his body and from inside like a snake, leaning that black motorcycle from side to side, cutting in and out of the slow line of cars to get there first, staring due-north through goggles towards Mount Moriah and switching coon tails in everybody's face was Wesley Beavers, and laid against his back, like sleep, spraddle-legged on the sheepskin seat behind him was Rosacoke Mustian who was maybe his girl and who had given up looking into the wind and trying to nod at every sad car in the line, and when he even speeded up and passed the truck (lent for the afternoon by Mr. Isaac Alston and driven by Sammy his man, hauling one pine box and one black boy dressed in all he could borrow, set up in a ladder-back chair with flowers banked round him and a foot on the box to steady it)—when he even passed that, Rosacoke said once into his back "Don't" and rested in humiliation, not thinking but with her hands on his hips for dear life and her white blouse blown out behind her like a banner in defeat.—Reynolds Price, *A Long and Happy Life*

No statistician is necessary to point out the obvious differences in sentence length. Anderson's sentences average 12.5 words, about the same as those of an average sixth-grader. Price's sentence unrolls to 190 words, almost half as long as some freshman themes. Neither passage is recommended as a model for the inexperienced writer. In expository writing, a passage of consecutive sentences as short as Anderson's could produce deadly monotony, and a nonstop sentence like Price's would be both confusing and exhausting. But in the narrative contexts, the sentence length in both passages can be justified. Anderson is telling a simple story of the tragic death of a simple woman in the simplest sentences and words he can find. The absence of variety in both sentence length and vocabulary captures the monotony of her drab existence. Price is capturing a swift moving picture, with its rapid transitions and striking contrasts; and the sweep and swoop of the rhythm suggests that there is no time in the breathless weaving world of the motorcyclist for the stops and starts of traffic lights—or periods.

In short, the problem of sentence length—like the problems considered in the rest of this chapter: economy, variety, and emphasis—is more a question of literary style than of elementary structure. It cannot readily be reduced to rules.

It makes some sense, however, to speak of a sentence as "too long for the middle of the twentieth century." In the days of crinolines and bustles, when the pace of life was still geared to the first rickety iron horse, when people had time to spend tedious months on patchwork quilts, to read three-volume novels and walk to the office, when ornate architecture was more fashionable in prose style, especially in the earnest rhetoric of parliamentary debate, a writer was more likely to construct sentences as synthetic as this one, balancing word against word, phrase against phrase, clause against clause, carefully building up the suspense until the final climax—or anticlimax. But the pace of modern life is different. Laborsaving devices have given us more leisure than our ancestors dreamed of. But we have not time to enjoy it. We are too busy being busy. We run up escalators to save three useless seconds. We read digests of digests. Radio and TV commentators give us all the news in fifteen hectic minutes. Newspapers and magazines shoot the facts at us like machine guns. So we are more likely to write sentences like these. Short, snappy, staccato sentences, or half sentences.

The dangers of both extremes should be apparent: they are equally artificial, equally tedious. But for better or worse, sentences are shorter than they used to be, and this generation of readers is accustomed to the staccato style. Despite the over-all gain in literacy, few people today have the patience to thread the maze of an elaborate sentence. The studies of Rudolf Flesch indicate that an average reader will have no trouble with a sentence average of seventeen words, but that as soon as the average reaches twenty-one, the level is "fairly difficult," and when it gets to twenty-nine, reading is "very difficult." An artist can hardly be expected to take such statistics seriously. Even in the machine age, a writer cannot be required to type with one hand and work a calculator with the other. But the bare figures should be sobering to a writer of simple exposition, whose chief aim is to get a point across to a reader with the least possible misunderstanding. Two British experts, Robert Graves and Alan Hodge, reduce the problem to a simple rule: "Sentences should not be so long that the reader loses his way in them."

If you write monotonous primer sentences that serve no stylistic purpose, you do not have to be told to err on the side of brevity in order to be fashionable. Nothing said here is meant to excuse primer prose. But when you find yourself tangled in a long construction, and all the rules of coordination, subordination, modification, and parallelism avail you nothing, do not be afraid to take the easiest way out: breaking up the long sentence logically into two or more short ones. Notice how the following exhausting sentences can be effectively broken up:

NONSTOP   The project of giving each school in the vicinity where there is a class of instrumental music two tickets to be used at each concert by the student making the most progress in musical studies between concert dates, which was announced in our last program, has been well received.

EASY STAGES   The project announced in our last program has been well received. Under this plan we distribute two tickets for each concert to every school in the vicinity with a class in instrumental music. They are awarded to the student making the most progress in musical studies between concert dates.

NONSTOP   The embedded ambition to become a surgical doctor, which was aroused by the sudden death of his mother, was retarded by a temporary illness of blindness initiated by an extensive reading of books late at night and by a poor condition of health due to neglect of his body, but after two years of illness the normal condition of health was restored by a rigid procedure prescribed by the physician.

EASY STAGES   The death of his mother fired him with the ambition to become a surgeon. For two years his studies were interrupted. Physical neglect had undermined his health, and the long hours of night reading had brought on temporary blindness. But by following a rigid procedure prescribed by his doctor, he completely recovered.

Of course, length is not the only culprit in these sentences. Both illustrate the general principle that nonstop sentences usually violate more fundamental rules of structure. The first example has a modifier (*which was announced* . . .) that is separated by thirty-seven words from the noun it modifies (*project*). In the second example, the writer is not only saying more in one sentence than it can handle but taking too many words to say it.

EXERCISE G

Break up the following passages into shorter sentences without omitting essential details or lapsing into primer prose:

1. At half-past nine on the morning of July 2, 1881, as President Garfield walked through the Baltimore and Potomac Railway Station on his way to take a train for Elberon, New Jersey, where his family had already gone, an assassin slipped up behind him and fired two shots from a forty-four caliber Navy revolver into his back, then turned to flee, leaving him fatally wounded and shocking a nation which only sixteen years before had been rocked to its foundation when a bullet from the gun of John Wilkes Booth killed Abraham Lincoln.

2. I am left-handed, which is not an unusual phenomenon, nor is it necessarily a handicap, but it has brought me more trouble than any other physical peculiarity I possess, and yet it helps in many different ways, so if I had the choice I would find it difficult to make up my mind whether to be left-handed or not, considering all my experiences as a southpaw.

3. He left on Monday, the sixteenth of September, shortly after I had received an old car from my mother in order to go back and forth to college, for my parents could not afford to have me live there, and I had resigned myself to four years of commuting, which sets me apart from the average students who live on the campus and spend most of their spare time hanging around the college book store.

4. Confirming our telephone conversation, I would like to say that I think it was very nice of you to agree to purchase one of the tickets which we are now offering for sale for our annual Police Benefit Ball, and in addition I would very much like to express my own personal gratitude for your very excellent cooperation in making a financial contribution to our efforts, which are principally directed toward raising a sufficient amount of money to keep twelve retired police officers on our pension list and also make it possible for twelve more, who have reached retirement age and are eligible to retire at any time from active police duties, to have their names placed on the inactive roster.

WORDINESS AND ECONOMY

Any wordy sentence is too long no matter how short it is. Repetition has already been discussed in connection with paragraphing (see pp. 65–68), and the lessons there are equally applicable within the sentence. But unnecessary repetition of the same words is only one brand of wordiness. Others are (1) *needless repetition of the same thought in different words;* (2) *circumlocutions;* (3) *the passive voice;* and (4) *overweight constructions.*

1. Same Thought Repeated in Different Words

WORDY Most people agree that a person should be literate and able to read and write before graduation from high school.
ECONOMICAL Most people agree that a person should learn to read and write before graduation from high school.

WORDY The undersigned students whose names appear below are required to report to the Dean's office.
ECONOMICAL The students whose names appear below are required to report to the Dean's office.

WORDY My favorite hobbies are sports, football, and tennis. (in this common construction the whole overlaps the parts)
ECONOMICAL My favorite hobbies are football and tennis.

WORDY They had a marriage based on deceit and deception rather than a union founded on trust and mutual faith.

ECONOMICAL   Their marriage was based on deceit rather than trust.

The *overlapping synonyms* in the last example are apparently the result of trying too hard for parallelism. Though no two synonyms have identical meanings, the second is usually redundant if their meanings overlap too much. This principle does not apply, however, when the writer makes the distinction clear, slight though it may be. (The book is both *learned* and *scholarly:* the author's immense knowledge has been intelligently sifted and organized.)

2. Circumlocutions

Do not go around the circumference of a verbal circle when you can cut across the diameter. Roundabout expressions can often be simply deleted from the sentence without rewriting.

Since most of my father's customers ~~consist of those who~~ are Polish and Russian, I acquired a smattering of both languages.

Common circumlocutions involve *there is, there are,* and *the fact that* (see p. 364).

I don't think ~~that *there is*~~ anyone ~~who~~ is completely unsuperstitious.

~~*There are*~~ three problems ~~which~~ are paramount in this discussion.

I could help the government in war because ~~of *the fact that*~~ I hold a radio license.

Sometimes rewriting is necessary:

WORDY   In connection with the difference between the two words, a distinction must be made in terms of connotation.
ECONOMICAL   The two words differ in connotation.

Experts in circumlocution frequently clutter their writing with expressions using the words *case, character, field,* and *nature*:

WORDY   In the *case* of Norman Mailer he can't resist writing about himself.
ECONOMICAL   Norman Mailer can't resist writing about himself.

WORDY   Of all my friends in the chemical *field*, he has the firmest grasp of problems of a scientific *character* (or *nature*).
ECONOMICAL   Of all my friends in chemistry, he has the firmest grasp of scientific problems.

3. The Passive Voice

Wordy writers often use the passive voice when the active is more economical. Though a kind of circumlocution, this usage is so common that it deserves a special category.

WORDY   On more than one occasion during my basic training, the whole group

was called together by the commanding officer for the purpose of giving us an opportunity to ask him questions pertaining to our problems.
ECONOMICAL   More than once during my basic training the commanding officer called the whole group together to enable us to ask questions about our problems.

WORDY   Several times during the term she was asked by the professor whether her lesson had been prepared or not.
ECONOMICAL   Several times during the term the professor asked whether she had prepared her lesson.

Notice how the shift from passive to active voice improves both examples ("*was called* . . . by the commanding officer" becomes "the commanding officer *called*"; "*was asked* by the professor" becomes "the professor *asked*"; "her lesson *had been prepared*" becomes "she *had prepared* her lesson"). It is unreasonable to outlaw the passive construction entirely. Sometimes it is effective, as in the anguished outcry of Willy Loman's wife in Arthur Miller's *Death of a Salesman:* "Attention, attention must be finally paid to such a person." But even in impersonal exposition, where some use of the passive is inevitable, it can often be replaced by a direct imperative. Instead of writing, "The acorn nuts are now attached to the bolts," why not say, "Now attach the acorn nuts to the bolts"?

4. Overweight Constructions

Many a construction, though not exactly a circumlocution, is too heavy for the light load of thought it carries. *Infinite predication*—the use of phrases with verbals instead of clauses with finite verbs—is one of the handiest aids to economy in the language. Flabby, overweight sentences can be reduced by converting clauses to phrases and phrases to single words.

WORDY   The first entrant *who solves the puzzle* will receive a pencil *which has four kinds of lead.*
ECONOMICAL   The first entrant solving the puzzle will receive a pencil with four kinds of lead.

WORDY   While *I was playing tennis*, I decided *that I would go for a swim in the lake.*
ECONOMICAL   While playing tennis, I decided to go for a swim in the lake.

WORDY   A woman *with a smiling face* sat in the corner.
ECONOMICAL   A smiling woman sat in the corner.

In the long run, of course, whether a word is preferable to a phrase or a phrase to a clause depends not only on the weight of the thought but also on the level of usage and the rhythm of the passage. Even in informal writing, you must not take so many shortcuts that your prose degenerates into shorthand.

100

EXERCISE H

Rewrite the following sentences, making them as economical as possible without omitting essential details:

1. The only thing which Mr. Cox does which is constructive is to encourage other people to be themselves.

2. After a while she eventually detested television because of the fact that the programs were so similar and alike from week to week.

3. As a quiet hush fell over the classroom I noticed that my fellow classmates were all staring at me.

4. Though I was not consistently lazy, there were many occasions during the course of the term when a higher standard of performance would have been achieved if I had not procrastinated and put off studying until later.

5. In the case of economics there are no important propositions that cannot be stated in plain language.—John Galbraith, "Writing, Typing, and Economics," *Atlantic*

6. I was told repeatedly that I should consider the following four principles in the writing of a paragraph: unity, coherence, emphasis, and completeness.

7. There are many politicians who use words in such a way so as to convey no meaning or significance to those who listen to them.

8. In comparison with his interest in studying in the medical field he was more strongly motivated by the desire to make a lot of money.

9. It was reported in the newspapers that the suspect who had apparently committed the crime was still at large.

10. Because of the fact that there are so many characters in the novel, the reader must be careful in order not to lose the thread.

VARIETY

If you can learn to avoid the monotony of primer prose by intelligently combining clauses, and to eliminate unnecessary repetition, you should write with a respectable minimum of variety. But only by reading widely and becoming aware of the great flexibility of sentence patterns can you hope to achieve a sentence variety that is more than the mere absence of monotony. Take, for example, this paragraph from the work of a distinguished novelist and critic:

(1) Before such power as this we are made to feel that the ordinary tests which we apply to fiction are futile enough. (2) Do we insist that a great novelist shall be a master of melodious prose? (3) Hardy was no such thing. (4) He feels his way by dint of sagacity and uncompromising sincerity to the phrase he wants, and it is often of unforgettable pungency. (5) Failing it, he will make do with any homely or clumsy or old-fashioned turn of speech, now of the utmost angularity, now of a bookish elaboration. (6) No style in literature, save Scott's,

is so difficult to analyse; it is on the face of it so bad, yet it achieves its aim so unmistakably. (7) As well might one attempt to rationalize the charm of a muddy country road, or of a plain field of roots in winter. (8) And then, like Dorsetshire itself, out of these very elements of stiffness and angularity his prose will put on greatness; will roll with a Latin sonority; will shape itself in a massive and monumental symmetry like that of his own bare downs. (9) Then again, do we require that a novelist shall observe the probabilities and keep close to reality? (10) To find anything approaching the violence and convolution of Hardy's plots one must go back to the Elizabethan drama. (11) Yet we accept his story completely as we read it; more than that, it becomes obvious that his violence and his melodrama, when they are not due to a curious peasant-like love of the monstrous for its own sake, are part of that wild spirit of poetry which saw with intense irony and grimness that no reading of life can possibly outdo the strangeness of life itself, no symbol of caprice and unreason be too extreme to represent the astonishing circumstances of our existence.—Virginia Woolf, "The Novels of Thomas Hardy," *The Common Reader, Second Series*

Although that passage, with an average sentence length of about twenty-seven words, is somewhat more formal and involved than most modern American prose, it amply illustrates the value of variety. The sentences range in length from the strikingly direct five-word third sentence to the relatively intricate final sentence of eighty-four words. The passage contains five simple sentences (numbers 3, 5, 7, 8, and 10), but these vary in structure from the third, with its simple subject and predicate, to the eighth, with its carefully balanced compound predicate. Woolf adds to the variety by using the rhetorical question (sentences 2 and 9), an effective device if employed sparingly to support meaning, not indiscriminately to evade it. Finally, notice that in four of the declarative sentences (1, 5, 8, and 10) the subject is preceded by one or more introductory phrases. Experienced writers understand the value of *putting something before the subject*—a phrase or a clause—in order to avoid sentence monotony. In contrast to primer prose, in which the simple sentences march jerkily down the page—subject-verb-object-period, subject-verb-object-period—like mechanical soldiers, Woolf's paragraph is a delight to read.

EMPHASIS

In ordinary conversation, the common methods of emphasis are obvious. We hit a word harder, pronounce it more carefully, underline it with a frown or a gesture. In trying to carry over these devices into the silent speech of writing, the inexperienced often rely too heavily on the artificial aids of punctuation, spraying the page with underlinings and exclamation points (see pp. 318, 337). But there are more subtle ways of achieving emphasis within the sentence. The four most common are (1) *isolation*, (2) *position*, (3) *repetition*, and (4) *parallelism*. (These methods are not, as you may notice, essentially different from those used for emphasis in the paragraph.)

1. Isolation

When a short, wiry sentence is isolated from more elaborate constructions, it stands out by contrast. This device is especially useful in the most important positions in the paragraph, the beginning and the end.

It was a life transformed. I was no longer a boarder at that hated brick barracks called St. John's, which had become so mysteriously changed from the home of a happy childhood, and I had no fear of the old routine of classes. Classes, when once I had outwitted and outgrown the gym, I had never hated, and I returned to them with the proud sense of having been a voyager in very distant seas.—Graham Greene, *A Sort of Life*

They were aghast that we could find anything appealing in the thought of a middle-class house on a middle-class street in a middle-class village full of middle-class people. That we were tired of town and hoped for children, that we couldn't afford both a city apartment and a farm, they put down as feeble excuses. *To this day they cannot understand us. You see, they read the books. They even write them.*—Phyllis McGinley, "Suburbia: Of Thee I Sing," *The Province of the Heart*

2. Position

WEAK   The history of English words is the history of our civilization in many ways.
MORE EMPHATIC   The history of English words is, in many ways, the history of our civilization.

WEAK   Arnold Toynbee is the outstanding historian of the twentieth century to the lay reading public.
MORE EMPHATIC   To the lay reading public Arnold Toynbee is the outstanding historian of the twentieth century.—Moses Hadas, "The Price of Power," *New York Times Book Review*

WEAK   The lyric grace of the river in its richest passage of the pastoral life begins above Albuquerque.
MORE EMPHATIC   Above Albuquerque begins the lyric grace of the river in its richest passage of the pastoral life.—Paul Horgan, "Pages from a Rio Grande Notebook," *New York Times Book Review*

Notice that Horgan achieves emphasis partly by inverting the normal order of subject (*grace*) and verb (*begins*).

WEAK   Use Listerine Antiseptic, the *extra-careful* precaution which instantly sweetens and freshens the breath . . . helps keep it that way, too . . . not for seconds . . . not for minutes . . . but for hours, usually.—Advertisement in *Redbook*
MORE EMPHATIC   Use Listerine Antiseptic, the extra-careful precaution which instantly sweetens and freshens the breath and helps keep it that way, not for seconds, not for minutes, but usually for hours.

After building up emphasis in several obvious ways—italicizing *extra-careful* and separating phrases with fancy dots and calculated parallelism—the advertising copywriter lets the whole sentence peter out in a ludicrous anticlimax.

Of course, anticlimax may be used purposely for satiric or comic effect:

Massive and paunchy in his baggy uniform, with a fleshy face adorned by a heavy, nearly white mustache and bushy eyebrows to match, with a clear youthful skin, calm blue eyes and a candid tranquil gaze, Joffre looked like Santa Claus and gave an impression of benevolence and naïveté—two qualities not noticeably part of his character.—Barbara Tuchman, *The Guns of August*

My father spoke nine languages and was a clod in every one.—Margery Finn Brown, "The Irregular Verb 'To Be,' " *McCall's*

Loose and periodic sentences

The importance of final position must not be pushed too far. Inversions can be awkward in English. Because we do not normally anticipate the end of sentences in conversation, the natural tendency is to put the main clause first. Sentences using this natural order, known technically as *loose sentences*, appear regularly in the best writing side by side with *periodic sentences*, which put the main clause, or complete the main point, at the end:

LOOSE Rachel was an outstanding student in chemistry, even though she had no special interest in science and was irritated by Professor Bunsen's punning.
PERIODIC Even though she had no special interest in science and was irritated by Professor Bunsen's punning, Rachel was an outstanding student in Chemistry.

PERIODIC With this type of person knocking about, and constantly crossing one's path if one has eyes to see or hands to feel, the experiment of earthly life cannot be dismissed as a failure.—E. M. Forster, "What I Believe," *Two Cheers for Democracy*
(Consider the loss of emphasis if Forster had reversed the order and begun with "The experiment of earthly life. . . .")

Occasionally a long periodic sentence can effectively achieve both emphasis and suspense:

Without arms, drained by starvation, inexperienced in military crafts, subjected to a system of brutality beyond description, and distrusted, sometimes even betrayed, by other European nationalities that were also being oppressed by the Nazis, the Jews of Eastern Europe were simply unable to hold back the "Final Solution."—Irving Howe, "The War Against the Jews," *New York Times Book Review*

But such a sentence must be used sparingly and constructed carefully. Too many readers are short on memory and patience. Moreover, like other elaborate rhetorical devices, the extended periodic sentence can call more attention to its syntax than to its substance.

3. Repetition

Used sparingly, conscious repetition can add emphasis within the sentence:

I didn't like the swimming pool, I didn't like swimming, and I didn't like the swimming instructor, and after all these years I still don't.—James Thurber, *My Life and Hard Times*

I have no memory of my trip to Vienna, no memory of a city I was never to see again, no memory of the name of the hospital, nor how I got to see it or in what language.—Lillian Hellman, *Pentimento*

A sentence should contain no unnecessary words, a paragraph no unnecessary sentences, for the same reason that a drawing should have no unnecessary lines and a machine no unnecessary parts.—William Strunk, Jr., and E. B. White, *The Elements of Style*

4. Optional Parallelism

Parallelism, which is sometimes required to avoid awkward shifts, can also be used for emphasis. But like repetition and the periodic sentence, it is a dangerous weapon in the hands of a novice. The day is past when words were weighed so carefully that a noun with three adjectives on one side of a conjunction could not possibly be balanced by a noun with only two on the other, and today's reader, more accustomed to the natural rhythms of easy conversation than to the contrived phrasing of formal rhetoric, is likely to be irritated by the pithy parallelism of Bacon's essays, the ponderous symmetry of Johnson's criticism, and the obvious balance of this sentence. But parallelism can sharpen the point of a short sentence:

We believe that teachers should be fired
‖ not in blocks of three for political wrongness
‖ but in blocks of one for unfitness.
                         "The Talk of the Town," *New Yorker*

It can be genuinely effective in a long sentence:

All this— ‖ the disillusionment,
         ‖ the braggadocio,
         ‖ the ‖ advertised and
             ‖ cultivated emancipation from the ‖ ideas and
                                               ‖ conventions
                                                 of the
                                                 nineteenth
                                                 century,
         ‖ the half-hearted hankering after strange foreign gods—

105

was an indication that the spokesmen for the people of the United States
‖ were losing some of the old instinctive confidence in themselves,
‖ were no longer altogether sure ‖ of the high significance of the nation's history,
 of the superiority of its institutions, or
‖ of the essential rightness of what the nation
‖ had done,
 was doing, or
 would in the future be doing.

Carl L. Becker, "What We Didn't Know Hurt Us a Lot," *Yale Review*

But such an intricate balanced sentence is rare in contemporary prose.

EXERCISE I

Rewrite the following sentences to make them more emphatic:

1. The great ship came home safely after the war with all our boys from foreign soil and she once again became the luxury liner of the seas and had all her beautiful ornaments replaced.

2. Little did the leaders of the temperance drive know that during the meeting that week there was a half case of the honey-flavored beer in the back closet of their clubhouse as I found to my surprise.

3. Developing new sources of energy to abolish our dependence on Arabian oil is one of the most important challenges of our time for a number of reasons.

4. Communism is a religion, not merely an economic theory, to many of its followers.

5. I was so excited that I started to tremble when the colonel announced that our outfit would probably move up to the front lines in two weeks or thereabouts.

6. I saw three spotted fawns two nights ago under the tree across the road.

7. They finally decided on a separation after seven years of continual bickering over issues that were trivial to say the least.

8. I didn't expect to win first prize and hear my name read over the radio by the Governor himself, though I felt I had done reasonably well for a beginner, considering the odds, law of averages, etc.

9. Warfare cannot be abolished from the globe as long as poverty exists, according to the speaker.

10. He argued that the people of the United States are obligated to help in Asia's fight against death, disease, and squalor.

SUMMARY

The essential doctrine of this chapter can be briefly summarized:

1. Write grammatically complete sentences unless the context justifies incomplete ones.
2. Combine clauses logically in accordance with the principles of coordination and subordination.
3. Relate each modifier clearly to the word it modifies.
4. Put parallel elements in parallel form.
5. Adjust the length of sentences to fit your purpose, avoiding primer prose and nonstop sentences.
6. Be economical, avoiding unnecessary repetition.
7. Aim for variety in sentence length and form.
8. Aim for emphasis without sacrificing naturalness.

EXERCISES (General review)

J. Rewrite the following sentences, giving a reason for each revision with specific reference to this chapter:

1. Even as an inexperienced author his book can be compared in many ways with the best writers of our time.

2. Although the professor in the course unquestionably knew his stuff, including an enormous amount of detailed factual information, but he simply couldn't get it across to beginners like me.

3. It became evident as the war progressed either that the United States had to throw their great power into the balance or stand idly by while Germany gobbled up the nations of Europe one by one.

4. Her sister was a statuesque blonde of indeterminate age and weight, and she was now being neglected by her third husband.

5. The speaker conceded that homicides with firearms could not be abolished by stricter controls on handguns, however, he insisted that such controls were a step in the right direction.

6. In the case of third parties it has been often observed by historians that they are seldom powerful enough in terms of political influence on account of the simple fact that they are usually too small.

7. Not having saved up enough money to finance my entire education, I had to work during the summer, and this made it impossible for me either to go to summer school to catch up on the subjects in which I was deficient or to do the reading necessary to improve my general background, for, though I had the time to do some of the latter, I was so tired after my eight hours on the night shift that I didn't want to do anything in the daytime except sleep or lie on the beach near my home.

107

8. Frost's attitude was that, though other poets were welcome to write in any form that suited them, that to him writing free verse was like playing tennis with the net down.

9. On hot summer nights, flying in erratic zigzags in search of insects, I watched the bats for what seemed like hours.

10. Having shown the most promise of the five children in the family as a schoolboy, his adult life was a disappointment, representing a dismal failure on the whole.

11. Scientists cannot expect to have sudden flashes of imaginative insight unless they have devoted long hours to acquiring a thorough knowledge of their subject, poring over the researches of others, and without patiently pursuing their own investigations.

12. Not only did Stephen Crane report the disaster for a newspaper but later "The Open Boat," one of the great short stories of American literature, appeared.

13. Evidently embarrassed at first, but soon at ease, because the girl, who introduced herself as Mildred Brown, said that it was about time women began repaying for drinks that men had bought for them, a view that reflected, though it didn't occur to him at the time, her stubborn faith in the single standard.

14. When it comes to the case of teen-agers, considering the tendency of the magazines and newspapers to either exalt them as a privileged group, the sensitive favorites of psychiatrists and the pampered darlings of the merchandisers, or, on the other hand, to imply that, if they are not all juvenile delinquents, it is all the result of either dumb luck or religion, the amount of confusion that does exist among our junior citizens can easily be explained, not so much in terms of their own inherent weaknesses, but as the inevitable result of environmental factors which are produced by the very adults who seem most concerned about the younger generation.

15. There were three aspects of the problem which particularly bothered him: (1) the calmness and complacency that were shown by his roommate in the face of all the accusations; (2) his roommate's indifference to moral standards in general; and (3) the weekend after the disappearance of the wallet an unaccustomed generosity had been displayed by his roommate on a double date on which they had gone together.

K. Comment on the sentence structure in the following passages, with specific reference to the ways in which the writers have aimed at emphasis or variety:

1. Of James' unusual intelligence there was no doubt.—K. M. Elizabeth Murray, *Caught in the Web of Words*

2. But of all team sports, baseball, with its graceful intermittences of action, its immense and tranquil field sparsely settled with poised men in white, its dispassionate mathematics, seems to me best suited to accommodate, and be ornamented by, a loner.—John Updike, "Hub Fans Bid Kid Adieu," *Assorted Prose*

3. To come all that way, rifle in hand, with two thousand people marching at my heels, and then to trail feebly away, having done nothing—no, that was impossible.—George Orwell, "Shooting an Elephant"

4. You wait to get inside the gate, you wait outside the great man's office, you wait for your agent to make the deal, you wait for the assignment, you wait for instructions on how to write what they want you to write, and then, when you finish your treatment and turn it in, you wait for that unique contribution to art, the story conference.—Budd Schulberg, *The Disenchanted*

5. The rolling period, the stately epithet, the noun rich in poetic associations, the subordinate clauses that give the sentence weight and magnificence, the grandeur like that of wave following wave in the open sea; there is no doubt that in all this there is something inspiring.—W. Somerset Maugham, *The Summing Up*

6. One learns first of all in beach living the art of shedding; how little one can get along with, not how much. Physical shedding to begin with, which then mysteriously spreads into other fields. Clothes, first. Of course, one needs less in the sun. But one needs less anyway, one finds suddenly. One does not need a closet-full, only a small suitcase-full. And what a relief it is! Less taking up and down of hems, less mending, and—best of all—less worry about what to wear. One finds one is shedding not only clothes—but vanity.—Anne Morrow Lindbergh, *Gift from the Sea*

7. So enchanted was the vision of a stateless society, without government, without law, without ownership of property, in which, corrupt institutions having been swept away, man would be free to be as good as God intended him, that six heads of state were assassinated for its sake in the twenty years before 1914.—Barbara Tuchman, *The Proud Tower*

8. Since time has not been generous with her memory, I had better remind some of the younger readers, and even, thank Heavens, some of the older ones, that Hedda Hopper, in her time a useful starlet, became, in her dotage, a feared columnist whose virtue was that she said what she thought, and whose vice was that what she thought didn't amount to much.—Peter Ustinov, *Dear Me*

9. He was always touchy about his pride not In his artistry but in his competence, and competence was something he greatly admired in any field, from writing to seaman-ship, drinking to statesmanship.—Alistair Cooke, *Six Men*

10. Although this photograph captures one beautiful moment of this diamond, no photograph can capture, in split second time, the true nature of this elusive spontane-ous beauty. Because every color is there. Everywhere. Never seeming to be in the same place twice. Jumping from a slash of red, to a glint of green, a glimmer of orange and yellow, then into a flash of blue. Over and over again. With an intensity and a "fire" that never dies.—Advertisement in *Travel and Leisure*

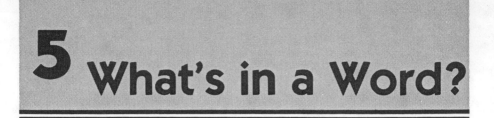

5 What's in a Word?

The Apostle tells us that in the beginning
was the Word. He gives us no assurance as to
the end.

George Steiner

There is no end to what should be known
about words.

Theodore Roethke

"The way to acquire a good vocabulary is to look up in the dictionary every word you don't understand and find out exactly what it means." At first glance this student sentence appears as foolproof as an axiom from mathematics. But the more it is examined by a critical reader, the more questions it raises. What is a good vocabulary? Is using the dictionary the only way to acquire one? What is "the dictionary"? What does it mean to "look up a word in the dictionary"? Can any dictionary tell you "exactly" what a word means? What does it mean to talk about what a word means? Although these questions bear a family resemblance to the annoying quibbles in which the classroom prosecutor often indulges, they are fundamental to an understanding of words. To anwer them in much detail would require a long excursion into the tangled jungle of *semantics*, the intricate study of the meaning of meaning. To answer them briefly is the purpose of this chapter.

BUILDING A VOCABULARY

It should be obvious that some of the shortcomings discussed in earlier chapters—primer prose, repetition, lack of variety—often result from an inadequate vocabulary. How large is your vocabulary? To begin with, it would be more accurate to speak of your vocabularies. The most obvious division is between the *recognition vocabulary*—words that you more or less understand on seeing or hearing them—and the *active vocabulary*—those that you use with reasonable frequency and precision. It is hard to determine the relative size of the two or the exact point at which any single word passes from one to the other. But your writing vocabulary is only as large as the number of words you can use readily, naturally, and intelligently. As Cyril Connolly says, "The vocabulary of a writer is his currency, but it is a paper currency and its value depends on the reserves of mind and heart which back it." A vast word hoard is valueless unless the owner's assets are readily negotiable, and wisely spent.

This does not mean, of course, that it is not important to acquire as large a vocabulary as possible. Assuming equal endowments of intelligence, tact, talent, language sense, and experience, those with a recognition vocabulary of 20,000 words will express themselves more effectively than those with only 10,000.

How should you build a large vocabulary? You can learn something about the meaning of words from well-chosen vocabulary lists, if you look the words up conscientiously in a good dictionary. You can also learn something by memorizing lists of prefixes, suffixes, and common stems: the difference, for example, between *ante-* and *anti-*, *hyper-* and *hypo-*, *pre-* and *pro-*, *-phile* and *-phobe*; or the fact that English words containing *-cede*, *-ceed*, or *-cess (precede, proceed, intercession)* are built from the Latin verb *cedere*, meaning *to move*. But after all is said and done, there is only one method of acquiring a large, versatile, useful vocabulary. That is the slow way—the long, patient, natural process of learning what words mean, not in isolated lists, but in their natural habitat of speech and writing. This requires attentive listening, thorough, wide-ranging reading, and consistent use, of course, of a good dictionary.

EXERCISE A

The following list contains a handful of the many scientific or technical terms in English with Greek or Latin ancestry. With the help of your dictionary explain the derivation of each word and match each with another word (not on the list) containing the same prefix, root, or suffix.

anarchy	cosmonaut	hypertension	orthodonture
anthropology	decathlon	hypothetical	polygamous
calculate	demagogue	kilogram	pornography
chronic	geriatrics	necrophilia	paranoid
claustrophobia	homogenize	neophyte	telepathy

CHOOSING A DICTIONARY

"Dictionaries," said Dr. Johnson, "are like watches; the worst is better than none, and the best cannot be expected to go quite true." The analogy is sound. But many people who would never think of using a sundial when fifteen dollars purchases a reasonably dependable watch will foolishly rely on an inaccurate, inadequate heirloom of a dictionary. You may speak loosely about "the dictionary" or "Webster," but you should know that there are dictionaries and dictionaries. And if you have come to college equipped with none at all, or at best with a child's garden of words that was given you as a prize for graduating from the sixth grade, you should go at once to the bookstore and buy an adult model.

There are, of course, several kinds that you may have occasion to use in the library (see pp. 221–222): dictionaries specializing in spelling, pronunciation, synonyms, clichés, dialects, slang, and the vocabularies of special fields; great "unabridged" dictionaries such as the one-volume *Webster's Third New International Dictionary* (1961), *The Random House Dictionary of the English Language* (1966), *The American Heritage Dictionary of the English Language* (1969), and the thirteen-volume *Oxford English Dictionary* (the OED or NED). But as a constant companion for continual reference, you might choose one of the following desk dictionaries:

The American Heritage Dictionary–New College Edition (Boston: Houghton Mifflin, 1978)—hereafter referred to as AHD.
Funk and Wagnalls Standard College Dictionary (New York: Harper & Row, 1977)—hereafter referred to as SCD.
The Random House College Dictionary (revised edition, New York: Random House, 1975)—hereafter referred to as RHD.
Webster's New Collegiate Dictionary (Springfield, Mass.: Merriam, 1977)—hereafter referred to as NCD.
Webster's New World Dictionary of the American Language (second college edition, Cleveland and New York: Collins and World Publishing Company, 1976)—hereafter referred to as NWD.

A good dictionary is a one-book reference library. It may contain biographical entries, with dates; geographical entries, with useful maps; rules for spelling and punctuation; common abbreviations; foreign phrases; instructions for preparing bibliographies and footnotes; proofreaders' marks; signs and symbols used in science; data on colleges and universities; the meanings of common given names; or even a vocabulary of rhymes. But it should be judged primarily for its completeness, clarity, accuracy, and reliability as a book on words.

WHAT WORDS TO LOOK UP

The number of words you look up during an evening's study will depend not only on the size of your vocabulary and the difficulty of the reading assignments but also on the aims of the course. One teacher may expect

112

you to read a hundred pages and get the author's main arguments; another may require you to read only ten but capture the full flavor of every phrase. Most students are quickly overwhelmed if they take too literally the familiar advice about looking up every strange word. A more sensible rule is this: in extensive reading, look up any word if your ignorance of its meaning makes it impossible to understand a main point; in intensive reading, look up every word whose meaning is not immediately clear from the context.

Inexperienced readers do not take full advantage of the extent to which the meaning of strange words is often implied or even defined in the context. For example, when Gilbert Milstein writes in the *New York Times Magazine*, "The putting together of every world's fair has been accompanied by an inordinate amount of *foofaraw*"—the general context of the article is a clear clue to the meaning of the unusual noun.

Though careful reading is not a guessing game, remember that of the thousands of words you can use more or less accurately, you have become familiar with all but a small number by hearing and seeing them in action. The most conscientious use of a dictionary in college should not cause you to abandon the natural habit of learning from context. Looking up any word in a good dictionary will give you information you cannot acquire by inference. But a more discriminating selection will enable you to devote more time to studying the words you do look up.

HOW TO LOOK UP A WORD

To make the most intelligent use of your dictionary, first familiarize yourself with the supplementary material in the introduction and appendix, not to absorb every detail but to learn, for future reference, the special features of your investment. In the front of NCD, for example, an Explanatory Chart illustrating two representative pages from the *p*'s is keyed to a series of Explanatory Notes which discuss in some detail various aspects of the entries throughout the text. This is followed by a short essay on "The English Language and Its History" and by guides to Abbreviations and Pronunciation Symbols.

The act of looking up a word should be more than a split-second glimpse; it should be a miniature problem in research. Too often a hasty student will look up the meaning of a word and misspell it, look up the spelling and misuse it, look up the meaning and spelling and ignore the grammatical function, jump at the first meaning given, pay no attention to the italic labels on any of the meanings, or skip impatiently over the small-print paragraph that makes the delicate distinctions between synonyms. Only by reading the whole story can you avoid these mistakes. Moreover, the words studied in this way are the ones most likely to become your own for life.

Take, for example, the word *curious* as it appears in NCD:*

> **cu·ri·ous** \'kyûr-ē-əs\ *adj* [ME, fr. MF *curios*, fr. L *curiosus* careful,
> inquisitive, fr. *cura* cure] **1 a** *archaic* : made carefully **b** *obs*
> : ABSTRUSE **c** *archaic* : precisely accurate **2 a** : marked by
> desire to investigate and learn **b** : marked by inquisitive interest
> in others' concerns : NOSY **3** : exciting attention as strange or
> novel : ODD — **cu·ri·ous·ly** *adv* — **cu·ri·ous·ness** *n*
> **syn** CURIOUS, INQUISITIVE, PRYING *shared meaning element* : inter-
> ested in what is not one's personal or proper concern. CURIOUS, the
> most general and the only neutral one of these words, basically
> implies a lively desire to learn or to know <children are *curious*
> about everything> <*curious* onlookers got in the way of the
> firemen> INQUISITIVE applies to impertinent and habitual curiosity
> and usually suggests quizzing and peering after information
> <*inquisitive* old women watching from behind drawn curtains>
> PRYING adds to *inquisitive* the implication of busy meddling and
> officiousness <I will not bare my soul to their shallow *prying* eyes
> — Oscar Wilde> *ant* incurious, uninterested

Carefully examined, this entry gives six different kinds of information in the following order:

1. *Spelling.* This also includes the correct division into three syllables
   (see p. 348). To a writer the dots indicate the acceptable points for
   dividing a word with a hyphen at the end of a line. The word *curious*
   has only one correct spelling. When more than one spelling of a word
   is acceptable, the main entry is usually headed by the most common
   form.
2. *Pronunciation.* The word is respelled phonetically in accordance
   with a pronunciation key at the foot of the page. NCD, like other
   dictionaries, supplies a more complete guide to pronunciation inside the front and back covers and in the introduction. A check with
   the footnote key shows that the first *u* in *curious* is pronounced, not
   surprisingly, like the *u* in *furious*, the *i* like *ea* in *easy*, and the *ou* like
   a in *abut*. The only accent comes on the first syllable (indicated in
   NCD *before* the phonetic k). Another word might have a heavy accent
   and one or more lighter accents.
3. *Grammar. Curious* is classified only as an adjective (*adj*). NCD also
   lists the adverb *curiously* and the noun *curiousness*. The usual noun,
   curiosity, is considered in a separate entry, as are *curio* and *curiosa*.
4. *Etymology (origin or derivation).* According to NCD, the word was
   adopted in Middle English (ME—roughly between 1100 and 1500)
   from the Middle French (MF) *curios*, which came from the Latin (L)
   curiosus, an adjective derived from the noun *cura* (meaning *cure*).
5. *Definitions.* NCD combines six meanings in three groups, listing the
   meanings in the probable order of their entering the language.
   Meanings no longer in use are labeled *obs*, or *obsolete*. Meanings
   labeled *archaic* are antiquated, surviving only in unusual contexts.
6. *Synonyms and antonyms.* NCD lists two synonyms, or words similar
   in meaning to *curious* (*inquisitive* and *prying*) and briefly explains
   the differences. The *antonyms*—or words of opposite meaning—
   incurious and *uninterested*, appear in separate entries.

*By permission. From *Webster's New Collegiate Dictionary*, © 1979 by G. & C. Merriam
Company, Publishers of the Merriam-Webster Dictionaries.

Until you familiarize yourself with the common symbols and abbreviations in your own dictionary by checking them a few times, this sort of investigation may seem somewhat tedious. But after a while it will become second nature and will pay increasing dividends.

Obviously some dictionary entries are briefer than the story of *curious*, others much longer. Not every entry includes all six kinds of information, and the importance of the information in each category varies with the word. A more detailed analysis will indicate the relative importance of the different parts of the story.

PRONUNCIATION

Spelling is discussed in Chapter 12 (pp. 340–357). The allied problem of pronunciation is only indirectly related to good writing, but it cannot be entirely ignored in any rounded discussion of the use of the dictionary. Consider the following points:

1. Because not all educated persons speak the same dialect, a dictionary often lists more than one pronunciation of a word. The first is not necessarily preferred or significantly more frequent. In many heated arguments about "correct pronunciation" (ad·ver'tise·ment vs. ad·ver·tīse'ment, rä·tion vs. rā·tion, re·search' vs. re'search, to·mä·to vs. to·mā·to) the combatants are wasting their breath. A good dictionary records both, and either (which may be pronounced īther) is acceptable. If a pronunciation is appreciably less common among presumably educated speakers, NCD, for example, puts *also* before it. By consulting the introduction, you can learn the practice in *your* dictionary.

2. As with spelling, society will often attach more importance to "correct pronunciation" than to intelligent communication. The United States has been called "the only civilized country where social and intellectual standing cannot be told by the voice quality of the speaker." But a pronunciation like *pitcher* for *picture* is evidence enough to many listeners that the speaker is uneducated.

3. Anyone who struggles too hard to shift from one dialect to another overnight is likely to end up speaking a strange, unnatural mixture of the two.

4. Short of taking a special course with a sensible expert, you can best improve your pronunciation by listening attentively to the natural speech of educated people in your community and by checking all strange words and doubtful pronunciations in a good dictionary. In this way, you should gradually eliminate the more obvious local and "uneducated" pronunciations from your vocabulary.

115

EXERCISE B

According to your dictionary, how are the following words pronounced? When more than one pronunciation is given, is there any difference in meaning?

agape	debris	geyser	liaison
apartheid	defense	harass	lingerie
banal	demesne	indefatigable	penalize
chaise longue	exquisite	isthmus	

GRAMMAR AND IDIOMS

A good dictionary will help with problems in grammar and idiom.

1. Parts of speech   If you look up the word *affect* in RHD, you will find thirteen different meanings listed. On looking further, you will discover that eleven of these uses are verbs and only two are nouns. Of the two nouns, the first is a technical term from psychology, the second is obsolete. There is no general use of *affect* as a noun. Yet many students use *affect* and *effect* interchangeably as nouns meaning *result*. The italic abbreviations for the parts of speech (*adj., adv., n., prep., pron., conj., interj., v.i.,* and *v.t.*) must be carefully observed. Is *beside* a preposition or an adverb? Is *like* a preposition or a conjunction? When is the verb *set* intransitive? When is *lay* intransitive? Is *rise* ever transitive? Similar examples could be multiplied endlessly.

2. Inflectional endings   A good dictionary supplies irregular plurals of nouns, the comparison of irregular adjectives and adverbs, and the principal parts of irregular verbs. What are the plurals of *alumnus, analysis, formula,* and *phenomenon*? Is *worser* acceptable as the comparative of *bad*? What are the principal parts of *lie* and *lay*? What is the past tense of *swim*? Is there any difference between *dived* and *dove, hanged* and *hung, lighted* and *lit, proved* and *proven, sang* and *sung, waked* and *woke*?

3. Problems of number   When are *athletics, mathematics,* and *politics* singular? When are they plural? Can *data* be used with a singular pronoun or verb? Is *none* singular or plural?

4. Idioms   An idiom is a commonplace expression that has grown naturally in a language without necessarily conforming either to logic or to the usual grammatical patterns. For example, you can order *a cold glass of beer* without noticing that the adjective is "misplaced," and that what you really mean is *a glass of cold beer*. You can *lose your head*; then,

116

shouting *at the top of your voice*, give the bartender *a piece of your mind*. To the despair of many who are not born to the language, prepositions present a special problem in English: *fill in* means *fill out*, *burn up* is synonymous with *burn down* and *slow up* with *slow down*; but *dress up* means neither the same as *dress down* nor the opposite.

When your ear will not supply the proper idiom, a good dictionary will often come to the rescue. For example, the entry for the verb *hold* in NCD includes definitions of *hold a candle to, hold forth, hold one's own, hold the bag, hold the line, hold water,* and *hold with.* A few special problems of idiom that may not be considered in your dictionary appear in the Glossary of Usage. If neither of these sources helps, consult a specialized dictionary of usage (see pp. 221–222).

The vigor of a language depends heavily on the variety of its idioms. Good writing is idiomatic. A purist who insists illogically on condemning an idiom because it "doesn't make sense" (*center around* for *center in*) may be sacrificing natural expression to an idolatrous worship of "correctness."

EXERCISE C

Consult your dictionary for answers to the following questions on grammar.

1. What parts of speech are *advise, censure, prophesy*?

2. Is *invite* ever a noun?

3. What is the singular of *insignia*? *species*?

4. What are the plurals of *cactus, criterion, curriculum, medium, mother-in-law, stadium*?

5. Are *measles, mumps,* and *phonetics* singular or plural?

6. What is the present tense of *wrought*?

7. What is the past tense of *heave*?

8. What does your dictionary say about: *It is me; she drove slow*?

9. What does your dictionary say about the mood of *were*?

10. How does your dictionary define *linking verb*?

ETYMOLOGY

It is pedantic to argue that a reader cannot understand the meaning of any word without knowing its origin. It can be equally pedantic to limit a word to its original sense after centuries of usage have broadened the meaning. For example, *crusade,* which once referred only to a journey to defend the Christian cross (Latin, *crux*), can now mean any "remedial enterprise undertaken with zeal and enthusiasm"; *candidate*, from the Latin *candidatus*—clothed in white—does not refer today to the togas in which the Romans competed for office; and *cockpit* is no longer limited to a pit for cock-fighting.

But the historical development of a language is a fascinating study, and particular word origins are interesting to anyone with a minimum of intellectual curiosity. It is intriguing if not exactly useful to know that *ticket* and *etiquette* have the same ancestor and that a bedroom *sheet* and a nautical *sheet* have two different ones; to know that *neighbor* and *boor* are related but *babble* and *Babel, island* and *isle* are not.

A knowledge of some derivations will both clarify meaning and guard against error. A journalist who hears thunder in *astonish* and sees the baleful stars in *disaster* will be less likely to scatter those words around at random. A freshman who knows the Greek *autos (self), bios (life), biblia (books),* and *graphein (to write)* can hardly make the familiar mistake of calling a theme *An Autobiography of My Life* or ending a research paper with *A Bibliography of Books*. The student who knows the Latin *et (and)* and *cetera (other things)* will not write *and etc.* or fall into the common misspelling *ect.* And an understanding of the Greek words *sophos (wise)* and *moros (fool)* should be a sobering influence during the second year of college.

Nor is the etymology of all English words confined to tracing them back for centuries to ancient languages. Many familiar expressions owe their origins to historical celebrities and nonentities (*bowie knife, boycott, chauvinism, Chesterfield, fuchsia, gerrymander, nicotine, sadism, sandwich, teddy bear*), to scientists or inventors (*ampere, guillotine, macadam, ohm, shrapnel, volt, watt*), or to characters in literature (*Babbitt, Lothario, malapropism, oedipal, Pollyanna, quixotic simon-pure*). *Goon* and *jeep* are from the comic strips; *bazooka* is from radio; *cellophane, Dictaphone, Kodak, Muzak, nylon, Polaroid, Xerox,* and scores of others are trademarked words that have drifted into general use. Dictionaries capitalize those that are still protected by copyright. If you form the habit of examining the origin of words when you look them up in the dictionary, you not only take out extra insurance against forgetting them but open up new vistas of knowledge.

EXERCISE D

The two words in each of the following pairs are related etymologically to each other. Explain the relation.

agonize – protagonist	egregious – gregarious	lace – lasso
augment – eke	eradicated – radish	masticate – moustache
clan – plant	glamour – grammar	prayer – precarious
contact – tactful	gossip – sibling	pun – punctuation
coronary – crown	grenade – grenadine	rodent – rostrum

118

DEFINITIONS

In 1755 Dr. Johnson confessed that, in beginning the seven years of drudgery on his famous dictionary, he had vainly hoped that the work would "fix our language, and put a stop to those alterations which time and chance have hitherto suffered to make in it without opposition." Today no responsible dictionary makers would flatter themselves with this illusion. Modern lexicographers don't attempt to fix the language or sit in stern judgment on it. They are recorders, not regulators. They describe usage; they do not prescribe it. The people who speak and write the language, who use and abuse it, who give birth to new words and let old words die—they are both the lawmakers and the judges.

Responsible lexicographers go through a complex process: collecting far-flung examples from writing and speech; transferring them in context to "citation slips," each carefully labeled with author, title, and date of source; arranging all citations for the same word in a single bank of the file—all this before an experienced editor sifts and studies the accumulated evidence to decide what words to include and how to define them.

But even this elaborate process—which is only a corporate systematizing of the technique that any trained reader or listener uses—does not make any dictionary an infallible rule book.

The false assumption that it is gives rise to two common illusions about definitions: (1) that there is a "right" meaning for every word (the "one-word, one-meaning fallacy"); and (2) that if a word is "in the dictionary" it is "correct" regardless of the restricting labels, the context in which a person uses it, or the user's intelligence, taste, or tact.

Thousands of words have more than one meaning. The semanticists Ogden and Richards once listed 16 main meanings of the word *meaning*. SCD—a compact desk dictionary—gives (including idiomatic phrases) 58 meanings for *round*, 66 for *pass*, 117 for *run*, 121 for *take*, and 126 for *turn*. Notice the difference when a random handful of meanings of *run* are put into sentences:

The track man *runs* the mile.
The train *runs* into the station.
The river *runs* into the ocean.
The driver *runs* into a pedestrian.
She *runs* into an old college roommate.
I shall *run* up to New York on the train.
Will he *run* for President again?
A tune kept *running* through his head.
The spendthrift quickly *runs* into debt.
The ships are planning to *run* the blockade.
The play had a long *run*.
The children were given the *run* of the house.

119

He played a fast *run* on his violin.
The right fielder hit a home *run*.
She has a *run* in her panty hose.

Such an exercise illustrates the absurdity of the one-word, one-meaning fallacy and the impossibility of defining words with perfect accuracy out of their context.

It also illustrates the importance of choosing carefully among different meanings of the same word. Regardless of what order your dictionary follows, you will come to grief if you habitually read only the first definition listed or the first one that happens to strike your eye. A college freshman once read an essay called "Fliers Are Inarticulate," in which the author makes the point that experienced aviators act so automatically in the air that they are unable to explain articulately the exact process of flying a plane. Stumped by the title, the student promptly consulted a dictionary and hastily read the first definition: "not jointed, having no joints." The picture of thousands of fliers without joints was so puzzling that the student never did get onto the track of the author's argument.

EXERCISE E

Choose one of the following words and compose ten short sentences illustrating ten different meanings: *pass, round, take,* and *turn.* See how many sentences you can concoct without consulting your dictionary.

Labels and Levels

The student who looked up *inarticulate* had evidently overlooked the *restrictive label* before the definition: *Zool.*, which is a warning that, in the sense of *not jointed*, the word is a technical term from zoology. Labels are widely employed in dictionaries, with varying abbreviations, to restrict the use of a word in accordance with (1) subject, (2) time, (3) place, and (4) level of usage.

1. Because an expert will often use a term in a sense entirely foreign to the layman, subject labels cannot be ignored. For example, the definitions of the noun *base* in SCD include special meanings from architecture, geometry, mathematics, military science, chemistry, biology, sports, linguistics, electronics, and heraldry. In an informal context, you may occasionally borrow a technical term for general use: you may write of "not getting to first base" in other realms than baseball or call a nonmilitary residence your "base of operations." But usually such terms are confined to more technical contexts.

120

2. If a word, or a particular use of a word, is no longer current, it will probably be restricted by one of two temporal labels:

obsolete—no longer in use. *Examples: affection* (meaning *affectation*); *dearth* (meaning *costliness*); *dowsabel* (*sweetheart*); *enchant* (meaning *delude*); *fondness* (meaning *foolishness*).
archaic—"obsolete in ordinary language but retained in special contexts, as in Biblical and legal expressions, in poetry, etc." *Examples: eftsoons (again, soon); methinks (It seems to me); pard (leopard); y-clept (called); ye (you).*

The exact point at which a word becomes archaic or obsolete is impossible to determine. The guiding principle for the general writer is simply this: don't use words with these labels unless you intend to convey a distinctly antique flavor: an ancient tombstone might be *graven* with an epitaph, but a shiny new wedding invitation is *engraved.* Because most students have few such words in their vocabularies anyway, the warning is largely academic.

3. If a word or phrase is restricted in place, it may be preceded by a specific regional label, reminding the reader, for example, that it is common in the United States but not in Great Britain, or common in New England but not in other sections of the country. Less exact labels classify a word as *dialectal* or *local,* implying that, though it is not used everywhere, it cannot be accurately restricted to a particular region. Examples of *localisms* are *boughten* (for *bought*), *goober* (for *peanut*), *poke* (for *bag* or *sack*), and *reckon* (for *think* or *suppose*). The local or dialectal label does not necessarily condemn a word as incorrect; it means that the word may be misunderstood, obscure, or unwelcome in a locality where it is not widely used. For this reason, unless you are intentionally representing a dialect, as in fiction, you should avoid localisms.

EXERCISE F

The following words are probably restricted in your dictionary in accordance with time or place. Explain the labels and (where necessary) define the words.

cate	dope (coke)	petrol
chirurgeon	drawing pin	quoth
corn pone	gaol	tonic (soft drink)
critter	jo	whilom

4. Levels of usage have already been briefly discussed in the first chapter (see pp. 15–20), and the three general levels are alluded to throughout this book. In approximating the usage level of an extended passage of prose, the trained reader considers several kinds of evidence, of which *diction*—the choice and use of words—is not always the most reliable. In making an educated guess about the status of an isolated word or phrase, one is limited not only by the absence of context but by the obvious fact that innumerable expressions are common to all three levels. But lexicographers—some with increasing reluctance—still use labels to estimate the social or stylistic status of words that are not generally acceptable.

Though the terms vary with the dictionary, the following labels, or their abbreviations, are common: *nonstandard, colloquial* (or *informal*), and *slang*. The labels *vulgar, illiterate,* and *substandard* also occur.

Nonstandard

Nonstandard applies, according to AHD, to "usages or varieties of language that do not conform to those approved by educated native users of the language." AHD pins this label on *ain't, irregardless, lay* (in "I want to *lay* down"), and *like* (in "Tell it *like* it is"). If your dictionary labels a word or phrase "nonstandard" (or "vulgar" or "illiterate" or "substandard"), avoid it in polite speech or serious writing, either formal or informal, unless you are intentionally recording the language of others, as in dialogue.

Colloquial

The word *colloquial* (from the Latin *loqui, to speak*) is sometimes mistakenly regarded as synonymous with *incorrect* or even *illiterate*. A reasonably accurate one-word definition would be *conversational*. A *colloquialism* is a word or phrase more common in speech than in writing.

In an age when informal writing closely reflects natural conversation, it is neither possible nor advisable to restrict colloquialisms to the spoken language. Contractions, for example, are the shortcuts of familiar conversation; but such common contractions as *it's, I'll, I'm, can't, don't,* and *isn't* turn up everywhere in informal writing and occasionally appear in contexts decidedly formal. Persistent use of such expressions as *does it not* and *is it not* can make writing not only formal but wooden and affected. On the other hand, indiscriminate use of contractions not only gives the impression of rapid, casual talk but implies that the writer's taking as many shortcuts as possible because he's in a hurry to finish what he's saying.

Generally speaking, colloquial expressions are out of place in formal writing, including undergraduate critical essays, and should be used with discretion on the informal level. There is a rough proportion between the frequency of colloquialisms and the informality of style and tone. Some dictionaries, because *colloq.* has been so widely misunderstood, now use the label *informal.* Both labels are clues to the flavor of the word, not final verdicts on its appropriateness in a particular context. Neither should be accepted as a commandment meaning "Thou shalt not ever use in serious prose."

Do not confuse *colloquialisms* with *localisms.* Though many colloquialisms are also localisms and most localisms are colloquial, the terms are not interchangeable. One of the commonest colloquialisms in English—*OK*—is international.

Slang

The line between colloquialisms and slang is hard to draw. Slang is certainly colloquial in the sense that it is more common in spoken English than written; *The Oxford English Dictionary* calls it "highly colloquial." The difference is an elusive flavor that is easier to taste than define. NCD characterizes slang as "an informal nonstandard vocabulary composed typically of coinages, arbitrarily changed words, and extravagant, forced, or facetious figures of speech." H. W. Fowler called it "the diction that results from the favorite game of the young and lively of playing with words and renaming things and actions." Another British expert, Eric Partridge, listed thirteen different reasons for slang-making, including humor, novelty, picturesqueness, surprise, intimacy, fashion, and sheer high spirits. F. L. Lucas once condemned slang as "a kind of linguistic fungus; as poisonous, and as short-lived, as toadstools." That is an extreme view.

At its best, slang is concrete, direct, fresh, and lively. In informal writing a carefully chosen slang expression can be effective:

The ads caused top California winemen to *pop their corks.—Time*

The pal teams in these movies have intuitive rapport. They *hang loose* when they're together.—Pauline Kael, *New Yorker*

If the intellectual thinks of himself as a man apart, it is probably because so many Americans have been accustomed to distrust doctrine and preferred to operate *off the* pragmatic *cuff.—*Russell Lynes, "Intellectuals vs. Philistines," *New York Times Book Review*

Be it crutch, cop-out, or genuine faith, his religion does make up for what Hayes has missed in basketball.—John Papanek, "The Big E Wants an MVP," *Sports Illustrated*

Where slang is appropriate, it should be used without apologetic quotation marks, unless your instructor requires them as a means of distinguishing levels of usage (see p. 332).

An inexperienced writer with an undeveloped awareness of usage levels should use slang with care, even in informal writing. The trouble with slang is not, as many people assume, that it is always "vulgar" or "bad English." The trouble is that much of it is (1) forced, (2) local, (3) overworked when alive, and (4) soon dead.

1. The very quality that makes some slang appealing in speech makes it irritating in writing. Good writing doesn't call too much attention to itself; many slang expressions are as flashy as red neon signs on a dark street. Though some slang fills a real need, much of it results from overexuberance and exhibitionism.

2. A slang expression is likely to be a localism. A popular word in one place may have an entirely different meaning in another. Today's favorite in Chicago may never invade New York. The tribal chatter on one campus is so different from that on another that old friends sometimes have trouble communicating when they go home for the holidays. A professor who should be *au courant* (up-to-date, in-the-know, savvy, hip, with it) is hard put to keep up with the latest student coinages. Many slang expressions are the private property of occupational groups both within and without the law. Gangsters, baseball players, rock musicians, mechanics, movie-makers, fliers, and sailors all have their own special vocabularies; and though a term will occasionally stray into general English, much of it is double-talk to the general public. This does not mean, of course, that all technical language or occupational shoptalk is slang.

3. Most slang expressions are fads. Like flagpole sitting and channel swimming, hula hoops or beehive hairdos, moron jokes or elephant jokes or Polish jokes, they are overdone for a day or a season. For a time, everybody is using an expression merely because everybody's hearing it. This unthinking imitation is stressed in Ambrose Bierce's satirical definition of slang: "The speech of one who utters with his tongue what he thinks with his ear, and feels the pride of a creator in accomplishing the feat of a parrot."

One of the surest ways of *not* building a vocabulary is to give too much houseroom to the fashionable slang. Many slang expressions are versatile words-of-all-trades, words that mean everything and nothing, verbicides freely murdering other words that might be more accurately used in their place. In Chicago during the 1940s, a newspaper reporter tried to find out from a group of teenagers why they wore zoot suits, and every member of the group parroted the same uninformative answer: "Because they're *sharp*." A similar inarticulate group in a later generation might have expressed their passion for blue jeans by chorusing: "Because they're *mellow*." In recent years, millions of Americans have learned that they can characterize any human error, mistake, slip, oversight, *faux pas*, boner, or blunder with one indispensable verbicidal verb: *to goof* (meaning to *make a boo-boo*). *Bag* and *thing* have become the omnibus slang words for any conceivable occupation, action, or attitude (That's not my *bag*; I do my own *thing*). As this sentence is being written, it is no longer fashionable to express your involvement with, say, chemistry, by explaining whether you are majoring in it, taking a course in it, reading about it, generally interested in it, or gainfully employed in it; all you have to say is: "I'm *into* chemistry." Nor is it up-to-date to say that anything deplorable is *the living end*; it is *the pits*.

4. Some slang expressions live to become respectable: *mob* (short for *mobile vulgus*) was slang in the eighteenth century, *carpetbagger* in the nineteenth. Other words stay on the slang level for years or even centuries. *Bunk*, dating back to 1820, bids fair to outlast its more respectable relations *buncombe* and *bunkum*, and will probably still be going strong when such literary expressions as *balderdash, poppycock, tommyrot*, and *twaddle* have long since died; but *bunk* is still generally classified as slang. *Phiz* (for *physiognomy*) has been slang since the eighteenth century, *invite* (for *invitation*) since the sixteenth, *bones* (for *dice*) since the fourteenth. Undergraduates who are pleased to presume that they are *sweating out* an examination or course in the latest slang might be surprised to know that Huck Finn once "tried to sweat out a verse or two" in memory of Emmeline Grangerford. But much of the slang of the 1920s (*spoon, sheik, lounge lizard, moo juice*—milk, *it*—sex appeal, *the bee's knees, the cat's ankle, the cat's pajamas, says you, so's your old man, twenty-three skidoo*) is dead and unmourned.

The value of labels

No writer should place too high a value on the accuracy of usage labels in any dictionary. The United States is a country where education is being strenuously democratized and the walls of caste are under heavy siege. Mobility—both social and vehicular—is blurring the differences of sect and section. Informality is a way of life. Magazines for the millions tend to present a "homogenized culture"—the cream of the vocabulary no longer separated from the milk. In such a society it is impossible for the dictionaries to keep pace with the diction.

Lexicographers and other linguists are constantly reminding us of the vast, spreading vocabulary that is common to all levels of usage. They warn us that their own designations are inexact, and they prove the point by frequently disagreeing about the status of individual words. But it is not wise to ignore the doctors because they often disagree. Responsible writers use whatever professional help they can get to supplement their own firsthand observations of the language in action.

For the writer who does not aspire to be a linguist, the chief value of observing usage labels is not to prevent an occasional expression from sneaking in where it is not ordinarily invited, but to build up an immunity against chronic fluctuation from level to level.

Of course, an experienced writer who is well aware of usage levels may shift gears with conscious suddenness to produce a particular effect such as abrupt emphasis or humor:

We exchanged the well-worn talismans, the hoary anecdotes, and the smiles of self-satisfaction with a deference usually reserved for serious or original ideas. In short we were real gone.—"Mr. Harper," *Harper's*

But such a device should not be overworked.

EXERCISE G

Depending on the dictionary consulted, some of the following expressions are slang, some colloquial (or informal), some unlabeled, some unlisted. Test your own judgment first before consulting your dictionary.

blind date	for the birds (worthless)	quiz (*n.*)
chicken (scared)	gut (easy course)	shrink (psychiatrist)
creep (offensive person)	jock (athlete)	shut-eye
flu	nerd	total (demolish)
flunk (*v.*)	prof	up-tight

SYNONYMS AND ANTONYMS

When a character in Somerset Maugham's comedy *The Circle* says, "There are no synonyms in the English language," he obviously means "no exact duplicates." In everyday use, of course, when we say that two words "mean the same thing," we mean "nearly the same thing in most contexts." That is what the dictionaries mean by *synonym*. An *antonym* is "a word of opposite meaning."

Sometimes a dictionary entry will merely list synonyms without discriminating between them. Sometimes it will contain a special paragraph distinguishing carefully between words of similar meaning; sometimes it will refer the reader to such a paragraph under another entry. The important point to remember is that you invite trouble if you merely go eeny-meeny-miney-mo among the synonyms. Do *curious, inquisitive,* and *prying* have the same meaning? In a loose way, yes. But notice the distinctions in the NCD synonymy on page 114.

Often you will have a word in the back of your mind that stubbornly refuses to come to the front, or a general meaning with no word to carry it. Because synonym lists in general dictionaries are necessarily limited, you may find help in a thesaurus. But such a thesaurus as Roget's must be used with special care. The words in a single entry range all the way from twins to second or third cousins, and no attempt is made to explain the difference. Formed on a different principle, *Webster's New Dictionary of Synonyms* attempts to discriminate carefully among meanings in context.

126

DENOTATION AND CONNOTATION

The problem of discriminating among synonyms is complicated by the obvious fact that all words have connotation as well as denotation. Denotation can be roughly defined as the basic, literal meaning of a word, connotation as its overtones. *Stout, portly, plump, rotund, chubby, fat, corpulent, obese*—all have the same essential denotation: "thick in body because of the presence of superfluous flesh or adipose tissue." But they are by no means interchangeable. *Stout* suggests or connotes robust health; *portly*, slow-motion dignity; *plump*, a pleasing fullness of figure; *rotund*, a spherical shape; *chubby*, the bouncy roundness of a cherub or a well-fed baby. *Fat*, the most general of them all, often carries an uncomplimentary connotation; *corpulent* suggests an unbecoming bulkiness; and *obese* implies an unhealthy excess of fat. Connotation makes all the difference between a compliment and an insult.

It is an inaccurate commonplace to say that a dictionary gives only the denotation of a word. A dictionary may define *horse* as "a large, solid-hoofed quadruped, Equus caballus." But in distinguishing *horse* from *jade, nag, palfrey, plug, steed*, and *charger*, it must invade the misty region of connotation. It cannot, however, give the complete connotation—all the infinitely various images, associations, and emotions that a word may possibly suggest. To one reader the word *steed* may conjure up a favorite scene from *Ivanhoe*, to another a Tennysonian vision of Sir Galahad. To one the word *plug* may suggest a sway-backed farm horse out of childhood; to another the equine hero of an old-fashioned comic strip called *Barney Google*; to a third the smell of a glue factory. Even the neutral word *horse* can come alive with connotation. When Richard III cries desperately, "A horse! a horse! my kingdom for a horse!" no imaginative reader conceives a picture as prosaic as "a large, solid-hoofed quadruped, Equus caballus."

Obviously connotation is inseparably related to context. Whenever an alert reader meets a familiar word in a sentence, its connotation for that reader personally is a blend of recollections of the word from other encounters (the reader's private, unwritten "citation slips") and the new coloring supplied by the new context; and in its broadest sense the context means not only the surrounding words in the passage but the entire social milieu—time, place, and circumstances—in which the word occurs. To see how connotation changes with context, consider the italicized words in these two sentences:

Dressed in his *new* uniform, which was *freshly torn* where his *parent* had already sewed it once, Junior was hitting an imaginary *ball, whirling—intensely hot*—around the bases, *rushing* over the *black* soil of his backyard *universe* on a *path* and at a *speed* that were not *controlled* by any respect for his mother's zinnias.

127

The *new* earth, *freshly torn* from its *parent* sun, was a *ball* of *whirling* gases, *intensely hot, rushing* through the *black* spaces of the *universe* on a *path* and at a *speed controlled* by immense forces.—Rachel Carson, *The Sea Around Us*

On turning to a good dictionary, you could find at least two distinct meanings for the words in each of several pairs. NWD, for example, defines *path* as: "1. a track or way worn by footsteps; trail"—which loosely fits the context of Junior's world—and "3. a line of movement; course taken [the *path* of the meteor]"—the essential meaning in the second passage. But no series of dictionary definitions could capture all the connotative differences that widen the gulf between a playful picture of childhood recreation and an awe-inspiring description of cosmic creation.

It might be argued that a student interested in literature or "creative writing" must be more sensitive to the suggestive power of words than the undergraduate who is mainly concerned with developing a clear expository prose style. But an acute awareness of the subtleties of connotation is one of the basic requirements of literacy. This important aspect of language will be discussed at greater length in the next chapter (see especially pp. 147–151).

EXERCISE H

The words in each of the following pairs are more or less alike in meaning. With the help of your dictionary (and, for the starred pairs, the Glossary of Usage), distinguish carefully between them.

ability, capacity	empiricism, pragmatism
agnostic, atheist	ethics, morals
ambiguity, obscurity	*famous, notorious
anxious, eager	*farther, further
apparent, evident	generality, generalization
authoritarian, authoritative	healthful, healthy
*average, median	historic, historical
*bimonthly, semimonthly	ill, sick
character, personality	*imply, infer
*childish, childlike	irony, sarcasm
coherent, cohesive	*luxuriant, luxurious
cohort, companion	monologue, soliloquy
common, mutual	nauseated, nauseous
contemporary, modern	*oral, verbal
*continual, continuous	practicable, practical
difference, differential	provocative, provoking
*disinterested, uninterested	sanatorium, sanitarium
economic, economical	*sensual, sensuous
egoist, egotist	sentiment, sentimentality
elemental, elementary	simple, simplistic

128

THE LIMITATIONS OF A DICTIONARY

For all its remarkable virtues, then, even the best dictionary has limitations that are fixed by the nature of language. From *aardvark* to *zymurgy*, not a single word in the English language can be perfectly defined. The best dictionary definition is merely an attempt to express in other words the approximate picture in the minds of most people when a word is used in a representative context. In or out of context, even a simple "concrete" word like *table* will not conjure up identical images in any two minds. A person's own name never "means the same thing twice" for the obvious reason that the mortal to whom it refers changes with the passing seconds. The best way to define *dog* is to go to a kennel and point to one, and that defines only *a dog*, or as the semanticists might put it, *dog₁*, at a given moment in time. This is not the discovery of twentieth-century semantics. The learned scientists of Lagado in *Gulliver's Travels* (1726) decided "that since words are only names for *things*, it would be more convenient for all men to carry about them such *things* as were necessary to express the particular business they are to discourse on. . . . I have often beheld," continues Gulliver, "two of those sages almost sinking under the weight of their packs, like pedlars among us; who, when they met in the streets would lay down their loads, open their sacks, and hold conversation for an hour together; then put up their implements, help each other to resume their burthens, and take their leave." Since such semantically pure conversation is obviously impractical (and impossible with such abstractions as *love*, *hate*, and *democracy*), we still have to carry on with elusive words, using them as accurately as possible with the help of a good dictionary.

EXERCISE I (Review)

The following definitions are selected from Samuel Johnson's Dictionary (1755). Using your own dictionary when necessary, comment on the extent to which each of Dr. Johnson's definitions would be acceptable in a dictionary today. Carefully consider both the words defined and the words in the definitions.

adult. A person above the age of infancy, or grown to some degree of strength; sometimes full grown: a word used chiefly by medicinal writers.

alamode. According to the fashion: a low word. It is used likewise of shopkeepers for a kind of thin silken manufacture.

caterpillar. A worm which, when it gets wings, is sustained by leaves and fruits.

humanist. A philologer; a grammarian.

lass. A girl; a maid; a young woman: used now only of mean girls.

lexicographer. A writer of dictionaries; a harmless drudge, that busies himself in tracing the original, and detailing the signification of words.

129

lucubration. Study by candlelight; nocturnal study; any thing composed by night.

network. Any thing reticulated or decussated, at equal distances, with interstices between the intersections.

nowadays. (This word, though common and used by the best writers, is perhaps barbarous.) In the present age.

oats. A grain, which in England is generally given to horses, but in Scotland supports the people.

puberty. The time of life in which the two sexes begin first to be acquainted.

purist. One superstitiously nice in the use of words.

rotgut. Bad beer.

sonnet. (1) A short poem consisting of fourteen lines, of which the rhymes are adjusted by a particular rule. It is not very suitable to the English language, and has not been used by any man of eminence since Milton.

to traipse. (A low word, I believe, without any etymology.) To walk in a careless or sluttish manner.

trait. A stroke; a touch. Scarce English.

unkempt. Not combed. Obsolete.

6 Words in Action

Words, like eyeglasses, blur everything that
they do not make clear.

Joseph Joubert

What is above all needed is to let the
meaning choose the word, and not the other
way about.

George Orwell

RIGHT AND WRONG WORDS

Mrs. Malaprop, in Sheridan's comedy *The Rivals*, took special pride in her use of the King's English: "Sure, if I reprehend anything in this world, it is the use of my oracular tongue, and a nice derangement of epitaphs!" Such speeches have earned her a personal memoir in the dictionary, the word *malapropism*. It is an insult to the memory of that "old weather-beaten she-dragon" to define *malapropism* as simply an inappropriate or malapropos word. It belongs to a comic tradition centuries older than Mrs. Malaprop and as new as Archie Bunker: the tradition of words that come close to others in form but miss by a mile in meaning.

Malapropisms make fascinating reading. They can be ludicrous (The referee penalized the team for unnecessary *roughage*); charming (To do this will take more than *wistful* thinking); informative (Many writers who possess an *infirmary* make the most of it); or monstrous (I arrived home safely, greeted the rest of my family, and after consuming some of my mother's *vitals*, went happily to bed). Most weary theme readers would hate to see them completely abolished. Yet they remain the most illiterate, though not the most common, of all errors in diction.

But few errors in diction miss by as much as a mile. There are many degrees in what Carlos Baker has called "that scale of word values which descends from the inevitable through the appropriate and down to the unfortunate." Usually an instructor who scrawls the symbols for faulty diction in the margin (WW or D) doesn't mean "This word is

131

entirely wrong" but "Couldn't you have used a more appropriate word in this context?" The discord may not be as astounding as Mrs. Malaprop's; the word may be closely related in meaning as well as in spelling. But to a careful writer, a near relative is not enough. "Use the right word," wrote Mark Twain on one occasion, "not its second cousin"; and on another, "The difference between the right word and the almost right word is the difference between lightning and the lightning bug."

EXERCISE A

The following sentences contain errors in diction ranging from absurd malapropisms to "second cousins." Identify and correct each error, supplying, where possible, the word the writer apparently intended.

1. I would have won the contest if I hadn't missed the target by a hare's breath on my last turn.

2. In spite of my poor work habits, I managed to graduate in the first decibel of my high-school class.

3. By describing the interior and other members of the house, Poe conjures up the vision of a haunted graveyard.

4. The novel was written in the 1960s but published posthumorously.

5. Why is the mention of anything so vital to everybody as death always to be shunned?

6. It was a great anticlimax for me when the championship game was postponed because of inclimate weather.

7. When Holmes argues in his essay that we should not study too hard, he directly antagonizes the advice that most parents give to the entering freshman.

8. In deciding whether to go to college or look for a job I was presented with an insolvent stigma.

9. I agree with the author that such classics as English, history, Spanish, and physics should be stressed in the curriculum.

10. Whenever I meet an interesting person, I think of putting him in a story, hoping he will fulfill the void in my imagination.

11. The innocuous fumes from exhaust pipes add immeasurably to air pollution.

12. Since you had to wear all the clothes you owned, they eventually became prevalent with lice.

13. Though my uncle has made a comfortable living as a mortuary, I am not intrigued by that profession.

14. As I lay in bed that night thinking back on my behavior at the party, my consciousness began to trouble me.

132

15. Chuck Peters is a typical, clean-cut American boy in the middle of his high-school generation.

16. She had a mischievous look on her face as if she had just diverged a secret that would change my whole life.

17. The most prominent feature in the play is Cyrano's enormous nose, to which constant reminder is made.

18. Though she was an intelligent student, her dereliction for shooting pool kept her from her books night after night.

19. The Battle of Lexington is a memento to the courage of the Minute Men who fought and died there.

20. When I first came to the mountains, I found the morning air so enervating that I would rise at 6 A.M, and run around the lake just to work off my animal spirits.

FRESH AND TIRED WORDS

Some words are not exactly wrong; they are merely worn out from overwork. Many presumably respectable words suffer, like slang, from the abuse of popularity. Examples of such *vogue words*—currently or recently overworked—are *bottom line, breakthrough, ethnic, fallout, feedback, impact, input, interface, lifestyle, parameters, paranoid, sexist, supportive,* and *uptight.* Such words often have precise scientific or technical meanings that become badly blurred when they roam at large in the general vocabulary.

Many tired words are not cursed with such spurious novelty; they are simply ordinary, everyday, unpretentious expressions that have slowly grown weak and vague through the years—the victims of their own versatility. When such commonplace words are used too loosely to have precise meanings, they are called *counterwords.*

Many counterwords are adjectives-of-all-work to express approval: *darling, exciting, fabulous, grand, great, interesting, lovely, marvelous, nice, perfect, super, swell, terrific, tremendous, unique, wonderful, worthwhile.* Some are used unthinkingly to express disapproval: *awful, dreadful, frightful, horrible, lousy, terrible.* Some have been bludgeoned lifeless by advertising: *colossal, exclusive, glamorous, latest, smart, thrilling, ultimate* (after "the ultimate in drip-dry fabrics," what next?). Others have been diluted by news reporting (*Crisis* is a very mild word this year.—Richard Rovere, *New York Times*). Still others have been weakened by social and intellectual pretentiousness: *brilliant, culture, lady, refined.* A few, such as *definitely, most, so,* and *very,* are overworked in an honest effort at emphasis. Many, such as *etc.* and *thing,* betray mental laziness.

When a word is overworked in a general sense, its more precise meanings gradually die of neglect. *Awful* is hardly awe-inspiring in any context; *terrible* and *terrific* no longer terrify. Consider these differences between discriminating and indiscriminate use of counterwords:

DISCRIMINATING "It was an *awful* sight of money when it was piled up."—*The Adventures of Huckleberry Finn*
INDISCRIMINATE What *awful* weather we're having!

DISCRIMINATING a *fine* wire mesh; a *nice* distinction; a *grand* view of the canyon; a *dreadful* monster
INDISCRIMINATE a *fine* or *nice* or *grand* or *dreadful* day, girl, football team, young man, drink, book, meal, baby, idea, game of rummy

DISCRIMINATING *colossal* Mount Everest
INDISCRIMINATE This film is the most stupendous epic-making, *colossal* production of this year or any other year! (until next week)

DISCRIMINATING *culture:* a knowledge of "the best that has been thought and said in the world."
INDISCRIMINATE The clientele of this establishment is restricted to persons of *culture* and refinement.

DISCRIMINATING Homer's *Iliad* and Vergil's *Aeneid* are among the *classics* of *epic* poetry.
INDISCRIMINATE Mammoth U. beat Lilliputian Tech in an *epic* struggle during the annual Cumquat Festival Basketball *Classic*.

It would be pedantic to expect anybody to exclude such handy counterwords as *fine* and *nice* from daily conversation. Small talk cannot be abolished: a polite guest must still tell her hostess that it's very *nice* of her to have her over to see such a *grand* view of the Bushkill Creek and walk in such a *lovely* garden on such a *fine* day. But in most writing, counterwords should be saved for contexts in which they carry an exact meaning.

Coinages (Neologisms)

In your search for fresh words, you may not resist the temptation to coin new ones to suit the context. In doing this, you are exercising a legitimate right that thousands have exercised before you. Without word-makers the language would stagnate. Some *coinages* (called *neologisms* when they are still new) become quickly and firmly entrenched in the general vocabulary. Thomas Henry Huxley coined the indispensable word *agnostic*. Gelett ("Purple Cow") Burgess invented *blurb, bromide* (a bore or cliché), and *goop*. A nineteenth-century temperance lecturer named R. Turner gave the world *teetotaler*. In 1956 a doctor called Humphrey Osmond created *psychedelic*. But many neologisms are stillborn or doomed to a brief, private existence.

Some coinages are ingenious: James Thurber's *bragdowdy* (a woman who proudly admits she has let her hair go); Vladimir Nabokov's *mauvemail* (a mild form of blackmail); Lawrence Lipton's *moneytheism* (dollar worship); Red Smith's *videot* (a TV addict); or even Ring Lardner's *blute* (a smoker who doesn't inhale). Others are presumably required by science, technology, war, or commerce: *cosmonaut, fan-jet, fastback, filter tip, hallucinogen, infrastructure, megadeath, overkill, petrodollars, software, stagflation, xerography.* Many are neither original nor necessary.

In these days of flashy journalism and advertising, *blends* (or *portmanteau words,* to use a coinage by Lewis Carroll) have been minted indiscriminately: *astrodome, cafetorium, dialogyness, mirthquake, Oldsmobility, psychedelicatessen, snoopervise, Schweppervescence, scenicruiser,* and the prolific families of hybrids ending in *-ama, -burger, -mania,* and *-athon.* Closely related is the tribe of verbs ending in *-ize: decriminalize, finalize, functionalize, ghettoize, maximize, personalize, prioritize*—some uglier than others. Such promiscuous neologizing defies control.

To call attention to this mushrooming is not to outlaw entire word-families as verbal outcasts. Any coinage must be weighed in terms of its usefulness and appropriateness. *Motel* is a reasonable blend of *motor* and *hotel,* but why use *guesstimate* when every estimate is a guess? *Homogenized* is a useful adjective to describe milk or contemporary culture, but *brotherized* converts a sentimental ritual (fraternity initiation) into a mechanical process.

Most English instructors will gladly permit students to coin new words if they can prove that a new word fits the context and fills a genuine need. Even an occasional *nonce word*—a word used only once and then discarded—can be defended: in reviewing *Webster's Third New International Dictionary,* Dwight Macdonald found it convenient and natural to refer to the headaches peculiar to the *unabridger.* But useful coinages are uncommon in undergraduate writing. Even Keats could hardly be forgiven for thinking that *purplue* made an excellent name for a color halfway between purple and blue.

EXERCISE B

None of the following "new words" appears in Webster's unabridged dictionary, published in 1961. In commenting on each word, answer the following questions: (1) Is it in your dictionary? (2) Does it appear to be a necessary or useful addition to the language? (3) If so, why? If not, why not?

ad glib	middlescence
anchormanese (TV)	pizzarama
apathete	pornoflic
autodating (computer dating)	quasar
biodegradable	skyjacking
consumerism	spacefaring
docudrama	workaholic
intermissionary entertainment	
(show between the halves)	

Clichés

Most words, of course, do not occur to a writer as isolated units; they come embedded in phrases. These phrases may be tailored to fit the context or they may be ready-made. Many ready-made phrases are the unavoidable idioms no writer can do without. But others are combinations which, however original they may have been at birth, have become thoroughly trite from overuse. The technical term for them, *cliché*, is taken from a French verb meaning stereotype. It is also related to a German noun meaning *a doughy mass.*

A random selection of clichés, grouped to show how they conform to common patterns, will give some indication of their extent:

1. Trite comparisons

brave as a lion	quick as a flash
brown as a berry	quiet as a mouse
cold as ice	red as a rose
cool as a cucumber	sharp as a tack
drunk as a lord	sick as a dog
fit as a fiddle	sober as a judge
green as grass	soft as silk
hard as nails	steady as a rock
old as the hills	warm as toast
pretty as a picture	white as snow

2. Canned adjective-noun combinations

acid test	fair sex
almighty dollar	fast buck
bitter end	feverish energy
blessed event	freedom-loving Americans
blood-curdling yell	hasty retreat
blushing bride	hearty breakfast
briny deep	imperialist warmongers
budding genius	mad scramble
clinging vine	naked force
constructive criticism	ominous silence
deafening roar	watery grave

3. Overworked proverbs and fragments from literature

A rolling stone gathers no moss.
Absence makes the heart grow fonder.
Accidents will happen.
All is not gold that glitters.
All work and no play make Jack a dull boy.
Birds of a feather flock together.
Blood is thicker than water.
Hope springs eternal in the human breast.
In the spring a young man's fancy lightly turns to thoughts of love.

136

It's better late than never.
It's never too late to mend.
Life is what you make it.
Silence is golden.
Variety is the spice of life.
You only live once.

4. Pseudopoetic personification

arms of Morpheus	Mother Nature
at Death's door	the fickle finger of Fate
Dame Fortune	the Grim Reaper
Father Time	the irony of Fate
Fortune's Wheel	the long arm of Coincidence

5. Platform platitudes and rhetorical crutches

a man who needs no introduction	It goes without saying
as every schoolboy knows	It is interesting to note
at this point in time	so to speak
I am reminded of a story	Time (space) will not permit
In closing I would like to say	to coin a phrase
in the final analysis	to make a long story short

6. Miscellaneous

bolt from the blue	rear its ugly head
break the silence	shadow of a doubt
by leaps and bounds	shot in the dark
calm before the storm	sight for sore eyes
chip off the old block	six of one and half a dozen of the other
from pillar to post	time of your life
never to be forgotten	tired but happy
none the worse for wear	trite but true

No writer can avoid using an occasional cliché. What wears the reader down is the mass production of secondhand phrases. James J. Kilpatrick makes the point in the *Saturday Review* while condemning the style of a biography of Adlai Stevenson:

> Thus, one shudders to contemplate the fateful day when shadows lengthened and seeds of suspicion were planted; after a hearty breakfast, one encounters a storm of controversy, a storm of protest, a stream of visitors, a flood of letters. Barn doors are locked after horses are stolen; young people dance into the wee hours; sirens are always screaming and briefcases are always stuffed.

Since originality is a relative term at best, it is not easy to draw the line between an accepted idiom and a trite phrase, an effective allusion and a hackneyed quotation. Nor is it possible to devise a system by which students who neither read widely nor listen carefully can be sure to recognize a cliché when they see one. But a few further hints should help:

1. Be wary of quotations from traditional literature   If you are not widely read, you are probably familiar with only hackneyed proverbs and overquoted purple passages from the schoolboy canon.

2. If you do use a familiar quotation because of its aptness, (a) introduce it unobtrusively and (b) reproduce it accurately

a. Do not telegraph it pretentiously in advance:

This point is clearly illustrated by a quotation from the celebrated Bard of Avon, William Shakespeare, who has well said: "The quality of mercy is not strained."

Do not emphasize its triteness:

An oft-repeated phrase that has been in use a long time is: "Necessity is the Mother of Invention." I found this out when I went camping.
BETTER   When I went camping, I really found out that necessity is the mother of invention.
BEST   When I went camping, I took a required course in resourcefulness.

Familiar allusions can be successful if they are woven naturally into the sentence or slightly altered for the occasion:

Where an Adams scrupled to tread, it is not for the stranger to rush in.—John Buchan, *Pilgrim's Way* (from Alexander Pope: "For fools rush in where angels fear to tread")

When a new style swims into our ken, as Hemingway's did in the 1920s, it is new, or was new, in respect to a historical situation.—Walker Gibson, *Tough, Sweet & Stuffy* (from John Keats: "When a new planet swims into his ken")

Optics is the language in which seeing is seeing and nothing else—not even believing.—J. Bronowski, *The Common Sense of Science* (from the proverb, "Seeing is believing")

The common practice is to omit quotation marks, giving the reader the slight pleasure of identifying the allusion without signposts (see p. 331).

b. Do not assume that you are so familiar with a familiar quotation that you can quote it accurately without checking in a reliable source (see p. 224); and if you do cite the original source, cite the right source. Do not guess that Shakespeare must have said it or take refuge in such playful or cautious uncertainties as "Someone has said somewhere" or "Wasn't it Pope who said?"

3. If you do use a trite phrase don't label it with quotation marks (see p. 332) or apologize for it in humble or facetious words; don't introduce one cliché with another

If I may be forgiven the cliché, I must admit that I never yet felt "as fit as a fiddle" after physical training class.
It slid like water off a duck's back, *to coin a phrase.*

4. Relax and write as naturally as possible   This advice may seem strange if you are a natural cliché expert. But with inexperienced writers more triteness probably results from struggling for effect than from indifference to good diction. Often a student's favorite phrases are innocently lifted from the dictionary of clichés.

5. Don't be eccentric in an effort to avoid triteness   *Briny deep* may be a cliché, but it is better than *saline depths.* Possibly *ocean* or *sea* would do the job admirably. As Fowler wrote, "the obvious is better than obvious avoidance of it."

Of course, the problem of avoiding clichés is far more complex than examining a representative list and reading a few general hints. Many of the clichés with which we presume to express ourselves are not the timeworn examples of the handbooks. They are today's slogans and catch phrases, stale almost as fast as they are manufactured (*back to basics, consciousness raising, search for identity*). A seasoned cliché expert, whether found in a magazine, on a political platform, in the columns of a newspaper, or at either end of a college classroom, is not merely a master of trite diction. Such a person is a victim of something that goes much deeper. The British logician L. Susan Stebbing has aptly called it "potted thinking." The word *cliché* may refer not only to a phrase but also to a moldy idea or convention. The student who thinks in clichés will inevitably write in clichés. The best advice to a cliché expert is this: Think for yourself.

EXERCISE C

Comment in detail on the diction of the following passage:

Members of the graduating class, this is only the commencement. In these hallowed halls you have spent the four happiest years of your lives. But that is only a fraction of the three score years and ten that we are permitted in this vale of tears. In the outside world you will find that there are two kinds of people who play the game of life: those who carry the ball and those who merely stand on the sidelines. I don't mean to infer that you should be as busy as bees or as eager as beavers twenty-four hours a day, for all work and no play makes Jack a dull boy. I mean that when you play, you should play hard, and that when you work, you should keep your noses to the grindstone. As the great poet Rudyard Kipling has well said, and I quote, you should fill the unforgetful minute with sixty seconds worth of distant run. Your Alma Mater sends you forth in troublous times. Life is no bed of roses, young ladies and gentlemen; it is a fierce struggle for existence in which the law of the survival of the fittest prevails until the bitter end. But the struggle is not for filthy lucre only but for all the wonderful things that money can buy in this prosperous land of ours. Last but by no means least, it is a struggle for the finer things in life which the almighty dollar can never buy. I am green with envy when I consider your golden opportunities in the years that lie ahead. You youth of today will be the adults of tomorrow. It is a challenge that you will meet, with heads held high, before the Grim Reaper cuts the threads of your existence. As I look into the sea of faces before me and know that you are part of the wave of the future, I feel confident this nation cannot fail.

LONG AND SHORT WORDS

When we speak of fifty-cent words as opposed to ten-cent words, we are usually distinguishing them roughly according to size. The distinction is, of course, a distortion of values. A person with a large vocabulary will "know a lot of big words" and probably be more successful than a person with a small vocabulary composed almost entirely of small words. Educated people will naturally use more long words than un-educated people, not necessarily to parade their learning—though they may be pedants or show-offs—but because they will more often make distinctions that cannot be adequately conveyed without resorting to long words. But it does not follow from this that a long word in any context is more valuable than a short one. Sometimes a fifty-cent word is not worth a nickel.

The objection to long words is not new. In the first century B.C., Horace spoke of "sesquipedalia verba"—"words a foot-and-a-half long." Oliver Goldsmith predicted that if Dr. Johnson made little fishes talk, they would talk like whales. But the reaction in our time has been especially strong. Widespread indignation against the interminable terms of government employees, sociologists, psychologists, educationists, literary critics, and others addicted to "gobbledygook" (see pp. 174–178) has led to spasmodic public campaigns for shorter words.

On the whole, this propaganda for plain talk is sound. Every generation needs to deflate its windbags and cut its pedants down to size. But when the love of short words is combined with an undiscriminating distrust of long ones, the reason is often not a genuine affection for simple language but mental laziness.

The old classroom rule—"Never use a Latin word when an Anglo-Saxon word will do just as well"—is of little use. It not only assumes some knowledge of Latin and Old English, but it tends to ignore the large number of indispensable short words from the Latin: *act, age, air, brief, cent, clear, date, face, long, move, pay, peace, spend, state,* and *trade*—to name only a few without which we would be all tongue-tied. A related rule—"Never use a long word when a short word will do just as well"—is a safer guide—if students don't interpret it as an excuse for refusing to enlarge their own vocabulary and for automatically suspecting every speaker or writer who uses words that lie beyond its narrow boundaries. The rule is in key with the modern tendency to say simple things in natural, informal language. It can be an effective antidote against the big-word disease. Notice how the following fuzzy passages

140

are clarified and simplified by substituting short words (notice also that big-word writing is usually wordy writing as well):

LONG WORDS The specialization in which the Marquis Company has consistently concentrated is principally directed towards the compilative methodism of searching out those actually or more likely to be subject to reference interest.—Quoted from *Who's Who in America* in a review by Hubert Herring, *New York Times Book Review*

SHORT WORDS The Marquis Company has always tried to choose names which the general reader is most likely to look up.

LONG WORDS In order to substantiate our desire to accommodate our guests we would appreciate your coopcration to anticipate your credit requirements before departure.—Sign in a Washington hotel, cited by Charles Morton, *Atlantic*

SHORT WORDS If you wish to cash a check, please let us know before leaving.

It might be argued with some logic that the second translation gains in directness and simplicity but loses in politeness. There is a difference in levels of usage as well as in length of words. "Your presence is requested" is on one level; "Please come to my party" is on another. The same kind of difference exists between "Trespassing on these premises is expressly forbidden" and "Keep out of this yard." This raises again the inevitable question of appropriateness. After all, an experienced writer doesn't ask: "Is this word too long?" or "Will that short word do just as well as this long one?" but habitually asks: "Is this the best word to convey my meaning? Is it appropriate in this context?" Once these questions are answered, the question of whether a word is short, long, or medium no longer matters.

CONCRETE AND ABSTRACT WORDS

The trouble with many long words is that they are too abstract. The chapter on grammar contains a distinction between a concrete noun—naming "something that can be seen, heard, touched, smelled, or tasted"—and an abstract noun—naming a quality or idea that cannot be perceived by the senses. This is an oversimplification. Just as all words have connotation as well as denotation, all words have some abstractness. *Boat* stands for something that can be touched and sometimes heard and smelled, but it also stands for the *boatiness* of boats in general. *Concrete* may have a "concrete" meaning in one sentence (a *concrete* sidewalk) and an "abstract" meaning in another (a *concrete* idea). The same is true of the word *abstract*. However arbitrary, the distinction between concrete and abstract words is still evident. *My dog Rover*, which has a specific *referent*, presumably in a specific kennel, is obviously more concrete than *dog*, just as *dog* is more concrete than *quadruped*. By the same token, *disease*, *vehicle*, and *educational institu-*

141

tion are more abstract than *mumps, Cadillac,* and *junior high school.* In short, *abstract words are general; concrete words are specific.* Good writing is specific.

The Value of Concreteness

Obviously you can't spend all your time writing on such tangible subjects as "My Dog Rover." It is easier for a short-story writer to use concrete words than for a philosopher. But much vague writing is vague because it is unnecessarily abstract.

See how the concrete words make the following paragraph come alive:

> And one summer I worked nights in the Post Office, that great gray building wherein are many stories. I sweated with the others, tossed mail hour on hour, my body swaying, my arms moving, my mind going dead, my eyes reading the addresses. We were supposed to sort fifty letters a minute. Figure that out, folks. I must have tossed a few billion while I was there, and where those letters went I did not care, and if the letters had black borders, if they carried sad news, I didn't care either; I kept on tossing them into the small squares. It was some job, and it taught me plenty. It taught me how to stand on one spot until the bell rang. There were long lines of mail-cases and a thousand men on the floor, and the hard chatter of over a hundred canceling machines went on all night. Who knows big business? Who knows all the big mail-order firms, those houses that dump loads and loads of mail into the Post Office? The belts rumbled on, carrying the mail away, and merchandise rattled down the chutes.—Albert Halper, *On the Shore*

Take out most of the concrete words and what is left? Something like this:

> One summer I was employed nights in the Post Office, a large, tall building. I became terribly tired of sorting so much mail. We were supposed to sort a certain number of letters in a certain length of time. I don't know how many I sorted in all; I just continued working without caring what the letters contained. I certainly didn't learn much from that job about big business. But who does understand big business? All I remember is a lot of mail and machinery and noise and confusion.

The sharp outlines of the picture are gone. The motion, the heat and sweat and noise and music, the bitter irony—all are gone. Nothing is left but a frame and a blurred excuse for a picture. The writer has *told* the readers something, but has *shown* them nothing.

Notice how much clearer the following passages are when translated into concrete English:

ABSTRACT In this study, as in all others, accessibility of books was a potent factor in determining the effectiveness with which the objectives of the program in reading were achieved.

CONCRETE   Like all other studies, this proves that the easier it is for students to get their hands on books, the sooner they will learn to read.

ABSTRACT   The utilization of any intellectual endowment in cases of retardation among children is dependent on parental reaction toward them in the domestic environment.
CONCRETE   How much backward children use their intelligence depends on how their parents treat them at home.

ABSTRACT   Facility of comprehension in a literary situation is not readily effected by indifferent interpersonal communication.
CONCRETE   It is not easy to understand a writer who does not try to be clear.

Often, when the layers of abstractions are peeled off, there is nothing at the core but an empty truism. The high-sounding abstract words are merely a disguise for an intellectual vacuum. Sometimes this disguise is unconscious. Sometimes it is a conscious effort to dress up nothing and make it look like something. Then the sin is not only bad writing but insincerity.

Every field of discussion has its favorite abstractions: economics (*property, inflation, deflation, value, depression, recession, prosperity, employment, capitalism, free enterprise, monopoly*); literary criticism (*romanticism, realism, naturalism, expressionism, impressionism, art, beauty, truth, masterpiece, genius, poetry, major poetry, minor poetry*); education (*culture, orientation, activation, communication, implementation, correlation*); politics (*democracy, communist, socialist, fascist, imperialist, patriotic, liberal, radical, reactionary, conservative*). A reputable expert will use these terms discreetly with some conception of their meaning for other experts. A propagandist will use them craftily to conceal distortions of the truth. We non-experts—and most of us pose as experts at times on almost any subject—will often use them carelessly without the vaguest notion of what we mean by them.

It is vain to argue that such words should be abolished from a person's vocabulary because they mean all things to all people. It is absurd to insist that abstractions should always be used with "their right meaning"; the right meaning is usually my meaning, the wrong meaning yours. It is utopian to assume seriously that any authority, whether it is a dictionary or a committee of the United Nations, can make all people agree on the same meaning for each word—though a powerful propaganda agency can come close to this goal. But a conscientious writer can observe these two principles:

Two Ways of Being Concrete

1. Whenever possible, write about concrete realities, not about words or abstract phenomena   A detailed description of a political program in action is worth more than an eloquent hymn in praise of "liberalism" or "conservatism." As soon as the discussion of a political regime no longer refers directly to the individuals who run it, the acts they perform, and the human beings it presumably serves, it loses contact with reality. As soon as human beings become *personnel*, they become impersonal. When a political discussion becomes a comparison of *isms*, it is likely to degenerate into an argument about words, not realities. By the same reasoning, a clear analysis of a single romantic poet is more valuable than an interminable discussion of *romanticism* without concrete illustrations. A specific objection to a particular ruling in the Dean's office makes a better editorial than a sprawling attack on "the Administration." A brief explanation of how one curriculum works is better than thousands of glowing words about *correlation* or *the humanities*. Because he chose to write about the concrete reality of *teaching*, Jacques Barzun's *Teacher in America* is a better book than a hundred that mull over the abstraction called *education*. See how concretely he states his aim:

Both political and educational theory are for the rare genius to grapple with, once in a century. The business of the citizen and the statesman is not political theory but politics. The business of the parent and the teacher is not education but Teaching. Teaching is something that can be provided for, changed, or stopped. It is good or bad, brilliant or stupid, plentiful or scarce. Beset as it is with difficulties and armed with devices, teaching has a theory too, but it is one that can be talked about simply and directly, for it concerns the many matters that affect our lives, from the three R's to electronics. To deal with it in that fashion is in fact what I am going to do in this book: very simply and literally I am going to tell tales out of school.

2. When an inevitable abstract word has a key position in a passage, make your meaning clear by definition or illustration (compare pp. 58–61)

The writer of the following passage explains an abstract technical term with two concrete illustrations:

Laplace suggested a different origin for the planets and satellites. The central condensation that eventually became the sun, also began to rotate upon its axis. It spun faster as contraction went on, by virtue of a well-known principle of mechanics called by the technical phrase "the law of conservation of angular momentum."

Angular momentum is a phenomenon well known to ballerinas or fancy skaters. For example, a skater or dancer wishing to execute a whirl starts spinning slowly upon one foot with both arms and one leg extended. An ice skater often goes into a crouching position at the beginning of the maneuver. Then the person draws the arms and leg closer to the body, trying to achieve pencil slimness as far as possible. The nearer the arms and legs reach the axis of rotation the faster the spin becomes.

Anyone possessing a rotable desk chair or piano stool can make an even more spectacular demonstration. Holding two fairly heavy books at arm's length,

144

start yourself spinning. Pull the books in toward your body and the speed of rotation increases noticeably. In fact, you can pull the books in only with considerable effort. They tend to fly off unless you hold them tightly.—Donald H. Menzel, "Other Worlds Than Ours," *Atlantic*

The law of conservation of angular momentum may be a physical reality well known to students of mechanics. But to most readers, even of an adult magazine such as the *Atlantic*, the phrase is abstract double-talk. Menzel brings the problem into the layman's sights by presenting a choice of two homely illustrations, either of which might reflect the reader's own experience. The reader has the further privilege of performing at least one of the two experiments. This device of domesticating scientific phenomena for the average reader is one of the standbys of popular science writing. It is merely a method for giving concrete reality to abstract terminology.

No definition of an abstract term is of much use unless it is in more concrete language than the term defined. Dr. Johnson's celebrated definition of *network* as "any thing reticulated or decussated, at equal distances, with interstices between the intersections" is a neat example of a definition that chases the reader in the wrong direction. It is equally futile to define a word in terms of the word itself. Shakespeare's Bardolph unconsciously illustrates this: "Accommodated, that is, when a man is, as they say, accommodated: or when a man is, being, whereby a' may be thought to be accommodated: which is an excellent thing." A more common practice is to define a word in terms of synonyms that are equally abstract. To define *democracy* as "a system guaranteeing liberty and justice" or *culture* as "an appreciation of the humanities" may move the readers by pleasant associations, but it doesn't get them much nearer the tangible truth.

If you find yourself trapped in such a circular definition, you might remember that the best way to define *dog* is to go to a kennel and point to one. A simple precept follows from this: *The best definition of an abstract term is a good illustration.*

EXERCISES

D. Without omitting any essential details, rewrite the following passages, substituting specific, concrete words (preferably short) for general abstractions:

1. A female relative of mine made it financially possible for me to pursue the study of a musical instrument, and she followed my attainments with great interest until further practice was interrupted by illness.

2. Whenever any of the participants encountered any difficulty on the field, the coach always rendered counsel and assistance which would make a recurrence unlikely.

3. The acquisition of higher education cannot be attained without considerable amounts of both persistence and financial competence.

4. My relations with the opposite sex have never been entirely satisfactory as regards mutual participation in social occasions.

5. They argued over whether anyone with radical ideas about the system in which all patriotic Americans believe should be denied the privileges of freedom.

6. The theory that differences in pupil capacity and status can be eliminated by uniform instruction and evaluation does not receive my approbation.

7. No individual can be properly comprehended unless both the temporal and geographical factors of the person's environment are taken into account.

8. It is inadvisable to attempt an evaluation of prospects that are still in an embryonic stage of development.

9. The actions and attitudes directed by one member of a group activity toward another should be such as the former would desire the latter to direct toward him in retaliation.

10. The sociologist maintained that individuals habituated to similar behavior are characterized by a tendency toward societal organization among themselves.

E. Write an essay of at least 300 words in which you define and illustrate your conception of one of the italicized abstract terms on page 143.

Euphemisms

A special example of the tendency to escape from concrete reality into abstractions is the *euphemism*—the substitution of a presumably inoffensive word for one that might give offense. Euphemisms are common in newspapers *(job action* for *strike, criminal assault* for *rape)*, and in the business world *(heating engineer* for *plumber; tonsorial artist* for *barber; adjuster of delinquent obligations* for *bill collector; mortician* for *undertaker; grief therapist* for *mortician; memorial park* for *cemetery,* once a euphemism for *graveyard; adult books* for *pornography)*. Many euphemisms are what Fowler called *genteelisms:* they reflect the presumed delicacy of people who pride themselves on their refinement *(perspiration* for *sweat, odor* for *smell, powder room* for *toilet)*. When they also reflect prudery or hypocrisy, they are more offensive to genuinely decent people than the blunt words they replace.

Some political euphemisms are a criminal abuse of language; George Orwell illustrated them this way:

Defenseless villages are bombarded from the air, the inhabitants driven out into the countryside, the cattle machine-gunned, the huts set on fire with incendiary bullets: this is called *pacification*. Millions of peasants are robbed of their farms and sent trudging along the roads with no more than they can carry: this is called *transfer of population* or *rectification of frontiers*. People are imprisoned for years without trial, or shot in the back of the neck or sent to die of scurvy in

Arctic lumber camps: this is called *elimination of unreliable elements.*—George Orwell, "Politics and the English Language," *New Republic*

His list could be extended indefinitely. *Escalation, device (bomb), effective ordnance delivery (accurate bombing), intelligence collecting (spying), strategic withdrawal (retreat), deep interrogation (torture), termination with prejudice (political assassination)*—a frightening glossary of euphemisms could be gathered from the history of warfare alone.

The calculated processing of presumably harmless labels to disguise disturbing truths or even cover up crimes is one of the evil arts of bureaucracy. Such language permeates government Officialese and corporate Commercialese and befogs honest communication in other walks of life. At its worst, it deserves a less euphemistic label than *euphemism: doublespeak.*

In daily conversation, euphemisms are occasionally necessary out of common decency. There is no point in insisting that a man has *died* if his widow prefers *passed away*. It may be kindness or diplomacy to call the poor *disadvantaged* or *underprivileged*, the crippled *handicapped*, the insane *mentally ill*, the mentally defective *retarded* or *unusual*, the aged *senior citizens*, slum dwellers *occupants of substandard housing*, or backward countries *emerging nations*. It may serve a psychological purpose for the Air Force to call a jail a *confinement facility* or the police to call a riot a *serious crowd-control situation*. But the private writer, uncontrolled by bureaucracy, should suspect any euphemism for its power to disguise or distort the plain truth.

This does not mean that a student should swing to the other extreme, reveling in the shock value of earthy words in order to advertise emancipation from Victorian taboos. A writer can call a spade a spade without digging up dirt for its own sake.

EXERCISE F

Without repeating any example in this book, make a list of ten euphemisms from varied sources.

CHARGED AND NEUTRAL WORDS

Gertrude Stein once made this characteristic comment on her own writing:

I didn't want, when I said "water," to have you think of running water. Therefore I began limiting my vocabulary, because I wanted to get rid of everything except the picture within the frame. While I was writing, I didn't want, when I used one word, to make it carry with it too many associations. I wanted as far as possible to make it exact, as exact as mathematics; that is to say, for

147

example, if one and one make two, I wanted words to have as much exactness as that. When I put them down they were to have this quality.—Gertrude Stein, "How Writing Is Written"

This is one writer's statement of her effort to solve a problem that sooner or later confronts all writers. Scientists have yearned for a language without a hint of emotional flavor—a perfect, detached, denotative language, an ideal scientific instrument. Not content with the restricted symbols of mathematics, some of them have dreamt of an English vocabulary free from the "birdsong" or "tweet-tweet" of connotation.

It is unlikely that the dream will come true in the near future. The most familiar phrases from Gertrude Stein—"rose is a rose is a rose is a rose" and "Pigeons on the grass alas"—are rich in associations. Whatever Shakespeare may have said about a rose by any other name smelling as sweet, the very word gives off a special fragrance. And James Thurber once devoted an entire essay to pointing out that *alas* carries too many pathetic overtones for pigeons.

Even the scientists' technical terms have unscientific overtones. E. B. White once wrote in *The Wild Flag:*

The latest element to turn up is called plutonium—which is Disney with a touch of mineral water. The word uranium had a mighty sound, a solemn sound, an awful sound. Plutonium is a belly laugh. Plutonium, incidentally, is not known in the stars; the stars are too high-minded. Plutonium is just a mouthwash used by Mandrake. Plutonium is just something belonging to the comical race of people who started their first atomic fire under a football stadium.

This discussion comes back to a point made in Chapter 5 (see pp. 127–128): all words have connotation as well as denotation. But a writer can still make a useful, if arbitrary, distinction between words that are *charged* with considerable bias or emotion and words that are relatively *neutral*. Charged words carry a heavy load of connotation, either unfavorable or favorable; neutral words are more strictly denotative.

CHARGED	NEUTRAL
propaganda	doctrine
controversial	debatable
bureaucrat	government official
drunkard	alcoholic
pedagogue	teacher
bookworm	student
pig-headed	obstinate
cravat	necktie
shrink	psychiatrist
guts	courage
hype	publicity

CHARGED	NEUTRAL
magnetic	attractive
slothful	lazy
money-changer	banker
fuzz	police
slumber	sleep
Quoth the raven, "Nevermore!"	"Never again," said the blackbird.

Because it cannot go far with connotation, a dictionary definition is often of little help to a writer with making these distinctions. Take, for example, the definitions of *controversial* in AHD: "1. Of, subject to, or marked by controversy. 2. Fond of controversy; disputatious." Neither definition hints that, to many people, a "controversial subject" may cloak a dangerous doctrine and a "controversial figure" suggests sinister designs, questionable loyalty, or at least instability. Nor does any of the three meanings of *realism* in NCD convey a hint that either the noun or the undefined adjective (*realistic*) or adverb (*realistically*) has an unpleasant taste for many. Writes Mary McCarthy, "Whatever the field, whenever you hear that a subject is to be treated 'realistically,' you expect that its unpleasant aspects are to be brought forward." That this is a personal view makes it no less a part of the word's total connotation.

You must keep your ears and eyes open to the associations that such words acquire from their contexts. In a special context, a harmless neutral expression like *that man* can be loaded with love or hatred ("I can't help loving *that man*" vs. "*That man* in the White House!"). The abstract phrase *law and order* has been used to mean both "democracy's bulwarks against anarchy" and "brutal suppression of legitimate dissent."

Perfect neutrality is as unattainable in language as in diplomacy. One person's neutral expression is another person's euphemism: it can be argued that *public medicine* or *national health* is biased as much on one side of the issue as *socialized medicine* on the other. But there are occasions when a responsible writer will carefully select neutral words. In technical exposition, where strict factual accuracy is all-important, emotional bias is out of place. A reputable journalist tries to make a careful distinction between objective reporting and editorializing, and to distinguish honestly between the legitimate slanting of a responsible columnist and the inflammatory slurs of an irresponsible gossip-caster. Any writer trying to arrive calmly and objectively at the truth in a controversy will try to avoid overloaded words. They will lead into the fallacy of begging the question—assuming in advance the truth of something that remains to be proved (see p. 203).

But in many kinds of writing neutrality is undesirable. The magic of words doesn't have to be the black magic of a propaganda minister. When you have no reason to steer a neutral course in the interest of accurate reporting or fair discussion, you may move the reader to feel beauty or wonder or terror or anger—whatever emotion you are trying to convey. You may take full advantage of the connotative value of charged words.

Read these two passages carefully:

A very trivial circumstance will serve to exemplify this. Suppose you go into a fruiterer's shop, wanting an apple,—you take up one, and, on biting it, you find it sour; you look at it, and see that it is hard and green. You take up another one, and that too is hard, green, and sour. The shopman offers you a third; but, before biting it, you examine it, and find that it is hard and green, and you immediately say that you will not have it, as it must be sour, like those that you have already tried.

Nothing can be more simple than that, you think; but if you will take the trouble to analyse and trace out into its logical elements what has been done by the mind, you will be greatly surprised. In the first place, you have performed the operation of induction. You found that, in two experiences, hardness and greenness in apples went together with sourness. It was so in the first case, and it was confirmed by the second. True, it is a very small basis, but still it is enough to make an induction from; you generalize the facts, and you expect to find sourness in apples where you get hardness and greenness. You found upon that a general law, that all hard and green apples are sour; and that, so far as it goes, is a perfect induction.—Thomas Henry Huxley, *Darwiniana*

So I wandered through the labyrinth of sunlight and shadow in the bazaar, watching, smelling, hearing, touching. I saw the long serpentine threads of sunlight sifting through the shade and fingering the booths of the jewel merchants; earrings, anklets, bracelets, neckbands, headbands, amulets, talismans; tooled leather from the southern ports, varnished metals from Indo-China, glittering worthless stones from Ceylon, vermilion and magenta silks from Tashkent, blue velvets from Bokhara, green rugs from Syria, great rippling shawls from Kashmir—no longer fresh, any of them, all of them spotted and stained by the wet seasons or the touch of hands. And beyond these the sweetmeats, clotted syrups soft in the sun's rays, raw spices, dark granular honey, dried citron and figs and dates buzzing with a thousand little golden flies; caskets and bowls and ewers and medicine-bottles twisted out of blue glass; strangely shaped receptacles of iron and bronze and copper; salves and perfumes sickening the nostrils. Something false and pathetic about it all, as pathetic as the faces that hovered over them like moths.—Frederic Prokosch, *The Asiatics*

The point is not, of course, that the first passage is bad writing because it is colorless and unexciting and the second good writing because it is colorful and exciting. Nor is the first passage good merely because it is plain talk for the man in the street and the second bad because it is fancy language for the poet in the attic. They are both good writing, but of two entirely different kinds. Huxley, a scientist and teacher, is defining the abstract process of induction, with the help of a homely concrete illustration. He uses neutral words—*shop, apple, hard, green, sour*— because he wants nothing to distract the reader from the bare statement of a simple scientific fact. Prokosch, a poet and novelist, uses exotic language rich with associations—*labyrinth, bazaar, serpentine, amulets, talismans, vermilion, magenta*—to awaken all the reader's senses to the atmosphere of Asia. One passage is first-rate exposition; the other is admirable description. Taken together, they are evidence that the choice between charged and neutral words depends entirely on the writer's purpose.

In most informal prose, there is a happy medium between the unemotional neutrality of the passage from Huxley and the richly spiced poetic prose of Prokosch. Students with an ingrained prejudice against literature, especially poetry, will too often swing consciously or unconsciously to a prosaic extreme. Picturing themselves, perhaps with some pride, as straightforward, sensible, tough-minded, "practical" writers interested only in the hard, cold facts of a problem, they will squeeze all the warmth and color out of language, leaving it as cold and pale as the directions on a can of baking powder. Other students—either sincerely in love with beautiful words or under the illusion that overloaded writing is expected in an English course—will flavor the most prosaic subject with inappropriate emotions and uncalled-for emphasis. Of the two extremes, the second kind of writer is doing more damage to the language. The undergraduate who pours strong emotions into trivial contexts is like the journalist to whom every scoop is a *sensation,* every political defeat a *landslide,* every diplomatic note an *ultimatum,* or the advertisers who have long since reached the dead end where even *super-deluxe* is a synonym for *commonplace.*

EXERCISE G

Analyze the diction of the following passages to show how each writer has used charged words to achieve a particular purpose:

1. The whole bag of tricks of the average business man, or even of the average professional man, is inordinately childish. It takes no more actual sagacity to carry on the everyday hawking and haggling of the world, or to ladle out its normal doses of bad medicine and worse law, than it takes to operate a taxicab or fry a fish. No observant person, indeed, can come into close contact with the general run of business and professional men—I confine myself to those who seem to get on in the world, and exclude the admitted failures—without marveling at their intellectual lethargy, their incurable ingenuousness, their appalling lack of ordinary sense. The late Charles Francis Adams, a grandson of one American President and a great-grandson of another, after a long lifetime in intimate association with some of the chief business "geniuses" of that paradise of traders and usurers, the United States, reported in his old age that he had never heard a single one of them say anything worth hearing. These were vigorous and masculine men, but intellectually they were all blank cartridges.—H. L. Mencken, "In Defense of Women"

2. I decline to accept the end of man. It is easy enough to say that man is immortal simply because he will endure; that when the last ding-dong of doom has clanged and faded from the last worthless rock hanging tideless in the last red and dying evening, that even then there will still be one more sound: that of his puny, inexhaustible voice, still talking. I refuse to accept this. I believe that man will not merely endure; he will prevail. He is immortal, not because he alone among creatures has an inexhaustible voice, but because he has a soul, a spirit capable of compassion and sacrifice and endurance. The poet's, the writer's, duty is to write about these things. It is his privilege to help man endure by lifting his heart, by reminding him of the courage and honor and hope and pride and compassion and pity and sacrifice which have been the glory of his past. The poet's voice need not merely be the record of man, it can be one of the props, the pillars to help him endure and prevail.—William Faulkner, "The Stockholm Address" (Nobel Prize Acceptance Speech)

3. I remember sharing the last of my moist buns with a boy and a lion. Tawny and savage, with cruel nails and capacious mouth, the little boy tore and devoured. Wild as a seedcake, ferocious as a hearthrug, the depressed and verminous lion nibbled like a mouse at his half a bun and hiccupped in the sad dusk of his cage.—Dylan Thomas, *Quite Early One Morning*

4. Shadows lope along the mountain's rumpled flanks; they elongate like root tips, like lobes of spilling water, faster and faster. A warm purple pigment pools in each ruck and tuck of the rock; it deepens and spreads, boring crevasses, canyons. As the purple vaults and slides, it tricks out the unleafed forest and rumpled rock in gilt, in shape-shifting patches of glow. These gold lights veer and retract, shatter and glide in a series of dazzling splashes, shrinking, leaking, exploding. The ridge's bosses and hummocks sprout bulging from its side; the whole mountain looms miles closer; the light warms and reddens; the bare forest folds and pleats itself like living protoplasm before my eyes, like a running chart, a wildly scrawling oscillograph on the present moment.—Annie Dillard, *Pilgrim at Tinker Creek*

THE SOUND OF WORDS

"The mind's eye" is a familiar expression. We could as logically speak of "the mind's ear," for it is possible to imagine sounds as well as sights. Because the ear of a trained reader is never completely at rest, word sounds are important, even in writing not intended for oral delivery. The relation between sound and sense is extremely subtle. Robert Frost once spoke of "the sound of sense" as "the first qualification of a writer." No word chemist, not even a poet, can separate the pure essence of audible beauty or ugliness from the other elements of connotation. Is *gush* as beautiful a word as *hush* or *ripe* as ugly as *gripe*? Is *lullaby* beautiful for its own sake or because it suggests madonnas and sleeping babies and Brahms? Why, as Felix S. Cohen has asked, do we use so many one-syllable words ending in *unk* "to designate so many unhonored objects:—*e.g., bunk, chunk, dunk, drunk, flunk, funk, hunk, punk, sunk, skunk, slunk, stunk*"? "Take care of the sense and the sounds will take care of themselves," said the Duchess to Alice. But the Duchess was wrong. All writers, even if they have neither the talent nor the ambition to write poetry, should be alert to the enemies of euphony (pleasing sound) and aware of the common sound effects in language.

Enemies of Euphony

The most common enemy of euphony in prose is the careless repetition of similar sounds. It may be unintentional true rhyme (*lice, nice*), identical rhyme (*vice, device*), or assonance (same vowels, different consonants: *vice, fine*). It shouldn't take a poet to catch the following distracting echoes:

I am not the *type* to *gripe,* and I don't *say* I deserve an *A* every *day.*

As she grew older, her face acquired a beauty that sur*passed* that of her *past.*

Fresh sup*port* for the troops has been recently re*port*ed in the *port* city.

My re*action* to this *faction* is that they should keep their dissatis*faction* to themselves. (The writer of this sentence denied intentionally playing with words.)

The introduc*tion* of the idea of muta*tion* marks nothing less than revolu*tion* in our scheme of interpreta*tion.* What also is the no*tion* of emergent evolu*tion* save recogni*tion* of the most novel, unexpected, unpredictable?

Marjorie Gregg, citing the last example in a letter in the *Saturday Review,* aptly called such bumping along from abstrac*tion* to abstrac*tion cobblestone rhetoric.* Special offenders are words ending in *-ation.* Tin-eared experts in several disciplines are addicted to jingling jargon like "the evaluation of the examination situation with relation to integration in education."

Intentional rhyme is uncommon in serious prose. Intentional assonance is a delicate device that even experienced writers must handle with care. Two other figures of speech are more common, *alliteration* and *onomatopoeia.*

Alliteration

Alliteration is the repetition of an initial sound, usually a consonant, in two or more words of a group. Except during the last two decades of the sixteenth century, it has never been as common in prose as in poetry. Today it is still widely used in advertising (*A*llstate's *A*ffordable *A*nswer, *W*atch *Wh*atever *Wh*enever, *P*eople who *p*rize Scotch *p*ay the *p*rice for *P*inch) and in flashy journalism (The war against the English language is thus a many-pronged offensive, waged amid *j*ungles of *j*argon, *o*ver *o*ceans of *O*fficialese, *p*rairies of *p*edantry, *m*ountains of *m*eringue, while the air *o*scillates with electric frenzy.—Lincoln Barnett, "Who Is Behind the Assault on English?" *Horizon*). Like parallelism and other forms of repetition, alliteration can be effective in speeches and slogans (*B*an the *B*omb, *W*in *w*ith *W*illkie, *T*ippecanoe and *T*yler *T*oo). But persistent al-

153

literation, even when it does not run the risk of requiring the reader to trip on tongue-twisters, is an artificial device that calls too much attention to itself. A writer must not neglect the sense to play games with echoes.

Onomatopoeia

Onomatopoeia—the use of words and phrases imitating sounds—is an effect that inexperienced writers are less likely to overwork. It is a familiar device in storytelling and description, not so common in exposition or argument. The English language has a generous supply of onomatopoetic words, whatever their etymology: *crack, growl, hiss, murmur, mutter, roar, rumble, snarl, thunder, tintinnabulation, whistle*—to name a random handful. The writer's problem often consists of selecting audible words (The ice *cracked* open as the boulders *crashed* down from above) instead of leaving the sound to the reader's imagination (The ice opened up as the boulders fell on it). But if no appropriate word exists in the dictionary, this is one realm in which writers may occasionally coin their own:

Analyzed, it is simply the old piano blues style (a sort of *oink-ily, oink-ily, oink-ily* effect).—Otis Ferguson, "Piano in the Band," *New Republic*

The pounding of the cylinders increased: *ta-pocketa-pocketa-pocketa-pocketa-pocketa.*—James Thurber, "The Secret Life of Walter Mitty," *My World and Welcome to It*

Tires *booped* and *whooshed*, the fenders *queeled* and *graked*, the steering wheel rose up like a spectre and disappeared in the direction of Franklin Avenue with a melancholy *whistling* sound, bolts and gadgets flew like sparks from a Catherine wheel.—James Thurber, *My Life and Hard Times*

Its [the train's] sound occasionally varied on the final click: *der-der-der-dun, der-der-der-dun, der-der-der-dack, der-der-der-dun.*—Alan Sillitoe, *The General*

"Weelawaugh, we-ee-eeelawaugh, weelawaugh," shrilled Mother's high voice. "But-and, but-and, but-and!" Father's low *mumble* would *drone* in answer.—Robert Lowell, *Life Studies*

Rhythm

Finally, remember that all prose has rhythm and some extended passages of prose have a regular rhythmic pattern, or meter. Compare these two sentences:

These mailmen work in all kinds of weather.

Neither snow, nor rain, nor heat, nor gloom of night stays these couriers from the swift completion of their appointed rounds.

Only an acutely sensitive ear would be concerned with the rhythm of the first sentence; only an insensitive reader could ignore the rhythm of the second. A simple analysis will show that the first ten words of the famous inscription from the New York City Post Office—with the exception of the first two—fall into a regular line of iambic pentameter (five "feet," each with an unstressed syllable followed by a stressed syllable):

x x ´ x ´ x ´ x ´ x ´
Neither snow, nor rain, nor heat, nor gloom of night

The difference between the two sentences lies partly in the choice of words—notably the contrast between "prosaic" *mailmen* and "poetic" *couriers*. But it is the pulsing rhythm of the inscription that makes the main difference here between information and emotion, between "literature of knowledge" and "literature of power." In other words, rhythm is one of the fundamental aspects of connotation.

Prose rhythms are not restricted to "emotive" or "ornate" prose (see pp. 168–172). The simplest balanced sentence from the most prosaic context has a symmetrical rhythmic pattern, though it might not be reducible to one of the standard verse meters:

To remove the connector, push it in, turn to the left, and pull it off the terminal.

Occasionally a sentence in strictly serviceable prose trips strangely along in a standard meter—as in this dactylic hexameter, gleaned by the *New Yorker* from the label on a wine bottle:

´ x x ´ x x ´ x x ´ x x ´ x x ´ x
Bottled in perfect condition, but care must be used in decanting

The rhythm of prose is not imprisoned within the phrase or sentence. It permeates the paragraph and may be sustained—especially in prose narrative—throughout the entire work, though this is not always revealed by such evident devices as parallel structure, metrical phrasing, or refrains. For sensitive readers the ear will not close at the end of each separate sentence of prose. They will not only hear the monotonous meter and distracting rhyme of that sentence but will be aware, subconsciously at least, that this one reverts to a more pedestrian rhythm. To Herbert Read, the paragraph, not the sentence, is "the first complete and independent unit of prose rhythm."

Writers who have reached the stage where they depend consciously on the rhythm of words to produce emotive effects—as in narrative, description, or impassioned argument—must remember that a sustained lyrical singsong or a tub-thumping beat or a self-conscious balancing act may irritate the eardrums of even the silent reader. The student who is primarily concerned with simple exposition should not forget that a broken rhythm may throw the simplest sentence off balance and destroy its emphasis.

The main lesson for the inexperienced writer in this whole discussion of sound is a reminder of a point already made in Chapter 2: *Read the theme aloud before you make your final draft,* not only to *see* what you have written but to *hear* it.

EXERCISE H

Rewrite each of the following sentences to make it more euphonious:

1. Once more order and quiet were restored, but the quiet was different, for now there was a sense of tenseness and apprehension.

2. Inevitably, a declaration of the Negro's changed perception of his own position creates a changed racial situation.—Nathan Wright, Jr., *Black Power and Urban Unrest*

3. From the treading of happy feet the hardwood floors were worn bare at the doors.

4. The urgency of the emergency is attested by the turmoil that touched off the terror in Tanzania.

5. I believe that one's ability to cope with problems requiring decisions that lead to action is in proportion to his ability to formulate apprehensions into words.—Margaret K. Bonney, "An English Teacher Answers Mario Pei," *Saturday Review*

6. When they found that the sound could not be kept down, the serious students began studying consistently in the stacks.

7. The police caught up with George on the way back to the house, but they did not arrest the rest of the culprits.

8. The President's explanation of the perils of inflation was broadcast to the entire nation.

9. I may have been rash to take off without cash, but I was thankful that I had a tank full of gas.

10. She was filled with elation when the Administration informed her of the decision on admission.

SIMILE AND METAPHOR

Most high-school graduates know that a *simile* is a direct comparison, usually with *like* or *as,* a *metaphor* an implied comparison without *like* or *as.* The definitions are accurate enough. But the common mistake is to assume that these two figures of speech are the monopoly of poets. This is far more misleading than to have the same illusion about alliteration and onomatopoeia. For simile and metaphor are not incidental ornaments (metaphor) to be laid on like the decorations on a birthday cake (simile). They are the lifeblood of language (metaphor). A dictionary is a cemetery of dead metaphors (metaphor); the word *metaphor* itself has a metaphorical origin (the Greek means *carry-over*). We could

156

not *eliminate* them (a dead metaphor meaning *put them out over the threshold*) if we tried.

Here is a passage of informal prose:

The way our sophisticated modern critic will read complex innuendos into what is elemental is enough to wear one's patience to the bone. Must poor old Homer father a lot of esoteric things? Is the *Iliad* to have four or five layers of meaning, one below the other, like a pile of sandwiches? This digging up of unsuspected meanings goes too far. It spoils a poem to be all the time spading it or boring through its imagery with a steam drill. These critics spend too much of their time underground, and they look pale and unwholesome when they come up. And it often happens that what they bring up is something they have dropped themselves. There are commentators who have been digging all their lives and come up with their own pocket handkerchief. They expect you to be glad about it. They think a poet, like a dog, no sooner happens on a good thing than he wants to bury it.—Frank Moore Colby, "Literary Burrowing," *Imaginary Obligations*

Of the ten sentences in that paragraph, only one is strictly literal, without a living simile or metaphor: *They expect you to be glad about it.* The key metaphor of burrowing is carried further than is common today in expository prose; a humorist may take more liberties with figurative language than a more serious essayist. But notice that in themselves the figures are all easy, natural, homely, essentially "unpoetic." And notice also that by using similes and metaphors, the writer is treating the highly abstract subject of literary criticism in the most concrete terms.

Now consider a different sort of example:

And these Saturdays are worst in the late winter when the snow has lost its novelty and its shine, and the school seems to have been reduced to only a network of drains. During the brief thaw in the early afternoon there is a dismal gurgling of dirty water seeping down pipes and along gutters, a gray seamy shifting beneath the crust of snow, which cracks to show patches of frozen mud beneath. Shrubbery loses its bright snow headgear and stands bare and frail, too undernourished to hide the drains it was intended to hide. These are the days when going into any building you cross a mat of dirt and cinders led in by others before you, thinning and finally trailing off in the corridors. The sky is an empty hopeless gray and gives the impression that this is its eternal shade. Winter's occupation seems to have conquered, overrun and destroyed everything, so that now there is no longer any resistance movement left in nature; all the juices are dead, every sprig of vitality snapped, and now winter itself, an old, corrupt, tired conqueror, loosens its grip on the desolation, recedes a little, grows careless in its watch; sick of victory and enfeebled by the absence of challenge, it begins itself to withdraw from the ruined countryside. The drains alone are active, and on these Saturdays their noises sound a dull recessional to winter.—John Knowles, *A Separate Peace*

This passage, from a serious modern novel, illustrates a less mundane, more versatile use of metaphor than that in Colby's playful essay. The first five sentences of the paragraph are a blend of literal observation ("the snow has lost its novelty and its shine" ... "thinning and trailing off in the corridors") and unobtrusive metaphors ("network of drains" ... "mat of dirt and cinders"). Only one metaphor might seem a trifle forced—"Shrubbery loses its bright headgear"—but the key image, suggesting as it does the glossy globe of a white football helmet, can hardly be called inappropriate in a novel with a school setting.

In the fifth sentence—without taking his eye completely off the object—Knowles gives his fancy a looser rein. Building a more complex metaphor in a carefully balanced sentence, he transforms winter, the inevitable season of the year, into Winter, the degenerating general. This is not incidental decoration. Both tone and language have been anticipated by the imagery of gray despair in the first part of the paragraph and are continued in the gurgling recessional of the final short sentence. The dominant metaphor—appropriate in a novel that also has a war setting—is artfully sustained, each word consistent with the dreary anticlimax of a military occupation.

This discussion does not mean that either writer has consciously said: "I shall sprinkle the page full of similes and metaphors to make my meaning clear." Such imagery is the natural result of an effort to give concrete form to an abstract idea (Colby) or *realize* an intangible atmosphere (Knowles). Similar figures inevitably come to all observant writers who are trying hard to express themselves clearly and concretely. They naturally reach out for new ways to present old ideas or to capture their unique personal views of life. Without coining neologisms wholesale, they try putting old words in new contexts, new arrangements—and give birth to fresh metaphors. This is one aspect of the natural growth of language.

Aristotle asserted wisely that a mastery of metaphor, based on "the intuitive perception of the similarity of dissimilars," cannot be learned from others. You are in for trouble if you consciously set out to write more metaphorically. The self-conscious struggle to sustain a metaphor can produce prose (or poetry) that is not fanciful, only fancy—the unnatural nonsense illustrated on page 21. But you can learn a few tests for measuring the effectiveness of the similes and metaphors that do occur to you. Most ineffective figures of speech are either (1) trite, (2) inappropriate, or (3) mixed.

1. Triteness

Trite similes and metaphors have already been considered in the discussion of clichés (see pp. 136–139). Such inevitable comparisons as *brown as a berry* and *brave as a lion* are similes; and many of the canned adjective-noun combinations—*acid test, budding genius, clinging vine*—are metaphors, though custom has staled their metaphorical flavor. George Orwell's rule for avoiding such metaphorical clichés is strict but sensible: "Never use a metaphor, simile or other figure of speech which you are used to seeing in print." Their consistent use betrays a writer who is too lazy to create original figures through the natural process of looking intently at the object. To the mature reader they are annoyingly familiar and have lost their power to evoke a clear-cut picture. And that power is the only justification for the existence of a simile or metaphor.

The difference between trite and fresh figures should be obvious at a glance:

TRITE   He was as bald as a billiard ball.
FRESH   The whites of his eyes were discoloured, like ancient billiard balls.—Aldous Huxley, "Young Archimedes," *Young Archimedes and Other Stories*

TRITE   A man who is filled with the spirit of adventure will hitch his wagon to a star.
FRESH   For an adventure differs from a mere feat in that it is tied to the eternally unattainable. Only one end of the rope is in the hand, the other is not visible, and neither prayers, nor daring, nor reason can shake it free—William Bolitho, *Twelve against the Gods*

TRITE   He is a complete bonehead.
FRESH   Intellectually he is a nothingness, like interstellar space—a vast vacuum occasionally crossed by homeless, wandering clichés—John Gunther, *Inside U.S.A.*

TRITE   There is a grind in the class who is always shooting his mouth off.
FRESH   The well-crammed youngster is like a siphon bottle. Press the handle and he fizzes in a welcome relief from pressure.—Henry Seidel Canby, *Alma Mater*

2. Inappropriateness

The test of appropriateness applies as surely to a figure of speech as to a single word. A simile or metaphor may be inappropriate because it is too grand for the context or too vulgar, too serious or too comical—because, in short, the picture it conjures up is hanging in the wrong gallery. Even without a broader view of their context, the following student figures are questionable:

The night was dark as ink and the heavens were *perspiring a cold sweat* that blanketed everything.

He was in full evening attire except that his black tie had vanished and all that remained was a grey collar bent *like a river as it winds its way among the mountains.*

Beautiful colored evening gowns filled with *little bunches of mirth and laughter* flitted around the floor attracting the attention of many a young gentleman.

The radio certainly was an inspiring discovery, and its place in the average home was once *like that of the saddle on a horse.*

In the first example, *dark as ink* is trite and the picture of a cold sweat blanketing might be condemned as mixed. But the main question is

159

whether it is appropriate for the *heavens* to *perspire a cold sweat*. *Heavens* is poetic; *perspire* is a genteel euphemism; *cold sweat* is an informal phrase commonly used to describe a physical symptom of fear. In the second sentence, the student has used a forced "poetic" simile absurdly out of place in a prosaic context, if not inaccurate geologically. The questionable image of the *gowns flitting*, in the third sentence, might be explained away as whimsy or *synecdoche*, a figure of speech in which the part is used for the whole. But *bunches*, a word commonly associated with celery or grapes or flowers, is a singularly inappropriate metaphor for young women. In the fourth example, the only point of comparison between the radio and the saddle is their presumed indispensability. If the student had written, "The radio was as important in a house as a saddle is on a horse," the comparison might be unobjectionable, though hardly inspired. But by failing to specify the point of comparison, the student leaves the reader to conjure up such irrelevant images as that of grandfather sitting astride the old Philco on the ridgepole.

3. Mixed Metaphors

It would be more accurate to call a *mixed metaphor* "a mixture of metaphors," for it usually consists of more than one. There are three common kinds:

A. *A mixture of living metaphors*

If the victorious allies had tried to put a fence around Japan and let her stew in her own juice, they would have created a festering sore.

He is convinced that the gravy of the capitalist is the sweated blood of the struggling wage-earner from whom the cream of life has been taken and whose milk has soured.

In the first example, the writer has asked readers to transfer their attention in rapid succession from a corral to a kitchen to a clinic. Though the pictures are consecutive, they follow each other so quickly that the reader gets the effect of a triple exposure. In the second sentence, the switch from dining room to sweatshop to dairy is also too rapid. It is impossible to draw a hard-and-fast line between a legitimate switch from metaphor to metaphor and one that is too sudden. Occasionally a writer will prepare the reader for a change ("to change the metaphor"), but this sort of apology can become tiresome. A general rule of thumb is this: *Once you have set sail in a metaphor, don't change horses in midstream until you have at least finished the sentence.*

B. *Two or more dead metaphors*
These come to life and fight when they are put side by side.

160

The United States can no longer use atomic power as an ace in the hole to hold over the heads of other world powers.

Some of them move outside the universities as well, joining hands with this or that political splinter.—Russell B. Lynes, "Intellectuals vs. Philistines," *New York Times Book Review*

By itself, *ace in the hole* would probably not come to life in this context as a picture from card playing; it is a familiar idiom even to people who have never sat in on a game of stud poker. Used alone, *hold over the heads* is also a commonplace idiom, familiar to many who have never heard of the sword of Damocles. But when the two are brought together, the reader may get a ludicrous picture of a poker player flourishing an ace in the hole over other players' heads. This is, of course, the last thing in the world he would do with it. In the second sentence, *joining hands* and *splinter* both come to life, and the reader conceives an image of a hand full of splinters.

C. A careless mixture of the figurative and the literal

Hester Prynne wore a scarlet A, while the Reverend Dimmesdale put on a false front.

My aunt was instrumental in my musical studies. Being a rather adept pianist, she entertained high hopes that I should follow in her footsteps.

We would like to take this opportunity to announce an amazing breakthrough in frozen chicken pie.—Radio commercial

For all its symbolic overtones in *The Scarlet Letter*, Hester's A for adultery is actually sewed on her dress. Placed beside it in the same sentence, Dimmesdale's false front looks like a literal addition to his wardrobe. The writer of the second passage doesn't want the reader to take *instrumental* literally, but in a musical context, it evokes a picture of trumpets and trombones. Worse still, the dead metaphor in the second sentence—*follow in her footsteps*—is reincarnated in this context and presents a vision of the aunt trampling up and down the keyboard with both feet. The copywriter for the ad is apparently eager to exploit the figurative meaning of the vogue word *breakthrough*. But instead of a picture of a culinary genius shouting "Eureka," the ad conjures up a grotesque image of a plunge through a broken piecrust.

EXERCISE I

Analyze the figures of speech in the following passages, distinguishing the effective ones from those that are trite, inappropriate, or mixed:

1. My mother kept all her troubles bottled up inside of her until one day the bottle broke and she took to drink.

161

2. To have tackled "The Alchemist" at all and to have reached even sight of the goalpost is no mean feat.—Charles Markowitz, *New York Times* (play review)

3. Sisterhood, as introduced by the women's movement, did not fall on my parched soul like rain on a desert.—Jane Howard, *A Different Woman*

4. In all the questioning about what makes a writer, and especially perhaps the personal essayist, I have seen little reference to this fact; namely, that the brain has become a kind of unseen artist's loft. There are pictures that hang askew, pictures with outlines barely chalked in, pictures torn, pictures the artist has striven unsuccessfully to erase, pictures that only emerge and glow in a certain light. They have all been teleported, stolen, as it were, out of time. They represent no longer the sequential flow of ordinary memory.—Loren Eiseley, *All the Strange Hours*

5. Her eyes were deep pools of blue, her cheeks were roses without thorns, her lips were like cherries without pits.

6. And with her good slice of the paternal mind, she had also been burdened with a slice of the paternal temper which took the unlovely form of bursting into tears when her feelings were hurt or even stamping her feet on the floor.—Louis Auchincloss, *Portrait in Brownstone*

7. For a moment his mind was bent to the contortions of his thought as the wall of a womb bends to the savage writhings of an unborn shark embryo at the moment of escape from the mother's darkness to the sea. But no words came out.

8. The first film was a slickly prefabricated bathtub of movie sentimentality, at the heart of which was a gallant young woman facing real hardships.—Vincent Canby, *New York Times*

9. In his youth Ted Williams was a wild young buck who got the goat of the sports writers.

10. For years my father kept too many irons in the fire, patiently hoping that one of them would bear fruit and that his ship would finally come in.

11. Snow covered the airfield.
  It had come from the north, in the mist, driven by the night wind, smelling of the sea. There it would stay all winter, threadbare on the gray earth, an icy, sharp dust; not thawing and freezing, but static like a year without seasons. The changing mist, like the smoke of war, would hang over it, swallow up now a hangar, now the radar hut, now the machines; release them piece by piece, drained of color, black carrion on a white desert.—John Le Carré, *The Looking Glass War*

12. He sprinted out of the chute like a bat out of hell and streaked like greased lightning down the straightaway.

13. It takes a long time to struggle through to your own being, to uproot all the weeds of a certain kind of education, of a certain kind of locker-room scepticism, which evolves as the barnacles of other people's experiences and of other people's prejudices begin to stick to you and imperceptibly hamper your progress.—Peter Ustinov, *Dear Me*

14. Do our brief candles shine fruitlessly in the night or do they cast a light so that others may see?

162

15. Erica and Danielle are still best friends, but their friendship now is full of Swiss-cheese holes in which sit things which cannot be discussed.—Alison Lurie, *The War Between the Tates*

SUMMARY

The discussion in this chapter cannot be reduced to a simple formula. But these generalities are safe guides if they are not taken too literally:

1. Use fresh words, not tired words, but beware of neologisms, vogue words, and straining to avoid clichés.
2. Prefer short words to long words if they will convey your meaning with equal accuracy.
3. Wherever possible, express yourself in concrete words, not in abstractions. Be wary of euphemisms.
4. Use neutral words in objective reporting, formal exposition, and logical argument; in other contexts use charged words freely without slipping into overemphatic, overloaded writing.
5. Read your paper aloud, alert to the blending of sound and sense; beware of unintentional rhymes and excessive alliteration.
6. Use similes and metaphors to make your writing more clear and concrete, not to decorate it.
7. The final test of any word or expression is this: Is it appropriate in its context?

Remember this above all: no word or phrase can, with much certainty, be labeled right or wrong, fresh or tired, too short or too long, too concrete or too abstract, neutral or charged, smooth or jarring without considering the context; and no student can learn what words mean or how they behave without alert listening and wide-ranging reading. William Hazlitt put the main lesson of this chapter briefly and simply more than a century ago: "The proper force of words lies not in the words themselves, but in their application. A word may be a fine-sounding word, of an unusual length, and very imposing from its learning and novelty, and yet in the connection in which it is introduced, may be quite pointless and irrelevant. It is not pomp or pretension, but the adaptation of the expression to the idea that clenches a writer's meaning. . . ."

EXERCISE J (Review)

After carefully considering the implications of each of the following statements, select one and, in an essay of at least 500 words, discuss it with specific illustrations from your reading and listening:

163

1. Some changes of the language are to be regretted, as they lead to false inferences, and society is always a loser by mistaking names for things. Life is a fact, and it is seldom any good arises from a misapprehension of the real circumstances under which we exist. The word "gentleman" has a positive and limited signification. It means one elevated above the mass of society by his birth, manners, attainments, character and social condition. As no civilized society can exist without these social differences, nothing is gained by denying the use of the term. If blackguards were to be called "gentlemen," and "gentlemen," "blackguards," the difference between them would be as obvious as it is to-day.—James Fenimore Cooper, *The American Democrat* (1838)

2. It is a curious fact that modern English has no general word which can be used without embarrassment to express favourable aesthetic appraisal. "Beautiful" has practically dropped out of use except in descriptions of scenery in Guide Books and the advertisements issued by travel agencies. "Pretty" is derogatory and "admirable" patronizing. None of these can be used to describe the symphonies of Brahms or the tragedies of Shakespeare. "Sublime" now sounds pompous, and "excellent" and "first class" belong to examiners. So we are reduced to saying "very good" or possibly "great."—T. D. Weldon, *The Vocabulary of Politics*

3. Remember . . . that the American vocabulary is pulverized between two stones, refinement and overstatement.—Evelyn Waugh, "An Open Letter to the Honorable Mrs. Peter Rodd (Nancy Mitford) on a Very Serious Subject," *Noblesse Oblige*

4. A word cannot be vulgarized except by being misapplied.—Leo Stein, *Appreciation*

5. . . . We must be careful to avoid thinking that, whereas poetry is a language based upon metaphor, science always gives us direct, unvarnished, prose statement. The fact is that all languages, except those of mathematics, have frequent recourse to metaphor. The scientist speaks of electric charges "attracting" or "repelling," of matter "obeying" certain laws. He finds such animistic expressions convenient. But he will use metaphor and analogy, as the poet does, not only for expressing but for discovering. Let us compare the nervous system to a clock and see what this tells us, said Descartes. Let me compare my love to a red, red rose, and see what follows, said Burns.—C. Day Lewis, "The Poet's Way of Knowledge"

6. The list of purely verbal entities which sages and ordinary people have taken seriously—sometimes seriously enough to kill and be killed for them—is almost endless. . . . —Joseph Church, *Language and the Discovery of Reality*

7. In the case of a word like *democracy,* not only is there no agreed definition, but the attempt to make one is resisted from all sides. It is almost universally felt that when we call a country democratic we are praising it: consequently the defenders of every kind of regime claim that it is a democracy, and fear that they might have to stop using the word if it were tied down to any one meaning.—George Orwell, "Politics and the English Language"

8. The copy writer cannot afford to turn up his nose at clichés. Our bread and butter comes from such tired words as "new . . . amazing . . . improved . . . easy." They may be shopworn but they work.—David Ogilvy, quoted by Peter Bart, *Saturday Review*

9. If you've just sent a youngster off to college for the first time or plan a homecoming weekend back at the old alma mater, you'll need to brush up on campus slang to be able to understand what the kids are talking about.

Some of yesterday's standbys are still around—"grinds" can be found in the library, "jocks" on the athletic field and "BMOC's" wherever the girls are, but those of you who once thought you were "hip" to collegiate "jive" will have to learn a new lingo.—Bethany Kandel, "A Parent's Guide to Collegiate 'Slanguage,' " *Family Weekly*

10. War does things to the language, and the language in revenge refuses to cooperate in helping us to understand what we are talking about.—Russell Baker, *New York Times*

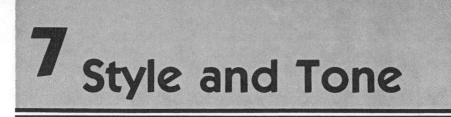

7 Style and Tone

An author's style is his written voice; his
spirit and mind caught in ink.
> *John Mason Brown*

He who has nothing to assert has no style
and can have none; he who has something to
assert will go as far in power of style as its
momentousness and his conviction will
carry him.
> *Bernard Shaw*

There are styles, but no style; there are great
styles and there are little ones: there are also
non-styles.
> *J. Middleton Murry*

WHAT IS STYLE?

In the broad sense in which the word is used in this chapter, *style* means
the way thought is expressed in writing. Much of this book is about
style. The general topics of the first two chapters; the organization of
paragraphs; sentence structure, especially the problems of length,
economy, variety, and emphasis; the choice of words and figures of
speech; even the most mechanical aspects of grammar, punctuation,
and spelling—all are matters of style. Thus this chapter, though it may
introduce you to several new concepts, should be a useful review of
some of the important aspects of good writing.

In the vast literature on the subject of style, three critical com-
monplaces appear again and again, each represented by a quotation at
the beginning of this chapter:

1. Style reflects the writer's individuality Buffon's time-worn
epigram—"the style is the man himself"—may be an oversimplification. Some good writing is meant to be impersonal, and not much writing has such a distinctly personal trademark as a typical passage by
Charles Lamb, Henry James, James Joyce, or William Faulkner. It
would not always be accurate, even if it were tactful, for the instructor
to say to the college freshman, "This is a dull theme because you are a
dull person." But in the long run, you reveal yourself on paper whether
you mean to or not—your sincerity or insincerity, your interest or lack
of interest in the subject, your sense of humor, your powers of observa-

tion, your moral and intellectual standards, your intelligence, the limitations of your whole view of life. You reveal yourself, at least in intermittent glimpses, not only in what you say but in how you say it. "An author's style *is* his written voice; his spirit and mind caught in ink." This should be a sobering thought to any writer, especially to the student who naively assumes that the year's written exercises reflect nothing more than ability to write "correct English." It also suggests that there is a limit to what you can learn by consciously aping the style of any other writer.

2. A writer should have something to say before considering the style in which to say it   "He who has nothing to assert has no style and can have none; he who has something to assert will go as far in power of style as its momentousness and his conviction will carry him." Perhaps Shaw's comment, made with his customary cocksureness, underestimates the conscious artistry behind good writing. It doesn't follow that a student with something worth saying will inevitably write in a style worth reading. But the essential point is clear. An effective prose style is not a mechanical mannerism that can be turned on like a spigot, or a collection of glittering ornaments to hang on the bare limbs of sentences. It grows naturally out of the writer's thoughts instead of being superimposed upon them. No good writer puts style before substance; no one can succeed in developing a manner that will compensate completely for the absence of matter. (See pp. 5–6)

3. The appropriateness of any style varies in accordance with the time, place, occasion, subject, the reader addressed, and the writer's purpose   As the quotation from J. Middleton Murry implies, there is no eternally suitable style. When responsible critics speak of the prose style of nineteenth-century English literature, they can only be generalizing about a kind of writing that was common at that time in England, as opposed to the general tendencies of the eighteenth or the twentieth century. When they speak of the style of Carlyle, they can only be alluding to the tendencies that most clearly distinguish "a characteristic" work by Carlyle from one by, say, Arnold or Newman. Although the style of any good writer may clearly show the imprint of the writer's age and country, as well as of the individual personality, it will naturally change in accordance with the particular occasion, the subject the writer has chosen, the reader for whom the work is intended, and the purpose it is meant to achieve. When he aimed only to clarify a scientific principle for workingmen, Thomas Henry Huxley could write the plainest down-to-earth prose (see p. 150); when he mounted a rostrum to spread the gospel of evolution, he sometimes soared away on the wings of rhetoric. The significant relation of style to purpose can be seen in the complex plan of Bonamy Dobrée's book *Modern Prose Style*. He devotes separate sections to "Descriptive," "Explanatory," and "Emotive" prose; and under "Explanatory Prose" he discusses the different styles appropriate to Science, Law, Philosophy, Morals, Theology, Political Science, History, and Literary Criticism.

The problem is not to cultivate a style and cling to it stubbornly regardless of what you are writing, where, when, for whom, and why. The problem is to find the right balance between the aim and the art, between the idea or emotion and the language chosen to convey it. *Reduced to its lowest terms, a good style is an appropriate adjustment of the means to the end.*

The Plain and Ornate Styles

Sooner or later most discussions of prose style arrive at an arbitrary distinction between two broad areas of writing. Matthew Arnold called them "Attic prose" and "Asiatic." Cyril Connolly distinguished between the "vernacular" manner and the "Mandarin." in this chapter they will be called "plain" and "ornate." Each has its virtues and its dangers; neither is either good or bad until writing makes it so. By examining a series of passages which have been chosen to represent both kinds, you should learn to distinguish between them in your own reading and begin to apply useful tests of style to your writing.

Read the following passages aloud:

I ate the ham and eggs and drank the beer. The ham and eggs were in a round dish—the ham underneath and the eggs on top. It was very hot and at the first mouthful I had to take a drink of beer to cool my mouth. I was hungry and I asked the waiter for another order. I drank several glasses of beer. I was not thinking at all but read the paper of the man opposite me. It was about the break through on the British front. When he realized I was reading the back of his paper he folded it over. I thought of asking the waiter for a paper, but I could not concentrate. It was hot in the cafe and the air was bad. Many of the people at the tables knew one another. There were several card games going on. The waiters were busy bringing drinks from the bar to the tables. Two men came in and could find no place to sit. They stood opposite the table where I was. I ordered another beer. I was not ready to leave yet. It was too soon to go back to the hospital. I tried not to think and to be perfectly calm. The men stood around but no one was leaving, so they went out. I drank another beer. There was quite a pile of saucers now on the table in front of me. The man opposite me had taken off his spectacles, put them away in a case, folded his paper and put it in his pocket and now sat holding his liqueur glass and looking out at the room. Suddenly I knew I had to get back. I called the waiter, paid the reckoning, got into my coat, put on my hat and started out the door. I walked through the rain up to the hospital.—Ernest Hemingway, *A Farewell to Arms*

And for a moment all the silver space was printed with the thousand forms of himself and Ben. There, by the corner in from Academy Street, Eugene watched his own approach; there, by the City Hall, he strode with lifted knees; there, by the curb upon the step, he stood, peopling the night with the great lost legion of himself—the thousand forms that came, that passed, that wove and shifted in unending change, and that remained unchanging Him.

And through the Square, unwoven from lost time, the fierce bright horde of Ben spun in and out its deathless loom. Ben, in a thousand moments, walked the Square: Ben of the lost years, the forgotten days, the unremembered hours; prowled by the moonlit facades; vanished, returned, left and rejoined himself, was one and many—deathless Ben in search of the lost dead lusts, the finished enterprise, the unfound door—unchanging Ben multiplying himself in form, by all the brick facades entering and coming out.

And as Eugene watched the army of himself and Ben, which were not ghosts, and which were lost, he saw himself—his son, his boy, his lost and virgin flesh—come over past the fountain, leaning against the loaded canvas bag, and walking down with rapid crippled stride past Gant's toward Niggertown in young pre-natal dawn. And as he passed the porch where he sat watching, he saw the lost child-face below the lumpy ragged cap, drugged in the magic of unheard music, listening for the far-forested horn-note, the speechless almost captured pass-word. The fast boy-hands folded the fresh sheets, but the fabulous lost face went by, steeped in its incantations.—Thomas Wolfe, *Look Homeward, Angel.*

Each of those passages comes near the dramatic close of a celebrated American novel published in 1929. Each passage portrays a moment of intense emotion in the life of the hero. Frederic Henry in *A Farewell to Arms* is trying to eat a calm supper between visits to the nearby hospital, where Catherine Barkley, who has just borne his child, is on the threshold of death. Eugene Gant in *Look Homeward, Angel* wanders in a dream through the city square of his birthplace, haunted by the inescapable memories of his dead brother. But there the resemblance ends. The ear alone can catch much of the difference. In the Hemingway passage the sentences are short and jerky; they are free from the traditional devices of platform rhetoric; their rhythm is the staccato pace of rapid conversation. Wolfe's sentences are long and swinging. He freely uses calculated repetition ("There, by the corner . . . Eugene watched . . . there, by the City Hall, he strode . . . there, by the curb . . . he stood"; "Ben, in a thousand moments . . . Ben of the lost years, the forgotten days, the unremembered hours . . . deathless Ben in search of the lost dead lusts . . . unchanging Ben multiplying himself in form"). Through his sentences sweeps the music of a meter that soars above the irregular rhythms of conversation—time-honored blank verse (unrhymed iambic pentameter—see p. 155).

And for a moment all the silver space . . .
there, by the curb upon the step, he stood . . .
that wove and shifted in unending change. . . .
And through the Square, unwoven from lost time,
the fierce bright horde of Ben spun in and out
its deathless loom. Ben, in a thousand moments . . . ;
Ben of the lost years, the forgotten days . . .

his son, his boy, his lost and virgin flesh . . .
leaning against the loaded canvas bag,
and walking down with rapid crippled stride . . .
toward Niggertown in young pre-natal dawn. . . .

Even a superficial glance at the diction reveals a similar contrast. The first passage contains only one phrase (*paid the reckoning*) that might not fit naturally into the relaxed pattern of everyday talk. In fact, there isn't a single living metaphor in the entire passage. The quotation from Wolfe is a rich tapestry of metaphor: "all the silver space was printed with the thousand forms of himself and Ben"; "peopling the night with the great lost legion of himself"; "the fierce bright horde of Ben spun in and out its deathless loom"; "in young pre-natal dawn"—to mention a random handful. It is not hard to see why a good-sized anthology has been quarried from the "poetical passages" in Wolfe's novels and short stories.

But it would be misleading to characterize the Hemingway passage as prosaic. For it conveys an underlying emotion that is intensified by the contrast with the matter-of-factness on the surface. In this selection Hemingway derives much of his effect from what he leaves unsaid. He soft-pedals the feelings of his hero, whereas Wolfe pulls out most of the stops. Hemingway understates, or at most merely states; Wolfe consistently overstates. Hemingway relies for effect on the eloquence of stark simplicity, Wolfe on the rhetorical artifice of traditional poetry or "poetic prose." The passage from *A Farewell to Arms* is written in a plain style, the passage from *Look Homeward, Angel* in an ornate style.

As a second illustration of the difference between the plain and ornate styles, consider passages from two different books by the same writer:

I continued in this unpretentious situation for nearly a year. However, by being so long in the lowest form I gained an immense advantage over the cleverer boys. They all went on to learn Latin and Greek and splendid things like that. But I was taught English. We were considered such dunces that we could learn only English. Mr. Somervell—a most delightful man, to whom my debt is great—was charged with the duty of teaching the stupidest boys the most disregarded thing—namely, to write mere English. He knew how to do it. He taught it as no one else has ever taught it. Not only did we learn English parsing thoroughly, but we also practised continually English analysis. Mr. Somervell had a system of his own. He took a fairly long sentence and broke it up into its components by means of black, red, blue, and green inks. Subject, verb, object: Relative Clauses, Conditional Clauses, Conjunctive and Disjunctive Clauses! Each had its colour and its bracket. It was a kind of drill. We did it almost daily. As I remained in the Third Fourth . . . three times as long as anyone else, I had three times as much of it. I learned it thoroughly. Thus I got into my bones the essential structure of the ordinary British sentence—which is a noble thing. And when in after years my school-fellows who had won prizes and distinction for writing such beautiful Latin poetry and pithy Greek epigrams had to come down again to common English, to earn their living or make their way, I did not

170

feel myself at any disadvantage. Naturally I am biassed in favor of boys learning English. I would make them all learn English: and then I would let the clever ones learn Latin as an honour, and Greek as a treat. But the only thing I would whip them for is not knowing English. I would whip them hard for that.— Winston Churchill, *My Early Life, A Roving Commission*

I have myself, full confidence that if all do their duty, if nothing is neglected, and if the best arrangements are made, as they are being made, we shall prove ourselves once again able to defend our Island home, to ride out the storm of war, and to outlive the menace of tyranny, if necessary for years, if necessary alone. At any rate, that is what we are going to try to do. That is the resolve of His Majesty's Government—every man of them. That is the will of Parliament and the nation. The British Empire and the French Republic, linked together in their cause and in their need, will defend to the death their native soil, aiding each other like good comrades to the utmost of their strength. Even though large tracts of Europe and many old and famous States have fallen or may fall into the grip of the Gestapo and all the odious apparatus of Nazi rule, we shall not flag or fail. We shall go on to the end, we shall fight in France, we shall fight on the seas and oceans, we shall fight with growing confidence and growing strength in the air, we shall defend our Island, whatever the cost may be, we shall fight on the beaches, we shall fight on the landing grounds, we shall fight in the fields and in the streets, we shall fight in the hills; we shall never surrender, and even if, which I do not for a moment believe, this Island or a large part of it were subjugated and starving, then our Empire beyond the seas, armed and guarded by the British Fleet, would carry on the struggle, until, in God's good time, the New World, with all its power and might, steps forth to the rescue and the liberation of the old.—Winston Churchill, *Blood, Sweat, and Tears*

In one of the more peaceful chapters of a book of reminiscences, where the thunder roll of the rostrum would be highly inappropriate, Churchill could write plain, relaxed prose with the flavor of genuine, if somewhat genteel, conversation. When he faced the House of Commons in a critical hour after the retreat from Dunkirk, he rose to the historic occasion. The carefully wrought balance and rhythm of the longer sentences; the richly charged words (*duty, resolve, His Majesty's Government, British Empire, native soil, struggle, New World, power, might, rescue, liberation*); the taut alliterative phrases (*do their duty, nothing is neglected, defend to the death, grip of the Gestapo, flag or fail, subjugated and starving*); above all, the lavish expenditure of repetition—these are marks of the oratorical grand manner—a variety of ornate style.

Churchillian oratory is a dying art in these days when political prima donnas are carefully rouged and powdered for television to represent the epitome of folksy informality. Again the discussion comes back to appropriateness. This book has been slanted in favor of the plain style partly because the most characteristic American prose in the second half of the twentieth century is plain and unadorned, partly because the ornate style is inappropriate to the subjects on which the college undergraduate usually writes. A simple narrative, a simple piece of description, a simple explanation of an idea or a process—to deck these out in the grand manner, whether in an English course or a course in reinforced concrete, is like hiring a symphony orchestra to play a folk song or mounting a platform to harangue friends in your own living room.

Flat Writing and Fine Writing

It is important to remember that the plain style is seldom as simple as it appears. The trick is not to ignore art, but to conceal it: to create the illusion of artlessness. Hemingway's simplicity is misleading, as many of his imitators have learned to their sorrow. A careful examination of the first passage from Winston Churchill gives the game away. Listen again to these four sentences: "They all went on to learn Latin and Greek and splendid things like that. But I was taught English. We were considered such dunces that we could learn only English. Mr. Somervell—a most delightful man, to whom my debt is great—was charged with the duty of teaching the stupidest boys the most disregarded thing—namely, to write mere English." After the sentence about the splendors of Latin and Greek, the brief second sentence is a calculated anticlimax. The repetition of *English*, *only English*, and *mere English* is obviously no accident. Here is a schoolboy at England's fashionable Harrow in 1887 who is denied the traditional privilege of wrestling with the classics in company with his more scholarly classmates and is penalized with a triple exposure to—of all things—his native tongue, English. Imagine that! From his perspective of 1930 the author is enjoying the wonder of it, and he wants the reader to enjoy it too. Thus the drill with Mr. Somervell becomes, not a prosaic statement of fact, but a varicolored miracle. In a series of blunt short sentences Churchill carefully emphasizes his teacher's thoroughness ("He knew how to do it. He taught it as no one else has ever taught it. . . . It was a kind of drill. We did it almost daily. . . . I learned it thoroughly"). By the time he comes to the key sentence ("Thus I got into my bones the essential structure of the ordinary British sentence—which is a noble thing"), the reader is prepared for the trenchant metaphor and the romantic adjective *noble*. But this is not all. The writer must clinch the paradox of a triumph born in defeat by contrasting the solid, practical value of "common English" (the phrase is obviously ironic by now) with the elegant veneer of "such beautiful Latin poetry and pithy Greek epigrams" (equally ironic). And in driving home the point, again he resorts to repetition: "Naturally I am biassed in favor of boys learning English. I would make them all learn English. . . . the only thing I would whip them for is not knowing English. I would whip them hard for that." In its way, this plain paragraph is as artfully contrived as the impassioned oration after Dunkirk.

Reduce this passage to a mere statement of essential facts and what do you get?

I was so stupid in school that while all the bright boys were learning Latin and Greek, I had to study English. My teacher, Mr. Somervell, was a good English teacher, and he taught me grammar very thoroughly. When I grew up, I found that I was just as well off as my classmates, who had to learn English after all to get ahead in life. Latin and Greek are all right in their place, but I think everyone should be made to learn English.

Simple, natural, clear, correct English—but completely without flavor. The plain style doesn't have to be a bald style. *Good plain writing is not flat writing.*

At the other extreme, if you attempt an ornate prose style, you must beware of "fine writing." In this phrase, the adjective is ironic; the label is commonly applied to the false notes struck by writers who struggle so hard to be vivid or eloquent or "poetic" that they completely ignore the importance of saying simple things simply. Murry calls fine writing "a miserable procession of knock-kneed, broken-winded metaphors with a cruel cartload of ponderous unmeaning polysyllables dragging behind them."

An intelligent college freshman, who eventually learned to write with admirable simplicity, launched his first theme with this fanfare:

At my arrival at college I gazed in open-mouthed naiveté after the manner of all freshmen, at the spectacular galaxy of character and personality, including the best and the worst, the most common and the most unique that paradoxical humanity has to offer its apprentices. It was not until several months after my violent introduction into this seething maelstrom in which learning battles ignorance that I got a finger-hold on the drifting straw of perception and was carried to an elusive conclusion on which to buoy my mental weight. I found that I had lost my inspiration where the road forks toward wisdom or knowledge. This change of attitude altered my conviction that knowledge is the doorway to accomplishment and showed me that knowledge is merely the key to the door of the palace of wisdom. This ideal thrusts me far back into the kindergarten of wisdom's school. I find that I am not well on the road to education, but merely on a footpath leading to the highway of wisdom. Truly, I cannot expect startling and spectacular revelations at every bend in the road, but the trek to wisdom is a gratifying journey.

You have been warned against this sort of writing in the remarks on "Naturalness" in the first chapter (pp. 20–21). The student paragraph is bad writing because it is not natural; it is too self-consciously "literary." The genuine emotion is not strong enough to carry the heavy cargo of metaphors.

A less contrived example reveals a common symptom of fine writing, *adjectivitis*:

The *blue-green* waves from the lake can be heard as you approach the *rustic* cabin. In the midst of a *fragrant* pine forest the *contented* cabin rests, keeping a *watchful* eye on the *turbulent* lake. Located in a *remote* cove far from the *aimless* rushing of *little* men, the *lonely* cabin presents a *quiet, peaceful* scene to the *unwary* traveler as he seeks *blessed* relief from the *endless* ratrace of the *dusty* metropolis.

Apparently in an honest effort to use specific details in description, the student writes as if compelled by some sacred law to furnish every noun with one or more adjectives selected at random regardless of accuracy or economy. Competing with each other for the reader's attention, the adjectives weaken the nouns they are meant to support. The result is not only monotonous to the ear but confusing to the eye—a clutter of details without harmony or focus.

Gobbledygook (Jargon)

Self-consciousness about style may result in unnatural writing. But complete indifference to style may leave the writer an easy prey to a disease that has become increasingly fashionable in recent years. In a lecture published in 1916, Sir Arthur Quiller-Couch called it *jargon*. In a blast from Washington in 1944, Maury Maverick brought it out of the Freshman English laboratory and renamed it *gobbledygook* (also spelled *gobbledegook*). Because it also refers to the restricted vocabulary of a special group, the word *jargon* is misleading as a synonym for gibberish-in-general. Gobbledygook, an onomatopoetic imitation of the gobbling of a Texas turkey, has apparently found a permanent place in the language.

When the symptoms of gobbledygook are isolated, they turn out to be time-honored failings of bad writing that English instructors have been fighting for decades. But they are especially prominent in the writing of experts, who have never learned or have forgotten the lessons of Freshman English. Since most college undergraduates will some day be experts in something, gobbledygook is analyzed here as a final review and a warning (the reader of the "improved" versions must remember that genuine gobbledygook defies accurate translation):

1. Involved sentence structure

GOBBLEDYGOOK   It is difficult to find a word which expresses the whole self which is involved here as clearly and intelligibly as *behavior* and *attitude* describe the parts of the self which are involved in the first two learning reactions I have illustrated.

IMPROVED   It is hard to find a word expressing the whole self as accurately as *behavior* and *attitude* describe the parts of the self involved in the first two learning reactions illustrated.

This is a relatively inoffensive example, but the Chinese box construction (*which*-within-*which*-within-*which*) presents the reader with a puzzle, not a clear statement.

174

2. Unnecessary repetition

GOBBLEDYGOOK   A contract shall be considered a single premium life insurance or endowment contract if substantially all the premiums on such contract are paid within a period of four years from the date on which the contract is purchased.

IMPROVED   A single premium life insurance or endowment contract is one on which most of the premiums are paid within four years of its purchase date.

3. Circumlocutions

GOBBLEDYGOOK   Wherever children are dealt with by schools or other agencies, there has been relatively little clarity in making the differentiation as to whether the problem is primarily a lack of intrinsic stuff or whether the primary problem is a disorder in capacity to form relationships.

IMPROVED   Wherever schools or other agencies deal with a child, it is seldom clear whether his primary problem is a lack of intelligence or an inability to form relationships.

Experts in gobbledygook display a special fondness for the passive voice (see pp. 99–100): "It must be recognized that"; "It can be observed that"; "The taxpayer's home address must be supplied and a permanent business address may be added." They also like circumlocutions pivoting on the word *case* (see p. 99): When the authors of tax forms write, "In the case of a husband and wife living together," they apparently mean, "When a husband and wife live together"; when they write, "Except in the case of amounts attributable to deductions," they mean simply, "Except for amounts attributable to deductions." Other circumlocutions abound in the gobbledygook jungle: *due to the fact that* means *because; to the extent that* sprawls in place of *if; for the purpose of determining* equals *to determine; prior to* and *subsequent to* mean *before* and *after;* a human being cannot merely *know*, but must *be cognizant of;* cannot *believe*, but must *be of the opinion;* does not *pay*, but *makes payment of;* property is not *bought*, it is *acquired by purchase.* The list is endless.

4. A gobbledygook vocabulary

When concrete nouns are replaced by abstractions, simple words by pseudotechnical jargon, the result is gobbledygook.

GOOBLEDYGOOK   Two important factors constitute the grounds for the uniqueness of supervision as educational method: first, the content of social case work and its training goals for the worker; and second, the learning situation composed of two people, a supervisor and a student, instead of a class situation.

IMPROVED   In two important ways supervision in social case work differs from other teaching: (1) the worker has different problems and training goals; and (2) the teacher has only one student instead of an entire class.

In its garb of gobbledygook, that relatively unobjectionable passage has an awesome academic air. Eliminate the pseudotechnical jargon (*factors*, a favorite in gobbledygook; *learning situation; class situation*) and the assertion is absurdly simple.

Gobbledygook experts not only replace short, concrete words with long, abstract synonyms, but have a deplorable habit of stretching words like rubber by adding unnecessary syllables: *analysization* for *analysis, certificate* for *certify, orientate* for *orient, origination* for *origin, summarization* for *summary*. They freely fabricate unnecessary verbs in *-ize* (see p. 135). They are especially fond of *cobblestone rhetoric* (see p. 153): deprive them of the abstract nouns ending in *-ion* and *-ation* and they are inarticulate:

GOBBLEDYGOOK   In each semester in every higher institution, a relatively small proportion of students tends to consume a disproportionate amount of institutional effort for a variety of reasons. These causes may have been nonexistent or impossible to discern and unpredictable as of the date of the student's admission. The consequences appear as unsatisfactory deviations from original reasonable expectations of the University and of the student and parents. On the basis of the propositions that "a stitch in time saves nine" and "an ounce of prevention is worth a pound of cure," it is clearly desirable that such deviates be identified as early as possible as a first step in the direction of remedy of the unsatisfactory situation.

In view of the foregoing, your cooperation is hereby invoked as follows: If (and when) you observe in student performance indications which point your thought toward this request, pencil an informal memorandum including the student's name and an outline of your observation and send it to this office through campus mail. Or, if you prefer, telephone 6-4831.

IMPROVED   I would like you to help me find problem students so that I can help them before it is too late. If you know of any, will you please write me a note or phone 6-4381?

There are many species of the genus gobbledygook. The dean's memorandum just quoted is a mixture of *Pedagese*, the jargon of experts in education (*institutional effort, deviations from original expectations, remedy of the unsatisfactory situation*) and *Officialese*, the private language of bureaucrats big and little (*as of the date of, on the basis of the propositions, in view of the foregoing, is hereby invoked*). Pedagese is merely one branch of the tangled tree of academic jargon; psychologists, anthropologists, sociologists, literary critics, and linguists can write equally offensive prose. Officialese is related to *Commercialese*, the jargon of business, and both are close relatives of *Legalese*. *Journalese*, which typically reveals a snappier, more economic style than true gobbledygook, is a distant cousin of the rest. Other species are being identified and labeled—usually with *ese*—as fast as they invade the private gardens of the proliferating specialists. One of the more recent—christened *Spacespeak* in the *New York Times*—mixes the breezy shop-talk of the new technology (*Go, Go-no-Go, no-Go*) with the professional pretentiousness more common in gobbledygook (*affirmative* for *yes; negative* for *no; achieve orbital insertion* for *go into orbit; the launch vehicle has acquired a malfunction* for *something is wrong with the rocket; effect egress* for *get out*).

Obviously an expert should not be condemned for using technical terms intelligently, especially when writing for other experts. Genuine technical terms are more accurate, less ambiguous than the lay synonyms. It is often hard for the layman to distinguish between the indispensable language of technical precision and the verbal sludge resulting from professional snobbery, indiscriminate parroting, or the conscious effort to puzzle the reader with bafflegab. But experts should not become so completely dependent on technical language that they are unable to make sense to anyone who has not been initiated into the cult. No writer should habitually use high-sounding pseudotechnical jargon when familiar words will accurately convey the meaning. The psychiatrist who indiscriminately calls every quirk a *complex*, every worry a *neurosis*, every dislike a *phobia*, every insecure person *paranoid* is not obsessed by a semantic fixation, but is merely in a verbal rut.

The gobbledygook vocabulary of special groups is at its most annoying when it turns up in the general vocabulary. The executive may find it hard to carry on without *contacting prospects* about a *deal*; the lawyer may be unable to avoid occasional reference to *the aforesaid party of the first part*; the bureaucrat may be lost without *personnel*, the engineer without *factors*, the educationist without *classroom situation*. But the rest of us can leave this jargon generously to the experts.

The relation of technical jargon to gobbledygook has been emphasized because many undergraduates assume that as soon as they survive the elementary English courses of the first two years and enter the ranks of the majors, they can stop writing English and begin writing Economics, or Psychology, or Sociology, or Law. An expert understanding of the jargon of a single field presumably gives them a special license to violate the law of saying simple things simply. But genuinely distinguished people are seldom victims of this illusion. Take this passage, for example:

Persecution for the expression of opinions seems to me perfectly logical. If you have no doubt of your premises or your power and want a certain result with all your heart, you naturally express your wishes in law and sweep away all opposition. To allow opposition by speech seems to indicate that you think the speech impotent, as when a man says that he has squared the circle, or that you do not care wholeheartedly for the result, or that you doubt either your power or your premises. But when men have realized that time has upset many fighting faiths, they may come to believe, even more than they believe the very foundations of their own conduct, that the ultimate good desired is better reached by free trade in ideas—that the best test of truth is the power of the thought to get itself accepted in the competition of the market, and that truth is the only ground upon which their wishes safely can be carried out. That, at any rate, is the theory of our Constitution. It is an experiment, as all life is an experiment. Every year, if not every day, we have to wager our salvation upon some prophecy based upon imperfect knowledge. While the experiment is part of our system, I think that we should be eternally vigilant against attempts to check the expression of opinions that we loathe and believe to be fraught with death, unless they so imminently threaten immediate interference with the lawful and pressing purposes of the law that an immediate check is required to save the country.—Justice Oliver Wendell Holmes, Dissenting Opinion, *Abrams v. United States* (250 U.S. 616), 1919

There is a paragraph by an expert. The most distinguished jurist of his time, he could easily have cluttered up the page with *whereas's* and *aforesaid*'s, learned parenthetical allusions and high-sounding legal abstractions. Instead, he wrote simply, directly, concretely, without pomp or pretense, and gave posterity one of the clearest statements on one of the most important problems of civilized government.

Nobody has to write gobbledygook, not even an expert.

WHAT IS TONE?

In considering the elements that contribute to the choice of an appropriate style, tone was intentionally omitted, for it demands a more detailed discussion. It can be roughly defined as the writer's attitude toward the material as it is reflected in the style. Tone is obviously related to the writer's mood, for the temper of an angry person will probably color that person's writing. It is also related to the attitude toward the reader: a writer of children's books who overestimates the innocence of the audience will almost certainly write in a tone of cute condescension.

Tone, like style, strongly reflects the writer's individuality and varies widely with time, place, occasion, subject, and purpose. The denotation and connotation of the words chosen, their position and interrelation in the sentence, the length and rhythm of the sentences, the role played by figures of speech—these are the important clues to tone as well as to style. But to diagnose the one is not to identify the other. A piece of plain prose may convey a tone that is gay or somber, literal or ironic, sentimental or cynical, smug or modest, reverent or mocking, apprehensive or complacent, tough or tender—tones are as various as human attitudes and the adjectives that describe them.

No student is unaware of the importance of tone in everyday speech. "Are you kidding?" "Can he possibly be serious about that?" "She couldn't have meant what she said." Even when we can actually hear the sound of the voice and see the accompanying gesture or look—the shrug of the shoulders, the gleam in the eye—we are sometimes at a loss to catch the exact tone. But the transition from listening to reading, from warm speech to cold print, creates more dilemmas. As every politician must learn the hard way, a casual quip tossed off in the presence of reporters can appear in the headlines like an earnest pronouncement and mark the politician as a victim of foot-in-mouth disease. As every letter writer should know, the problem of tone looms larger as soon as the typewriter replaces the tongue. To write a sincere thank-you note for a useless wedding present or after a boring weekend; a letter of condolence that is neither cold nor trite; a friendly letter that catches the familiar flow of talk with the same friend; or a business letter that is direct but not blunt, courteous but not oily—these are all problems of tone as well as style. The tone of your writing reflects not only your command of language but the extent of your tact and your taste.

In listening and reading, you cannot ignore tone. In speaking and writing, you can try—unsuccessfully—to evade it by being always serious, literal, impersonal—and dull. But to write well you must learn to detect tone in your reading and control it in your writing. You can make a good beginning by carefully analyzing the tone of some representative passages of prose.

Examples of Tone

Here are two passages of student writing, both reminiscences of childhood:

His house rested on the adjoining hill. It was a small frame house, amply windowed, with a large, red-roofed porch to one side. The placement of the structure was such that the sloping ground to all sides gave it a certain eminence by exaggerating its not unusual height. The boy had a den beneath the porch which was referred to principally as "the cave." It was a black hole—at least half carved from the cold, musty earth itself. It had the smell of dampness and mold, and to be there was like being buried alive. Its drafts covered you. Its rawness ate beneath your skin. The boy loved it there, but often when he entered, his flashlight caught the shoe string tails of rats scampering nervously into the shadows. Often the gang—that was Jim and Chuck and Dick—held meetings there, in which they burned candles and sat shivering as the restless light did things to their faces. But the cave was not important only for the atmosphere it evoked. It was also unsurpassed as a hiding place for certain invaluables. The various nooks and crannies concealed obscure literature which dealt intimately with the great, the infinite, the mysterious. There was a book on black magic which explained the complex symbolism of beech trees and disclosed the variety of effects arising from the intelligent employment of two aspen limbs and a dead rat. The most valuable possession of all, however, was a fifty-page picture playground in which the sun-bronzed students of Charles Atlas paraded in spotted skins, cloths and belts. The mighty man himself was on one of the pages—his seventeen-inch arm cocked like a steel spring. He could pull a freight car as most men would pull a wagon. Tenpenny nails became like rubber under his grip. His signature was as forceful as a slap in the face and it seemed chiseled into the page. This was the greatest man in the world. A book on crime detection was also of unusual interest. It told how criminals are brought to justice by means of fingerprints. Crime does not pay, it said. Toward the front cover was a picture of a woman gangster. She had a rather sweet face, and Chuck said she looked like Mrs. Kuntz (Mrs. Kuntz lived up by the hospital and was having trouble with Mr. Kuntz at the time). Because of the atmosphere and the treasures it held, the cave was a big part of the boy's life. It excited him like Stevenson's picture. It was dark and changeful. It was the Soho Street of Mr. Hyde.

In an effort to supplement the family income and earn the dime the Saturday matinee at the Wilbur cost, my brother and I once organized a popcorn company. I say we organized it, but the organization took place only after my mother bought fourteen gross of the stuff and told us we were going to sell it.

I was to be district vice-president in charge of salesmen. Brother was to be president in charge of business in the home office. This meant I would have to peddle popcorn all over the Borough while he stayed home and counted the money I was earning. I felt that this was unfair. My mother's feelings concurred with my own, so a reorganization took place. We now had two district vice-presidents, each supplied with a basket of popcorn and some change, and a new president whose duties at home would keep her from taking unfair advantage of the other two members of the company. So one bright sunny morning I sallied forth into the business world with the enthusiasm of a man who has just eaten his first mashed potato sandwich.

You who have not sold popcorn at the tender age of nine and a half cannot imagine the heart-rending anxiety I felt as I approached the door of my first would-be customer. They say a dying man will have his life flash across his mind during his last moments. They say a condemned man will repent of his sins while he walks to the electric chair. I was firmly convinced that a fate as terrible as these lay behind the door in front of me. Summoning all the courage in my quivering little body, I reached for the bell. I rang the bell. I said a prayer. My prayer was answered. Nobody came to the door. I ran down the street.

In the first example, a passage of description, the writer combines two tones: the excitement of the boy and his gang and the amusement of the adult view of childhood. Assuming the third-person viewpoint, he projects the mysterious atmosphere of the boy's special world by a skillful choice of concrete details conveying dampness, darkness, and terror. The *black hole* conjures up the horrors of Calcutta; *buried alive* could remind the reader of a story by Poe; the *burned candles* might suggest the ghostly ritual of a Gothic romance. Though some of the details may be adapted from other pictures, "the shoe string tails of rats scampering nervously into the shadows" are sketched from life. In presenting the three books from the boy's angle (though not always in his words), the writer sustains the tone of innocent excitement while intentionally amusing the adult reader with his authentic, deadpan description of their spurious contents ("This was the greatest man in the world. . . .Crime does not pay, it said"). The prosaic reference to Mrs. Kuntz takes the reader temporarily back to the commonplace adult world above ground. But the final allusions to the romance and terror of Stevenson end the paragraph on a note of eerie excitement.

The writer of the second selection—a first-person narrative—may not reveal the same talent for creating an authentic atmosphere from his imagination and observation. The tone is lighter throughout. But on a more prosaic level he too blends amusement with excitement. The amusement, as in the other student selection, lies mostly in the contrast between the worlds of the child and the adult; but here the boy is not shivering happily in a private world of his own but trembling apprehensively on his debut in the public world of the grown-ups. The plain language in the first two paragraphs conveys no atmosphere of mystery; this is the practical business world. But the deadpan reference to the specialized organization of the juvenile firm indirectly ridicules the complex hierarchies of bigger business. The excitement is turned on abruptly in the final paragraph. Here the student proves to be something of a cliché expert (*tender age, heart-rending anxiety*, the conventional last moments of the dying or condemned man, *fate as terrible, Summoning all my courage*). But though the surprise ending may not be original, it would strike many readers as an effective comic anticlimax in key with the general tone of the story.

Now consider the tone of two passages of exposition:

There is another form of willful obscurity that masquerades as aristocratic exclusiveness. The author wraps his meaning in mystery so that the vulgar shall not participate in it. His soul is a secret garden into which the elect may penetrate only after overcoming a number of perilous obstacles. But this kind of obscurity is not only pretentious; it is short-sighted. For time plays it an odd trick. If the sense is meagre time reduces it to a meaningless verbiage that no one thinks of reading. This is the fate that has befallen the lucubrations of those French writers who were seduced by the example of Guillaume Apollinaire. But occasionally it throws a sharp cold light on what had seemed profound and thus discloses the fact that these contortions of language disguised very commonplace notions.—W. Somerset Maugham, *The Summing Up*

Complexity and obscurity have professional value—they are the academic equivalents of apprenticeship rules in the building trades. They exclude the outsiders, keep down the competition, preserve the image of a privileged or priestly class. The man who makes things clear is a scab. He is criticized less for his clarity than for his treachery.

Additionally, and especially in the social sciences, much unclear writing is based on unclear or incomplete thought. It is possible with safety to be technically obscure about something you haven't thought out. It is impossible to be wholly clear on something you do not understand. Clarity thus exposes flaws in the thought. The person who undertakes to make difficult matters clear is infringing on the sovereign right of numerous economists, sociologists, and political scientists to make bad writing the disguise for sloppy, imprecise, or incomplete thought. One can understand the resulting anger. Adam Smith, John Stuart Mill, John Maynard Keynes were writers of crystalline clarity most of the time. Marx had great moments, as in *The Communist Manifesto*. Economics owes very little, if anything, to the practitioners of scholarly obscurity. If any of my California students should come to me from the learned professions, I would counsel them in all their writing to keep the confidence of their colleagues. This they should do by being always complex, always obscure, invariably a trifle vague.—John Kenneth Galbraith, "Writing, Typing, and Economics," *Atlantic*

Maugham, a highly successful story-teller and dramatist, writes in his autobiography about the "willful obscurity" by which a writer intentionally hides meaning behind a mask of "aristocratic exclusiveness." The passage is not merely a piece of straightforward exposition; it is an elegant mockery of such a writer: "His soul is a secret garden" in which "the vulgar" may not trespass. His obscurity is "not only pretentious; it is shortsighted" because in time he may have no readers for his "meaningless verbiage" or reveal only "commonplace notions" beneath his "contortions of language." Maugham consistently chooses words to sustain a tone of ironic ridicule.

A deeper irony is in the contrast between the writer's pretentions and his fate: by choosing to write obscurely, he is finally consigned to obscurity, or at best to the ranks of the profoundly simplistic.

Galbraith, a renowned economist, also ridicules obscure writers. Though he puts more emphasis on their sloppy thinking than on their pretentiousness, he too places them in an exclusive aristocracy: "a privileged or priestly class." But Galbraith departs further than Maugham from straight exposition. His irony differs not only in degree (he is more bitter) but in technique. The essence of irony is contrast. In Maugham it is the contrast between expectation and outcome—what has been called "circumstantial irony." In Galbraith the contrast is between the literal and implied meanings of the words. Like a person who, on the most miserable day in March, says "Lovely weather we're having," writers, with malice aforethought, solemnly assert what they don't believe, often say the direct opposite of what they really think. Instead of deploring complexity and obscurity directly, Galbraith appears to praise their professional value in a world where a clear writer is a "scab," guilty of "treachery" to his trade. Even after asserting directly that sloppy writing is a disguise for sloppy thinking, Galbraith apparently dignifies such language as a "sovereign right" of social scientists. After a historical reference to famous economists who were known to write clearly, he goes to the extreme of actually promising to coach his own students for success in the learned professions by advising them to be "always complex, always obscure, invariably a trifle vague."

Galbraith's promise is not as monstrous as Jonathan Swift's *Modest Proposal* for marketing infants for the table, a bitterly ironic comment on the starvation in eighteenth-century Ireland. But he uses the same ironic technique.

Hints About Tone

Although no textbook formula can teach you how to distill the subtle essences of tone in your writing, a few general hints should help:

182

1. Adopt a tone appropriate to the subject   This is really a matter of good taste. A facetious tone is hardly fitting in a funeral oration or a sober air of pedantry appropriate in a discussion of the operation of a pinball machine. A good deal of strictly informative writing, as in a piece of technical exposition, is essentially toneless; add flesh to the skeleton of facts but do not apply rouge.

2. Beware of sudden shifts of tone in the middle of a paper   Consistency of tone is as important as consistency in levels of usage. Do not burst out in a belly laugh in the midst of a serious discussion or suddenly lapse into irony after a strictly literal introduction. The reader has a right to know when the tongue is in the cheek.

3. Be personal but not familiar   One trouble with Officialese is that it is so utterly impersonal. It is a machine grinding out directives for personnel, not a human voice talking to human beings. In most undergraduate papers it is natural for students to write frankly in the first person about their own reactions, whether or not the assignment is labeled "a personal essay." Only occasionally, as in a research paper or a technical report, is a personal tone likely to be out of place. This does not mean, however, that you should treat the reader habitually as one of your chums or make every paper a chatty, friendly letter to the instructor.

4. Beware of dogmatism and false modesty   As a college undergraduate, you are not expected to write on any subject with the tone of an expert who knows all the answers. You should be wary of authoritative pronouncements and glib, unsupported generalities. These sins are committed by some college editors who, though they may be modest and unassuming in the flesh, grow strangely arrogant in print, infected by what T. S. Eliot once called "the braggadocio of the mild-mannered man safely entrenched behind his typewriter." On the other hand, you are not required to wear your ignorance and immaturity on your sleeve, hedging every assertion with a humble apology ("It seems to me"; "Of course, this is only my personal opinion as a college freshman").

5. Beware of exaggeration (hyperbole)   Exaggeration is presumably one of the traits that distinguish the boastful American from the undemonstrative Englishman. It permeates American advertising ("the longest and tastiest hot dogs east of the Rockies"). It flavors political oratory ("the most cowardly act of treason ever perpetrated against the American people since the Founding Fathers wrote the Constitution"). It is the lifeblood of newspaper reporting (college football players on Saturday afternoon become "gallant warriors locked in a titanic struggle for supremacy in the gridiron world"). It has been both the blessing and the curse of American humor ("Bless your heart. Cooper hasn't any more invention than a horse; and I don't mean a high-class horse either; I mean a clothes-horse."—Mark Twain). It oils the wheels of social intercourse ("I am eternally grateful for your fabulous hospitality"). But it is a dangerous weapon in the hands of an inexperienced writer.

By exaggerating your feeling about your alma mater, your athletic coach, or your favorite cocker spaniel, you can easily pervert genuine emotion into sentimentality. By overdramatizing a story, you can bludgeon the reader into boredom so that the big moment reads like just another incident. By overloading an argument with unqualified superlatives (*the most, the greatest, the worst*), you can leave yourself wide open to the counterpunches of a more cautious opponent. Exaggerated irony—the "oh yeah" tone that creeps into many student editorials—degenerates into sneering sarcasm. Exaggerated humor becomes tiresome farce.

Generally speaking, intelligent modern readers do not want to be written *at*. If they feel that a writer is struggling too hard to open their tear ducts or tickle their ribs, they will automatically set up a resistance to tears or laughter. A general rule follows from this: let the emotion arise naturally from an accurate presentation; infuse it into the material but don't superimpose it.

6. Handle humor with special restraint Undergraduate writing contains a great deal of genuine humor. But the weekly theme pile sometimes turns up a few students with a chronic case of wisecracking. They can't begin their autobiographical first themes without straining for something funny in the simple fact that they were born ("In the beginning, of course, I was born"; "I was born in a little log cabin which I did not help my father to build"). They can't make a serious critical comment without killing it with an adolescent quip ("If I were asked to recite a few lines from Shakespeare's plays, I couldn't do it, because my teachers have never succeeded in getting me interested in Willy's weary works"). They can't refer to a member of the faculty or student body without a pseudo-Dickensian tag name (Professor Fossilpuss, Joe Bigshot, Bessie Birdbrain). Humor to these students is a series of forced gags strung together with all the incoherence of a stand-up comic's repertoire. They have never learned the first principle of comedy: "If what you're doing is funny, you don't have to be funny doing it."

The student who wants to write humorously can learn a lot from the professional masters. Take, for example, this paragraph:

I passed all the other courses that I took at my University, but I could never pass botany. This was because all botany students had to spend several hours a week in a laboratory looking through a microscope at plant cells, and I could never see through a microscope. I never once saw a cell through a microscope.

This used to enrage my instructor. He would wander around the laboratory pleased with the progress all the students were making in drawing the involved and, so I am told, interesting structure of flower cells, until he came to me. I would just be standing there. "I can't see anything," I would say. He would begin patiently enough, explaining how anybody can see through a microscope, but he would always end up in a fury, claiming that I could *too* see through a microscope but just pretended that I couldn't. "It takes away from the beauty of flowers anyway," I used to tell him. "We are not concerned with beauty in this course," he would say. "We are concerned solely with what I may call the *mechanics* of flars." "Well," I'd say, "I can't see anything." "Try it just once again," he'd say, and I would put my eye to the microscope and see nothing at all, except now and again, a nebulous milky substance—a phenomenon of maladjustment. You were supposed to see a vivid, restless clockwork of sharply defined plant cells. "I see what looks like a lot of milk," I would tell him. This, he claimed, was the result of my not having adjusted the microscope properly; so he would readjust it for me, or rather, for himself. And I would look again and see milk.—James Thurber, *My Life and Hard Times*

There may be a trace of exaggeration in that well-known passage: possibly the author did see a cell through a microscope. But this tendency to overstatement is neatly balanced by simple statement verging on understatement. ("I would just be standing there." "And I would look again and see milk.") The author has not souped up his material with a will to move the reader to hysterics at any price. In the whole paragraph there is not a wisecrack, not a cute or clever comment, not a single smart aside. The effect is produced almost entirely by straight reporting. Whether this particular incident ever happened at Ohio State University is beside the point. It is the kind of incident that has happened in every college laboratory in the country. Thurber has let the humor rise from his material. The passage is appealing not because it is so clever but because it is so genuine.

7. Do not confuse seriousness with solemnity Frederick Lewis Allen once made a useful distinction between the *goon* and the *jigger*. "A goon is a person with a heavy touch as distinguished from a jigger, who has a light touch. While jiggers look on life with a genial eye, goons take a more stolid and literal view." Goons may have a standardized sense of humor: they can laugh long and loud at a joke—if it is properly labeled. But they are baffled by people who can see anything funny in situations or magazine cartoons that are obviously not jokes. To goons, serious writing is sober writing, and humorous writing is funny writing, and never the twain shall meet. It doesn't strike them as somewhat absurd that many a college campus has a literary magazine that must not be humorous, a humor magazine that must never be either serious or literary, and a yearbook in which the prose is all deathless because it has never been alive.

On the other hand, the playful minds of jiggers enable them to see

that a light surface tone may add life to a piece of writing that is fundamentally serious. They know that a writer can be serious without being
solemn.

Take this passage, for example:

Clearly, Thursday shouldn't throw me into a dither, but I think I know why it
does. Every waking hour of every day affects me more or less the same way. I am
constantly reminded of how little I know about the world I live in. Putting paper
into a typewriter simply emphasizes the predicament. What ought to be a
statement of truth turns into verbal manipulation of ignorance. Not that I'm
against verbal manipulation. I love puns, limericks, double-crostics. Life would
be poor without word games. But the trouble is that we are living in a world of
word games, most of them so seriously contrived that we don't take them for
games at all. We can't tell a White paper from a charade. We read something
about India or Russia without realizing that the man who wrote it didn't know
what he was talking about. He was just a monkey with the typewriter keys
falling his way. He keeps up with the fashion in words, inexorable as fashions in
lipsticks—the central fact, the foreseeable future.—Thomas Hornsby Ferril, *I
Hate Thursday*

Obviously the passage has a light surface tone. The tone is conveyed
by the colloquial contractions, the natural use of the first-person pronoun, the informal use of prepositions at the end of two sentences, the
incomplete sixth sentence, the frank affection for puns and limericks,
the candid snapshots of the writer in an undignified dither and the
monkey at the typewriter. Yet the whole point is extremely important in
an age of semantic confusion and naiveté, and the writer is evidently
serious about it. To be sure, the tone would be too light for some contexts. But it would be old-fashioned to restrict such writing to a quaint
category called the *informal* (or *personal* or *familiar*) *essay*. The light
tone has long since escaped those confines.

**8. Do not compensate for the absence of tone by over-punctu-
ating**   The discussion of punctuation (see pp. 315–338) warns against
supplying emphasis by overunderlining, excitement by scattering exclamation points, irony by tucking question marks in parentheses or
using too many quotation marks. If the words don't convey the tone you
want, rewrite the paper.

EXERCISES

A. Answer these questions about the style of each of the following passages, supporting your conclusions with specific illustrations: (1) Is the writing plain or ornate? (2) If plain, is it effective or merely flat? (3) If ornate, is it
genuinely eloquent or is it "fine writing"? (4) Is the writer's style appropriate to
the apparent purpose?

186

1. Before constructing an imaginary life history of a typical wave, we need to become familiar with some of its physical characteristics. A wave has height, from trough to crest. It has length, the distance from its crest to that of the following wave. The period of the wave refers to the time required for succeeding crests to pass a fixed point. None of these dimensions is static; all change, but bear definite relations to the wind, the depth of the water, and many other matters. Furthermore, the water that composes a wave does not advance with it across the sea; each water particle describes a circular or elliptical orbit with the passage of the wave form, but returns very nearly to its original position. And it is fortunate that this is so, for if the huge masses of water that comprise a wave actually moved across the sea, navigation would be impossible. Those who deal professionally in the lore of waves make frequent use of a picturesque expression—the "length of fetch." The "fetch" is the distance that the waves have run, under the drive of a wind blowing in a constant direction, without obstruction. The greater the fetch, the higher the waves. Really large waves cannot be generated within the confined space of a bay or a small area. A fetch of perhaps 600 to 800 miles, with winds of gale velocity, is required to get up the largest ocean waves.— Rachel Carson, *The Sea Around Us*

2. We Americans have at last chosen sides; we believe that it may be idle to seek the Soul of Man outside Society; it is certainly idle to seek Society outside the Soul of Man. We believe this to be the transcendent stake; we will not turn back; in the heavens we have seen the sign in which we shall conquer or die. But our faith will need again and again to be refreshed; and from the life we commemorate today we may gain refreshment. A great people does not go to its leaders for incantations or liturgies by which to propitiate fate or to cajole victory; it goes to them to peer into the recesses of its own soul, to lay bare its deepest desires; it goes to them as it goes to its poets and its seers. And for that reason it means little in what form this man's message may have been; only the substance of it counts. If I have read it aright, this was that substance. "You may build your Towers of Babel to the clouds; you may contrive ingeniously to circumvent Nature by devices beyond even the understanding of all but a handful; you may provide endless distractions to escape the tedium of your barren lives; you may rummage the whole planet for your ease and comfort. It shall avail you nothing; the more you struggle, the more deeply you will be enmeshed. Not until you have the courage to meet yourselves face to face; to take true account of what you find; to respect the sum of that account for itself and not for what it may bring you; deeply to believe that each of you is a holy vessel unique and irreplaceable; only then will you have taken the first steps along the path of Wisdom. Be content with nothing less; let not the heathen beguile you to their temples, or the Sirens with their songs. Lay up your Treasure in the Heaven of your hearts, where moth and rust do not corrupt and thieves cannot break through and steal."—Judge Learned Hand, "Mr. Justice Brandeis" (at a memorial service in the Supreme Court), *The Spirit of Liberty*

3. The springs of your body release. You hurtle into the blast. Your ears "pop" in the sudden pressure. Your body falls and starts to turn. Then, with a sudden jerk, your body is stopped and yanked upright. Your helmet snaps down over your nose and bruises its bridge. The risers slap your shoulders and welt your neck. You recover quickly and push your helmet back out of your eyes. You pull a forward slip and check your canopy. Perfect! Everything's all right! You sag in the harness with a sigh of relief. You glance down at the fast approaching ground. You spot your landing point and slip towards it. You can relax for a few seconds and enjoy the view. A feeling of superiority sweeps over you as you float slowly and magnificently downward. You admire the sun shining through your canopy, dousing your body in splashes of green and brown reflections from your camouflaged 'chute. Then you realize that the landing is due. You glance around and see that the earth below is clear. You slip and turn until you are in a position to hit. You pull down on your risers. The ground comes nearer and nearer. Your knees are bent, your head up, your legs relaxed. You release your risers with a "pop," and your fall is momentarily checked. There is a slight pause. Wham! You hit and roll. It is all over.—Student theme

4. It is with the highest appreciation I venture to convey the admiration for your excellent editorial, "August's Deepening Colors." The rich flow of expression, as well as the marked significance of August's manifestations in the revealing of her natural pigments, brings the reader nearer, and at home, with the hidden gems of nature's distant unfoldments.

There is no doubt that he who has been unacquainted with the many expressions of the season's splendor is brought face to face with the living disclosures of her wonders in this presentation. Could anything be more sublime? The richness of letters are to be found in the distinct and prolific rendition of all compositions. Truth needs no embellishment for the apprehension of its idea. Life needs only the cognizant to give utterance to her features.

Only he who is capable of understanding nature in her true light and giving expression thereunto can leave the lasting impressions of beauty in poetry and epistolography. It is to him alone man may pay homage for the spark of the imagination that he may behold in the abstract that which has been already visibly concrete.—Letter by George F. Burnett in the *New York Herald-Tribune*

5. It may be taken as axiomatic that any statement of fact about the Middle Ages may (and probably will) be met by a statement of the opposite or a different version. Women outnumbered men because men were killed off in the wars; men outnumbered women because women died in childbirth. Common people were familiar with the Bible; common people were unfamiliar with the Bible. Nobles were tax exempt; no, they were not tax exempt. French peasants were filthy and foul-smelling and lived on bread and onions; French peasants ate pork, fowl, and game and enjoyed frequent baths in the village bathhouses. The list could be extended indefinitely.—Barbara Tuchman, *A Distant Mirror*

6. One afternoon while we were there at that lake a thunderstorm came up. It was like the revival of an old melodrama that I had seen long ago with childish awe. The second-act climax of the drama of the electrical disturbance over a lake in America had not changed in any important respect. This was the big scene, still the big scene. The whole thing was so familiar, the first feeling of oppression and heat and a general air around camp of not wanting to go very far away. In midafternoon (it was all the same) a curious darkening of the sky, and a lull in everything that had made life tick; and then the way the boats suddenly swung the other way at their moorings with the coming of a breeze out of a new quarter, and the premonitory rumble. Then the kettle drum, then the snare, then the bass drum and cymbals, then crackling light against the dark, and the gods grinning and licking their chops in the hills. Afterward the calm, the rain steadily rustling in the calm lake, the return of light and hope and spirits, and the campers running out in joy and relief to go swimming in the rain, their bright cries perpetuating the deathless joke about how they were getting simply drenched, and the children screaming with delight at the new sensation of bathing in the rain, and the joke about getting drenched linking the generations in a strong indestructible chain.

188

And the comedian who waded in carrying an umbrella.—E. B. White, "Once More to the Lake," *One's Man's Meat*

7. I am a jogger because I believe that every person, both young and old, should stay in good physical shape. People who do not exercise soon get out of shape, and jogging has been proved to be one of the best kinds of exercise. Also, jogging has certain social values. In spite of people kidding me about "the loneliness of the long-distance runner," I have found that my friends and I have a good time together when we are out jogging in a group. Though jogging may not build character, teach cooperation, and bring out leadership like team sports, it is surely good for your character when you "carry on" after you are completely exhausted. But I guess the main thing with me is that jogging is so much fun. And what is life without fun? "All work and no play makes Jack a dull boy."—Student theme

8. But though I was initially disappointed at being categorized as an extremist, as I continued to think about the matter I gradually gained a measure of satisfaction from the label. Was not Jesus an extremist for love: "Love your enemies, bless them that curse you, do good to them that hate you, and pray for them which despitefully use you, and persecute you." Was not Amos an extremist for justice: "Let justice roll down like waters and righteousness like an everflowing stream." Was not Paul an extremist for the Christian gospel: "I bear in my body the marks of the Lord Jesus." Was not Martin Luther an extremist: "Here I stand; I cannot do otherwise, so help me God." And John Bunyan: "I will stay in jail to the end of my days before I make a butchery of my conscience." And Abraham Lincoln: "This nation cannot survive half slave and half free." And Thomas Jefferson: "We hold these truths to be self-evident, that all men are created equal . . ." So the question is not whether we will be extremists, but what kind of extremists we will be. Will we be extremists for hate or for love? Will we be extremists for the preservation of injustice or for the extension of justice? In that dramatic scene on Calvary's hill three men were crucified. We must never forget that all three were crucified for the same crime—the crime of extremism. Two were extremists for immorality, and thus fell below their environment. The other, Jesus Christ, was an extremist for love, truth and goodness, and thereby rose above his environment. Perhaps the South, the nation and the world are in dire need of creative extremists.—Martin Luther King, Jr., "Letter from Birmingham Jail," *Why We Can't Wait*

B. Without changing the meaning significantly, translate each of the following passages of gobbledygook into plain English:

1. When the tax liability of an individual for 1978 is discharged and such tax liability is greater than the tax for 1979, the excess of 1978 over the 1979 tax liability is added to the 1979 tax liability.

2. In the case of the fourth child or student, a problem is presented which is impossible in terms of a solution.

3. During the days of the development of intensive psychiatric services, case work found in psychiatric and psychoanalytic knowledge the greatest contribution to its own equipment; today an equal absorption of economic information is essential for intelligent operation as a case worker in the field of relief administration.

4. By prioritizing grammatics in the classroom interface, the learning experience can be optimized and pupil communication skills maximized.

5. For the purpose of legitimizing the document hereinafter referred to as "the contract," said document must be signed by the individual prior to approval thereof.

6. The great value of the lecture is that it creates a situation in which simultaneous mass communication may occur, in which the emotional component, if not too strong, will transform in meaningful ways the relations of partially related subject matter and will assimilate the transformation as mental stuff for new understanding and exploration.—Beardsley Ruml and Donald R. Morrison, *Memo to a College Trustee*

C. The following comments on aspects of style in English prose are from five different periods, ranging from the beginning of the eighteenth century to the second half of the twentieth. Analyze each passage with these questions in mind: (1) Does the author provide useful advice for a writer today? (2) What are the significant characteristics of the author's own style? (3) To what extent does each author follow his own advice? Finally, consider the extent to which the five authors appear to agree with one another.

1. I could likewise have been glad, if you had applied yourself a little more to the study of the English language, than I fear you have done; the neglect whereof is one of the most general defects among the scholars of this kingdom, who seem not to have the least conception of style, but run on in a flat kind of phraseology, often mingled with barbarous terms and expressions, peculiar to the nation. Neither do I perceive that any person, either finds or acknowledges his wants upon this head, or in the least desires to have them supplied. Proper words in proper places, make the true definition of a style. But this would require too ample a disquisition to be now dwelt on: however, I shall venture to name one or two faults, which are easy to be remedied, with a very small portion of abilities.

The first is the frequent use of obscure terms, which by the women are called *hard words,* and by the better sort of vulgar, *fine language;* than which I do not know a more universal, inexcusable, and unnecessary mistake, among the clergy of all distinctions, but especially the younger practitioners. I have been curious enough to take a list of several hundred words in a sermon of a new beginner, which not one of his hearers among a hundred could possibly understand, neither can I easily call to mind any clergyman of my own acquaintance who is wholly exempt from this error, although many of them agree with me in the dislike of the thing. But I am apt to put myself in the place of the vulgar, and think many words difficult or obscure, which the preacher will not allow to be so, because those words are obvious to scholars. I believe the method observed by the famous Lord Falkland in some of his writings, would not be an ill one for young divines: I was assured by an old person of quality who knew him well, that when he doubted whether a word was perfectly intelligible or no, he used to consult one of his lady's chambermaids, (not the waiting-woman, because it was possible she might be conversant in romances) and by her judgment was guided whether to receive or reject it. And if that great person thought such a caution necessary in treatises offered to the learned world, it will be sure at least as proper in sermons, where the meanest hearer is supposed to be concerned, and where very often a lady's chambermaid may be allowed to equal half the congregation, both as to quality and understanding. But I know not how it comes to pass, that professors in most arts and sciences are generally the worst qualified to explain their meanings to those who are not of their tribe: a common farmer shall make you understand in three words, that his foot is out of joint, or his collar-bone broken, wherein a surgeon, after a hundred terms of art, if you are not a scholar, shall leave you to seek. It is frequently the same case in law, physic, and even many of the meaner arts.—Jonathan Swift, *A Letter to a Young Gentleman, Lately Entered into Holy Orders* (1719–20)

2. Every man speaks and writes with intent to be understood, and it can seldom happen but he that understands himself might convey his notions to another, if, content to be understood, he did not seek to be admired; but when once he begins to contrive how his sentiments may be received, not with most ease to his reader, but with most advantage to himself, he then transfers his consideration from words to sounds, from sentences to periods, and as he grows more elegant becomes less intelligible.

It is difficult to enumerate every species of authors whose labors counteract themselves; the man of exuberance and copiousness, who diffuses every thought through so many diversities of expression, that it is lost like water in a mist; the ponderous dictator of sentences, whose notions are delivered in the lump, and are, like uncoined bullion, of more weight than use; the liberal illustrator, who shews by examples and comparisons what was clearly seen when it was first proposed; and the stately son of demonstration, who proves with mathematical formality what no man has yet pretended to doubt.—Samuel Johnson, "The Bugbear Style," *Idler* (1758)

3. It is not easy to write a familiar style. Many people mistake a familiar for a vulgar style, and suppose that to write without affectation is to write at random. On the contrary, there is nothing that requires more precision, and, if I may say so, purity of expression, than the style I am speaking of. It utterly rejects not only all the unmeaning pomp, but all low, cant phrases, and loose, unconnected, *slipshod* allusions. It is not to take the first word that offers, but the best word in common use; it is not to throw words together in any combinations we please, but to follow and avail ourselves of the true idiom of the language. To write a genuine familar or truly English style is to write as any one would speak in common conversation who had a thorough command and choice of words, or who could discourse with ease, force, and perspicuity, setting aside all pedantic and oratorical flourishes. Or to give another illustration, to write naturally is the same thing in regard to common conversation as to read naturally is in regard to common speech. It does not follow that it is an easy thing to give the true accent and inflection to the words you utter, because you do not attempt to rise above the level of ordinary life and colloquial speaking. You do not assume, indeed, the solemnity of the pulpit, or the tone of stage-declamation; neither are you at liberty to gabble on at a venture, without emphasis or discretion, or to resort to vulgar dialect or clownish pronunciation. You must steer a middle course.—William Hazlitt, "On Familiar Style" (1821)

4. . . . According to the well-known saying, "The style is the man," complex or simple, in his individuality, his plenary sense of what he really has to say, his sense of the world; all cautions regarding style arising out of so many natural scruples as to the medium through which alone he can expose that inward sense of things, the purity of this medium, its laws or tricks of refraction: nothing is to be left there which might give conveyance to any matter save that. Style in all its varieties, reserved or opulent, terse, abundant, musical, stimulant, academic, so long as each is really characteristic or expressive, finds thus its justification, the sumptuous good taste of Cicero being as truly the man himself, and not another, justified, yet insured inalienably to him, thereby, as would have been his portrait by Raffaelle, in full consular splendour, on his ivory chair.

191

A relegation, you may say perhaps—a relegation of style to the subjectivity, the mere caprice, of the individual, which must soon transform it into mannerism. Not so! since there is, under the conditions supposed, for those elements of the man, for every lineament of the vision within, the one word, the one acceptable word, recognizable by the sensitive, by others "who have intelligence" in the matter, as absolutely as ever anything can be in the evanescent and delicate region of human language. The style, the manner, would be the man, not in his unreasoned and really uncharacteristic caprices, involuntary or affected, but in absolutely sincere apprehension of what is most real to him.—Walter Pater, "Style," *Appreciations* (1889)

5. There has risen lately in journalism a credo that writing should be simplified, that there shall be so many words and so many ideas, if any, to a sentence. Write as you talk, the mentors say. But most people should not even talk as they talk. And writing is different from speaking; it must have rhythm and accent and imagery. Good writing is not a thing to be measured with yardsticks; it comes out of what T. S. Eliot called the "agonizing ecstasy of creation."

Likewise with editing. The good editor is born and he cannot be made; he can only be unmade. He does not edit according to a Trendex or a Gallup Poll of his readers. That is fatal. As Herbert Bayard Swope said, the sure formula for success is not easily come upon, but the sure formula for failure is to try to please everybody. So the real editor edits for himself. If he has imagination and taste and judgment, he will succeed; if he has not, he is sunk and no pollster can salvage him.—Lester Markel, "The Real Sins of the Press," *Harper's* (1962)

D. The following passages are grouped in pairs to show that two selections on the same subject or similar subjects can have marked differences in tone. Analyze these differences within each pair, and discuss the relation between each writer's tone and apparent purpose.

A

1. In short, we reject the notion that excellence is something that can only be experienced in the most rarified strata of higher education. It may be experienced at every level and in every serious kind of higher education. And not only may it be experienced everywhere, but we must *demand* it everywhere. We must ask for excellence in every form which higher education takes. We should not ask it lightly or amiably or good naturedly; we should demand it vigorously and insistently. We should assert that a stubborn striving for excellence is the price of admission to reputable educational circles, and that those institutions not characterized by this striving are the slatterns of higher education.

We must make the same challenging demands of students. We must never make the insolent and degrading assumption that young people unfitted for the most demanding fields of intellectual endeavor are incapable of rigorous attention to *some sort of standards.* It is an appalling error to assume—as some of our institutions seem to have assumed—that young men and women incapable of the highest standards of intellectual excellence are incapable of any standards whatsoever, and can properly be subjected to shoddy, slovenly and trashy educational fare. College should be a demanding as well as an enriching experience—demanding for the brilliant youngster at a high level of expectation and for the less brilliant at a more modest level.—John W. Gardner, *Excellence*

2. ["The scene is in Hell at the annual dinner of the Tempters Training College for young devils." Screwtape, the speaker, is "a very experienced devil and guest of honour."] In that promising land the spirit of *I'm as good as you* has already become something more than a generally social influence. It begins to work itself into the educational system. How far its operations there have gone at the present moment I would not like to say with certainty. Nor does it matter. Once you have grasped the tendency, you can easily predict its future developments; especially as we ourselves will play our part in the developing. The basic principle of the new education is to be that dunces and idlers must not be made to feel inferior to intelligent and industrious pupils. That would be "undemocratic." These differences among the pupils—for they are obviously and nakedly *individual* differences—must be disguised. This can be done on various levels. At universities, examinations must be framed so that nearly all the students get good marks. Entrance examinations must be framed so that all, or nearly all, citizens can go to universities, whether they have any power (or wish) to profit by higher education or not. At schools the children who are too stupid or lazy to learn languages and mathematics and elementary science can be set to doing the things that children used to do in their spare time. Let them, for example, make mud pies and call it modelling. But all the time there must be no faintest hint that they are inferior to the children who are at work. Whatever nonsense they are engaged in must have—I believe the English already use the phrase—"parity of esteem." An even more drastic scheme is not impossible. Children who are fit to proceed to a higher class may be artificially kept back, because the others would get a *trauma*—Beelzebub, what a useful word!—by being left behind. The bright pupil thus remains democratically fettered to his own age-group throughout his school career, and a boy who would be capable of tackling Aeschylus or Dante sits listening to his coaeval's attempts to spell out A CAT SAT ON A MAT.—C. S. Lewis, "Screwtape Proposes a Toast," *The World's Last Night*

B

1. Maddy was what we called her familiarly. Madeline was her real name and she was a prima donna and a cat—in that order. Maddy was a cat that bowed, the only one I have ever encountered. She is part of my story, what one might call the elocution or stage part. We patronized each other. Maddy performed her act, and I assumed the role of her most ardent admirer. In discharging this duty I learned a great deal from Maddy, my patroness, whom I here acknowledge.

I have known a good many cats in my time—some that scratched, some that bit, some who purred, and even one who, by my standards at least, talked. I liked Maddy, I suppose, because we had so much in common. Maddy was an isolate. Maddy lived with three other more aggressive and talented animals who took the major attention of my host. Maddy, by contrast, was not so much antisocial as shy, when you came to know her. She wandered a little forlornly in back rooms and concealed herself under furniture or in a recess above the fireplace.—Loren Eiseley, *All the Strange Hours*

2. [This passage refers to the ruins of the Largo Argentina in Rome.] It is possible to walk among the venerable stones, but staring down from above, one hesitates. It is the cats, alert, fierce old pirates, ears chewed in fights, some filthy, some sleekly shining on their pedestals, the absolute lords of their manor of dark caverns and sun-splashed marble, terrifying in their numbers and confidence, sure of the old ladies who will bring plastic sacks full of entrails and last night's spaghetti for these kings of the jungle. Always mesmerizing and growing larger and more tigerish as one stares at them, they lose their menace only for a short time in the spring when the sterile old stones shoot forth flowers and the cats' tails swim through the blooms like swift, elusive fish.(Inhabitants of the neighborhood say they have observed an old woman creep into the ruins at night and out in the morning. They could be right. Between ruins Roman, medieval, Renaissance, and Hoovervilles, the city must have more than 50,000 squatters.)—Kate Simon, *Rome*

C

1. I see by the new Sears Roebuck catalogue that it is still possible to buy an axle for a 1909 Model T Ford, but I am not deceived. The great days have faded, the end is in sight. Only one page in the current catalogue is devoted to parts and accessories for the Model T; yet everyone remembers springtimes when the Ford gadget section was larger than men's clothing, almost as large as household furnishings. The last Model T was build in 1927, and the car is fading from what scholars call the American scene—which is an understatement, because to a few million people who grew up with it, the old Ford practically *was* the American scene.

It was the miracle God had wrought. And it was patently the sort of thing that could only happen once. Mechanically uncanny, it was like nothing that had ever come to the world before. Flourishing industries rose and fell with it. As a vehicle, it was hardworking, commonplace, heroic; and it often seemed to transmit those qualities to the persons who rode in it. My own generation identifies it with Youth, with its gaudy, irretrievable excitements; before it fades into the mist, I would like to pay it the tribute of the sigh that is not a sob, and set down random entries in a shape somewhat less cumbersome than a Sears Roebuck catalogue.—E. B. White, "Farewell, My Lovely!" *The Second Tree from the Corner*

2. As so often happens, when the minds of many people have been silently brooding over the same subject, there has recently been an outbreak of books, articles, and legislative investigations, all devoted to assessing the mechanical defects, the bodily hazards, and the mounting social disadvantages of the motor car. The tone of this discussion has been critical, not to say sacrilegious. Some of the critics have dared to say that the Sacred Cow of the American Way of Life is overfed and bloated; that the daily milk she supplies is poisonous; that the pasturage this species requires wastes acres of la ́ that could be used for more significant human purposes; and that the vast herds of sacred cows, allowed to roam everywhere, like their Hindu counterparts, are trampling down the vegetation, depleting wild life, and turning both urban and rural areas into a single smudgy wasteland, whose fancy sociological name is Megalopolis.

The priesthood of the Sacred Cow, very sensitive to the mildest heresy, now shows definite signs of alarm, alternating plaintive moos with savage bellows; for in their religion, the cult of the Sacred Cow is closely affiliated with an older object of worship, the Golden Calf. With justified trepidation, the priestly establishment feels religion itself (capitalized) is being challenged—that religion for whose evidences of power and glory the American people, with eyes devoutly closed, are prepared to sacrifice some 45,000 lives every year, and to maim, often irreparably, more than a million and a half more. Only war can claim so many premature deaths; for the death rate from motor cars is greater than the combined death rate from falls, burnings, drownings, railroads, firearms, and poisonous gases, plus some two thousand other deaths from unidentifiable causes. And though only roughly half as many Americans were killed outright by autos in the last four-year period as were killed in our armed forces during a similar term in the Second World War, nearly three times as many were injured.—Lewis Mumford, "The American Way of Death," *The New York Review of Books*

D

1. Watching television, you'd think we lived at bay, in total jeopardy, surrounded on all sides by human-seeking germs, shielded against infection and death only by a chemical technology that enables us to keep killing them off. We are instructed to spray disinfectants everywhere, into the air of our bedrooms and kitchens and with special energy into bathrooms, since it is our very own germs that seem the worst kind. We explode clouds of aerosol, mixed for good luck with deodorants, into our noses, mouths, underarms, privileged crannies—even into the intimate insides of our telephones. We apply potent antibiotics to minor scratches and seal them with plastic. Plastic is the new protector; we wrap the already plastic tumblers of hotels in more plastic, and seal the toilet seats like state secrets after irradiating them with ultraviolet light. We live in a world where the microbes are always trying to get at us, to tear us cell from cell, and we only stay alive and whole through diligence and fear.—Lewis Thomas, *The Lives of a Cell*

2. My family couldn't brush their teeth after every meal, but we had something more precious together. I guess you could call it "togetherness."

My mother and father did everything together, and so did we. I can't remember a single moment when there wasn't a family-size bottle of Coke on the indoor barbecue pit.

So many little scenes flash through my mind as I think of those years in Crestwood: my father, laughing through his smoke rings as he chortled, "Winston tastes good!"; Aunt Birdie, who came from Mobile, chirping roguishly, "Lahk a cigarette should!"; my mother seeing my teenage sister Shirley off to a dance with the heartwarming whisper: "Don't be half-safe!"

My mother was the most unforgettable character I had ever met. I see her now, rubbing her freshly ironed wash against her cheek and murmuring of its whiteness; or rushing to my father as he came home from work and crying, "Darling, have you heard the wonderful news? Professional laundries use *soap*, not detergents!" My mother had that kind of mind.—Marya Mannes, "Miltown Place, or Life with Sponsors," *More in Anger*

8 Clear and Cloudy Thinking

Bad writing is nothing more than the
outward and visible sign of bad thinking.
Oscar James Campbell

The new tinge to modern minds is a
vehement and passionate interest in the
relation of general principles to irreducible
and stubborn facts.
Alfred North Whitehead

As the first quotation at the head of the chapter implies, cloudy thinking
may be reflected in faulty organization, incorrect grammar, loose sentence structure, or careless choice of words. Part of the following discussion is concerned with principles of language that have already been
considered in Chapters 5 and 6. But this chapter will also consider some
common *errors in reasoning* that violate rules of logic. These errors—or
fallacies, as logicians call them—are rare in narrative and descriptive
writing, but they are by no means confined to the process of "taking
sides" on a controversial issue. If you say, "All footballs are made of
pigskin," you are committing, not a fallacy, but an error in fact. If you
say, "All footballs are made of pigskin because many people call them
pigskins," you are guilty of an absurd but alarmingly common fallacy.
You may have no desire of "starting an argument," but you have set one
forth. By merely pretending to give a reason for your assertion, you have
entered the realm of opinion, a treacherous region beset by fallacies on
every hand.

PREJUDICE VS. OPINION

When Ambrose Bierce defined *prejudice* as "a vagrant opinion without
visible means of support," he treated it as an inferior species of opinion.
But it is a useful aid to clear thinking to keep the two as distinct as
possible.

A prejudice is a *pre*judgment, a conclusion reached *before* any evidence is in. It has no basis in observable facts or sound reasoning. Born in ignorance, it lives in fear of knowledge, for knowledge can quickly slay it. Its natural habitat is the brain of the bigot, from which it emerges skulking behind dogmatic generalities, charged words, exaggeration, and name-calling. Although a prejudice may be cool or even cold, it commonly generates heat and often explodes in a blast of hot air, sealing the mind with debris.

An opinion is a judgment resulting from an honest atttempt to examine the evidence and reason logically from it. It is based on knowledge, however inadequate, and though new knowledge may destroy it, it is not afraid to succumb to a better opinion. Most at home in the mind of the responsible citizen, it expresses itself openly in tangible examples, neutral, unambiguous words, calm, reasonable tones. However strong, it is always flexible, never hardening into dogma. However warmly held, it always aims to supply not heat but light.

If you write an informal essay expressing a playful prejudice against parsnips, it is foolish to condemn you for not listing logical reasons. But in any serious attempts to express a point of view on paper, prejudice has no charms to soothe educated readers. They want evidence. To be sure, the evidence may be a strenuous effort to defend a preconception. When you begin organizing your thoughts on any subject, it is possible that, from reading and listening and random reflecting in the past, your mind has already taken a tentative stand. But if you frankly recognize this preliminary bias and are careful not to confine yourself to the evidence supporting it—a mental process inappropriately called *rationalizing*—you can still express a logical opinion. Even if your bias has hardened into a prejudice, your case is not hopeless unless you stubbornly insist on passing it off as a valid opinion. As Thoreau said, "it is never too late to give up our prejudices."

DEFINITION AGAIN

"If you wish to converse with me," said Voltaire, "define your terms." If the first step toward intelligent discussion is abolishing prejudice, the second is a clear understanding of what the discussion is all about. In any serious argument, you must make an unambiguous statement of your point of view, for it is obviously futile to assert *why* you take your stand until you show clearly *where* you take it. In some discussions, this involves a careful definition of words. Not that every opinion must begin with a dictionary definition (see p. 36). Arguments centering in "what Webster says" are notoriously futile because a dictionary is not the ultimate judge of meaning. But you should leave no doubt about what you yourself mean by the pivotal words in your argument.

The danger of loose, ambiguous terms and the problem of defining abstract words have been considered in detail elsewhere (see pp.

141–145). It should be clear by now that the most eloquent mouthing of abstractions is not logical argument, whether they are charged with noble sentiments (liberty, loyalty, Americanism, free enterprise) or with venom (tyranny, disloyalty, treason, fascism). Von Bülow's arrogant boast—"To the meaningless French idealisms, Liberty, Equality, and Fraternity, we oppose the German realities, Infantry, Cavalry, and Artillery"—contains a sobering lesson in semantics.

Do not forget that it is often wise to avoid the problem of definition entirely by simply limiting the scope of the discussion. For example, you are beaten at the start if you try to argue for or against "communism" or "socialized medicine" or "progressive education" in 500 words without any attempt at definition. If you set out to define them, fully aware of the complexity of the task, you can hardly avoid readjusting your lens to bring a formless blur into sharper focus. Thus a cloudy indictment of communism can become a clear argument against one aspect of the foreign policy of the Soviet Union; a fuzzy attack on "socialized medicine" can become a clean-cut objection to a single provision of one bill before Congress; a hopeless jumble of assertions about something called "progressive education" can be reduced to a convincing defense of the old-fashioned policy of teaching children the alphabet before puzzling them with reading and writing and spelling. You have, to be sure, fled from the disturbing dilemma of defining terms. But you have succeeded in defining your subject: *limiting* it to a reasonable size. You have shifted the grounds of the argument from words to issues.

One of the virtues of definition is that it is a safeguard against the common error of letting a word slip from one meaning to another in the course of the same argument:

> I have no objection to the sincere humanitarian aims of the proponents of this measure; they are all idealists of the highest order. But this is a hard, cruel, practical world, a world in which our leaders should keep their feet firmly planted on the ground. It is an age for practical men who are familiar with the problems of meeting a payroll. It is not an age for fuzzy-minded idealists.

All words change color from context to context, but the word *idealists* behaves in that passage like a chameleon. When first used, it carries approximately the first meaning listed in *The Random House College Dictionary:* "a person who cherishes or pursues noble principles, purposes, goals, etc." Surely the writer could not object to such an idealist in any generation; even the most practical people are urged to hitch their wagons to a star. But three sentences later the same *idealists*, with no warning from the writer, have acquired the connotation of meaning number two: "a visionary or impractical person," and the reader is left wondering whether the ambiguous author has any faith in ideals.

This fallacy—known to logicians as the fallacy of *equivocation*—may also crop up in arguments between two or more persons. Many a dormitory debate goes on half the night before somebody asks, "What do you mean by so-and-so?" and the disputants, finding themselves using the same label for two or more markedly different meanings, become suddenly aware that they have been tilting for hours at verbal windmills. When they have clearly defined the equivocal terms, the contestants often prove to have surprisingly similar views—a discovery they might have made in the beginning at a considerable saving of time and vocal energy.

IGNORING THE QUESTION

Although it often helps, defining the terms doesn't always isolate the issue. *Evading the issue* or *ignoring the question*—either consciously or unconsciously—is one of the commonest fallacies in everyday discussion.

There are many kinds of red herring in the marketplace, and the accomplished demagogue or propagandist is an expert at dragging them all across the trail to distract attention from the real point under discussion. The "band wagon" device ("Everybody's voting for Wintergreen. Don't you be left out"); the "plain folks" appeal ("Our candidate is just a plain humble farmer whose heart is still in the soil"); the testimonial (" 'Peppermint is my candidate,' says Debbie Taylor, distinguished star of stage and screen"); the appeal to flattery ("the thoughtful voters of this great city of Wilkes-Barre"), or pity ("He left the sickbed of a dying mother to speak to you tonight"), or fear ("Do you want your life savings swept away by economic crackpots?")—these are only a few of the emotional maneuvers used to convert an audience from thinking to throbbing.

The conscientious citizen, with no desire to imitate the demagogue, will often drag a red herring across the trail without being in the least aware that there is anything fishy about the argument. A familiar kind of unconscious evasion (though it may be conscious too) is the *argumentum ad hominem*—or "argument against the person." A speaker in a debate suddenly shifts from attacking an opponent's assertions to ridiculing the other's manners or morals; or a writer, pretending to discuss the shortcomings of a proposed law, concentrates the attack—with or without explicit name-calling—on the family background of the senator proposing it. There are, to be sure, occasions where the issue is the person—the wisdom of a presidential appointment, for example—and others where the person has made such an issue of his or her own personality that it is difficult for even the fairest opponent to judge the achievement impersonally. But despite the time-honored proverb, it is still not a pertinent criticism of the accuracy of stone-throwers to point out that they live in a glass house. Personal ridicule—"stooping to personalities"—is a favorite pastime with politicians, but it is not fair or logical argument.

199

A less obvious but extremely common kind of evasion is the *false dilemma*, also known as *either-or reasoning*. This is the popular device by which speakers or writers reduce a many-faceted problem to a neat argument with only two sides: their own, which is presumably pure white, and a hypothetical opponent's, which is clearly jet black. The propounders of such false dilemmas are fond of saying, "All who are not with me are against me." They commonly deny that there can be any compromise between two extremes, any conceivable M between their own unassailable A and the adversary's impossible Z. If they do concede the existence of more than one argument besides their own and their target's, they are likely to maintain that, since the opposition's proposals "differ only in degree," they are really the same—a technique as logical as protesting that gray cats of all shades are really black because they are not white. Thus the traditional debating society assumes that all controversial questions can be deftly divided by two, Affirmative and Negative, with never a fraction left over. The professional politician presents the voter with a simple choice between absolutes: between "free enterprise" and "government planning," between "freedom from entangling alliances" and "involvement in international war," between "our whole ticket and honest government" and "their whole ticket and corrupt bureaucracy." The packages are neatly wrapped in the over-simplification factory and plainly labeled *either this* and *or that* by experts in "potted thinking."

The thoughtful voter knows better. This doesn't mean that a writer limited by time and space can always examine "all sides of an issue" or that you should timidly avoid conclusions because "there is much to be said on both sides." It means that the dilemma with only two horns is a much rarer animal than proverbial wisdom implies—and even the two horns have a disturbing way of branching out like a deer's antlers. And the unicorn is still a myth.

DEDUCTION VS. INDUCTION

When you have vowed to avoid prejudice and isolate the issue, you have only laid the groundwork for sound argument. You should also be able to identify the kind of argument you are using so that you can avoid the fallacies that commonly accompany it.

Logicians make an important distinction between two kinds of argument: *deduction* and *induction*.

In a deductive argument, a person infers ("deduces") a conclusion from one or more statements, called *premises*. The reasoning is usually from the general to the particular (All women are mammals; therefore, Elizabeth Taylor is a mammal. All mice are rodents; therefore, Mickey Mouse is a rodent). In its simplest form, a deductive argument may

200

contain, like these illustrations, a single premise and a single conclusion. But the one most familiar to students of traditional logic is the three-part form called the *syllogism*:

All women are mammals. (*major premise*)
Elizabeth Taylor is a woman. (*minor premise*)
Therefore, Elizabeth Taylor is a mammal. (*conclusion*)

If the conclusion follows logically from the premises, a deductive argument is said to be *valid*, even if one or both premises are false.

Valid argument with major premise and conclusion false:

All mammals are fish. (*major premise—false*)
Elizabeth Taylor is a mammal. (*minor premise—true*)
Therefore, Elizabeth Taylor is a fish. (*conclusion—false*)

Valid argument with both premises and the conclusion false:

All mammals are men. (*major premise—false*)
Mickey Mouse is a mammal. (*minor premise—false*)
Therefore, Mickey Mouse is a man. (*conclusion—false*)

But *if the premises are true and the reasoning is valid, the conclusion must necessarily be true.* Thus you should ask yourself two questions: (1) Are my premises true? (2) Is the reasoning valid?

The author of an *inductive* argument also draws ("induces") a conclusion from one or more statements. But these statements are commonly called *evidence* (not premises); the typical reasoning is from the particular to the general; and the conclusion can never, strictly speaking, be inevitable or valid, but only "possible," "probable," "convincing," or "unconvincing"—depending largely on the weight of the evidence.

The conclusion of an inductive argument may be a *generalization*: the assertion that something is true of all or some members of a class of people or things. This is illustrated, as you may recall, by Huxley's well-known example of the apple-taster in the fruit shop (see p. 150). The example can be reduced to this simple pattern (*not a syllogism*):

Apple no. 1 is hard, green, and sour.
Apple no. 2 is hard, green, and sour.
It is therefore probable that apple no. 3, which is hard and green, will also be sour.

Or an inductive conclusion may be a *hypothesis*, a provisional explanation to account for the evidence:

Mrs. Thockmorton had obviously been alive when she called Rigby at 8:30 P.M.
Her body was discovered shortly after midnight with a paper cutter in the left shoulder blade.
The coroner who examined her at 1 A.M. conjectured that she had been dead at least two hours.

201

The window was open and in the snow outside were bloody male footprints
  pointing away from the house.
Therefore, the police concluded that the woman had been stabbed between 8:30
  and 11 P.M. by a man who had entered through the door and escaped through
  the window.

Inductive reasoning—the technique of a detective solving a crime, a
doctor making a diagnosis, a chemist analyzing a solution, or an engineer testing a structure—is the logical foundation of the scientific
method.

ERRORS IN DEDUCTIVE ARGUMENT

To detach the backbone of reasoning from a deductive argument, arrange it as a syllogism, detect the fallacy, if any, and give it the proper
technical label—these are skills that you cannot perfect without an
elementary course in logic. The following discussion is limited to two of
the commonest errors in deduction.

1. Faulty Assumptions

In speech and writing a deductive argument seldom appears in the neat,
bare form of a single syllogism; it often contains a number of syllogisms,
complete and incomplete, explicit and implicit. Here, for example, is a
passage from an editorial in which a student argues against converting
an all-male Alma Mater to coeducation:

> It is obvious that women require a different kind of education from men.
> Thus, to establish coeducation would mean, not only the expense of building
> new dormitories, with a fat salary bill for house mothers and additional campus
> policemen, but also the cost of establishing new courses in such fields as Home
> Economics and Child Psychology. The number of women attracted would not
> justify the added expense. If our aim is to attract more good students to the
> campus, it would be simpler and cheaper in the long run to put the college "on
> the map" with a winning football team.

It isn't necessary to stretch that argument on the frame of the syllogism to test its weakness; the reader need look no further than the first
premise. If it were obvious that women require a different kind of education from that required by men, one of the oldest educational squab-
bles could be permitted to die a peaceful death. Since the student has
built his argument on a doubtful premise, it is fundamentally weak, and
the most solid logic in the superstructure won't keep it from tumbling
down when an opponent attacks it. Of course, the superstructure is not
solid. The student's third sentence contains another assumption (that
the enrollment of women would not justify the expense); and the final
sentence—a sort of superfluous cupola on the main structure—contains

no fewer than three: (1) that winning football games would be simpler than converting to coeducation; (2) that it would be cheaper; and (3) that it would attract more good students to the college. An unmerciful opponent might point out that the evidence of recent years makes all three assumptions highly questionable. Another might point out that this analysis of the editorial mentions only the student's *explicit* premises and doesn't consider the truth of his *hidden* premises. How much, for example, does the student assume about the basic differences between men and women? And doesn't he assume, despite his passing reference to "good students," that the important tests of the value of any curriculum are (1) does it make a profit? and (2) does it bring the college publicity? The most unassuming argument often conceals a tangled network of the most dubious assumptions.

2. Begging the Question

The fallacy of assuming the truth of something that remains to be proved is known in logic as *begging the question*. A simple form of question-begging is *circular reasoning:* "The Smiths are an undesirable family because they moved into the Fifth Ward, where the homeowners don't want undesirable families like the Smiths." This is little different from saying, "The Smiths are undesirable because they are—undesirable." By stating the conclusion in the major premise, arguers end up exactly where they started, having proved absolutely nothing.

In an article entitled "The Alleged Failure of Democracy," Ralph Barton Perry shows that question-beggars—as they have been called—are often more subtle:

> People do not as a rule beg a question explicitly: they do not say in so many words that democracy is a bad thing because democracy is a bad thing. But there are those who argue against democracy in theory from their dislike of it in practice. Since the practice is precisely what the theory means, these critics are really not arguing at all, but are only expressing a prejudice.

The commonest kind of question-begging is the use of charged words or phrases (see pp. 147–151), especially the resort to *name-calling*. The polite pastel label *undesirable* is typical of the language of genteel prejudice. Henry Morton Robinson, arguing against students' working their way through college, begins by slanting the title ("Working Your Way—or Your Professor?") and throughout the discussion brands his victims as "scholastic hitchhikers," "academic parasites," "academic rabble," and "academic gate-crashers." And any newspaper is likely to reveal a columnist or a congressman who has discovered that it is easier to beg the question of someone's guilt by pinning a label on the person than to argue the question with impartial evidence. Despite the old proverb, names can hurt worse than sticks and stones. The game of fair argument should not be played with loaded dice.

PROBLEMS OF INDUCTIVE ARGUMENT

1. Finding the Facts

Although facts play a role in deduction, the very essence of sound inductive argument is "a vehement and passionate interest in the relation of general principles to irreducible and stubborn facts." Everybody concedes the importance of facts in modern life. We are impressed by the well-informed game show contestant on TV who can summon up remembrance of miscellaneous facts at a moment's notice; we admire the scientist who is trying to find the facts about cancer and the common cold; we applaud the politician who says, "My friends, let's look at the record." But like Dickens' Thomas Gradgrind ("In this life, we want nothing but Facts, sir; nothing but Facts!"), we pay lip service to the worship of fact while we calmly subscribe to the prejudices of popular superstition. As Felix Cohen has said, "Generally, the theories we believe we call *facts*, and the facts we disbelieve we call *theories*." Our hard, cold facts are often hard and cold only because enlightened minds have long since consigned them to the grave. The discoveries of modern science are a sobering reminder that some of our most cherished axioms no longer qualify as facts.

In its strict sense, as commonly used in scientific discussion, a fact is "a truth known by actual experience or observation." Is it a fact that parallel lines never meet, that a straight line is the shortest distance between two points, or that the sum of the angles of a triangle equals two right angles? These are not facts; they are merely the convenient assumptions of plane geometry. Is it a fact that blood is a transmitter of heredity? Studies in heredity present not the slightest evidence for it. Is it a fact that all peoples resort to war as a solution of their problems? Anthropologists have presented evidence that some "primitive" cultures cannot even conceive the possibility of a state of war. Is it a fact that you can't change human nature, that the Puritans burned witches in Salem, that the heart is on the left side of the chest, that there are superior and inferior races, that lightning never strikes twice in the same place, that the porcupine shoots its quills? All these "facts" are popular errors (Ashley Montagu and Edward Darling, *The Prevalence of Nonsense*). As Bergen Evans has said, "the civilized man has a moral obligation to be skeptical, to demand the credentials of all statements that claim to be facts."

Many so-called facts are not disguised folklore but concealed judgments. "The St. Louis Cardinals are a baseball team"; "oranges grow in California"; "stealing is a criminal offense in New York City"; "Shakespeare was born in 1564"—these are all facts that can be readily verified, the first three by firsthand observation, the last by reference to dependable documents. A *judgment* is a conclusion involving a personal evaluation of evidence. Even if the evidence overwhelmingly corroborates the conclusion, it can never be a fact. "The New York Yankees are the best baseball team in the world" is not a fact, even if they have just won the World Series. "Delicious oranges grow in California" may not be a fact to fanatical citizens of Florida. "Crime doesn't pay" is the expression of an ethical judgment bolstered by the sturdiest evidence from criminology—but it remains a judgment. And even if every responsible critic in the world supported it, the statement that "Shakespeare is the greatest playwright in English literature" could never become a fact. A careful writer doesn't lead off with "It's a well-known fact that" and follow with a judgment.

2. Interpreting Statistics

In its search for irreducible facts, the modern world has developed the science of statistics to an astounding degree. Techniques of mass interviewing and rapid calculating have been perfected to a point where the poor citizen untutored in the mysteries of modes and medians and graphs and incidences and correlations often feels strangely illiterate. In some circles, there is no deity but the digit and the pollster is its prophet. It is an established article of twentieth-century faith that "figures don't lie."

Unfortunately they often do. The lies of statistics range all the way from the little white lies that only slightly mislead to the most barefaced falsifications. The responsible experts who live with statistics are thoroughly aware of their limitations. For example, the first celebrated "Kinsey Report" (*Sexual Behavior in the Human Male*), after devoting 118 pages to a discussion of the complicated problem of collecting and evaluating statistical data, sounds this warning:

> Throughout the remainder of this volume, the raw data and the calculations based on the raw data are treated with a precision that must not be misunderstood by the statistically inexperienced reader. It has not been practical to carry this warning in every paragraph of every chapter. Neither has it been possible to qualify every individual statistic, as every statistic in any study of the human animal should be qualified. For the remainder of the volume it should, therefore, be recognized that the data are probably fair approximations, but only approximations of the fact.

"Only approximations of the fact." That is all a reader can demand of statistical evidence involving complex, fallible human beings. Yet careless writers and speakers still throw "facts and figures" around with the calm assurance that every figure is a fact.

The most elementary study of statistics is a whole college course. There is room here only to caution you with a general rule of thumb: *Do not put your faith in what statistics say until you have carefully considered what they do not say.*

Examples could be multiplied indefinitely to support the rule that in almost all statistical evidence something is left out. Thus, figures that announce a distressingly higher rate of mental illness in our age of anxiety than in 1900 omit eight decades of progress in psychiatric diagnosis and institutional growth. Statistics indicating a much higher per capita "crime rate" in A town than in B burg may ignore the point that a crime in A town, which has an alert modern police force and an uncorrupted judiciary, is merely a harmless wild oat in B burg, where the sheriff is not only in the pay of John Q. Gambler but married to the judge's favorite sister. And a student who comes to the common conclusion that Y college, where the passing grade is 70, has higher standards than Z University, where it is 60, may overlook the evidence tending to show that a 90 at Y is easier to get than a 75 at Z.

Finally, one of the biggest troubles with "hard, cold figures" is that they are hard and cold. The statistics on the number of people killed by the first atomic bomb dropped on Japan—an item that one commentator summarized as "considerable personnel damage"—cannot speak as eloquently as the human argument in John Hersey's *Hiroshima*. For all its virtues, our modern tendency to worship statistics can be dangerously inhuman. Charles Dickens tried to teach this lesson in *Hard Times* when statistical method was still in its infancy. Sissy Jupe confesses to her friend Louisa Gradgrind how miserably she has failed in Mr. M'Choakumchild's school of hard facts:

"And he said, Now, this schoolroom is a nation. And in the nation there are fifty millions of money. Isn't this a prosperous nation? Girl number twenty, isn't this a prosperous nation, and a'n't you in a thriving state?"

"What did you say?" asked Louisa.

"Miss Louisa, I said I didn't know. I thought I couldn't know whether it was a prosperous nation or not, and whether I was in a thriving state or not, unless I knew who had got the money, and whether any of it was mine. But that had nothing to do with it. It was not in the figures at all," said Sissy, wiping her eyes.

Statistics are often indispensable in supporting opinions. But a writer must be forever aware of what is "not in the figures at all."

3. Citing Authorities

In tracking down facts and figures to support an inductive argument, you can't always limit yourself to first-hand evidence; sooner or later you must depend on the authority of others. The medieval faith in Aristotle could hardly have been more submissive than our slavery to the power of print and the pronouncements of experts. Many people in this expert-ridden age put implicit belief in what "it says here" without ever stopping to ask themselves who says it where. In a century when it has become evident that millions will believe even the most incredible lie if it is repeated often enough, this is a dangerous habit.

The problem of discriminating among sources is discussed in more detail in the next chapter. But you should be warned now to be wary of citing any source in support of an opinion when your knowledge is limited to the fact that the author is someone named Doe, who has a Ph.D., and that the book has a blue cover. It is equally questionable to cite a distinguished expert in one field (the social life of fruit flies) as an authority on a problem that lies in another (Far Eastern diplomacy)— even though it is standard practice for advertisers to imply that a star second-baseman becomes automatically a connoisseur of cigarettes, beer, and shaving lotion. Finally, the most convincing evidence in an argument doesn't come from an authority biased by personal or party prejudice. A rabid Republican newspaper is not the most reliable source on the sins of the Democrats or a member of the Democratic National Committee the most detached critic of the corruption of the Republicans. Obvious as this may appear, many students remain uninterested in whether an authority is disinterested.

A conscientious writer takes care not only to choose authorities carefully but to represent them accurately. An obvious kind of misrepresentation is inaccurate paraphrase or misquotation. A more subtle kind is ignoring the context of a quotation. This is a calculated trick of experienced demagogues, who are masters of ripping a suspicious phrase from its setting and challenging their opponents to prove that they didn't say that. It is a natural technique in movie promotion, where the critic's assertion that "Jane Fonda's acting is only occasionally brilliant" becomes in the advertisement "Jane Fonda's acting . . . brilliant"—with or without the three dots denoting an omission. A more innocent student will sometimes build an entire theme or examination answer on a single phrase quickly read without benefit of context. "Lincoln was a radical," writes Rollo Walter Brown, and one student comes angrily to the great emancipator's defense without carefully reading the essay in which the author systematically defines his use of the adjective. "Even A.B.'s Must Eat," asserts Ernest Earnest in a title, and another student automatically assumes that the author is maintaining the impracticality of liberal education, though a careful reading of the article would show that he is doing nothing of the kind.

In the broadest sense, the context of a quotation not only includes the sentences immediately surrounding it but extends beyond the source to involve all the circumstances of its composition. Who said or wrote it? What were the circumstances of time and place? What was the writer's intention? Considering the author, the circumstances, and the intention, what can be inferred about the tone of the quotation? Are the words to be taken seriously or humorously, literally or ironically? All these questions are essential in honest criticism. Take, for example, the classic argument that America should isolate itself from the affairs of the world because our first president warned in his Farewell Address against "entangling alliances." In the first place, it is pertinent to point out that the phrase is not Washington's but Jefferson's; Washington wrote (and incidentally both Madison and Hamilton contributed to the speech): " 'Tis our true policy to steer clear of *permanent* alliances, with any portion of the foreign world." A glance at the immediate context of the phrase would reveal that, among other things, Washington condemned "infidelity to existing engagements" and specifically advocated "temporary alliances for extraordinary emergencies."Finally, the most superficial study of the larger context would raise the natural question of whether a policy recommended in the days of sailing ships, warning an infant republic against involvement in European wars, can have any logical application to the world's most powerful democracy in a time of long-range missiles carrying nuclear destruction.

4. Arriving at Conclusions

Paul B. Sears, in his study of Charles Darwin, tells the story of two scientists at the University of Illinois in the 1920s who were investigating the sense of balance, which is so important in aviation. They found that white rats, after long imprisonment in whirling horizontal cages, "naturally showed some motor disturbance, but usually recovered." However, when some of the offspring of these whirling vermin were born with a tendency to travel in circles, it looked as if the old moot problem of the inheritance of acquired characters had finally been solved. Cautious excitement prevailed until a skeptical fellow scientist at a convention raised a pertinent question: "Are you sure that those animals did not have a hidden strain of the 'waltzing' habit in their inheritance to start with?" Further investigation revealed that the waltzing offspring all had a disease of the inner ear having no apparent relation to inheritance.

The history of science is studded with such tales, and every one is a warning to scientists not to announce conclusions until they have made the most exhaustive investigation of the evidence—and even then to regard the conclusions as no more than credible hypotheses.

Unlike scientists, most writers can't seek sanctuary in the laboratory for years before they venture humbly forth with a tentative inductive conclusion. But there is a happy medium between a Charles Darwin studying evolution for more than twenty years before he printed his tentative conclusions in *On the Origin of Species* and a William Jennings Bryan thundering from the lecture platform: "If man is descended from the monkeys, why cannot we go into Africa today and see monkeys turning into men?" No writer can wait until "all the evidence is in" before coming to a conclusion; sooner or later all must take the "inductive leap" from the specific instances to the general rule. But careful writers will look before they leap.

The soundness of a generalization depends on whether the evidence presented is accurate, typical, relevant, and adequate. Obviously a conclusion cannot be valid if it is based on errors in fact or on a discriminating selection of exceptional instances, ignoring typical evidence. And only the flimsiest hasty generalization can be based on evidence having no discernible relation to the conclusion. For example, a luncheon speaker is reported in a newspaper to have said: "Members of service clubs become tolerant of each other's views and therefore are in a better position to fight the 'isms' which threaten our economic and political system." Even if the first half of this sentence is accepted as evidence, by what logic does the second half follow? The assertion is an extreme example of a *non sequitur*: "it does not follow." Another kind of *non sequitur* is represented by the common assumption that because B follows A, it was necessarily caused by A: "As soon as Coach Smith took over, the team lost to State for the first time in twenty-three years. Obviously bad coaching is the answer." The loyal alumnus guilty of this typical leap from fact to fancy probably doesn't know that Latin has a phrase for it: the fallacy of *post hoc, ergo propter hoc* "after this, therefore because of this."

The meaning of the arbitrary term "adequate evidence" will vary with the length and nature of the argument. A short essay in opinion may convincingly present three examples to "prove" a point; a doctoral dissertation may display 300. But you should be warned against leaping to a generalization from a single piece of evidence, however accurate, typical, and relevant.

Even when a generalization is supported by adequate evidence, it is wise to present it with caution. Words such as *all* and *every*, *never* and *always*, *best* and *worst*, *certainly* and *undoubtedly* may convey a dogmatic cocksureness unjustified by the evidence. A writer would do well to remember that, when Sir Joseph Porter, K.C.B., boasts that he is "never, never sick at sea," the skeptical chorus of the sisters and the cousins and the aunts makes him qualify it with "well, hardly ever." A writer who overdoes such qualifying, even in a scholarly article, may some day be permanently stuck on the fence. But it is better to do a little extra qualifying than to let an opponent invade your generalizations and rip them full of holes.

5. Arguing from Analogy

Which of the following arguments is the more convincing?

But the tendency of the time is much better illustrated by a group of professors of education who have just recently proposed that the list of "required reading" in schools should be based upon a study which they have just sponsored of the tastes of school children. . . . Would any pediatrician base the diet which he prescribed for the young submitted to his care simply on an effort to determine what eatables they remembered with greatest pleasure? If he knew that the vote would run heavily in favor of chocolate sodas, orange pop, hot dogs and bubble gum, would he conclude that these should obviously constitute the fundamental elements in a "modern" child's menu?—Joseph Wood Krutch,

"Should We Bring Literature to Children, or Children to Literature?" *New York Herald-Tribune Book Review*

For instance, the author may be arguing against social security or the theory that it is the Government's business to provide for its people individually as well as collectively. On the face of it, the author's contention seems inhumane. But the principle involved—the reason behind the reason—is that life is a struggle, only the fittest survive; that men become fitter only by struggling; and that the progress of civilization depends upon the survival of the fittest. Therefore, handouts undermine the will and the ability to stay fit.—Alvan E. Duerr, *Pledge Training*, National Interfraternity Conference

Krutch compares the educator prescribing a diet for children's minds to the pediatrician prescribing for their stomachs. Duerr supports a hypothetical argument with an implied comparison between the "struggle for existence" in modern society and the evolutionary process by which *Homo sapiens* has descended through untold ages from the beginning of time. Both arguments employ the extremely common device of *analogy*.

This book contains other analogies: for example, Huxley's customer at the fruiterer's unconsciously illustrating the process of induction (see p. 150). But Huxley is primarily bent on exposition, and the chief test of the analogy's effectiveness is whether it helps to make the point clearer. Krutch and Duerr are using analogies to carry the burden of argument. The main question is: Do they logically support that argument?

From the strict standpoint of logic, all analogical arguments are unsound. (It is sometimes maintained that they do not deserve to masquerade under the banner of induction, but represent a third kind of argument.) No matter how many points two things may have in common, the comparison always breaks down somewhere along the line. But a useful distinction can still be made between a *tight* analogy, which, though it may actually prove nothing, helps to support the argument, and a *loose* analogy, which leaves the writer wide open to attack from a skillful adversary.

Regardless of convictions about education or politics, a trained reader could hardly fail to see this difference in the passages cited. Why, says Krutch, should an educator let children draw up their own mental menu when no responsible pediatrician would dream of letting them prescribe their own physical menu? The question is hard to answer. It can be pointed out, of course, that pedagogues are not pediatricians and the mind is not the stomach. But are these differences significant in this context? Is there any reason why children need less guidance in feeding their minds than in feeding their bodies? On the contrary, whereas the stomach might teach them an immediate lesson, rebelling violently against a surfeit of chocolate sodas and orange pop, the brain could survive for years on a diet of comics and picture magazines before its owner became aware that chronic illiteracy had set in. Krutch has thrown an embarrassing spotlight on the professors' proposal; although his tight analogy is only a small part of the argument of a long article, it helps to support that argument.

By contrast, the analogy in the second passage conceals a fallacy that Huxley exposed in the 1890s:

> There is another fallacy which appears to me to pervade the so-called "ethics of evolution." It is the notion that because, on the whole, animals and plants have advanced in perfection of organization by means of the struggle for existence and the consequent "survival of the fittest"; therefore men in society, men as ethical beings, must look to the same process to help them towards perfection. I suspect that this fallacy has arisen out of the unfortunate ambiguity of the phrase "survival of the fittest." "Fittest" has a connotation of "best"; and about "best" there hangs a moral flavour. In cosmic nature, however, what is "fittest" depends upon the conditions.—Thomas Henry Huxley, "Evolution and Ethics," *Evolution and Ethics and Other Essays* (1893)

In other words, the familiar analogy between the "fittest" man in the economic struggle of modern times and the animal or plant best adapted to survive the evolutionary process through the ages—a fallacy based on the careless use of loose terms—is too loose to clothe even the ghost of an ancient argument. It is easier to find biological evidence for the contrary conclusion that the price of distinction is extinction.

An analogy can be regarded as an extended simile or metaphor (depending on whether the comparison is stated or implied) and can be put to the same tests of originality, appropriateness, and consistency already discussed in Chapter 6. For example, the "survival of the fittest" analogy not only is inappropriate but had already crystallized by 1893 into a trite metaphor. Today it takes its place beside Carlyle's scornful comparison of Democracy to a ship in a storm being run by the entire crew instead of by the captain, and Lincoln's analogy between swapping presidents in 1864 and swapping horses in midstream. These corroded coins still have a rhetorical glitter, but it is not the pure gold of sound logic.

EXERCISES

A. Which of the following statements are fact, and which are judgments?

1. A fish is cold-blooded.

2. Shakespeare was a greater playwright than Edward Albee.

3. In football the best offense is a good defense.

4. Women take longer to dress themselves than men.

5. Pearl Harbor was attacked by the Japanese on December 7, 1941.

6. There is no alternative to peace.

7. Students who wear beards are nonconformists.

211

8. No one can be happy under a dictatorial government.

9. A cat is an animal that is often kept as a pet or for killing mice.

10. *Moby Dick* is one of the great novels of American literature.

11. Coffee is grown in Brazil.

12. Coeducation is the only normal way of life for college undergraduates.

13. You are known by the company you keep.

14. Marijuana iṣ a narcotic that is commonly smoked in cigarettes.

15. Fraternities teach students the true meaning of brotherhood.

B. Identify the assumptions in each of the following statements:

1. Because Shakespeare was an actor, he wrote plays that have been highly successful in the theater.

2. A student who does not get high grades in courses in economics cannot be successful in business.

3. Having graduated with Honors in Child Psychology, she was one of the most capable mothers in the PTA.

4. Because of the abilities required of them in their profession, Public Speaking should be a required course for all potential lawyers.

5. The mayor should not be expected to help rebuild the slums in the Fifth Ward, because nobody there worked for him during his campaign.

6. Not yet over thirty, she was better able to understand the actions and attitudes of the students than the sexagenarian who headed the department.

7. Not having had any professional experience in education, he was ill-equipped to serve on the university's Board of Trustees.

8. The student committee concluded that the college should offer courses that are relevant in the second half of the twentieth century, not Middle English literature or Ancient History.

9. He had played team sports all through college and was therefore a man of high character who was calm under the pressures of business and able to cooperate smoothly with other members of the firm.

10. To improve the morals of the youth of the community, the police department should put a ban on all obscene books in the library.

C. Whenever possible, add a valid conclusion to each of the following pairs of premises (you are not asked to decide if the premises are true):

1. No student in the class received an F in Biology.
   Mabel received an F in Biology.

2. All kangaroos have marsupial pouches.
   Wombats have marsupial pouches.

3. All television programs are boring.
   The Tonight Show is a television program.

4. All members of Phi Phi Phi are undergraduates.
John is an undergraduate.

5. All citizens of the community are allowed in the swimming pool.
The Smiths are not citizens of the community.

6. No snakes have limbs.
Snakes are reptiles.

7. All basketballs are round.
This ball is not round.

8. No people have two heads.
Italians are people.

9. Some undergraduates smoke marijuana.
Tom smokes marijuana.

10. All houses on our street were damaged by the flood.
The Fosdicks' house is not on our street.

D. Each of the following passages illustrates one of these errors in reasoning: equivocation; *argumentum ad hominem*; false dilemma; faulty assumption; begging the question; loose analogy; *post hoc, ergo propter hoc*. Identify.

1. The federal government has no right to investigate the financial affairs of a private citizen, because a citizen's private affairs are none of the government's business.

2. The events of recent history have proved that we must either abolish communism from the world or surrender to it.

3. Depending on a dictionary that is derived from the usage of the general public is the same thing as letting murderers and thieves make the laws because they know more about killing than lawyers.

4. After eating snapping turtle soup once I had an upset stomach for three days. Obviously it doesn't agree with me.

5. A girl should not go to a coeducational college unless she is more interested in matrimony than in scholarship.

6. "Once or twice I have been provoked and have asked the company how many of them could describe the Second Law of Thermodynamics. The response was cold: it was also negative. Yet I was asking something which is about the scientific equivalent of: *Have you read a work of Shakespeare's?*"—C. P. Snow, *The Two Cultures*

7. It is hard for me to see how my neighbors and I should be blamed for discrimination when it comes to deciding who is to live in our neighborhood. We make discriminations all through life. If people are not allowed to discriminate, how can they make decisions in life between good and bad?

8. I cannot agree with the political philosophy of a man who has been twice divorced and remarried, especially when there are children involved.

9. You can't have it both ways: either we beat the Russians in the cold war or appease them.

213

10. I cannot vote for the bill advocating the construction of the dam because its sponsor is a corrupt swindler whose only concern is lining the pockets of his constituents.

E. Each of the following passages contains one or more analogies, either explicit or implicit. Which of the analogies strike you as convincing? Why? Which ones appear to be too loose to support an effective argument? Why?

1. We favor the registration of all firearms, long or short. The N.R.A. has done a good job of persuading its members that registration is the first step toward confiscation of all weapons. Nonsense. Americans register, among other things, their autos, their dogs and the births of their children. Yet confiscation of cars, cocker spaniels or infants has never been a great problem.—Editorial, *Life*

2. In spite of this [that an adequate volunteer army can be obtained for a relatively small expansion of the military budget], thoughtful men can seriously propose a lottery for the draft, though this makes no more sense than a lottery for the income tax in which some citizens are favored with no tax at all and others would pay a threefold tax.—Kenneth Boulding, "The Many Failures of Success," *Saturday Review*

3. Writing free verse is like playing tennis with the net down.—Robert Frost, "Address at Milton Academy"

4. As a result, when he crossed the ocean to bring to war-torn Europe a just and lasting peace, he put himself in the deplorable position of the benefactor who wishes to restore the eyesight of a patient but does not know the construction of the eye and has neglected to learn the necessary methods of operation.—Sigmund Freud and W. C. Bullitt, "Woodrow Wilson," *Encounter*

5. Chesterton once said that starting with half a reform and hoping the rest would follow was no way to get anything done. Suppose, he said, it is agreed that each man should have a cow; you give him half a cow to be going on with; he doesn't know what to do with it and he leaves it lying about. Then people say he never wanted any cow at all. Probably the half cow is actually the anti-cow brigade's way of making sure he never gets a whole one. . . . —Katharine Whitehorn, *Observer*

F. Analyze the reasoning reflected in the following passages, identifying by name any fallacies explained in this chapter.

1. In a democracy the office of president goes to the candidate receiving the largest popular vote. The election is over; the people have spoken. The winner has not yet made one official utterance or performed one official act. How then can critics argue that the winner is not popular?

2. Another advantage of football is that it builds strong physical specimens. It is no game for weaklings. You have to have a real physique to play sixty minutes of rugged football—strong legs and good wind and lots of coordination. The reader can see from this that football's value in building physiques can't be surpassed by any other sport.

3. We cannot protect the planet Mars against our enemies from the Earth if we permit these Earthists to flourish in our midst. Glog believes in freedom of speech; so do the Earthists. He believes in the right of trial by jury; so do the Earthists. He hates war as the Earthists do. He subscribes to the well-known Earthist philosophy that sin is a bad thing. I accuse him of being an Earthist of the most dangerous kind.

4. In our country the common people cannot be overlooked. The common people govern our democracy. They decide who operates the government. Actually the government is nothing but the servant of the common people. Throughout the years they usually have chosen men of their own caliber to the important offices. Seldom has a learned scholar with an I.Q. comparable to Einstein's been elected President of the United States. Because the common people prefer material progress to spiritual progress, they should be given the kind of education that will allow them to make a direct material gain from it.

5. Before that fatal day of July 4th I had not been swimming all summer. That afternoon some friends and I went into the woods to the old swimming hole for a dip. The outlet had been clogged with leaves and branches, and the water was stagnant and uninviting. But boys will be boys—especially on a hot summer day. The very next morning I was seized with the mysterious aches that turned out later to be the dreaded symptoms of polio. My system had obviously been invaded by some kind of bug in the polluted pool.

6. My worthy opponent calls herself a progressive because she advocates such "forward-looking" measures as higher salaries for teachers, fairer wages in industry, and a new town sewage system. Then she ridicules me for what she calls my "Victorian faith in the inevitability of progress." How can a person call herself a progressive when she doesn't even believe in progress?

7. In regard to the college magazine the administration can do one of two things. It can either abolish the office of the so-called "faculty adviser" and give the magazine back to the students, making them and them alone responsible for what appears in print, or it can give the adviser unlimited power to crib, cabin, and confine creative writing at this college with the most odious form of censorship. One course is democracy; the other is—fascism. As for me, give me journalistic freedom or require me to withdraw from college.

8. This man's reputation as a reformer of public morality has been built up amid the glamour of the television screen. How well it is deserved can be seen from a look at his own personal morality. The record shows that he has been twice divorced and that his first wife was given custody of the children by that "marriage." And this is the man who dares to prescribe public morality! Practice what you so unctuously preach, Smathers!

9. A college is a business just like a copper mine or a cement mill or a paper cup factory. No business can exist without advertising. Then why shouldn't those who run the business of the college be allowed to spend a decent amount of money for a good football team to advertise their plant and their product?

10. These so-called liberals must be seen for what they really are. The dictionary defines *liberal* as "favorable to or in accord with the policy of leaving the individual as unrestricted as possible in the opportunities for self-expression or self-fulfillment." It is the self-styled liberals who have voted for the laws that have crippled American industry in recent years. They are not worthy of the name. The real liberals are the conservatives.

11. When a government passes an unjust law, a citizen can either obey it without a murmur and be a slave or refuse to obey it and be free. The law requiring employers to collect taxes from their employees on a pay-as-you-go basis is obviously unjust. By what authority can the Congress compel me to be a tax-collector without pay? I see no alternative but to refuse to conform to this tyrannical law.

12. To get a clear picture of Shakespeare's taste in play-writing, one has only to look at *Titus Andronicus*. In the first act the hero sacrifices one of the three sons of the captive Gothic Queen, Tamora, and slays one of his own. In the second act the remaining two sons of Tamora murder Bassianus, and, after ravishing his wife, Lavinia, tear out her tongue and cut off her hands so that she can't squeal or put the finger on them. In the third act Titus cuts off one of his own hands, and two of his sons are decapitated. In the fourth act, after Tamora gives birth to a "blackamoor," her villainous lover, Aaron, kills both the nurse and the midwife to ensure secrecy. In the last act, Titus cuts the throats of Tamora's remaining sons, and Lavinia, after catching their blood in a basin, serves them up in a pie. But why pile on more evidence? How can anyone seriously argue that the author of this bloody butchery is a better playwright than the author of *Death of a Salesman*?

13. This policy is unsound because it is the work of crackpot college professors. How can anybody have faith in a plan drawn up by fuzzy-minded planners in mortarboards? If they had been kept in their ivory tower where they belong and never allowed to flock to Washington to run the government with their bureaucratic meddling, a plan as impractical as this would have never been born.

14. As an example of what I mean by saying that the romantic poets are poor guides for modern living, take Keats. At the end of his famous "Ode on a Grecian Urn," he argues that "Beauty is truth, truth beauty." I don't deny that this may be true. But when he goes on to say:

> that is all
> Ye know on earth, and all ye need to know

I rebel. How can we possibly get along in the modern world if all we know on earth is that beauty is truth, truth beauty? This is poetic nonsense of the silliest kind.

15. Some students can memorize and cram for a test and ring up a 95, while others won't study at all but rely entirely on what they learned at a lecture and emerge with an 80. But some time later, the latter have a better chance of retaining all they learned than the former. This proves that grades signify nothing as far as intelligence is concerned.

9 The Library Research Paper

Research is but diligent search which enjoys
the high flavor of primitive hunting.
James Harvey Robinson

Some articles are born documented, others
achieve documentation, but a good many
have footnotes thrust upon them.
William Riley Parker

WHAT RESEARCH IS

In the highest sense of the word, research is investigation resulting in an original contribution to knowledge. The scientist may discover a new alloy or drug in the laboratory; the historian, pursuing the quarry through faded newspapers and forgotten documents, may throw new light on the causes of a devastating war; the literary scholar may edit an unpublished manuscript or add an important piece to the puzzle of a great writer's life.

On rare occasions college undergraduates have made contributions of this sort. An undergraduate at Oberlin College was the first American to work out the method by which aluminum is produced. But the instructor who assigns a library research paper doesn't expect revolutionary discoveries. You will probably be laboring in a field that has been thoroughly plowed by scholars who have recorded their findings in books and articles in any good library. You will be expected to track down these references, sift out the materials that best suit your purpose, and synthesize them in a well-planned, well-written essay, carefully acknowledging indebtedness in accordance with a standard technique. You will also be expected to display a critical intelligence throughout and come to logical conclusions on the basis of the evidence presented.

Library research is not restricted to scholars, feature writers, and historical novelists. It is a task for thousands of unliterary citizens who are required to collect accurate information, not only for speeches and reports but in the routine pursuit of their daily jobs. The research paper is an assignment that you will meet again and again in college. The experience of writing one paper cannot make you a trained scholar; but it can introduce you to the library, teach you to organize materials more complex than the facts and fancies of your shorter themes, show you the proper technique of scholarly acknowledgment, and help you to develop the resourcefulness and independence without which genuine education is impossible.

WHAT A RESEARCH PAPER IS NOT

A research paper is not a series of quotations loosely stitched together with the tenuous threads of transition. (Zilch says this: Quote at length. Zupitz, on the other hand, maintains this: Quote at length.) This is not a research paper; it is a scrapbook.

A research paper is not a paraphrase of a single book or article, or even of two or three laid end to end. This is a précis, synopsis, or digest.

A research paper is not a simple transfer without acknowledgment from the printed page to the typed manuscript, however skillfully disguised with occasional alterations. This is literary larceny.

CHOOSING AND LIMITING A SUBJECT

In writing a 500-word theme, the problem of selecting a subject and "staking out a claim" (see pp. 30–33) is relatively simple. The preliminary choice of a topic for research is often highly tentative; the precise subject may not come clearly into focus until you have spent many hours in the library. During the hunt for material, a vast area (marine disasters) may be narrowed down to a workable claim (the sinking of the *Titanic*). The search for the answer to a presumably simple question (How did Truman win the nomination for Vice-President in 1944?) may lead into an intricate maze (American political strategy). A student beginning with a subject as infinite as evolution may run across accounts of the Tennessee "Monkey Trial" of 1925, become interested in the spellbinding politician who led the prosecution, and end up by writing on William Jennings Bryan's "Cross of Gold" speech in 1896.

Of course, if the instructor selects the topic, he or she will not want it to undergo a complete metamorphosis. But your instructor will expect the final size and shape of the subject to be intelligently adjusted to the length of the paper and the amount of information available. A 2,000-word paper entitled "The Uses of Atomic Energy," "The Poetry of Lord Byron," or "Labor Unions" can be nothing but the most superficial survey. "Radioactive Isotopes in Cancer Detection," "History and Fiction in 'The Prisoner of Chillon,'" "The Labor Policies of David

Dubinsky"—these titles reflect a better sense of proportion. Occasionally students choose a subject so limited that they quickly exhaust its possibilities, but it is far more common for inexperienced investigators to bite off more than they can even begin to taste.

FINDING MATERIAL

The only way to use the college library is to walk in and go to work. But if you are aware of some of the important sources common to all good-sized libraries, you can get off to a faster start than a classmate who wanders vaguely up to the delivery desk and asks the nearest assistant librarian where to look for a book on model airplanes. The following list may seem imposing, but it is only a limited list of the many sources you may have occasion to consult. You should be particularly familiar with those marked with an asterisk (*); you should know where they are in the library, what they are for, and how to use them.

* The Card Catalogue

A complete card catalogue lists every book in the library on at least three separate cards: by author, by title, and by subject. See the accompanying representative author card from the series issued by the Library of Congress.

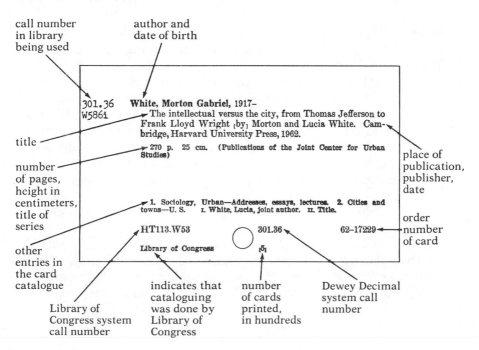

The title card for this same book is identical except that the title is inserted above the author's name. Each of the subject cards is identical except that the subject (Cities and towns—U.S., for example) appears above the author's name. Your library probably catalogues this book under both subjects indicated on the Library of Congress card, in addition to the joint author.

Periodical Indexes

Although the card catalogue may include the titles of all the magazines and newspapers in the library, giving a complete record of volumes, numbers, and dates, it cannot possibly index all the articles in those periodicals. The student who reports that there is nothing in the library on Citizens' Band Radio because there are no books listed under that subject in the card catalogue is ignoring the most obvious sources of information. Even if your subject is as old as "The Battle of Marathon," your most valuable source may be an obscure article tucked away in one of the bound volumes of a magazine. A well-equipped reference room contains both general and specific periodical indexes.

General indexes

Book Review Digest (1905–). Contains excerpts from representative book reviews indexed by author, title, and subject. A quick way to find an exact reference to a review and get a glimpse of a book's reception on publication.

International Index to Periodicals (1907–1965). Indexes by author, title, and subject the articles in many scholarly magazines not recorded in the *Readers' Guide* (see below), including those in foreign languages. Superseded in 1965 by *Social Sciences and Humanities Index*, which split in 1974 into *Humanities Index* and *Social Sciences Index*.

New York Times Index (1913–). An index (now twice a month) to the *New York Times* since 1913. This guide not only directs readers to the files (now in microfilm) of a newspaper notable for its complete, objective reporting, but also helps to date the events of recent history and to determine dates when the same event was reported elsewhere.

Poole's Index to Periodical Literature (1802–1906). A subject index to articles appearing in English and American periodicals for a century before the *Readers' Guide* (see below) was established.

Readers' Guide to Periodical Literature (1905–). An indispensable reference to contributions in the best-known current magazines, indexed by author, title, and subject. It appears twice a month (monthly in February, July, and August), and the bound volumes cover one-year periods.

Special indexes

Applied Science and Technology Index (1958–   ). Formerly *Industrial Arts Index* (1913–1957).
Art Index (1929–   ).
Biography Index (1946–   ).
Biological and Agricultural Index (1964–   ). Formerly *Agricultural Index* (1916–1964).
Business Periodical Index (1958–   ).
Dramatic Index (1909–1949).
Education Index (1929–   ).
Engineering Index (1906–   ).
General Science Index (1978–   ).
International Index to Film Periodicals (1973–   ).
Music Index (1949–   ).
Public Affairs Information Service (1915–   ).

Dictionaries

The use of a standard desk dictionary is discussed in detail in Chapter 5. The following are either more comprehensive or more specialized.

General unabridged dictionaries

*Craigie, Sir William A., and James R. Hulbert, eds. *A Dictionary of American English on Historical Principles*. 4 vols. (1936–1944).
The Oxford English Dictionary. 12 vols. and supplement. (1933). Originally issued as *A New English Dictionary on Historical Principles* (1888–1928). Supplements in progress (1972–   ). The OED or NED not only lists meanings in historical order but cites and dates passages in which these meanings appear. It gives the "complete history" of a word. Thus it is indispensable not only to students of language and literature but to all investigators who need an accurate understanding of any English word as a key to the past.
The Random House Dictionary of the English Language (1966).
Webster's New International Dictionary of the English Language (1934).
Webster's Third New International Dictionary (1961).

Special dictionaries

Cooperud, Roy H. *American Usage: The Consensus* (1970).
Evans, Bergen, and Cornelia Evans. *A Dictionary of Contemporary American Usage* (1957).
Fowler, Henry W. *A Dictionary of Modern English Usage*. 2nd ed. rev. by Sir Ernest Gowers (1965).

221

Kenyon, John S., and Thomas A. Knott. *A Pronouncing Dictionary of the English Language.* 2nd ed. (1953).

Klein, Ernest. *A Comprehensive Etymological Dictionary of the English Language.* 2 vols. (1966–1967).

March, Francis A., and F. A. March, Jr. *March's Thesaurus and Dictionary of the English Language.* rev. ed. (1968).

Partridge, Eric A. *A Dictionary of Slang and Unconventional English.* 7th ed. (1970).

Roget, Peter M. *Roget's International Thesaurus.* 4th ed. Rev. by Robert L. Chapman. (1977).

Webster's New Dictionary of Synonyms (1973).

Wentworth, Harold, and Stuart B. Flexner. *A Dictionary of American Slang.* 2nd ed. (1975).

Biographical References

Current Biography (1940–   ).

✻*Dictionary of American Biography.* 20 vols. and supplements (1928–   ). The DAB contains lives of distinguished Americans no longer living.

✻*Dictionary of National Biography.* 22 vols. and supplements (1885–   ). The DNB contains lives of the distinguished of Great Britain no longer living.

International Who's Who (1935–   ).

✻*Webster's Biographical Dictionary.* Rev. ed. (1972).

✻*Who's Who* (1849–   ). An annual guide to noteworthy living British subjects.

✻*Who's Who in America* (1899–   ). A biennial guide to the lives of noteworthy living Americans.

Encyclopedias and Other Reference Works

General

Chambers's Encyclopedia. New rev. ed. (1973).

Collier's Encyclopedia. 24 vols. (1965).

Encyclopedia Americana. 30 vols. (1949, annual revisions).

New Columbia Encyclopedia (1975).

New Encyclopaedia Britannica. 15th ed. 30 vols. (1974). Radically different from previous editions.

Special

AGRICULTURE

Bailey, Liberty Hyde, ed. *Cyclopedia of American Agriculture.* 4 vols. (1907–1909).

ART AND ARCHITECTURE

Britannica Encyclopedia of American Art (1973).

Bryan, Michael. *Bryan's Dictionary of Painters and Engravers.* rev. ed. 5 vols. (1903–05).

Canaday, John E. *The Lives of the Painters.* 4 vols. (1969).

Encyclopedia of World Art. 15 vols. (1959–1968).

Fletcher, Sir Banister. *A History of Architecture.* 17th ed. (1961).

BUSINESS AND ECONOMICS

Greenwald, Douglas, ed. *The McGraw-Hill Dictionary of Modern Economics.* 2nd ed. (1973).

Munn, Glenn G. *Encyclopedia of Banking and Finance.* 7th ed. by Ferdinand L. Garcia (1973).

CHEMISTRY

Thorpe, Jocelyn F., and M. A. Whiteley. *Thorpe's Dictionary of Applied Chemistry.* 4th ed. 12 vols. (1937–1956).

EDUCATION

Deighton, Lee C., ed. *Encyclopedia of Education.* 10 vols. (1971).

Ebel, Robert L., ed. *Encyclopedia of Educational Research.* 4th ed. (1969).

Monroe, Paul, ed. *Cyclopedia of Education.* 5 vols. (1911–1913).

FOLKLORE AND MYTHOLOGY

Frazer, Sir James G. *The Golden Bough.* 3rd ed. 13 vols. (1955).

GOVERNMENT

McLaughlin, Andrew C., and Albert B. Hart, eds. *Cyclopedia of American Government.* 3 vols. (1914).

Smith, Edward C., and Arnold J. Zurcher, eds. *Dictionary of American Politics.* 2nd ed. (1968).

HISTORY

Adams, James Truslow, ed. *Dictionary of American History.* 2nd ed. 6 vols. (1942–1963).

The Cambridge Ancient History. 3rd ed. 17 vols. including maps and plates (1970–1975).

The Cambridge Medieval History. 16 vols. including maps and plates (1911–1936).

The Cambridge Modern History. 2nd ed. 14 vols. including atlas (1902–1926).

Langer, William L., ed. *An Encyclopedia of World History.* 5th ed. (1972).

Morris, Richard B., and Graham W. Irvin. *Harper Encyclopedia of the Modern World* (1970).

223

LITERATURE AND QUOTATIONS

*Bartlett, John, ed. *Bartlett's Familiar Quotations.* 14th ed. (1968).
The Cambridge Bibliography of English Literature. 5 vols. (1941–1957).
   The New Cambridge Bibliography is in progress.
The Cambridge History of American Literature. 4 vols. (1917–1921).
The Cambridge History of English Literature. 15 vols. (1907–1933).
Evans, Bergen. *Dictionary of Quotations* (1968).
Hart, James D. *Oxford Companion to American Literature.* 4th ed. (1965).
Harvey, Sir Paul, and Dorothy Eagle, eds. *Oxford Companion to English Literature.* 4th ed. (1967).
Holman, C. Hugh. *A Handbook to Literature.* 3rd ed. (1972).
Kunitz, Stanley J., and H. Haycraft. *Twentieth Century Authors* (1942, first supplement 1955).
Manley, John M., and Edith Rickert. *Contemporary American Literature* (1974).
_____. *Contemporary British Literature* (1974).
Millett, Fred B. *Contemporary American Authors.* Rev. ed. (1970).
The Oxford Dictionary of Quotations. 2nd ed. (1953).
The Oxford History of English Literature. 12 vols. projected. (1945–   ).
Publications of the Modern Language Association (PMLA). Annual Bibliographies.
Smith, Horatio, ed. *Columbia Dictionary of Modern European Literature* (1947).
Spiller, Robert E., et al. *Literary History of the United States.* 3 vols. (1946). 4th ed. 2 vols. (1974).
Whitlow, Roger. *Black American Literature* (1973).

MUSIC

Blom, Eric, ed. *Grove's Dictionary of Music and Musicians.* 5th ed. (1955, supplement 1961).
Feather, Leonard G. *The Encyclopedia of Jazz* (1960).
_____. *The Encyclopedia of Jazz in the Sixties* (1967).
The New Oxford History of Music. 10 vols. (1954)
Thompson, Oscar, ed. *International Cyclopedia of Music and Musicians.* 10th ed. (1975).

PHILOSOPHY AND PSYCHOLOGY

Baldwin, James M., and B. Rand. eds. *Dictionary of Philosophy and Psychology.* New ed. 3 vols. (1940).
Edwards, Paul, ed. *Encyclopedia of Philosophy.* 4 vols. (1973).
Eysenck, H. J., et al., eds. *Encyclopedia of Psychology.* 3 vols. (1972).

RELIGION

Encyclopedia Judaica. 16 vols. (1972).
Hastings, James, ed. *Dictionary of the Bible.* Rev. ed. 5 vols. (1963).

Jackson, S. M., ed. *New Schaff-Herzog Encyclopedia of Religious Knowledge* (1908–12, supplement 1955).
The New Catholic Encyclopedia. 15 vols. (1962, supplement 1974)

SCIENCE AND TECHNOLOGY

Coolocott, T. C. *Dictionary of Science and Technology* (1971).
McGraw-Hill Encyclopedia of Science and Technology. 15 vols. 3rd ed. (1971).
Sarton, George. *Introduction to the History of Science*. 3 vols. (1927–1948).
Singer, Charles, et al., eds. *History of Technology*. 5 vols. (1954–1958).
Van Nostrand's Scientific Encyclopedia. 4th ed. (1968).

SOCIAL SCIENCE

Seligman, Edwin R. A., and Alvin Johnson, eds. *Encyclopedia of the Social Sciences*. 15 vols. (1930–1935).
Sills, David L., ed. *International Encyclopedia of the Social Sciences*. 17 vols. (1968).

THEATRE

Hartnoll, Phyllis, ed. *Oxford Companion to the Theatre*. 3rd ed. (1967).
McGraw-Hill Encyclopedia of World Drama. 4 vols. (1972).
New York Times Directory of the Theater (1973).

Yearbooks

The following annual publications contain up-to-date factual information:

The Americana Annual (1923–   ).
American Year Book (1910–   ).
Britannica Book of the Year (1938–   ).
Facts on File (1940–   ).
The Negro Almanac (1967–   ).
The New International Year Book (1907–   ).
The Statesman's Year-Book (1864–   ).
Yearbook of the United Nations (1946–   ).
The World Almanac and Book of Facts (1968–   ).

Atlases and Gazetteers

Encyclopaedia Britannica World Atlas (1949–   ).
National Geographic Atlas of the World. 4th ed. (1975).
Shepherd, William R., ed. *Historical Atlas*. 9th ed. (1964).
The Times Atlas of the World (1975).
Webster's New Geographical Dictionary. Rev. ed. (1972).

Booksellers' Guides

The following regular publications are indispensable for locating books on your subject or checking a book about which you have heard to find the publisher's name and address, the price, and whether it is still in print. Books are separately listed by subject, title, and author.

Books in Print (1948–   ).
Cumulative Book Index (1898–   ).
Paperbound Books in Print (1955–   ).
Subject Guide to Books in Print (1957–   ).

THE PRELIMINARY BIBLIOGRAPHY

After you have consulted the card catalogue and the pertinent books in the reference room, you should be able to make a preliminary list of sources you may use in preparing your paper. A book or article with a promising title may be crossed off the list when a quick survey of its contents—especially convenient if you have access to the open shelves—reveals that it doesn't cover the phase of the subject in which you are primarily interested; another may turn out to be merely a re-hash of a more thorough and reliable source. But it will save time and trouble in the long run if you carefully record all the promising items in the preliminary list as they would appear in the final bibliography. You can do this by entering each item on a separate 3 × 5 card and alphabetizing the cards—by author's last name, or, if no author is given, by title.

Final bibliographical entries must contain a prescribed minimum of essential information. The typical entries below (and the footnote form to be discussed later) follow the instructions in the *MLA Handbook* published by the Modern Language Association (1977). You may find eventually that scholars in the sciences use a different system or that your English instructor prefers some departures from the MLA rules. If your instructor does not, you should conform to the following rules down to the last mark of punctuation. *Do not devise your own system.*

It will help you with the punctuation if you remember that the three essential parts of a bibliographical entry—author, title, publication information—are separated by periods.

For a Book

1. *Author's name, last name first.* This order is used for alphabetizing. The last name is followed by a comma, the rest of the name, and a period. Unless an author is well known by initials (White, E. B.) or prefers a middle name (Maugham, W. Somerset), give the first name and any initial(s), using the title page as your guide. It is frustrating to

look in a card catalogue for *Smith, J.* If a book is a collaboration, list all authors after the first in normal (first name first) order (the first author's name is followed by a comma in that case). If a book has more than three authors, you may list the name of the first author followed by "et al." or "and others."

2. *Full title*—underlined (italicized) and followed by a period.

3. *Place* (colon), *publisher* (comma), and *date of publication* (period). Examples:

Book with a single author

Muller, Herbert J. <u>Issues</u> <u>of</u> <u>Freedom</u>. New York: Harper,
 1960.

Book with two authors

Irvine, William, and Park Honan. <u>The</u> <u>Book</u>, <u>the</u> <u>Ring</u>, <u>and</u> <u>the</u>
 <u>Poet</u>. New York: McGraw-Hill, 1974.

Work in more than one volume

Marchand, Leslie A. <u>Byron:</u> <u>A</u> <u>Biography</u>. 3 vols. New York:
 Knopf, 1957.

(If a multivolume work is published over several years, use this form: 1937–59.)

Edited book, second edition

Smart, William, ed. <u>Eight</u> <u>Modern</u> <u>Essayists</u>, 2nd ed. New
 York: St. Martin's, 1973.

Edition by somebody other than the author

Brontë, Emily. <u>Wuthering</u> <u>Heights</u>. Ed. V. S. Pritchett.
 Boston: Houghton Mifflin, 1956.

Work with more than three editors, revised edition

Allison, Alexander W., et al., eds. <u>The</u> <u>Norton</u> <u>Anthology</u> <u>of</u>
 <u>Poetry</u>. Rev. ed. New York: Norton, 1970.

Essay in a collection of pieces by different authors

McGinley, Phyllis. "Suburbia, of Thee I Sing." In <u>The</u> <u>Borzoi</u>

227

College Reader. Ed. Charles Muscatine and Marlene

Griffith. 3d ed. New York: Knopf, 1976.

For a Magazine (or Journal) Article

1. *Author's name, last name first.* The last name is followed by a comma, the rest of the name, and a period.

2. *Full title of article*—in quotation marks, followed by a period (inside the second pair of quotation marks).

3. *Name of magazine*—underlined (italicized) and followed by a comma.

4. If the page numbers are continuous throughout the year: volume in Arabic numerals; date in parentheses, followed by a comma; page number(s), followed by a period.

If each issue is paged separately, the volume number is omitted, and the date is set off by commas.

Examples:

Article in a magazine with continuous pagination

Estess, Sybil P. "Elizabeth Bishop: The Delicate Art of Map

Making." Southern Review, 13 (1977) 705-27.

Article in a magazine with each issue paged separately

White, Theodore H. "Growing Up in the Land of Promise."

Atlantic, Aug. 1978, pp. 13-51.

(Note that, when each issue is paged separately and no volume number is given, the abbreviation for *pages, pp.,* is inserted)

Unsigned article in a weekly magazine

"Big Casino on Wall Street." Time, 18 Sept. 1978, p. 62.

Book review

Burgess, Anthony. "No Health Anywhere." Rev. of Running Dog,

by Don DeLillo. Saturday Review, 16 Sept. 1978, p. 38.

For a Newspaper Article or Editorial

Follow the same form used for a magazine article, supplying edition (if pertinent) and column as well as page number. If the paper has two or more sections with separate paging, give the section number immediately after the date.

Examples:

Signed news story

Clymer, Adam. "Nation Votes Today in Skeptical Mood." <u>New</u>

    York <u>Times</u>, Late City Ed., 7 Nov. 1978, p. 1, col. 1.

Unsigned editorial

"Despite Vote Disgrace, New Era for Philadelphia." Editorial.

    <u>Philadelphia</u> <u>Inquirer</u>, 8 Nov. 1978, Sec. A, p. 14, cols.

    1-2.

For an Article in an Encyclopedia or Other Reference Work

List it like an essay in a collection (see pp. 227–228), but omit "in" before the encyclopedia title, omit the editor's name, and omit other facts of publication except edition and year. If the work is alphabetically arranged, you may also omit volume and page number(s), but must supply them if you refer to a single page of a multi-page article.
    Examples:

Signed encyclopedia article

Last, Geoffrey Charles. "Ethiopia." <u>Encyclopaedia</u>

    <u>Britannica</u>. 14th ed. (1963).

(The article is signed with initials identified in the Index volume.)

Unsigned article in a reference work

"Welles, Orson." <u>Who's</u> <u>Who</u> <u>in</u> <u>America</u>. 14th ed. (1978–79).

    In addition to this standard information, enter the library call number in the upper left-hand corner of each bibliography card (see p. 219). This is for your convenience, not for the final bibliography. For other examples of representative bibliographical entries, see the short bibliography at the end of the specimen research paper (pp. 275–276).

DISCRIMINATING AMONG SOURCES

Your ability to judge your sources will depend to a great extent on your previous knowledge of the subject under investigation. But even if you are starting from scratch, you should not accept as gospel everything you find in print. Ask yourself these questions:

1. Who is the author?   Is he or she a scholar pursuing the truth or a propagandist grinding an ax? Do other sources refer to the author as a recognized authority? Is this author merely a name or can you find reliable information about him or her in one or more standard reference works?

2. How was the book received?   Technical books are often reviewed by experts in the field. A glance at the *Book Review Digest* (see p. 220) or in the book review section in a pertinent scholarly periodical may serve as a rough guide to a book's reliability.

3. Where did the article appear?   An article in a reputable professional journal is likely to be more trustworthy than a feature story in a popular magazine or an undergraduate study guide; a news story in the *New York Times* will probably be a better source than one in the *Daily News*.

4. How recent is the source?   The latest word may not be the most dependable, but in many fast-changing fields, timeliness is highly important. An article on atomic energy published in 1940 would probably be an untrustworthy guide in 1980. The date of a book is often sufficient evidence that a book is dated.

5. How far is the author removed from the material?   You will usually be organizing secondhand material from the firsthand research of others. You will seldom use "primary sources" in the most limited sense of the term: unpublished diaries, memoirs, and other manuscripts. But you can learn to get as close to firsthand material as time and the resources of the library will let you. If you are writing about a literary work, for example, you should read the text carefully before you evaluate its critics. If a point turns on what happens in Act IV of *Hamlet*, you will read *Hamlet*—not confine yourself to what Jones says about Hamlet, or, worse still, what Smith says Jones says.

6. Does the source sound reliable?   A good liar can create the illusion of truth; a quack can sometimes pass as a scholar. But often an unreliable book or article will be betrayed by its own inconsistencies, unsound generalities, or obvious sensationalism. Experienced readers can detect quackery even in fields where they are rank beginners. In discriminating among sources, you should apply what you know about

230

the use and abuse of words (Chapters 5 and 6), style and tone (Chapter 7), and logic (Chapter 8).

NOTE-TAKING

Seasoned scholars often develop their own personal methods of taking notes on their reading. An inexperienced student would do well to follow a common procedure such as this:

1. Take notes on one side of 4 × 6 or 5 × 8 cards, limiting each card to a single source. (Use a larger size for notes than for bibliography.)
2. Identify each card at the top with a caption concerning the subject and with the source of the material. If the source is already listed in your preliminary bibliography, you don't need to add place and date of publication.
3. In the left-hand margin write the number of the page from which each part of the material is taken, clearly indicating the exact point at which you go from one page to the next.
4. Distinguish carefully among (1) direct quotations—in quotation marks, (2) paraphrase, and (3) your own incidental comments [in square brackets]. When you quote directly, *quote exactly*—word for word, punctuation mark for punctuation mark. Check all quotations against your source to make sure you have done this. If you omit part of a direct quotation, insert three dots, plus end punctuation if the omission comes at the end of the sentence. When you paraphrase or summarize a passage, put it as nearly as possible into your own words. If your paraphrase retains a key phrase from the original, set it off in quotation marks (see p. 236).
5. If material from a single source covers more than one note card, number each card and identify it with caption and source.

A sample note card containing material used in the research paper in this chapter (see p. 261) is shown on p. 232. The number 2 in parentheses in the upper right-hand corner means that this is the second of two or more cards based on Cantril's book, for which complete bibliographical information is recorded on a bibliography card.

THE OUTLINE

A 500-word theme may be neatly organized without an outline, but the more complex problem of weaving together the materials from a number of sources into a research paper four or five times as long makes page numbers   subject heading   source identification   2nd card based on this source   researcher's reaction in brackets

Public reaction   *Cantril, Invasion* (2)

➤58   20% of listeners thought it was news bulletin." 70% of them "frightened or disturbed."

➤60   Increase of 39% in phoning in metropolitan No. Jersey during broadcast hour [which doesn't seem like much].

➤67   Quotes Dorothy Thompson (NYH-Trib., Nov. 2, 1938): "Nothing whatever about the dramatization was in the least credible, no matter at what point the listener might have tuned in." Cantril adds that first few minutes were "almost credible to even relatively

67/8 sophisticated / listeners.... The sheer dramatic excellence of the broadcast must not be overlooked."

slash in quote where new page begins   period plus three dots indicate omission   Cantril quotes another source

some sort of outline indispensable. If you are required to submit one with your paper, you should observe these conventions:

1. Use the standard system of subordination

I.
  A.
    1.
      a.

2. Make either a topic outline or a sentence outline

A topic outline is made up of *words* or *phrases*; a sentence outline is made up of *complete sentences*. For the sake of parallelism, avoid mixing the two.

Part of a topic outline

I. Renaissance forerunners of modern thought
  A. Copernicus
  B. Machiavelli
  C. Montaigne
    1. Comparison between man and animals

2. Man's ignorance of nature
3. The failure of man's senses

Part of a sentence outline

I. Modern thought was influenced by three great Renaissance minds.
  A. Copernicus upset the Ptolemaic concept of the universe.
  B. Machiavelli called man incapable of good action.
  C. Montaigne questioned man's traditional place in the "great chain of being."
    1. He found man only another animal.
    2. He stressed man's ignorance of nature.
    3. He maintained that man cannot even trust his senses.

3. Avoid overlapping, illogical subordination, and single subdivision

Overlapping

I. Kinds of fruit
  A. Oranges
  B. Apples
  C. Melons
  D. Cantaloupes

(Cantaloupes are melons, not a distinct "kind" like oranges and apples.)

Illogical subordination

I. Kinds of fruit
  A. Oranges
  B. Apples
  C. Vegetables

(Vegetables should not be subordinated under "Kinds of fruit.")

Single subdivision

I. Kinds of fruit
  A. Oranges
  B. Apples
    1. Crabapples
II. Kinds of vegetables

(If a topic is divided, there should be at least two subdivisions. Example:
  B. Apples
    1. Crabapples
    2. Pippins)

A complete topic outline for a research paper appears on page 247.

After finishing the outline, go back through your notes, mark them with an appropriate symbol from the outline (IA; IB1), and arrange them in the approximate order you will follow in the first draft.

WRITING THE PAPER

After all the preliminary digging and planning, too many students consider the actual writing of the paper a kind of mechanical splicing operation requiring few of the skills of composition. The laws of good writing—of paragraphing, grammar, sentence structure, punctuation, diction, style, tone and logic—are not repealed in research. Because the style appropriate to a research paper is usually more formal than that of most other assignments, the danger of gobbledygook is increased. Although the typical tone is more impersonal and informative—allowing less scope for charged words, for humor and irony—you must not assume that you are only a neutral recorder who is expected to hold no opinions and arrive at no conclusions. The best research paper reveals a critical intelligence expressing itself in readable writing.

The actual work of writing presents two more problems that do not loom large on a 500-word theme: (1) the use of quotation and paraphrase; and (2) the acknowledgement of indebtedness in footnotes.

Quotation and Paraphrase

The amount of quoting will vary greatly with the nature of the research; the study of a poet's work is more likely to contain frequent direct quotations than does an analysis of economic theory. As a general rule, undergraduates quote too much. Although direct quotation is extremely common in dealing with primary sources, with secondary sources paraphrase will most often suffice. Generally speaking, quote directly only

1. when you are clinching an important point;
2. when the exact phrasing of the source is essential to clarify a controversial detail or illustrate a writer's style;
3. when the passage is so strikingly written that a paraphrase would squeeze out all the flavor; or
4. when the phrasing of the original is so well known that paraphrase would sound like parody.

Prose quotations of no more than four lines of typing should be incorporated in the double-space text in quotation marks. Longer prose quotations are usually typed single-space and set in from the margin *without quotation marks* (see p. 235). They are usually introduced by a colon. Quote at length, however, only when the passage is particularly significant.

In quoting poetry be careful to reproduce the verse form of the original, showing line divisions, indentions, capitals, and punctuation marks as the poet intended them. In quoting a single line or part of a line, run it on in your prose text in quotation marks (see pp. 326–327). If you quote no more than three lines, you may run the passage on in your text if you separate the lines by a slash (/):

```
     None of these point to what Byron had in mind when he

wrote, "O pleasure! you're indeed a pleasant thing. / Although

one must be damn'd for you no doubt."--Lionel Trilling, Beyond

Culture.
```

234

A passage of more than three lines should be indented in a separate "paragraph" without quotation marks.

Whatever you quote, in prose or poetry, reproduce the text with painstaking accuracy unless you alert the reader to any changes. If you do not distort the essential meaning, you may omit words either in the middle or at the end of a quotation. When you do, insert three spaced dots plus end punctuation (see p. 336). If you insert a comment of your own in the middle of a quotation, be sure to set it off in square brackets [thus], *not* parentheses (see pp. 335–336). If your typewriter lacks square brackets, insert them in ink.

If you incorporate a quotation into a sentence of your own text, be sure that the blend is grammatical. Confusion often results, for example, from the failure to distinguish between direct and indirect discourse:

CONFUSING (MIXTURE OF INDIRECT AND DIRECT DISCOURSE) Samuel Butler once said that he did not mind lying, but "I hate inaccuracy."
CLEAR (DIRECT DISCOURSE) Samuel Butler once said: "I do not mind lying, but I hate inaccuracy."
CLEAR (INDIRECT DISCOURSE) Samuel Butler once said that he did not mind lying but hated inaccuracy.

Much of the confusion and unintentional dishonesty in undergraduate research papers results from ignorance or carelessness about the difference between quotation and paraphrase. Study the following illustrations carefully:

1. Direct quotation

Since this is a long quotation, it is indented single-space without quotation marks. Notice also the use of spaced dots to indicate an omission, the careful reproduction of the author's italics (underlining), and the quoter's interpolation in brackets.

In his candid analysis of the English character E. M.

Forster carefully distils the essence of English hypocrisy:

> The Germans are called brutal, the Spanish cruel, the
> Americans superficial, and so on; but we are perfide
> Albion, the island of hypocrites, the people who have
> built up an Empire with a Bible in one hand, a pistol in
> the other, and financial concessions in both pockets. Is
> the charge true? I think it is; but while making it we
> must be quite clear as to what we mean by hypocrisy. Do
> we mean <u>conscious</u> deceit? Well, the English are
> comparatively guiltless of this. . . . Do we mean
> <u>unconscious</u> deceit? Muddle-headedness? Of this I
> believe them to be guilty. When an Englishman has been
> led into a course of wrong action, he has nearly always

> begun by muddling himself. A public—school education
> [Americans would say private school] does not make for
> mental clearness, and he possesses to a very high degree
> the power of confusing his own mind.

2. Half-baked paraphrase

The words of Forster and the student are indiscriminately confused. *Unacceptable*.

Forster says that, whereas Germans are called brutal, the Spanish cruel, the United States citizens superficial, the English are perfide Albion, the people who have built up an Empire with a Bible in one hand, a gun in the other, and pockets full of financial concessions. He goes on to say that, though this charge is true, English hypocrisy is not conscious deceit, but unconscious deceit. When an Englishman has been misled into a wrong action, he has nearly always begun by muddling himself. A public—school education, says Forster, does not make for mental clearness, and the Englishman possesses to a great degree the power of confusing his own mind.

3. Partial paraphrase

Brief quotations from Forster are properly identified. *Acceptable*.

In his analysis of the English character Forster carefully considers the indictment of England as "the island of hypocrites," a nation of Empire—builders "with a Bible in one hand, a pistol in the other, and financial concessions in both pockets." Although admitting the essential truth of this charge, he finds his countrymen guilty not of conscious hypocrisy but of "<u>unconscious</u> deceit" or "muddle—headed-ness"—a quality which the public schools have helped to develop.

236

4. Complete paraphrase

Forster's main point is put into the student's own words. *Acceptable*.

Although Forster admits that the English have built an
Empire on hypocrisy, he concedes that their hypocrisy is
usually the unconscious by-product of a mental confusion
partly fostered by the public schools.

FOOTNOTES AND ENDNOTES

In a short theme, indebtedness to others may be acknowledged infor-
mally in the text in accordance with the general principles listed in
Chapter 1 (p. 7). In a research paper, the writer cites sources in more
formal detail.

Occasionally these citations are made in parentheses in the text. This
is a convenient method if the number of necessary acknowledgments is
small and there is no danger of cluttering up the page with interruptions. If you use parenthetical acknowledgments, they should contain
all the information common to footnotes. Example:

In her biography of her grandfather, <u>Caught in the Web of
Words</u>, K. M. Elizabeth Murray writes that as a young man the
great editor of the <u>Oxford English Dictionary</u> was a
"compulsive collector" of rocks, ferns, and flowers (New
Haven: Yale Univ. Press, 1977, p. 34).

Parenthetical notes are often convenient for brief references—for
example, to act, scene, and line of a play, or to page numbers in a book
clearly identified elsewhere.

Though the *MLA Handbook* prescribes *endnotes* for undergraduate
research papers, many people still prefer *footnotes*, regardless of the
typing problem involved. Whether or not you place notes at the foot of
the page, you will be following a common convention if you call them
all *footnotes*. Identify them with Arabic numerals, slightly elevated and
not followed by any punctuation, and numbered consecutively
throughout the paper. Place numbers in the text where they will not
interrupt the flow of the sentence. Do not use asterisks or daggers.

Use a footnote (see p. 7):

1. whenever you quote another person's actual words;
2. whenever you use another person's idea, opinion, or theory, *even if it
   is completely paraphrased in your own words*;

3. whenever you borrow facts, statistics, or other illustrative material, unless (like the site of the Gettysburg Address) the information is common knowledge.

These rules must, of course, be applied with discretion or the text of the manuscript will be drowned by the rising tide of footnotes. As Frank Sullivan once said, if you give a footnote an inch, it will take a foot. You don't need to annotate quotations that are familiar to any educated reader or ideas that are generally accepted.

"Substantive footnotes" may also be used—sparingly—to record explanations and interesting sidelights that do not fit conveniently into the text of the paper (see pp. 269–273).

Complete Footnotes (First References)

In your first footnote reference to each source, give complete information even if it all appears in the bibliography. Short footnotes are for subsequent references (see pp. 241–242).

A complete footnote contains the same information as a bibliographical entry, but there is no reason to put the last name of the author first, and the exact page number is usually cited for both books and articles. Compare and contrast the following notes with the corresponding bibliographical entries on pages 226–229. Notice particularly the differences in punctuation: though the three parts of a bibliographical entry are separated by periods, a footnote is regarded as a sequential entry in which all three items are hooked together by commas. See also the notes for the specimen research paper on pages 269–273.

For a Book

1. *Author's full name in normal order*—preceded by a slightly elevated arabic numeral and followed by a comma.
2. *Full title*—underlined (italicized) and followed by a comma unless the next detail is in parentheses.
3. *Place of publication* followed by a colon; *publisher's name* followed by a comma; and *date of publication*—all three enclosed in parentheses.
4. *Page number(s)* preceded by a comma and followed by a period.
Examples:

Book with a single author

   [1] Herbert J. Muller, Issues of Freedom (New York: Harper, 1960), p. 48.

Book with two authors

   [2] William Irvine and Park Honan, The Book, the Ring, and the Poet (New York: McGraw-Hill, 1974), pp. 360–61.

238

Work in more than one volume

   [3] Leslie A. Marchand, <u>Byron:</u> <u>A</u> <u>Biography</u> (New York:
Knopf, 1957), II, 920–21.

Edited book, second edition

   [4] William Smart, ed., <u>Eight</u> <u>Modern</u> <u>Essayists</u>, 2nd ed.
(New York: St. Martin's, 1973), p. 71.

Edition by somebody other than the author

   [5] Emily Brontë, <u>Wuthering</u> <u>Heights</u>, ed. V. S. Pritchett
(Boston: Houghton Mifflin, 1956), p. 187.

Book with more than three editors, revised edition

   [6] Alexander W. Allison et al., eds., <u>The</u> <u>Norton</u> <u>Anthology</u>
<u>of</u> <u>English</u> <u>Poetry</u>, rev. ed. (New York: Norton, 1970), p. 276.

Essay in a collection of pieces by different authors

   [7] Phyllis McGinley, "Suburbia, of Thee I Sing," in <u>The</u>
<u>Borzoi</u> <u>College</u> <u>Reader</u>, ed. Charles Muscatine and Marlene
Griffith, 3d ed. (New York: Knopf, 1976), pp. 392–93.

For a Magazine (or Journal) Article

   1. *Author's full name in normal order*—preceded by a slightly elevated arabic numeral and followed by a comma.
   2. *Full title of article*—in quotation marks, followed by a comma (inside the second pair of quotation marks).
   3. *Name of magazine*—underlined (italicized) and followed by a comma.
   4. If the page numbers are continuous throughout the year: *volume* in arabic numerals; *date* in parentheses, followed by a comma; page number(s), followed by a period. The abbreviation for *page(s)* (*p.* or *pp.*) is omitted when the volume number is supplied.
   If each issue is paged separately, the volume number can be omitted and the date set off in commas.
   Examples:

Article in a magazine with continuous pagination throughout the year

   [8] Sybil P. Estess, "Elizabeth Bishop: The Delicate Art of
Map Making," <u>Southern</u> <u>Review</u>, 13 (1977), 706.

Article in a magazine with each issue paged separately
   9 Theodore H. White, "Growing Up in the Land of Promise,"
Atlantic, Aug. 1978, p. 36.

Unsigned article in a weekly magazine
   10 "Big Casino on Wall Street," Time, 18 Sept. 1978,
p. 62.

Book review
   11 Anthony Burgess, "No Health Anywhere," rev. of Running
Dog, by Don De Lillo, Saturday Review, 16 Sept. 1978, p. 38.

For a Newspaper Article or Editorial

Follow the same form as for a magazine article, supplying edition (if
pertinent) and column as well as page number. If the newspaper has
two or more sections with separate paging, give the section number
immediately after the date.
   Examples:

Signed news story
   12 Adam Clymer, "Nation Votes Today in Skeptical Mood,"
New York Times, Late City Ed., 7 Nov. 1978, p. 1, col. 1.

Unsigned editorial
   13 "Despite Vote Disgrace, New Era for Philadelphia,"
Editorial, Philadelphia Inquirer, 8 Nov. 1978, Sec. A, p. 14,
cols. 1–2.

For an Encyclopedia Article or Other Reference Work

List like an essay in a collection (see p. 239) but omit "in" before the
title, omit the editor's name, and omit other facts of publication except
edition and year. If the work is alphabetically arranged, you may also
omit volume and page number unless you refer to a single page of a
multi-page article.
   Examples:

Signed encyclopedia article
   14 Geoffrey Charles Last, "Ethiopia," Encyclopaedia
Britannica, 14th ed. (1963).

(The article is signed with initials identified in the Index volume.)

Unsigned article in a reference work

[15] "Welles, Orson," Who's Who in America, 40th ed.
(1978–79), II, 3425.

For a Quotation at Second Hand

[16] Noel Annan, Leslie Stephen: His Thought in Relation to
His Time (Cambridge: Harvard Univ. Press, 1952), p. 99, as
quoted in Gertrude Himmelfarb, Victorian Minds (New York:
Knopf, 1968), p. 218.

(Check the original source whenever possible.)

For a Biblical Reference

[17] Exodus 20.17.

(Book—not underlined—chapter, and verse)

For a Play

(if author and title are clearly given elsewhere)

[18] IV.iii.6–9.

(Act, scene, lines) Notice in the last two examples that no space is used
between the numbers.

Short Footnotes (Subsequent References to a Source Already Annotated)

Give a complete footnote the first time you refer to each source. For a
subsequent reference to the same source, you may use a short form. If
you cite no other work by the same author or no other author with the
same name, give only the author's last name and the page(s):

[19] Muller, p. 96.

Where necessary to avoid confusion, give both author and an abbre-
viated title:

[20] Muller, Issues, p. 96.

Sometimes in a long paper, the writer will supply a key to short footnotes frequently recurring or will announce subsequent shortening the
first time a work is mentioned in a footnote:

[21] George Lyman Kittredge, ed., The Complete Works of

<u>Shakespeare</u> (Boston: Ginn, 1936), p. 1524—hereafter cited as
<u>Works</u>.

Though their popularity is dying, the following Latin abbreviations
are still used for footnote references after the first. You should know
what they mean but avoid using them.

Ibid.	An abbreviation of *ibidem*, meaning *in the same place*. Refers to the same page of the same source *which was referred to in the footnote immediately preceding*.
Ibid., p. 324.	Refers to another page of the same source *which was referred to in the footnote immediately preceding*.
Muller, op. cit., p. 84	An abbreviation of *opere citato*, meaning *in the work cited*. Refers to page 84 of the work by Muller cited several pages back. If only one work by Muller has been cited and the complete footnote is nearby, the Latin abbreviation tells the reader nothing; it is one of the vestigial remains of scholarly tradition.
Op. cit., p. 84.	The author's name may be omitted from the footnote if it is mentioned or clearly implied in the text.
Loc. cit.	An abbreviation of *loco citato*, meaning *in the place cited*, i.e., the passage referred to in a recent note. *Loc. cit.* is never followed by a page number.

Other abbreviations

You may have occasion to use the following abbreviations in either
footnotes or bibliography:

c. or ca.	Abbreviation for Latin *circa* (about), used with approximate dates (c. 1568).
cf.	compare (cf. p. 83). Unless a comparison is intended, use *See*, which is now common for all cross-references.
ch. or chap. chs. or chaps.	chapter(s)
ed., eds.	editor(s), edition(s): Eric A. Partridge, ed., *A Dictionary of Slang and Unconventional English*, 7th ed. (New York: Oxford, 1970), p. 241.
et al.	and others (*et alii*). Used in footnotes and bibliography after the name of the first author when a source has more than three.
f., ff.	and the following page(s) or line(s): pp. 13 f. or ff.; ll. 93 f. or ff. Preferable: pp. 13–26; ll. 93–100.
1., ll.	line(s). Often clearer if spelled out.

242

n., nn.	note(s): p. 76, n. 4; p. 57n.
n.d., n.p.	no date, no place. Inserted in square brackets when the date or place of publication is not given.
rev.	revised (by), revision; review. (Spell out *review* if the abbreviation for it might be confusing.)
sic	thus. Inserted in square brackets in a quotation to indicate that you are quoting exactly when an error or an obviously absurd or extreme statement is made, or when you want to call attention to part of the passage quoted (not an abbreviation and thus not followed by a period).
vol., vols.	volume, volumes: Leonard Huxley, *Life and Letters of Thomas Henry Huxley*, 2 vols. (London: Macmillan, 1900), p. 73. When citing one volume of a multivolume work: Leonard Huxley, *Life and Letters of Thomas Henry Huxley* (London: Macmillan, 1900), II, 73.

When drawing information consistently from one source, you may occasionally avoid a profusion of unnecessary footnotes with a comprehensive note of this sort:

The facts in my account of Johnson's life are taken from

W. Jackson Bate, Samuel Johnson (New York: Harcourt, 1977).

THE FINAL BIBLIOGRAPHY

Do not confuse footnotes and bibliography. Footnotes usually give exact page references for specific borrowings and are commonly placed either at the foot of the page or in a separate list at the conclusion of the text (endnotes) before the bibliography (see pp. 269–273). A bibliography is a general list of sources; it usually follows the endnotes and contains no page references to books and only general page references to periodical articles. In a short research paper, where you have acknowledged indebtedness carefully in footnotes, a bibliography is not always required. If the instructor requires one, you must decide whether to present an *extensive* bibliography which gives a thorough listing of available source material on the subject or a *selected* bibliography listing only the sources you found most useful. Because many long undergraduate bibliographies are copied uncritically from the card catalogue and *Readers' Guide*, most college instructors would rather see a bibliography limited (like the one on pages 275–276) to the sources actually used.

In listing sources in the final bibliography, follow the same form prescribed for the preliminary bibliography (see pp. 226–229). Alphabetize sources by author's last name, either in a single list or in separate lists according to classification; it is unnecessary in a short bibliography to list books and magazine articles separately. When no author is given, alphabetize an entry by the first important word in the title.

REMINDERS

It would be vain to try to summarize all the details in this chapter. Unless you have an exceptional memory, you will not be able to remember the form for every variety of footnote or bibliographical entry. But in preparing your paper you should make frequent reference to the examples. Remember to follow these models carefully, making exceptions only when the instructor recommends them. *Do not manufacture your own system.* Notice, for example, that the standard abbreviation for *page* is a small *p.*, not a capital or a *pg.*, and that it is followed by a period. Remember that the titles of magazine articles are in quotation marks and that the titles of books are underlined. Don't forget to alphabetize your bibliography. Trivial as these matters may seem, they are important simply because if all individualists had their way, the language of scholarship would be chaotic.

The research paper is not a glorified scrapbook to be judged only as evidence of thorough investigation and punctilious acknowledgment. It is a comprehensive test of your ability to read with critical intelligence, sift your sources with discrimination, organize a large body of material in an orderly manner, and present the evidence and your conclusions in readable form. For this reason, it is often regarded in the elementary composition course as a sort of valedictory exercise, and, in more advanced courses, in whatever department, as convincing evidence of whether a student has absorbed the lessons of freshman English.

A SPECIMEN RESEARCH PAPER

Study the following research paper. Because it is significantly longer than most freshman papers, you can use it as a comprehensive review of the principles and details stressed in this chapter. The title page presents a minimum of essential information, carefully spaced and framed for the sake of appearance. The instructor may require other details. If a title page is not requested, place the same information (not including the title) in the upper right-hand corner of the first page of the paper. A research paper is unfolded and may be enclosed in an outside cover. The specimen paper also contains a short topic outline. Whether a topic or sentence outline is required, you should make yourself one as a guide, but not as a straitjacket.

MARTIANS AND MASS HYSTERIA

Woodruff Howe

English 102

Mr. McCluskey

May 12, 1979

Outline

I. Introduction to Mars and the broadcast

II. The impact of the broadcast

    A. The initial panic

    B. Later public reaction

III. Reasons for panic

    A. The jittery America of October 1938

    B. Faith in radio news reporting

    C. Convincing acting

    D. Good theater in the script

        1. The warnings against credulity

        2. Alternation of calm and crisis

IV. Incredible aspects of the script

    A. The defiance of time and distance

    B. The immortal Professor Pierson

    C. Familiar literary devices

        1. Martians in science fiction

        2. "On-the-spot" reporting in other literature

V. The neglect of other evidence

    A. Failure to check the story

    B. Rationalizing the evidence from inadequate checks

VI. From yesterday to tomorrow

    A. The persistence of the story

    B. The possibility of an encore

    C. The dream of an earthly Mars

    D. A challenge to education

No page number on page 1

Title not underlined or in caps or
quotation marks

The sections of the outline are in the
margin to show you the organization of
the paper.

Short sentence as transition between
paragraphs and topics

Direct quotations distinguished from
paraphrase

248

Martians and Mass Hysteria

When it swings closest to the earth, the planet Mars is   I
still about thirty-five million miles away.[1] When the
unmanned Viking spacecraft bridged that gap with its historic
landing in the summer of 1976, scientists hoped to learn at
last if even the lowest forms of plant or animal life
existed--or ever had existed--in the unfriendly atmosphere of
the red planet. After months of sifting the evidence, the
results were inconclusive.[2]

For reputable scientists in the twentieth century, the
age-old question "Is there life on Mars?" had never included
the probability of living, intelligent beings even remotely
human.[3] But the popular imagination, with its infinite
capacity for self-delusion and superstition, is seldom
concerned with scientific evidence. On Halloween in 1938 a
fictitious Martian invasion of the earth, broadcast as news
over the Columbia radio network by Orson Welles and the Mercury
Theater of the Air, panicked a million radio listeners.[4]

The fear was nationwide. In Newark, New Jersey, one of   II.A
the primary objectives of the invaders, more than twenty
families in a single block rushed from their homes, their faces
covered with wet towels and handkerchiefs as protection
against a gas attack. A woman in Pittsburgh was found in a
bathroom with a bottle of poison in her hand screaming: "I'd
rather die this way than like that." In "a small southwestern
college," sorority girls "huddled around their radios
trembling and weeping in each other's arms."[5] Church services

Plain arabic numeral for page number
in upper right-hand corner

Topic sentence summarizing later
public reaction

Transitional sentence introducing new
topic

Quotation of more than four lines
indented and single-spaced without
quotation marks

were interrupted in New Jersey and Indianapolis; and in the
state of Washington, more than three thousand miles away from
the scene of the invasion, women fainted from fear when the
lights went out during the height of the broadcast.[6] Not until
the Columbia Broadcasting System had repeatedly reminded its
listeners that the broadcast was only a Halloween adaptation
of H. G. Wells's half—century—old thriller, The War of the
Worlds, did the gullible victims finally go trembling to their
beds.

After the wave of hysteria had passed, the general public   II.B
reacted with a mixture of indignation, admiration, and
amusement.[7] Some wrote outraged letters to newspapers and
magazines advocating reprisals against Welles and the Columbia
Broadcasting System and proposing stricter radio censorship.
Others had nothing but praise for the dramatic artistry of the
production. Still others exploded in laughter. A group of
Princeton undergraduates promptly formed a "League for
Interplanetary Defense," with a platform advocating an embargo
on Martial——with a Capital M——music.

Undoubtedly the radio public had been conditioned for   III.A
disaster by the recurrent shocks of recent history. Frederick
Lewis Allen neatly describes the atmosphere of doom that hung
over the Depression decade:

> A feeling of insecurity and apprehension, a feeling that
> the world was going to pieces, that supposedly solid
> principles, whether of economics or of politics or of
> international ethics, were giving way under foot, had
> never quite left thoughtful Americans since the collapse
> of Coolidge—Hoover prosperity in 1929 and 1930. It had
> been intense during the worst of the Depression, had been
> alleviated somewhat as business conditions improved, and
> had become more acute again as the international
> aggressors went on the rampage (and as, simultaneously,
> the United States slid into the Recession).[8]

In September 1938, Hitler, already master of Austria,

Short quotation blended into sentence without comma

Transitional sentence followed by topic sentence

Short paragraph as transition between topics

had put the finishing touches on the coup that brought
Czechoslovakia into the Nazi fold. On September 30, after
frantic days of dread, Chamberlain returned to London from
Munich to tell cheering crowds that a pact with Hitler had
brought "peace for our time." And day and night through it
all, the precise, commanding voice of H. V. Kaltenborn had
carried the crisis into every living room with a radio. In the
eerie twilight before the darkness of total war, Americans,
despite Chamberlain's promises, were actually jumpy. "I doubt
if anything of the sort would have happened four or five months
ago," wrote Heywood Broun after the Welles broadcast. "The
course of world history has affected national psychology.
Jitters have come home to roost."[9]

    During the weeks before the Martian invasion, the radio   III.B
had done more than give America a bad case of jitters. It had
given the nation a brave new faith in radio news reporting.
Many listeners, especially those with little education, had
succumbed to the easy habit of listening to the news rather
than reading it. The thousands of listeners who had been kept
in a state of nervous excitement by the radio flashes on the
Munich crisis, and who believed implicitly that radio news was
always news, were likely to be ready dupes of a Martian
melodrama masquerading as a sensational scoop—even without
the customary voice of H. V. Kaltenborn.[10]

    But neither the jitters of the age nor its childlike faith
in Marconi's miracle is enough to account for all the hysteria
of the Halloween invasion. What of the broadcast itself?

    Listening to a recording of the broadcast forty years   III.C
later, aware that it is a souvenir of a monstrous hoax, a
living-room critic can still be impressed by the authenticity
of the acting. Surely Orson Welles comes across as a

Indented quotation; see p. 251

Three spaced dots plus punctuation
show omission from quotation

Transitional sentence introducing new
topic

254

convincing Professor of Astronomy from Princeton (for that was his acting role). It would be three years before he made the classic movie <u>Citizen Kane</u>, but at the time of the Halloween broadcast, Welles, at only twenty-three, had already earned a nationwide reputation as a "boy wonder" for both acting and directing.

The key role during the early part of the broadcast was that of Carl Phillips, the radio announcer. It demands a convincing transition from the matter-of-factness of the reporter interviewing Professor Pierson about the strange new "meteorite" that has landed near Princeton to the horror of the stunned Earthling watching his first Martian monsters wriggling through its topside exit:

> Just a minute! Something's happening! Ladies and gentlemen, this is terrific! This end of the thing is beginning to flake off! The top is beginning to rotate like a screw! The thing must be hollow! . . . Good heavens, something's wriggling out of the shadow like a grey snake. Now it's another one, and another. They look like tentacles to me. There, I can see the thing's body. It's large as a bear and it glistens like wet leather. But that face. It . . . it's indescribable.[11]

Ripped from its context, this pulp-fiction excitement is hardly believable. But Frank Readick, who played the part, had an inspiration. He obtained the recording of the <u>Hindenburg</u> disaster—the famous report in which Herbert Morrison, covering a routine landing at Lakehurst, is suddenly aware that the giant dirigible has burst into flames in mid-air; and he played it over and over until he captured the authentic note of horror in his own voice.[12] The effect was—and still is—strangely convincing.

Apart from the authenticity of the acting, the script III. itself is effective theater. The writer, Howard Koch, conditioned the audience to accept the fantastic climax, not

Throughout this paragraph the writer blends paraphrase of the script with carefully selected direct quotations. The passage not only illustrates Koch's "warnings against credulity" but captures the flavor of the dialogue.

Another transition that serves also as a topic sentence

256

only by the dry factual tone of the first reports of "gas
explosions" on Mars, but by insisting, through his "scientific
experts," that the listener attach no undue importance to
these phenomena.   The first direct word from Professor (Orson
Welles) Pierson is a calculated anticlimax--"Nothing unusual
at the moment"--followed by incidental information that the
chances are a thousand to one against "living intelligence as
we know it" existing on Mars.[13]   Mars, he reminds us, is
approximately forty million miles from the earth.   "Well,"
answers Carl Phillips, making the obvious banal comment of the
lay interviewer, "that seems a safe enough distance."   Later,
when word comes of the shock near Princeton, the Professor
calmly denies that it can have any connection with the
disturbances on the red planet: "This is probably a meteorite
of unusual size and its arrival at this time is merely a
coincidence."[14]   Even after the "meteorite" has turned into a
Trojan horse and the first leathery monsters have emerged, a
news bulletin cautions the listener against credulity:
"Professor Indelkoffer, speaking at a dinner of the California
Astronomical Society, expressed the opinion that the
explosions on Mars are undoubtedly nothing more than volcanic
disturbances on the surface of the planet."[15]   Interviews
after the broadcast would reveal what Koch must have
anticipated when he was writing the script: the more the
experts protested that there was nothing to fear, the more
certain were the listeners that sinister secrets were being
withheld and that the fictitious invasion was a terrifying
fact.[16]

    Koch not only prepared the audience psychologically for   III.D.2
the climax, but made full use of the playwright's device of
alternating calm and crisis.   The first intimations of trouble

Again the writer blends paraphrase
with direct quotations from the script.

Transitional paragraph from III to IV

"Familiar" quotation not annotated

on Mars are carefully interspersed with selections from "the music of Ramon Raquello and his orchestra" playing in "the Meridian Room in the Hotel Park Plaza in downtown New York."[17] The maestro's program includes "the ever-popular 'Star Dust.'" When the landing of the "huge flaming object" at Grovers Mill, New Jersey, is reported and the broadcasting system's "special mobile unit" is hurrying to the scene, the listeners' excitement is suspended in mid-air while they hear twenty seconds of dance music by "Bobby Millette and his orchestra" from the "Hotel Martinet" in Brooklyn.[18] When the monsters are wriggling toward Phillips and he retreats desperately to a new position, the interlude is filled with the music of a lone piano. A moment later, when the broadcast from Grovers Mill is cut off amid "screams and unearthly shrieks," the noise of a crashing microphone is followed by dead silence; then comes the reassuring bulletin from California, then the piano again, playing "Clair de Lune," then a flash bringing the startling bulletin that at least forty people, including six State Troopers, lie dead in a field east of the village, "their bodies burned and distorted beyond all possible recognition."[19]

At a distance of forty years it is easy to smile at such obvious contrivance and to wonder how any alert listener could have missed the cosmic variation on the old gag about the Californians' refusal to confess to stormy weather or the obvious double entendre in the titles of the music. But it is hard to deny that on Halloween in 1938 the production must have been convincing enough to induce, even in a sophisticated listener, "that willing suspension of disbelief for the moment which constitutes poetic faith." Still it is one thing to surrender one's skepticism temporarily to the wiles of the

The writer uses some material from the note card on p. 232.

Topic sentence summarizes this paragraph.

Square brackets around interpolation by author of paper

playwright and another to give way to genuine panic. Neither
the anxiety of the times nor the effectiveness of the
presentation could adequately explain the fears of a million
radio listeners--if those listeners had reacted like
intelligent adults. "Nothing whatever about the dramatization
was in the least credible," wrote Dorothy Thompson after the
event.[20]

As any intelligent listener should have known, the   IV.A
immutable laws of time and space and common sense, though they
might not apply to Martian visitors, would hardly be suspended
in New Jersey for the special benefit of the Columbia
Broadcasting System--even on Halloween in an eerie decade. As
Welles was quick to point out in his own anguished defense, the
tale is actually not told in the present at all: "The broadcast
was performed as if occurring in the future and as if it were
then related by a survivor of a past occurrence."[21] The total
destruction was carried out in less than twelve minutes; the
entire broadcast from the first faint Martian rumors to the
fall of Manhattan took less than forty; yet in that time "men
traveled long distances, large bodies of troops were
mobilized, cabinet meetings were held, savage battles were
fought on land and in the air, and millions of people accepted
it emotionally if not logically."[22]

Other improbabilities should have struck home even to   IV.B
listeners with no sense of time. Confronted with the problem
of supplying on-the-spot accurate information about the
"meteorite" to the radio audience, Professor Pierson throws
scientific caution to the winds:

    Phillips: Can you tell us the meaning of that scraping
               noise inside the thing?
    Pierson: Possibly the unequal cooling of the surface.
    Phillips: Do you still think it's a meteor, Professor?
    Pierson: [who has been standing at a safe distance] I

> don't know what to think. The metal casing is
> definitely extra-terrestrial . . . not found
> on this earth.[23]

Obviously this is not the time for careful laboratory
experiments. But, of course, Pierson has an extra-terrestrial
quality himself; he leads a charmed life. The last gasping
speech of the ill-fated Phillips describes the Professor
fearlessly reconnoitering around the mysterious object while
three of Grovers Mill's finest advance toward the emerging
Martians hopefully flaunting a white handkerchief tied to a
pole. Phillips has retreated to a distant point; but after the
invaders launch their first attack with their deadly weapon,
the announcer's charred body is found in the wreckage, while
the Professor, now safely ensconced in a farmhouse, ventures a
"conjectural explanation" of the death-dealing heat ray.[24] He
lives on in accordance with the inexorable law that a lone
survivor can and must survive all danger--especially if he is
played by Orson Welles.

Without either scientific knowledge, time sense, or IV.C.1
common sense, any listener with the thinnest veneer of
literary sophistication should have been insulated against
belief in the broadcast. By 1938, more than half a century of
far-fetched science fiction, from Jules Verne and H. G. Wells
to Buck Rogers and Flash Gordon, had reduced the man from Mars
to a cliché no more horrendous than a Halloween goblin.[25] As
one unfooled listener remarked, "just the word Martian was
enough even without that fantastic and incredible
description. . . . I knew it had to be a play."[26] The IV.C.2
technique of radio newscasting may have been new, but the
technique of disguising a fantastic fiction as sober fact,
painstakingly documented with credible details of actual time
and place, is as old as literature itself.

9

The more one contemplates the script of the invasion, the less one wonders that the author himself considered abandoning it in embryo as too fantastic even for radio. "Under no circumstances," Koch had feared, "could it be made interesting or in any way credible to modern American ears."[27]

It can be argued, of course, in defense of the duped that many of them switched from Charlie McCarthy only after the Martians were devastating New Jersey and that they didn't stay with the program long enough to hear any of the three subsequent announcements clearly identifying it as a dramatization. But the disturbing truth remains that thousands of those listeners believed the evidence of their ears implicitly without making any intelligent effort to check on it. If a spin of the dial had taken them from Charlie McCarthy to Martian monsters, another spin would have taken them back again to a station that was carrying on its routine broadcast calmly while Manhattan fell to the invaders.

V.A

Many of those who did check made the mistake of rationalizing the new evidence as consistent with their worst fears. One scared listener would run to the window, and seeing no cars in the street, conclude that they had all been obliterated by the Martians; another would see the street teeming with traffic and assume that people were fleeing for their lives.[28] All this in a nation that prides itself on its mastery of the careful techniques of scientific investigation!

V.B

In the years since 1938 the story of the Halloween invasion has become firmly fixed in the record of American gullibility. Cantril's conclusions are earnestly discussed in learned journals on social psychology and in college textbooks concerned with panic behavior.[29] In the persistent literature on UFO's it has become a commonplace to compare the reports of more recent extra-terrestrial visitors with Welles's Martian

VI.A

The writer uses a series of rhetorical
questions to introduce the broader
implications of the subject and prepare
for the conclusion.

Omission from quotation: three dots
and period

invaders.[30] The recording of the broadcast has been a best-seller, popular with collectors of curiosities and played annually on radio stations for Halloween entertainment.[31] More than thirty years after the event, an enterprising developer was offering building lots in Grovers Mill at "fancy prices" by advertising their location as the historic site of the landing of the Martians.[32]

Given the special combination of circumstances and talent, could a similar hoax--perhaps a "news report" on TV--ever persuade a gullible America to relive the panic of 1938? Even after the Viking landing, do most Americans care or even know about the scientific evidence that Mars may not be habitable for even the lowest forms of life, let alone a frightfully efficient task force of humanoid invaders? Considering the unflagging enthusiasm for sci-fi, including the amazing impact of _Star Wars_ and its monstrous progeny, can Americans draw a sharper line between fact and fiction--or are we more prone than ever to accept the possibility of doom from outer space?   VI.B

Specific answers to such questions can be no more than educated guesses. But two general predictions would be hard to refute.

One is that Earthlings will not easily abandon their age-old dream that the planet Mars is inhabited by intelligent creatures called Martians. Professor Bruce Murray of Cal Tech has put it this way: VI.C

> Mars somehow has extended and endured beyond the realm of science to so grab hold of man's emotions and thoughts that it has actually distorted scientific opinion about it. So it isn't just the popular mind that has been misled, but the scientific mind as well. . . . The reason this has happened is that man as a human species has been guilty of wishful thinking collectively. We want Mars to be like the Earth.[33]

The writer concludes with a critical comment on the significance of the event.

11

Why we insist that the dream be a nightmare, assuming that the fellow-inhabitants of our universe must be enemy aliens, can only be ascribed, Koch believes, to our national xenophobia, an unreasoning fear of foreigners or strangers, no matter what planet they inhabit.[34]

Another prediction has broader implications: Whether VI.D confronted by an actual invasion or by the terrifying rumors of an enemy skilled in propaganda, the American people cannot afford to behave again like the frightened million of October 1938. Orson Welles may have sworn off playing hobgoblin on Halloween, but the difference between a Martian heat ray and the devastating flash of an actual nuclear bomb is of little concern to the panic-stricken. We can take some comfort in Cantril's finding that "only about half as many people with a college education, as compared to those with a grammar school training, believed the broadcast was a news report."[35] The preventive for mass panic is not to train every citizen in the facts of science or the intricacies of foreign policy and propaganda analysis. The answer is to develop in as many citizens as possible the sound judgment and healthy skepticism that distinguish the educated adult from the easy victim of the propagandist, the rumormonger, and the demagogue. The story of the radio invasion from Mars is a challenge to American education.

Endnotes beginning on new page.
First line indented. Double-spaced
typing

Complete note for a book

Complete newspaper reference

Article in a collection, edition specified

Comprehensive note. See p. 243.

Short note—complete information in
note 4

Indirect source. See note 20.

Substantive note. See p. 238.

12

Notes

[1] Samuel Glasstone, Sourcebook on the Space Sciences (Princeton: Van Nostrand, 1965), p. 700.

[2] "Martian Chronicle," New York Times, Late City Ed., 24 July 1977, p. 29, cols, 1-2.

[3] See, for example, Sir James Jeans, "Is There Life on Other Worlds?" in A Treasury of Science, ed. Harlow Shapley, 2nd ed. (New York: Harper, 1946), pp. 83-88.

[4] Hadley Cantril, The Invasion from Mars: A Study in the Psychology of Panic (Princeton: Princeton Univ. Press, 1940), p. 58. Unless otherwise noted, all details concerning the invasion are from the original report in the Times: "Radio Listeners in Panic, Taking War Drama as Fact," New York Times, Late City Ed., 31 Oct. 1938, p. 1, cols. 4-5 and p. 4, cols. 4-8.

[5] Cantril, p. 53.

[6] Frederick L. Allen, Since Yesterday: The Nineteen-Thirties in America (New York: Harper, 1940), p. 329.

[7] See, for example, the letters in the New York Times, Late City Ed., 2 Nov. 1938, p. 22, col. 6 and in Time, 21 Nov. 1938, p. 4.

[8] Allen, p. 37.

[9] "It Seems to Me," New York World-Telegram. 2 Nov. 1938, as quoted by Cantril, p. 202.

[10] In his radio version of the Mercury Julius Caesar, Welles had already helped to obscure the difference between radio news and radio drama by having Kaltenborn read a running commentary out of Plutarch's Lives.

Article in a monthly magazine

See note 9.

Unsigned news story

Substantive note

Substantive note

[11] Cantril, pp. 15–16. All references to the script are to the printed version in Cantril's book.

[12] John Houseman, "The Men from Mars," Harper's, Dec. 1948, p. 79.

[13] Cantril, p. 8.

[14] Cantril, p. 10.

[15] Cantril, p. 18.

[16] Howard Koch, The Panic Broadcast: Portrait of an Event (Boston: Little, Brown, 1970), pp. 27–28. Koch also reprints the script.

[17] Cantril, pp. 5–7.

[18] Cantril, p. 11

[19] Houseman, p. 79, and Cantril, pp. 18–19.

[20] New York Herald–Tribune, 2 Nov. 1938, as quoted by Cantril, p. 67.

[21] "FCC to Scan Script on 'War' Broadcast," New York Times, Late City Ed., 1 Nov. 1938, p. 26, col. 3. The New Yorker, however, blamed the confused time picture for some of the panic: "People anchored to the present listening to a future event described by an invisible man to whom it happened in the past are in a bad way to begin with, and are going to be uneasy no matter what is said." ("Notes and Comment," 12 Nov. 1938, p. 15.)

[22] Houseman, p. 80.

[23] Cantril, p. 15.

[24] Cantril, p. 10.

[25] See Life, 14 Nov. 1938, pp. 2–5.

[26] Cantril, p. 91.

[27] Houseman, p. 76. Koch asserted that he had pleaded to be relieved of the assignment because so little in H. G. Wells's novel was usable and he was confronted with concocting

Another book by Cantril—complete
note

Collaboration. See notes 30 and 33.

Book with more than three authors

Short title to distinguish from other
book by Cantril in note 28

an almost completely original hour-long play in six days.
Welles, however, would not permit his "favorite project" to be
scrapped (Koch, p. 13).

[28] Hadley Cantril, The Psychology of Social Movements
(New York: Wiley, 1941), p. 71.

[29] See Eleanor E. Maccoby, Theodore M. Newcomb, and
Eugene M. Hartley, eds., Readings in Social Psychology, 3rd
ed. (New York: Holt, 1958), also Duane P. Schultz, Panic
Behavior (New York: Random House, 1964), pp. 16-17, 28, 59, 66.

[30] Carl Sagan and Thornton Page. eds., UFO's--A
Scientific Debate (Ithaca: Cornell Univ. Press, 1972), pp.
216-17.

[31] "The Night the Martians Didn't Land," Life, 19 Feb.
1971, p. 56B.

[32] Koch, p. 15.

[33] Ray Bradbury et al., Mars and the Mind of Man (New
York: Harper, 1973), p. 22.

[34] Koch, p. 28.

[35] Cantril, Invasion, p. 112.

Alphabetized on separate page. First
lines at margin, others indented.
Double-spaced typing

For forms of entries, see pp. 226–229.

Collaboration. The second and third
authors are listed first name first.

Bibliography

Allen, Frederick L. Since Yesterday: The Nineteen-Thirties in
    America. New York: Harper, 1940.

Bradbury, Ray, et al. Mars and the Mind of Man. New York:
    Harper, 1973.

Cantril, Hadley. The Invasion from Mars: A Study in the
        Psychology of Panic. Princeton Univ. Press, 1940.

--------. The Psychology of Social Movements. New York:
    Wiley, 1941.

"FCC to Scan Script of 'War' Broadcast." New York Times, Late
    City Ed., 1 Nov. 1938, p. 1, col. 4 and p. 26, cols. 2-3.

Glasstone, Samuel. Sourcebook on the Space Sciences.
    Princeton: Van Nostrand, 1965.

Houseman, John. "The Men from Mars," Harper's, Dec. 1948, pp.
    74-82.

Jeans, Sir James. "Is There Life on Other Worlds?" In A
    Treasury of Science. Ed. Harlow Shapley. 2nd ed New
    York: Harper, 1946.

Koch, Howard. The Panic Broadcast: Portrait of an Event.
    Boston: Little, Brown, 1970.

Life, 14 Nov. 1938, pp. 2-5.

Maccoby, Eleanor E., Theodore M. Newcomb, and Eugene M.
    Hartley, eds. Readings in Social Psychology. 3rd ed.
    New York: Holt, 1958.

"Martian Chronicle," New York Times, Late City Ed., 24 July
    1977, p. 29, cols. 1-2.

New York Times, Late City Ed., 2 Nov. 1938, p. 22, col. 6.

"The Night the Martians Didn't Land." _Life_, 19 Feb. 1971, 56B.

"Notes and Comment." _New Yorker_, 12 Nov. 1938, p. 15.

"Radio Listeners in Panic, Taking War Drama as Fact." _New York Times_, Late City Ed., 31 Oct. 1938, p. 1, cols. 4–5 and p. 4, cols. 4–8.

Sagan, Carl, and Theodore Page, eds. _UFO's——A Scientific Debate_. Ithaca: Cornell Univ. Press, 1972.

Schultz, Duane P. _Panic Behavior_. New York: Random House, 1964.

Time, 21 Nov. 1938, p. 4.

A Guide to Correctness

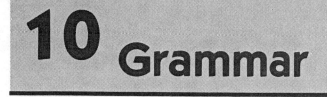

10 Grammar

There are moments when anyone resents
gravitation very much, as, say, Mr.
Alexander Woollcott resents grammar. But
you do not repeal the law of gravity if you
step off a cliff into thin air. You only
illustrate it.

Wilson Follett

All I know about grammar is its infinite
power.

Joan Didion

If you remember the discussion of correctness in Chapter 1, you will not
take Wilson Follett's analogy at the head of this chapter too literally.
The "laws" of grammar are not as immutable as the law of gravity. For
example, a hoary law that would insist on changing the first *as* in the
previous sentence to a *so* has all but faded from the books, relegated to
the same limbo as the convention that would insist on *an* before *hoary* in
this sentence. It is hard to walk through a modern English sentence
without stepping on the grave of a dead grammatical rule. Some so-
called laws—the distinction between *among* and *between*, for
example—not only do not conform to usage now but never did. Some
rules that were violated by literate people are now strictly observed;
educated people today do not say *he don't*, like their nineteenth-century
ancestors. Still other laws—on the use of *who* and *whom*, for
example—have reached the point in their evolution where strict obser-
vance depends on the level of usage. It would be easy in this chapter to
pretend that all that's not white is black, every expression not formally
grammatical is illiterate. But that simply isn't so.

Acutely aware of the wide gulf between "traditional formal grammar" and "current English usage," some students of language insist
that a new grammar is long overdue. They argue that the traditional
rules became embedded in the popular mind during the eighteenth
century when grammarians ignorant of modern linguistic science tried
to build a systematic English grammar on the wrong foundations: the
grammar of classical Latin or, worse still, the myth of a universal language. The new grammar, they maintain, must be based on the assump-

tion that English—even American English—has a structure of its own, which must be analyzed with scientific objectivity as it is revealed, not in writing, but in spontaneous speech. All preconceived notions of "correctness" or "propriety" must be ruled out as unscientific prejudices. Where the old terminology does not fit the new observations, it must be scrapped and replaced.

Whatever the value of recent research in exposing some of the outdated rules, our society still preaches the value of a traditional standard of grammatical correctness; it is widely regarded as an important badge of education, if not of intelligence. In preparing to live in a world in which businessman, lawyer, doctor, or engineer may be as concerned with "good grammar" as the English professor, you cannot ignore the formal conventions. Most of your college instructors, not only in English, will expect you to apply them consistently in your written work.

The treatment of grammar in this chapter follows a traditional order and uses conventional terminology. The parts of speech are first defined and illustrated, then classified according to kinds and uses. The common grammatical errors are discussed where they are most pertinent: for example, errors in case and reference under pronouns, tense under verbs, and agreement—which concerns more than one part of speech— in a separate section. The discussion ends with a brief consideration of phrases and clauses which serves as a bridge to sentence structure. The chapter does not pretend to present a complete English grammar or to contain all the minor grammatical rules that a writer might conceivably violate; it aims only to describe those terms and conventions that may help you in your writing.

Some matters that might be considered under "grammar" are treated elsewhere: for example, sentence fragments (p. 78), the comma fault (p. 319), misplaced and dangling modifiers (pp. 88–90), restrictive and nonrestrictive clauses and phrases (p. 322), the possessive forms of nouns (p. 347), the double negative (p. 363), the split infinitive (p. 371), and the use of such verbs as *lie* and *lay*, *raise* and *rise*, *set* and *sit*, and *shall* and *will* (see the Glossary of Usage).

In this chapter, the problems that bother undergraduates most are starred for emphasis (✶).

When you read the chapter, with special attention to the starred sections, do not parrot all the rules and definitions, for they can be only approximations at best; try instead to understand how they reflect actual usage by carefully examining the illustrations and testing your grasp of grammar-in-action in the exercises.

THE IMPORTANCE OF TERMS

The beginning of wisdom in the study of grammar is the ability to recognize *and name* the grammatical elements. The *and name* is stressed because there is a widespread classroom illusion that a student can understand a subject without benefit of terminology. Up to the point where they degenerate into needless jargon, technical terms are indispensable to understanding. "Every self-respecting mechanic," said John Dewey, "will call the parts of an automobile by their right names because that is the way to distinguish them." The mechanic cannot convey intelligence by resorting to the lazy habit of calling everything a *gizmo* any more than a biologist can get away with calling an amoeba a *wiggly piece of gelatine* or a physicist can define *Archimedes' principle* as *what happens to a body in a bathtub*. You may forget many of the terms after accuracy becomes habitual. Many seasoned writers have. But as long as you are slipping grammatical cogs, you and the instructor must talk a common language. If you write "Between you and I, George and Mary is going to the Interfraternity Ball," the instructor can hardly get anywhere by sputtering: "Words like *between, among, in, on*, and so forth, are followed by words like *me, him, her*, and *whom*; and when you have two people who *do* or *are* something, they *do* or *are* it, not *does* or *is*." The instructor can convey intelligence by saying: "A preposition takes an object in the objective case; a compound subject takes a plural verb."

Nor is identifying grammatical elements valuable only in the study of grammar. Grammar, sentence structure, and punctuation are subtly interrelated; handbooks must draw arbitrary distinctions for teaching purposes. This chapter defines a *clause* (grammar); Chapter 4 discusses the combination of clauses known as a *compound sentence* (sentence structure); and Chapter 11 considers the use of commas and semicolons in the combination of clauses known as a compound sentence (punctuation). This is a house that you can build only by learning to recognize a clause in the first place.

THE PARTS OF SPEECH

Traditional grammarians distinguish eight *parts of speech* in English:

Substantives

1. *Noun*—the *name* of a person, place, or thing:

   Smith went to *Washington* to see the *monument*.

2. *Pronoun*——a word used in place of a noun:

   The man *who* helps *himself* will be successful if *he* does not get caught.

Verbs

3. *Verb*—a word used to assert action, state, or being:

   Girl *kisses* boy. (action)
   Girl *feels* happy. (state)
   Girl *is* happy. (being)

Modifiers

4. *Adjective*—a word used to *modify* (that is, describe, limit, or qualify) a noun or pronoun:

> *A small red* ant in *an* anthill may be *busier* than *the strongest* man.
> (*a, small,* and *red* modify *ant; an* modifies *anthill; busier* modifies *ant; the* and *strongest* modify *man. A* and *an* are *indefinite articles; the* is the *definite article.*)

5. *Adverb*—a word used to modify a *verb, adjective,* or other *adverb*:

> Alice ran *slowly.* (The adverb *slowly* modifies the verb *ran.*)
> She was an *incurably* stubborn woman. (The adverb *incurably* modifies the adjective *stubborn.*)
> She ran *very slowly.* (The adverb *very* modifies the adverb *slowly.*)

Connectives

6. *Preposition*—a word used to connect a noun or pronoun (its object) with some other word in the sentence and show the relation between them:

> George went *to* the dance. (*To* connects *dance* with *went.*)
> He danced *with* her. (*With* connects *her* with *danced.*)

7. *Conjunction*—a word used to connect words, phrases, or clauses (see pp. 311–312):

> ham *and* eggs (connects words)
> of the people, by the people, *and* for the people (connects phrases)
> Daniel Webster was a great statesman, *though* he never became president. (connects clauses)

Interjections

8. *Interjection*—an expression of emotion, unrelated grammatically to the rest of the sentence.

> *Hurray,* we won!
> *Zowie,* what a ball game!

Among other things, this list illustrates three important facts about grammar:

1. *No word can be safely classified as a part of speech without considering the part it plays in relation to other words.* (That is why every word in the list is illustrated in context.) For example, what is *up* in each of the following sentences?

> He climbed *up* a tree.
> Whatever goes *up* must come down.

282

The time is *up*.
He has his *ups* and downs.
Speculators always *up* the price.

The answers are, respectively, preposition, adverb (modifying *goes*), adjective (modifying *time*), noun, and verb. By the same token, *for* can be a preposition (He ran *for* home) or a conjunction (He ran, *for* home was near); *home* can be a noun, adjective, adverb, or verb; *down* can be a noun, adjective, adverb, verb, or preposition. You can ship a man or man a ship, walk a block or block a walk, run a show or show a run, study in a dream or dream in a study—the list is endless. This flexibility is one of the distinctive traits of the English language.

Thus when a word that is normally cast in one grammatical role turns up unexpectedly in another, the cry of "bad grammar" is hardly relevant. When space experts say "All systems are *Go*"—a new adjectival use of a word that is commonly a verb and sometimes a noun—they are using the fashionable shorthand of their trade. When advertising copywriters say that a cigarette "*gentles* the smoke," they should not be made to cite three gentle-verbs and two gentle-nouns in the unabridged Webster to silence those who complain that they have misused an adjective. Whatever their sin, it isn't syntax.

2. *No definition can include all you need to know to distinguish one part of speech from another.* For example, *green* in *a green shamrock* might be mistakenly classified as a noun because it is the name of a color; *hastily* might be misnamed as a verb because it asserts action; the traditional definition of a preposition is hardly adequate to distinguish it from a conjunction. Since the same part of speech may function in a number of different ways in a sentence, no single statement can adequately define a noun or a verb. You can learn to identify the parts of speech only after carefully considering their subtypes, properties, and uses as these are discussed and illustrated in the rest of this chapter.

3. *Six of the eight parts of speech can be conveniently grouped in three pairs in accordance with the parts they play.* Nouns (or names) and pronouns (or substitutes for names) are paired as *substantives*, a general term which includes nouns and other words or phrases functioning as nouns. Adjectives and adverbs both act as *modifiers*. Prepositions and conjunctions serve as *connectives* between more important words.

Interjections, which raise no grammatical problems, can be respectfully left in peace.

The characteristic use of the preposition is illustrated in a number of places throughout the chapter. Nouns and pronouns, verbs, adjectives, and adverbs, and—to a lesser extent—conjunctions require separate discussion.

EXERCISES

A. Name the part of speech of each word in the following sentences. (Use your dictionary if necessary.)

1. Politicians are people whose words shout louder than their actions.

2. Oh, what a tangled web we weave when first we practice to deceive!

3. Some students fail to recognize verse when it is written as prose.

4. An old Greek named Antiphanes of Macedonia accused grammarians of digging up the poetry of others by the roots.

5. In a pluralistic society the frequency of errors in agreement is a singular fact.

B. Each of the following words has been used as more than one part of speech. The number of different classifications, according to *Webster's New Collegiate Dictionary*, follows in parentheses. Name all the classifications and make up a sentence to illustrate each.

but (5)	effect (2)	prime (3)
double (4)	empty (3)	right (4)
down (5)	head (3)	round (5)
dry (3)	out (5)	true (4)

Nouns

Five kinds of nouns are usually singled out. (They are not mutually exclusive.)

1. A proper noun is the name of a particular person (*Henry Kissinger*), place (*Perth Amboy*), or thing (*R.M.S. Queen Elizabeth*). It is usually capitalized. (See further examples on pp. 345–346.)

2. A common noun names any member of a class of persons or things, as distinguished from a proper noun:

man, woman, boy, girl, horse, potato

3. A collective noun names a group of persons or things:

gang, team, family, navy, congregation, flock

4. A concrete noun names something that can be seen, heard, touched, smelled, or tasted:

boat, bell, fur, perfume, caviar

5. An abstract noun names a quality or idea that cannot be perceived by the senses:

happiness, apathy, pessimism, democracy, Communism, Existentialism

Nouns have gender and number. (The only distinctive "case ending' is the possessive, which is considered under Spelling Conventions on page 347.)

Gender

In French, the pencil (*le crayon*) is *masculine,* but the pen (*la plume*) is *feminine*. In English the facts about sex are more logical. Males are *masculine* (*man, boy*), females *feminine* (*woman, girl*), others *neuter* (*parlor, bedroom, sink*). In a poem the sun may be personified as *he* or a Grecian urn as *she*, but these exceptions need not worry the undergraduate writer. Whereas the student of French or German must memorize the article (*le* or *la; der, die,* or *das*) with each new noun in the vocabulary, *a, an* (*indefinite* articles), or *the* (*definite* article) will serve in English for all genders. There are only a few borrowed English nouns whose sex is denoted by a special ending (*alumnus, alumna; fiancé, fiancée*). Nor is the American student in any real danger of failing to make the gender of the pronoun agree with that of the noun. For all practical purposes the gender of English nouns can be forgotten.

Number

The greater importance of number will become apparent in the discussion of Agreement on pages 304–310. As every schoolchild should know, a noun referring to one person, place, or thing is *singular* (*boy, lunch, mouse*), to more than one is *plural* (*boys, lunches, mice*). Most English plurals merely add *s* or *es* to the singular. *Mice* is an exception; grammatically, two spouses are not *spice*. Some of the common exceptions are discussed in the Glossary of Usage.

Uses

In addition to its possessive use, a noun can be used as a *subject,* an *object,* a *subjective complement,* an *objective complement,* an *appositive,* or a word in *direct address.*

1. Subject   The subject of a sentence is the person, place, or thing about which an assertion is made or a question asked:

The *horse* ran down the street.
Did the *horse* run fast?
The *horse* and the *rider* were both killed. (compound subject)

2. Object: direct object   The direct object is a person, place, or thing directly affected by the action of a transitive verb (see p. 293):

Herbert passed the *butter*.

Indirect object   The indirect object is indirectly affected by the action of a transitive verb. It precedes the direct object:

Herbert passed *Homer* the butter.

3. Subject (or subjective) complement A subject complement follows a linking verb (see p. 293) or a passive transitive verb (see p. 294) and renames or modifies the subject. It may be a *predicate noun* or *pronoun (predicate nominative)* or a *predicate adjective*. These terms indicate that it belongs to a part of the sentence that *predicates* or asserts something about the subject:

You are a *student* of English grammar. (The predicate noun *student* follows the linking verb *are* and renames the subject *you*.)

She felt *bad* about her friend's accident. (The predicate adjective *bad* follows the linking verb *felt* and modifies the subject *she*.)

4. Object (or objective) complement An object complement renames or modifies a direct object:

He called his roommate a *liar*. (*Liar* renames *roommate*, the direct object of *called*.)

She considered the dress a *bargain*. (*Bargain* renames *dress*, the direct object of *considered*.)

She considered the dress *ugly*. (The adjective *ugly* modifies *dress*, the direct object of *considered*.)

5. Appositive An appositive is a noun or phrase that repeats the meaning of (is in *apposition* with) a grammatical element immediately preceding:

George Washington, the *father* of his country, died in 1799. (*Father* is in apposition with *George Washington*.)

Popular error has confused Frankenstein, *Mrs. Shelley's hero*, with the monster he created. (*Mrs. Shelley's hero* is in apposition with *Frankenstein*.)

6. Noun in direct address

Children, come home.
Farewell, cruel *world*.

Pronouns

1. Personal pronouns The personal pronouns are *I, you, he, she*, and *it* in the singular and *we, you*, and *they* in the plural—called personal because they distinguish between the person speaking, the person spoken to, and the person or thing spoken about. In the third person they show gender—masculine, feminine, and neuter—in the forms *he, she*, and *it*. Personal pronouns also have different forms reflecting case (see pp. 288–289).

2. Relative pronouns The relative pronouns are *who, which, that, what* (meaning *that which*), *whoever, whichever*, and *whatever*—called relative because they introduce subordinate clauses that *relate* back to antecedents (see p. 290). Of these, *who* has a different form for each case (see pp. 289–290).

Who commonly refers only to persons and animals, *which* to animals and inanimate things, and *that* to any of the three.

The relative pronoun *that* is always restrictive (see pp. 322–323):

The woman *that* I saw was looking the other way.

Which can be either restrictive or nonrestrictive (see pp. 322–323):

The horse *which* stumbled broke a leg. (restrictive)
This horse, *which* is called Pegasus, broke a leg. (nonrestrictive)

Some writers use *that* for all restrictives, *which* for nonrestrictives; others use either *that* or *which* for restrictive clauses according to their ear.

3. Interrogative pronouns   Interrogative pronouns are used to introduce questions: *who, which, what, whoever, whichever, whatever*. The interrogative *who* has the same case forms as the relative *who*. (See p. 289.)

4. Indefinite pronouns   The long list of indefinite pronouns includes *any, anybody, anyone, anything, each, either, everybody, everyone, everything, neither, nobody, none, one, somebody, someone,* and *something*. The main problem with these pronouns is number; it is treated under Agreement on pages 304–310.

5. Demonstrative pronouns   Demonstrative pronouns are used to demonstrate or point out: *this,* plural *these; that,* plural *those*.

6. Reflexive pronouns   A reflexive pronoun usually serves as the direct or indirect object of a verb and refers back to the subject. (Plagiarists fool only *themselves*.) Such pronouns are formed by adding *self* or *selves* to certain of the personal pronouns: *myself, yourself, himself, herself, itself, ourselves, yourselves, themselves*.

7. Intensive pronouns   Intensive pronouns have the same forms as reflexives but are used for emphasis:

I'll marry her *myself*.
You did it *yourself*.

8. Reciprocal pronouns   The reciprocal pronouns are *each other* and *one another*. They may be used interchangeably whether referring to only two or more than two.

*Case of pronouns

Personal, relative, and interrogative pronouns are unique in having distinct case forms for subjects, possessives, and objects. Personal pronouns have the most forms:

	SINGULAR	PLURAL
	FIRST PERSON (*all genders*)	
SUBJECTIVE*	I	we
POSSESSIVE	my, mine	our, ours
OBJECTIVE	me	us
	SECOND PERSON (*all genders*)	
SUBJECTIVE	you	you
POSSESSIVE	your, yours	your, yours
OBJECTIVE	you	you

	THIRD PERSON			
	masc.	*fem.*	*neuter*	*all genders*
SUBJECTIVE	he	she	it	they
POSSESSIVE	his	her, hers	its	their, theirs
OBJECTIVE	him	her	it	them

The only possessive form to give trouble is *its. Notice that it does not have an apostrophe*; the form *it's* is a contraction of *it is*.

Other forms can be troublesome when they appear as compound subjects or objects. Such errors as these are common:

You and *me* want dinner (objective case for subject)
Do Mary and *her* both love me? (same error)
Johnny hit Bob and *I*. (subjective case for object of verb *hit*)
Don't say that about Harold and *she* (subjective case for object of preposition *about*)

The most elegant speakers may launch a pet rumor with "Just between you and I"—apparently under the illusion that they are avoiding the "vulgar error" in *It is me*. Ironically, though *between you and I* (subjective case as the object of a preposition) is still nonstandard, *It is me* (objective case as predicate nominative) has won general acceptance in informal English. (Does Augie think they're ludicrous, or is it just me and the assumed author?—Walker Gibson, *Tough, Sweet & Stuffy*) In fact the formally correct usage has become such a joke that the best advice to a student might be: When you say, "It is I," smile. It is one of the quirks of usage that other violations of the same grammatical principle (It is *us*, It is *her*, and so on) are more generally frowned upon.

To sum up, you may permit yourself some leeway, especially in speech, with the use of the first person of the personal pronoun as a predicate nominative. (The occasion doesn't arise often in writing, any-

---

*Note: The Latin labels for these cases are, respectively, *nominative, genitive, accusa-tive*.

how.) But for the other uses of personal pronouns you should stick close to the cases of the regular declension on page 288, using the subjective case as the subject of a sentence and the objective as the object of a verb or preposition:

The river lay between *her* and *me*. (formal and informal)
The river lay between *she* and *I*. (nonstandard)

That amused Throckmorton and *me*. (formal and informal)
That amused Throckmorton and *I*. (nonstandard)

It is *I* who tapped the wires. (formal)
It is *me* who tapped the wires. (informal)
I am the one who tapped the wires. (acceptable and most natural)

The relative or interrogative pronoun *who* has three case forms:

	SINGULAR AND PLURAL
SUBJECTIVE	who
POSSESSIVE	whose
OBJECTIVE	whom

The only problem with the possessive is one of spelling. Notice that *whose*, like the possessive *its*, has no apostrophe: *who's* is a contraction of *who is*.

The labors of generations of English instructors to persuade students to distinguish properly between *who* and *whom* have brought forth a comic legend of the same family as the *It is I* gag. In one cartoon the well-educated owl on the limb outside the English building is hooting "Who-o-o-m!" In another a frail professor is standing in the office of the President at "State U." saying, "You've decided to fire *who* from the English department?" And the well-meant *between you and I* is matched by James Thurber's caricature of correctness *Whom are you anyways?*

This problem too has been exaggerated, for in informal speech and writing, the dilemma is normally evaded simply by omitting the annoying pronoun. Whereas formal writing might have *Dr. Livingston was the surgeon to whom my father sent me*, the informal version would probably be *Dr. Livingston was the surgeon my father sent me to*. Not even the best-educated comedian says: "Who was that lady with whom I saw you last night?"

In *formal* writing:

1. Use <u>who</u> as the subject

Who owns the house with the pink roof? (subject of *owns*)
I know a man *who* sleeps only four hours a night. (subject of *sleeps*)
Adlai Stevenson, *who* many people thought was the best candidate, finally agreed to run again. (*Who* is the subject of *was*, not the object of *thought; many people thought* is parenthetical.)
It is not easy to decide *who* will make the best president. (*Who* is the subject of *will make*, not the object of *decide*; the object of *decide* is *who will make the best president*.)

Note carefully that the case of a pronoun is determined by its use within the clause, regardless of the case of the word it refers back to.

2. Use <u>whom</u> as the object of a verb or preposition

Whom did the speaker mean when he mentioned the termites feasting on the ship of state? (object of *mean*)

I know the man *whom* he condemned. (object of *condemned*)

My roommate, *whom* many consider to be well-dressed, wears my clothes as if she owned them. (object of *consider*)

Did you see the woman to *whom* the president of the Deke House gave his pin? (object of preposition *to*)

If you have trouble with the formal use of *who* and *whom*, try substituting *he* or *she* for *who,* and *him* or *her* for *whom.* Tested this way, *It is not easy to decide whom will make the best president* becomes *It is not easy to decide him (or her) will make the best president*—obviously incorrect.

Who did the speaker mean? (informal)

I knew the woman *who* the president of the Deke House gave his pin to. (informal)

EXERCISE C

In accordance with the conventions of *formal* grammar, choose the correct case of the pronouns in each of the following sentences and explain your choice:

1. The man (who, whom) the witness had seen leaping over the fence turned out to be the one (whose, who's) handkerchief was later found in the kitchen wastebasket.

2. Although he had seen my sister and (I, me) many times, he was still under the impression that I had the same innocent eyes as (she, her).

3. In deciding (whom, who) will make the best president, (its, it's) often a choice between personalities, not issues.

4. After shouting for several seconds to (whoever, whomever) was on the other end of the phone, she finally discovered that she was addressing a recording.

5. Between you and (me, I), Smathers is the kind of teacher (who's, whose) popularity with the students is achieved by always taking their side against the administration.

*Reference of pronouns

The word or group of words to which a pronoun refers is called its *antecedent* (something that "goes before"). Be sure there is no doubt about the antecedent of any pronoun.

There are four common kinds of *faulty reference:*

1. No reference (a pronoun has no antecedent)

Even after I was old enough to drive, the family rules were so strict that I always assumed in advance that he would turn me down when I asked to borrow the car. (The antecedent of *he* is probably "my father," but, because he is not specifically identified, the reader can only guess. The antecedent could, of course, be clearly mentioned in a previous sentence.)

2. Remote reference (the antecedent of a pronoun is buried too far back for the reader to exhume it handily)

Shakespeare wrote for a theater that was appreciably different from ours. Today we are accustomed to realistic settings with their elaborate scenic and lighting effects. We wait patiently between the acts while stagehands trundle heavy flats into place. In Elizabethan times *it* had a simple platform stage with no proscenium arch. (*It* refers to *theater*, which is buried three sentences back.)

3. Wrong reference (a pronoun apparently refers to the wrong antecedent)

I clenched the arms of my chair until *they* turned red. (*They* apparently refers to the arms [of the chair]. Presumably it was the speaker's hands that turned red.)

4. Squinting reference (a pronoun is cross-eyed from referring to two antecedents at once, only one of which is correct)

Older people believe that eighteen-year-olds are not fully developed socially and intellectually. *They* pay very little attention to political problems. (*They* might conceivably refer either to *older people* or to *eighteen-year-olds*. To assume that it refers automatically to the nearer antecedent is misleading here, because a reader tends to infer that the subject of one sentence will be the subject of the next unless explicitly told otherwise.)

The conventions of strict usage also forbid *broad reference*, in which the pronoun refers to the whole idea embodied in the previous clause, phrase, or sentence:

BROAD (BUT CLEAR)   I saw nobody, which was welcome enough in one way but suggested that the pubs had been shut long enough to give local drinkers time to walk home.—Kingsley Amis, *That Uncertain Feeling* (*Which* refers broadly to the whole statement of the previous clause.)

STRICT (BUT AWKWARD)   I saw nobody, a welcome enough fact in one way, but one suggesting that the pubs. . . .

or I saw nobody, a fact which was welcome enough in one way, but which suggested that the pubs. . . .

BROAD (AND AMBIGUOUS)   I knew nothing about the subject, which my professor had not learned.

CLEAR   My professor had not learned that I knew nothing about the subject.

Faulty reference can often be cured by rearranging the words in the sentence so that the pronoun is as near as possible to its antecedent:

AMBIGUOUS   A car was in the middle of the river which had obviously been washed off the road at the height of the flood. (*Which* apparently refers to *river*.)
CLEAR   In the middle of the river was a car which had obviously been washed off the road at the height of the flood.

Do not repeat the antecedent after the pronoun to clarify a vague reference:

CLEAR BUT AWKWARD   Through his use of picturesque words he plays upon the reader's imagination so eloquently that he (the reader) feels exactly what the writer feels.
IMPROVED   Through his use of picturesque words he plays upon the reader's imagination so eloquently that the reader feels exactly what the writer feels.

No pronoun is worth saving at the expense of clarity. If, after a reasonable effort to recast a sentence, you are still requiring the reader to track down the antecedent, throw out the pronoun and repeat the noun.

EXERCISE D

Rewrite the following sentences, correcting faulty or questionable reference of pronouns:

1. He suggested that since the father holds all the trump cards, he should use them whenever he pleases, telling them they are naughty, comparing them with other children, and employing even more devious strategies.

2. Last year I saw a deer with three fawns, which is rather rare.

3. I think the moral decay of the new morality, if it really exists, is partly a result of acquiring the facts of sex before they are old enough to understand it.

4. The stock market crash of 1929 was a national disaster. Many affluent investors lost all their savings. Some committed suicide. Others lost their faith in capitalism and turned to socialism. Its political, economic, and psychological effects profoundly changed the nation.

5. The dichotomy of concrete and abstract has occasioned much controversy, at least partly because people insist on dichotomizing it, whereas in fact we can recognize many forms and degrees of abstractness and concreteness.—Joseph Church, *Language and the Discovery of Reality*

6. I have become increasingly annoyed by the rabid fans who are getting into the act at basketball games. Watching them is not my favorite way of spending an evening.

7. I must have driven a hundred golf balls in practice that morning before they (my drives) began to straighten out.

8. My critical analysis of the poem, which was not a brilliant piece of writing, struck my professor as a reproach to both art and scholarship.

292

9. His wife did not share his prejudices and eventually ran away with a sea captain, which was about the best solution for all concerned.—Peter Ustinov, *Dear Me*

10. Lucille interested him more than Louise, though she could be highly appealing at times. This made it hard to consider a permanent relationship.

Verbs

There are four kinds of verbs.

1. A transitive verb needs a direct object to complete its meaning:

I *opened* the shutters quickly. (*Shutters* is the direct object.)

2. An intransitive verb does not require a direct object:

When the door *opened*, the murderer *lay* still in the corner.

Most verbs, like *open* in these illustrations, can be either transitive or intransitive, but some—like *lie*—are intransitive only. When in doubt about whether a verb can take a direct object, consult a dictionary, where the abbreviations *v.t.* and *v.i.* are commonly used.

3. A linking verb connects the subject with a predicate noun or pronoun (see p. 286) or predicate adjective (see p. 302):

Carter *became* President in 1977. (*President* is a predicate noun.)
Many people *felt* happy about it. (*Happy* is a predicate adjective.)
My name *is* Superman. (*Superman* is a predicate noun.)
Dressed as Clark Kent, I *look* commonplace. (*Commonplace* is a predicate adjective.)

The following commonly function as linking verbs: *appear. be, become, feel, look, seem, smell, sound,* and *taste.*

4. An auxiliary verb is used with another verb to denote number, person, mood, voice, or tense (see p. 295).

I *can* do anything better than you.
He *is* going to the dogs.
We *will* never surrender.
She *should have* died hereafter.

Common auxiliaries are *be, can, could, have, may, might, must, ought, shall, will, should,* and *would.*

Verbs have number, person, mood, voice, and tense. Number and person have already been considered with nouns and pronouns and will be discussed again under Agreement (see pp. 304–310). Mood and voice can be disposed of quickly.

293

Mood
English has three moods.

1. Indicative—to make a statement or ask a question:

Cold *makes* people shiver.
Is winter your favorite season?

2. Imperative—to command:

Come and *get* it.

3. Subjunctive—to express (1) wishes, (2) doubt, or (3) conditions contrary to fact; and (4) in *that* clauses after such verbs as *demand, recommend, require,* and *urge:*

(1) I wish I *were* rich.
(2) He wondered if he *were* going blind.
(3) If I *were* you, I could get away with it.
(4) He recommended that she *go* with him; she urged that he *find* somebody else.

Notice that the first three examples all involve the past subjunctive of *to be,* which is *were* in all three persons and both numbers. The fourth example illustrates the only common construction in current English where any verb except *to be* occurs in a distinctive subjunctive form: the third person without the -s ending.

Most of the other uses of the subjunctive are stiffly formal (If that *be* treason, make the most of it) or included in stereotyped expressions (I move that this *be* stricken from the record; *Come* what may; *Be* that as it may; Resolved that Mrs. Fewsmith *be* given a rising vote of thanks for supplying the peonies). Use of the subjunctive in such expressions is automatic.

Voice
A verb is in the *active voice* when the subject does the acting, in the *passive voice* when the subject is acted upon:

ACTIVE   The Dodgers *beat* the Mets.
PASSIVE   The Mets *were beaten* by the Dodgers.

Where a logical choice exists between the two, use the active voice because it is more direct. *John threw the football* is obviously more natural than *The football was thrown by John.* (See pp. 99–100.)
Do not mix the active and passive voices in the same sentence:

INCONSISTENT   When you stop for gas, the motor should be turned off.
CONSISTENT   When you stop for gas, you should turn off the motor.

294

*Tense

English has six basic tenses:

	FIRST PERSON SINGULAR, INDICATIVE, ACTIVE VOICE
PRESENT	I *study* today.
PAST	I *studied* yesterday.
PRESENT PERFECT	I *have studied* since yesterday.
PAST PERFECT	I *had studied* hard the day before yesterday, but yesterday I studied harder.
FUTURE	I *shall (will) study* again tomorrow.
FUTURE PERFECT	I *shall (will) have studied* by tomorrow night for three straight days.

Notice especially the three "past forms," which colloquial usage tends to lump under a single tense. The past represents past time not continuing to the present; the present perfect stands for past time continuing to the present; and the past perfect signifies the "past before the past."

Of course, this brief picture hardly begins to indicate the versatility of English verb forms. For example, the present tense may be used for future time (I *take* my final examinations tomorrow): past time (the *historical present*: It *is* early morning of December 7, 1941, and all *is* peaceful at Pearl Harbor); or to make a statement that is presumably true at any time (Birds of a feather *flock* together).

With the use of *auxiliaries* a vast number of verb forms can be made. For instance, we use the forms of the auxiliary *be* to express progressive action (I *am* eating, I *was* eating, I *have been* eating, and so on) and the auxiliary *do* for emphasis (I *do* love you, I *did* say it). Some of the distinctions between auxiliaries (*shall* and *will*, *should* and *would*, *can* and *may*) are breaking down in informal English (see the Glossary of Usage).

Consistency of tenses

The problem of consistency of tenses can get complicated, but if you apply the following general rules, you will avoid the most common errors:

1. If the verb in the main clause is past tense or past perfect, make the verb in a subordinate clause past tense or past perfect:

WRONG I *knew* that war *is* coming.
RIGHT I *knew* that war *was* coming.

WRONG I *had known* for some time that war *is* coming.
RIGHT I *had known* for some time that war *was* coming.

2. Use the present perfect tense, not the present or past tense, to indicate past time continuing to the present:

WRONG   Since I *arrived* here I *have* nothing interesting to say.
RIGHT   Since I *arrived* here, I *have had* nothing interesting to say.

WRONG   I *was* here since eight o'clock.
RIGHT   I *have been* here since eight o'clock.

3. Use the past perfect tense whenever it is necessary to distinguish between two times in the past:

WRONG   Now that peace *came*, Germany was in disgrace for the destruction she *brought* on the world.
RIGHT   Now that peace *had come*, Germany was in disgrace for the destruction she *had brought* on the world.

4. Do not use *would* in conditional if-clauses:

WRONG   If I *would have done* that, he would have been happy.
RIGHT   If I *had done* that, he would have been happy.

5. Avoid all unnecessary shifts in tense:

WRONG   Major Rathbone *attempted* to intercept him, but Booth *slashes* him in the arm with a knife.
WRONG   He *does not characterize* the boy or his father by saying, "The old man was short and fat and had bushy hair." Instead, he *presented* the man in action. He *shows* him puffing as he *jogged* along the road.
RIGHT   He *decided* not to fight a man twice his size because discretion *is* the better part of valor. (Necessary shift from an occurrence in the past to a statement that is presumably as true today as ever.)

Awkward shifting between past and present is especially common in essays on literature, where the writer is discussing a work written in the past but being analyzed in the present. You can avoid confusion by using the past for facts directly concerned with literary history or biography (When Shakespeare *wrote The Rape of Lucrece*, the theaters *were* closed) and resorting to the present for your analysis of the text, including plot summary (The poem *is* rich with sensuous detail).

EXERCISE E

Rewrite the following sentences, correcting any errors in the use of verbs:

1. I wish I was able to remember everything that happened since yesterday.

2. It all began when I spoke to a slender blonde whom I previously stared at in silence.

3. A student who leaps blindly into writing an essay will overlook important aspects of organization, and the final product becomes incoherent.

4. I was sitting before the TV for an hour when Joe burst into the room and ostentatiously turned down the volume.

5. When I was finally convinced that my educational philosophy is logical, I began asking my classmares which colleges they applied to and why.

6. If I would have known the difference between red and green, the accident never would have happened.

7. She went to the store to buy provisions, and enough groceries were brought back to feed an army.

8. *A Midsummer Night's Dream* contained a group of "mechanicals" whose grotesque antics add a loud note of farce to the proceeding. This balanced the more subtle comedy of the moonstruck lovers and gives variety to the play.

9. Her frozen body lay in the snow looking like marble, and people came to stare as if she was an exhibit in a sideshow.

10. If my father did not help me with my college education, I never would have made it all the way through.

✶ *Verbals*

Any verb limited to a specific person and number (He *drinks*—third person singular) is called a *finite verb*. *Verbals* are not limited by person and number. They are parts of verbs that do the work of nouns, adjectives, and adverbs but do not carry the entire verb load in a sentence. If you can readily distinguish between a finite verb and a verbal, you are less likely to write fragmentary sentences (see p. 78).

There are three verbals: the *infinitive*, the *participle*, and the *gerund*.

1. Infinitive   Most versatile of the verbals, the infinitive may be used as a noun, an adjective, an adverb, or as part of a finite verb. Its forms are

	ACTIVE	PASSIVE
PRESENT	(to) try	(to) be tried
PERFECT	(to) have tried	(to) have been tried

As a noun, the infinitive may be

SUBJECT   *To write* for a living is not easy.
OBJECT OF A VERB   Soon after the war, the nations began *to fight* again.
OBJECT OF A PREPOSITION   His roommate did nothing but *sleep* and *eat*. (The *to* is often omitted.)
PREDICATE NOMINATIVE   His only ambition was *to get* a degree.

297

As an adjective:

> Early morning is the best time *to jog*. (modifying *time*)
> The place *to go* is the nearby woods. (modifying *place*)

As an adverb:

> I come *to bury* Caesar, not *to praise* him. (modifying *come*)
> *To get* home, he walked through the cemetery. (modifying *walked)*

With an auxiliary as part of a finite verb:

> You can't *go* home again.

2. Participle   The participle may be used as an adjective, as part of a finite verb, and in an absolute construction. Its forms are

	ACTIVE	**PASSIVE**
PRESENT	singing	being sung, sung
PAST	having sung	having been sung, sung

As an adjective:

> Pascal called man a *thinking* reed. (modifying *reed*)
> The heroine succumbed to a *broken* heart. (modifying *heart*)
> *Staring* wildly, the hero vowed revenge. (modifying *hero*)

As part of a finite verb:

> I am *dying*, Egypt, *dying*.
> I have *been* faithful to thee, Cynara, in my fashion.

In an absolute construction (a phrase independent grammatically of any other part of the sentence):

> The gun *having jammed*, Bond escaped again.

3. Gerund   The gerund has the same form as the present participle (ending in *ing*) but is used as a noun:

SUBJECT (ACTIVE AND PASSIVE)   *Rowing* is good exercise, but *being rowed* is more fun.
OBJECT OF A VERB   I prefer *walking*.
OBJECT OF A PREPOSITION   Huxley devoted his life to *popularizing* science.
PREDICATE NOMINATIVE   His favorite indoor sport was *making* money.

The old rule that the subject of a gerund must be possessive has been belied by divided usage. The possessive is usually considered more formal, and the possessive pronoun is more frequent than the noun:

FORMAL   I could see no reason for *Tom's* acting that way.
INFORMAL   I could see no reason for *Tom* acting that way.

298

FORMAL   Scarcely a week goes by without *someone's* publishing a new book of travels in the bright continent.—John A. Kouwenhoven, "What's American About America?" *Harper's*

INFORMAL   Also the mere fact of *everyone* being jammed together helps to create in an audience a feeling of unanimity.—Tyrone Guthrie, *A Life in the Theater*

Sometimes the choice of case with a gerund appears to make a difference in emphasis:

I never though of *Sylvia* winning a beauty contest. (Of all persons)
I never thought of *Sylvia's* winning a beauty contest. (Slightly more charitable)

EXERCISE F

In the following sentences, classify all finite verbs as transitive or intransitive and all verbals as infinitive, participle, or gerund:

1. Jogging has added a new hazard to driving a car.

2. Although playing one of the hardest schedules in the country, the team will probably win most of its games before the season is over and be national champion again.

3. When he wrote *The Red Badge of Courage,* Stephen Crane had never seen a battle.

4. If it were not for the common assumption that a major in economics guarantees success in business, many students would never have decided to enter that crowded department.

5. Not having lived in New York for more than ten years, I feel strange on Times Square even on New Year's Eve.

6. My belief that seeing is believing has often been shaken by optical illusions.

7. In a year and a half he had been converted from a rather indifferent freshman, not caring seriously about college, into a first-rate student who showed every indication of becoming a scholar.

8. She tried so hard to be popular that all the sharp edges of her individuality were quickly worn away.

9. When the leaders of all the nations are as tired of wars as those who have to fight them, peace may come to the world.

10. Only yesterday she looked hale and hearty, striding down the street as if she were going to live forever.

Principal parts
The *principal parts* of a verb are the *present infinitive; past tense* (first person singular); and *past participle* (some grammarians include the

299

present participle). Most English verbs are *regular*, forming the past tense and past participle by merely adding *ed* or *d* to the infinitve (*jump, jumped, jumped; blame, blamed, blamed*). The omission of a verb ending from a regular verb is almost always due to carelessness, except where it represents a particular dialect (The horse *gallop* down the road). Many *irregular* verbs make trouble. Some of these are represented in the Glossary of Usage. See *born, borne; get, got, gotten; lay, lie; lead, led; leave, let; lighted, lit; proved, proven; raise, rise; set, sit;* and *irregular verbs*. The principal parts of these and other verbs are listed in a good dictionary.

EXERCISE G

Using the Glossary of Usage or your dictionary if necessary, correct all faulty verb forms in the following sentences:

1. The scene was so inviting that I could have laid down in the sun and gone to sleep.

2. When Donna entered the room, Dolores raised from the bed, smiling sleepily.

3. Having borne the package all the way from the post office, I sat it down on the table with a sign of relief, and soon my roommate opened it and dived in.

4. When I asked him to leave me study in peace, he walked off, letting crumbs and papers all over the floor.

5. When she told me she had got a place on the team and had swam in every meet, my estimate of her ability rose abruptly.

*Adjectives and Adverbs

How to tell them apart

The only safe way to tell adjectives from adverbs is to find out what they modify. By definition, an adjective modifies a noun or pronoun; an adverb modifies a verb, adjective, or other adverb. If you can't readily distinguish them, the old-fashioned test is useful:

Adjectives answer these questions:

1. How many? (*nine* Muses)
2. What kind? (A *snap* course)
3. Which one? (*That* boy stole *his* dog.)

The third example shows how words that often function as pronouns can be used as adjectives (*pronominal adjectives*).

Adverbs usually answer these questions:

1. How? (Please drive *carefully*.)
2. When? (The circus is coming *tomorrow*.)
3. Where? (The bride went *home* to mother.)
4. How much? (The world is *less* peaceful than in 1900.)

Not included in these categories are *conjunctive adverbs (however, moreover, nevertheless, therefore*—see p. 327); and *adverbs of assertion and concession (yes, no, not, maybe, probably).*

Many adverbs end in *ly*, and many of these are formed by adding *ly* to the adjective or, if the adjective ends in *y*, by changing the *y* to *i* before adding *ly: badly, sweetly, gaily, happily*. But the *ly* ending is not a safe recognition feature for these reasons:

1 Some adjectives also end in *ly:*

courtly, heavenly, holy, princely, ungodly, unearthly

2. Some adverbs have no *ly* form:

now, there, then, up, down, far (the last four of which can also be adjectives)

3. Some adverbs have two forms, one with *ly* and the other without:

loud, loudly	slow, slowly	tight, tightly
quick, quickly	soft, softly	wrong, wrongly

With some adverbs in this group (*direct, directly; late, lately; low, lowly; hard, hardly; right, rightly*), there is a clear difference in meaning between the two forms. (Though she tried *hard*, she could *hardly* make the grade.) With the others, the choice depends on sound and on level of usage. The *ly* ending is more common in formal writing; it is the usual form when the adverb precedes the verb. (*Slowly* she ambled down the street.) The form without *ly* appears frequently after short verbs in informal English, especially in commands. (Come *quick*, drive *slow*, hold on *tight*). The *ly* is unnecessary in *firstly, secondly, thirdly*, and *thusly*.

Comparison

Forms   Adjectives and adverbs have no inflection for person, number, or case. Instead they are compared in three degrees:

ADJECTIVES

POSITIVE	COMPARATIVE	SUPERLATIVE
strong	stronger	strongest
glum	glummer	glummest
lovely	lovelier, more lovely	loveliest, most lovely
beautiful	more (less) beautiful	most (least) beautiful
good	better	best

ADVERBS

near	nearer	nearest
quickly	more (less) quickly	most (least) quickly
beautifully	more (less) beautifully	most (least) beautifully
well	better	best

301

Words of one syllable are usually compared by adding *er* for the comparative, *est* for the superlative. Words of two syllables often have these forms as well as the forms with *more* and *most*; the choice is determined by rhythm and emphasis. Words of three or more syllables are compared only with *more* (*less*) and *most* (*least*.)

Use In strict formal writing the comparative degree is used in comparing two things; the superlative, with three or more:

John is the *faster* of the two.
He is the *handsomest* of seven children.

In speech and informal writing, the superlative is often used for two:

May the *best* team win.
Put your *best* foot forward.

But objections to the use of the superlative-for-two are still widespread.

So-called *absolutes* cannot, strictly speaking, be compared. Logically, there is only one degree for *dead, possible, perfect,* or *unique.* But here usage has all but conquered logic, and the purists are fighting a losing rearguard action. In informal writing such words are often compared. This is partly for emphasis (*deader* than an iced catfish), partly because some of these words have virtually lost their absolute meaning. (Nearly two centuries ago, the Founding Fathers wrote of forming "a *more perfect* union.") In *a most unique occasion, unique* has become a loose synonym for *rare.* The damage has come not from comparing *unique* but from overworking the word until it is drained of its uniqueness (see p. 372).

Position of adjectives

When the *thirsty* traveler saw the stream, *cool, clear,* and *inviting,* he did not know that it would taste salty.

In that sentence, the adjective *thirsty* precedes the noun *traveler,* which it modifies. On the other hand, *cool, clear,* and *inviting* follow their noun, *stream.* This order is less common but entirely acceptable in many contexts.

Salty is a *predicate adjective* following the linking verb *taste,* modifying the pronoun *it.* Thus an adjective, like a noun, often serves as a subjective complement after a linking verb (see p. 286).

When an adverb is used after a linking verb, either it is incorrect or it expresses a different meaning from the comparable adjective:

INCORRECT   It tastes *saltily.* The rose smells *sweetly.* This house looks *shabbily.*
CORRECT   He looked *sharply* at his opponent. (with a fixed stare)
He looked *sharp* in his new jacket. (stylish)

The choice of *bad* or *badly* and *good* or *well* presents a special problem after some linking verbs. The formally correct expression is "I feel (or look) *bad*" (predicate adjective). But "I feel (or look) *badly*" is more common in speech and informal writing. Some authorities consider *badly*, in this expression, an *ly* adjective conveying a different meaning (*unhappy*, not *unwell*) from *bad*; others insist that "I feel (or look) *badly*" conveys a weak sense of touch or sight. Because both *good* and *well* can be adjectives, the difference between "I feel (or look) *good*" and "I feel (or look) *well*" is clearly one of meaning, not grammar (see p. 365).

EXERCISE H

Choose the correct form of the two in parentheses and identify it as an adjective or an adverb. If both forms are permissible in writing, suggest any differences in meaning or level of usage.

1. If I had my school days to live over again, I would try to listen more (attentive, attentively) to my teachers.

2. Nobody could have felt more (foolish, foolishly) than I did when I was aware of having done the entire problem (wrong, wrongly) from beginning to end.

3. A politician ought to examine each issue (thorough, thoroughly) on his own before giving in to the demands of constituents who insist that he can do (well, good) only by voting their way.

4. Although he pitched (real, really) (good, well) throughout his career, he never threw a no-hitter.

5. Of the two leading Republicans, Schmidt appeared to have the (bigger, biggest) number of followers; in fact, the polls gave her the (more, most) votes of any candidate being considered.

6. They walked (slow, slowly) holding (tight, tightly) to each other's hands.

7. He did not feel (bad, badly) after the fall except for a sharp pain that came (throbbing, throbbingly) into his left leg at frequent intervals.

8. The old-fashioned art of crooning a song (sweet, sweetly) and (low, lowly) was unknown to Ricky Dink's fans, who obviously felt that the (louder, more loudly) he shouted the greater he was.

9. Although the food tasted (sour, sourly), he was in no mood for being (particular, particularly) about what he ate.

10. Because so much modern music sounded (discordant, discordantly) to him, he could not be convinced by the argument that when an artist is exposed to new influences he must express them (different, differently).

Conjunctions

There are four kinds of conjunctions:

1. Coordinating conjunctions

and, but, for, or, nor, yet (these should be memorized)
A coordinating conjunction joins words, phrases, or clauses of equal grammatical rank:

of the people, by the people, *and* for the people
Many are called, *but* few are chosen.

2. Subordinating conjunctions

although, as, because, if, since, unless, while, and others
A subordinating conjunction joins elements of unequal grammatical rank:

Although many are called, few are chosen.
While seated one day at the organ, she found a lost chord.

3. Correlative conjunctions

both . . . and, either . . . or, neither . . . nor, not only . . . but also, and others
Correlative conjunctions are used in pairs in a parallel construction:

The food appeared to be *neither* fish, flesh, *nor* fowl.
She *not only* passed the bar examinations *but also* became an assistant district attorney.

4. Adverbial conjunctions (*conjunctive adverbs*)

however, moreover, nevertheless, therefore, and others
An adverbial conjunction is used as a transition between two sentences or to connect main clauses in a compound sentence:

In this book, the adverbial conjunction is classed as a conjunction. It is also known, *however*, as a conjunctive adverb.
He was disturbed by the noise in the dormitory; *therefore*, he decided to study in the library.

The different uses of these four kinds are further discussed in the chapters on Sentences and Punctuation.

✻AGREEMENT

Statistics have indicated that mistakes in agreement are the commonest *grammatical* errors in undergraduate writing. The general formal rules for agreement can be briefly stated (though the following discussion

304

gives some examples of informal usage, you may be required to observe the formal conventions in your college papers):

1. A verb must agree with its subject in number and person.
2. A pronoun must agree with its antecedent in number, gender, and person.
3. A demonstrative adjective (formed from a demonstrative pronoun) must agree with its noun in number.

Mary *takes her* lamb to *this* school.

The verb *takes* agrees with *Mary* in number (both are singular) and person (both are third person). The pronoun *her* agrees with its antecedent, *Mary*, in number (singular), gender (feminine), and person (third). The demonstrative adjective *this* agrees with *school* in number (singular). This much is simple.

But there are numerous agreement problems, several of them presenting borderline instances of *divided usage*. In these the writer is often confronted with a conflict between grammar and meaning.

1. Two or more subjects joined by *and (compound subject)* take a plural verb:

Beaumont and Fletcher *were* successful collaborators.

EXCEPTION: when both subjects refer to the same person or thing:

My lord and master *is* coming.

2. When two or more subjects are joined by *or* or *nor*, the number of the verb is determined by the subject nearest the verb:

Either you or he *has* to lose.
Neither the girl nor the boys *were* able to answer the question.
I wonder if John or his friends *are* going.
I doubt if the professor or the president *insists* on that kind of education.

In informal writing *either . . . or* and *neither . . . nor* sometimes take a plural verb even when both subjects are singular:

INFORMAL   Neither Reagan nor Rockefeller *were* nominated.

3. A singular subject followed by a phrase beginning with *along with, as well as, in addition to, together with,* or *with* takes a singular verb in formal English but sometimes appears with a plural verb in informal writing:

FORMAL   Stanley as well as the American people *was* overjoyed.
INFORMAL   The style in which books are written, as well as the format in which they are produced, *are* determined by the social context.—August Heckscher, "Reading in America," *Reading for Life*

Because of the dilemma of number, the expression *both ... and* is often a smoother substitute: Both the style in which books are written and the format in which they are produced *are* determined. . . .

4. a. The following indefinite pronouns take a singular verb: *anybody, each, every, everybody, everyone, nobody, no one, somebody, someone*:

I wonder if anybody *is* home; everyone *seems* to be gone away.

b. In formal writing, a pronoun referring to any of those indefinite pronouns is also singular:

The scoutmaster expects everyone to do *his* duty.
When the lieutenant asked for volunteers, everybody made *herself* inconspicuous.
The teacher went around the class giving individual help to anyone having trouble with *his* work.

c. In informal writing, the pronoun referring to *anybody, anyone, each, every, everybody,* or *everyone* is often plural:

INFORMAL   Each of the voters decided according to *their* attitudes.
INFORMAL   Now is the time for everybody to come to the aid of *their* party.

d. Formal usage treats *either* and *neither* as singular pronouns, but they often appear as plural in informal writing:

FORMAL   I do not know if either of them *is* going to throw *his* hat into the ring.
INFORMAL   Neither of the girls *intend* to continue *their* studies.

There are two reasons for the divided usage of some of these pronouns. One is that, though grammatically singular, they often convey a distinct plural meaning. *Everybody* may refer grammatically to only *onebody*, but to a reader it conveys the notion of *manybodies*. The other reason is that the English language possesses no singular pronouns that serve equally well for both sexes—pronouns that are neutral without being neuter. Sentences like "If every man and woman does his or her best to consult his or her conscience before casting his or her ballot" are obviously absurd. Since new pronouns cannot be established by emergency legislation, the choice still lies between insisting on *his* as the bisexual possessive—accepting a masculine prerogative that may be outmoded—or falling back on the plural *their*, a form that many educated people, trained in traditional grammar, are still reluctant to use. If you are reluctant to be accused of either sexism or faulty grammar, you can often dodge the issue by revising the sentence: "If all voters do their best" and so forth.

e. The pronoun *any* is normally treated as plural; *none* may be either, depending on your emphasis, but its singular use is less common.

Are any of them going to the picnic?
None of them but George *have* signed up yet.

306

None (meaning *not one*) of her friends or relatives *was* with her when she died. . . .—Lawrance Thompson, *Robert Frost: The Early Years*

5. When a collective noun (*class, group, family, mob, number, team*) is considered as a whole, it takes a singular verb and pronoun; when the individuals are considered separately, it takes a plural verb and pronoun:

The Lackawanna football team *overwhelms* its traditional rival annually.
The squad *receive* their letters for playing in this game.
Its crew never *refer* to it by name: To *them* it is always "this bucket."—Thomas Heggen, *Mr. Roberts*

6. a. In formal writing a pronoun takes a verb of the same number and person as its antecedent:

"It *is* I who *am* the law in this community!" shouted the educated dictator. (The antecedent of *who* is *I*; hence the verb *am* is first person singular.)
He was one of those patriots who *are* always shouting about the American Way out of one corner of *their* mouths and spewing *their* odious prejudices out of the other. (The antecedent of *who* is *patriots*; hence the verb *are shouting* and the pronoun *their* are third person plural. Notice also that *mouths* and *prejudices* are plural for the sake of consistency.)
Fowler's "Modern English Usage" is one of those books that *delight* certain people in an intense and personal way.—Dwight Macdonald, "Sweet Are the Uses of Usage," *New Yorker*

b. In informal writing the *one of those who* construction often takes a singular verb and pronoun:

"Faith" is one of those words that *connotes*, however irrationally, some kind of virtue in *itself*.—Louis J. Halle, "Bringing about Change," *New Republic*
It is one of those words that *sounds* as though *it* were loaded. . . .—Russell Lynes, "Dirty Words," *Harper's*
The enjoyment of physical possession of things would seem to be one of the prerogatives of wealth which *has* been little impaired.—J. Kenneth Galbraith, *The Affluent Society*

c. Remember that, though the number, gender, and person of a pronoun are determined by its antecedent, the *case* of a pronoun is governed by its use within the clause, regardless of the case of its antecedent (see p. 290):

Helen Keller was a woman *whom* handicaps did not conquer. (The antecedent of *whom*, *woman*, is predicate nominative, but in its own clause, *whom* is the direct object of *conquer* and therefore objective.)
Thousands cheered the punch-drunk boxer, *who* was lying prostrate on the canvas. (The antecedent of *who*, *boxer*, is the direct object of *cheered*, but *who* is nominative because it is the subject of *was lying*.)

7. a. When the subject and complement differ in number, the verb *to be* usually agrees with the subject:

A complete game *is* four quarters of fifteen minutes each. Twelve lectures *are* a week's teaching for anybody.

b. In sentences introduced by a *what* clause, the verb *to be* can be either singular or plural if it is followed by one or more plural nouns:

What satisifies him most *is* (or *are*) snow-capped mountains. What he dislikes *is* (or *are*) turnips, parsnips, and squash.

8. a. Ordinarily *there is* and *there was* are used when the subject is singular, *there are* and *there were* when it is plural:

There *is* many a slip 'twixt the cup and the lip.
There *are* smiles that make us happy.

b. When the first part of a compound subject is singular, though other parts are plural, *there is* and *there was* are permissible:

There *is* an aardvark, a wapiti, and two platypuses in the local zoo.

In the sentences in (a) and (b), *there* is not the real subject but an anticipatory subject or *expletive*. The word *it* (*It* is time for a change) often serves the same purpose.

9. The expressions *these kind* (*sort, type*) and *those kind* often occur in speech and informal writing, followed by a plural verb and pronoun, but formal grammar requires consistent agreement:

FORMAL *This* kind of man *is* faithful to *his* trust.
FORMAL *These* kinds of people *are* stingy with *their* money.
INFORMAL *Those* kind of women *are* fastidious about *their* clothing.

10. Do not be misled in applying any of these conventions by the intrusion of other words between subject and verb, pronoun and antecedent. Notice the following student sentences:

WRONG The rhythm of the words *sound* like music to the ear. (The subject is *rhythm* not *words*.)
RIGHT The rhythm of the words *sounds* like music to the ear.

WRONG Each of these items *are* checked as the system is traced. (The subject is *each*, not *items*.)
RIGHT Each of these items *is* checked as the system is traced.

WRONG Only the high spots and important background of each game *is* at the disposal of the writer. (The compound subject is *spots and background*, not *game*.)
RIGHT Only the high spots and important background of each game *are* at the disposal of the writer.

WRONG Everybody from the highest ranking officer down to the private *are* briefed on the method to be used in taking the town. (The student would not write everybody *are briefed*, but a whole army has squeezed in between subject and verb, and the student is carelessly thinking of all the soldiers as the subject.) **RIGHT** Everybody from the highest ranking officer down to the private *is* briefed. . . .

11. a. Even in a situation where the choice of number is optional, be consistent throughout. Beware of unnecessary shifts in number and person. Notice the inconsistent use of pronouns in the following sentences·

No state would be able to lay up *their* own store of atom bombs and then on some dark night go out and conquer all of *its* neighboring nations. (shift in number)

I have learned never to trust them behind *your* back. (shift in person)

The majority *was* treated unjustly because *they* lacked the power to vote. (shift in number—either singular or plural is permissible with the collective noun *majority*, but not both)

To be able to speak what *you* want is something that makes a *person* feel more at ease than anything else. (shift in person)

It was a truly picturesque home, the kind *anybody* would like to own as long as *you* had a small family. (shift in person)

The *individuals* described above are completely lacking in insight, more so than any other type of mental disorder except possibly the lowest grade of mental deficiency. *He* is incapable of love in even the most primitive sense of the word. However, there is something about the hidden immaturity of *these people* that women seem to be attracted to. *He* is often a very attractive person superficially and often makes a strong impression when one first meets him. (shift from plural to singular to plural to singular in four sentences)

b. Slavish consistency in the use of the impersonal pronoun *one* is an awkward concession to formality:

When *one* speaks of *one's* old teachers, it is generally to *one's* college teachers that *one* refers. For it is then, if *one* is lucky, that *one* comes in contact with men who communicate and articulate the things and ideas which become the seeds of *one's* later intellectual and imaginative life.—Irwin Edman, *Philosopher's Holiday*

One gets weary of that sort of thing, doesn't one? It is not only permissible but preferable to refer to the impersonal *one* with the personal pronouns *he, his, him, she,* and *her:*

Without some modicum of thinking *one* cannot write at all, and it is emphatically true that *one* cannot ever write any better than *he* can think.—O. T Campbell, "The Failure of Freshman English," *English Journal*

In informal writing the impersonal *you* is more natural than *one:*

The advantage of "teaching" is that in using it *you* must recognize—if *you* are in *your* sober senses—that practical limits exist. *You* know by instinct that it

309

is impossible to "teach" democracy, or citizenship or a happy married life.—
Jacques Barzun, *Teacher in America*

EXERCISE I

Correct the errors in agreement in the following sentences. In instances of divided usage, distinguish between the formal and informal levels. If you decide to make no change in a sentence, defend your decision.·

1. His range of conversational topics were limited to sports, rock music, and women.

2. Because they are like all other little boys, the only thing my brothers are interested in watching on TV are Westerns.

3. The mature individual must make decisions, and if he wants to indulge in the things our society thinks is not beneficial to his development, it is his right and privilege as a citizen to do so.

4. The sentence structure is uncomplicated, and this, along with the fact that there are few obscure words, create a definite air of informality.

5. It is doubtful that either of them are going to complete their work.

6. In his poetry, the Objectivist expressed life in any way he could regardless of accepted poetical forms. If they could have, the Objectivist would have liked to make poems out of real objects so that the reader could cut it, or squeeze it, or taste it. What they achieved was something more: they were able to make the intangible qualities of an object or an incident into tangible sensations.

7. What he has often given us are half-truths that are no less misleading than half-lies.—Gertrude Himmelfarb, *Victorian Minds*

8. The average family in the world today is paying more in taxes to support the arms race than to educate their children.—James Reston, *New York Times*

9. Students interested in membership should request a written nomination from the professor who knows him or her best.

10. It is doubtful that many of these men will make a home for their families in Brookford because neither job opportunities nor new building are likely to attract them.

11. As a result, a mess of inconsistent laws and court rulings still discriminate against women.—"The Talk of the Town," *New Yorker*

12. When my father or older brother try to correct my golf swing, I ignore their suggestions because I don't think those kind of lessons should come from close relatives.

13. Economics is one of those subjects that become more interesting with the passage of time.—Tom Bethell, "The Wealth of Washington," *Harper's*

14. The interior of the nests are like a three-dimensional maze, intricate arrangements of spiraling galleries, corridors, and arched vaults, ventilated and air-conditioned.—Lewis Thomas, *The Lives of a Cell*

15. The combination of well-qualified professors, visiting lecturers, and movies make Engineering Fundamentals an enjoyable and valuable course.

PHRASES AND CLAUSES

Although the discussion of grammar so far has concentrated on the role of individual words, it has not been entirely possible to avoid mentioning two grammatical terms for groups of words: *phrase* and *clause*. If you know the parts of speech, you should have little trouble with phrases and clauses, for they usually do the same jobs as nouns, verbs, adjectives, and adverbs.

A phrase is any group of two or more grammatically related words, without a subject and finite verb, acting in a sentence as a single part of speech. Phrases can be classified in two ways:

According to form

PREPOSITIONAL	to the house	at the game
INFINITIVE	He played *to win,* not *to be beaten.*	
PARTICIPIAL	an old city *sleeping in the sun* a game *halted by darkness*	
GERUND	*Crossing the street* is dangerous. I liked *his doing that.*	
VERB	am coming, have arrived	

According to function

NOUNS

Tossing the javelin takes coordination. (A gerund phrase is used as the subject. It is just as if the writer were saying merely: "Track takes coordination.")

Many people have tried *swimming the English Channel.* (gerund phrase used as the object of the verb *have tried*)

He was jailed for *stealing a car.* (gerund phrase used as the object of the preposition *for*)

To tell the truth is not always easy. (infinitive phrase used as the subject of the sentence)

He managed *to open the safe.* (infinitive phrase used as the object of the verb *managed*)

VERBS

I *am coming* in a minute. He *has done* it again.

ADJECTIVES

The woman *in the black dress* is a secret agent. (prepositional phrase modifying *woman*)

The man *running the store* is my uncle Murad. (participial phrase modifying *man*)

She is a woman *to admire.* (infinitive phrase modifying *woman*)

ADVERBS

The horse jumped *over the barrier.* (prepositional phrase modifying *jumped*)

311

He swerved *to miss the child*. (infinitive phrase modifying *swerved*)

A *clause* is a group of related words containing a subject and a finite verb and forming part of a compound or complex sentence.

An *independent (main, principal)* clause is one that can stand alone as a complete sentence: a *dependent (subordinate)* clause is incapable of standing alone. (For exceptions see pp. 79–81.)

DEPENDENT CLAUSE   Although a dependent clause may grow like this one to a considerable size, adding phrase after phrase like the branching twigs of a tree,

INDEPENDENT CLAUSE   it still needs a main trunk like this to support it.

A *dependent* clause may serve as a noun, an adjective, or an adverb:

That he would eventually return to his black-eyed Bess was the highwayman's bold promise. (noun clause, subject)

Nobody knows *what enormous loads of wood a woodchuck can chuck*. (noun clause, object of the verb)

On the fifth page of her paper he came to *what was obviously her key point*. (noun clause, object of the preposition *to*)

A man *who has no music in his heart* may be merely tone deaf. (adjective clause modifying *man*)

Where many had failed before him, the great Unus alone succeeded in standing on a single digit. (adverbial clause modifying *succeeded*)

To distinguish easily between dependent and independent clauses is to solve the most elementary problem of sentence structure (see pp. 77–78).

Coordinate clauses are independent clauses of equal grammatical rank joined by a coordinating conjunction: (see pp. 83–86)

Thelma came to the party, but *she did not stay*.
She talked to a few friends, and *she slipped away quietly*.

Elliptical clauses are those in which certain words are understood but not expressed:

She is shorter than I [am]. (second verb unexpressed)
I couldn't see the point [that] he saw. (conjunction unexpressed)
Her dog was a purebred, his [dog was] a mongrel. (Second subject and verb unexpressed)
When [you are] in Rome. do as the Romans do. (first subject and verb unexpressed)
Though [she was] only a child, she had an adult vocabulary. (first subject and verb unexpressed)

If properly related to the rest of the sentence, elliptical clauses are important aids to economy in writing. If left *dangling*, they cause confusion (see p. 89).

312

EXERCISES

J. In the following sentences, identify all phrases and dependent clauses and explain the function of each. (*Example*: That is a horse of a different color. *Of a different color* is a prepositional phrase used as an adjective modifying *horse*.)

1. Although rapid reading can be useful for undergraduates, it should not replace slow, meditative reading.

2. Tired of studying, he went to the movies at the foot of the hill.

3. Starting down the trail, he found soon that his skis had no intention of remaining parallel.

4. She was in no apparent danger of losing the match even if she tried experimenting with her shots.

5. As soon as he had discovered the atom bomb, man immediately forgot that science is an international language.

6. She jumped into the lake with all her clothes on to save the carefree youth who had fallen through the ice.

7. Few lovers of Joyce Kilmer's "Trees" pause to consider that the same God who makes the trees makes the fools who make the poems.

8. He argued that if Liberal Education is to be revived, the faculty will have to be less liberal in approving miscellaneous electives that have no place in a serious curriculum.

9. The game of bridge is all that stands between some people and a life of continuous boredom.

10. After the game ended, every loyal alumnus stood at embarrassed attention faithfully trying to improvise the Alma Mater.

K. (General review) Rewrite the following sentences, correcting all errors in grammar and explaining your corrections. In instances of divided usage, distinguish between levels or meanings.

1. I would never of gone to church at all if it wasn't for a woman named Mrs. Sturgis who took care of my brothers and I when I was eight.

2. Almost everybody has important ambitions they want to fulfill, which requires dealing with other people.

3. In any society it takes perceptive observers to identify those whom are called liberal.

4. He tries to dissect the poem as if it was a grasshopper or a worm laying on a table in a biologist's laboratory.

5. No man who's afraid to express himself has a right to be hurt when someone sees their silence as the cowardice it really is.

6. Even though he is obviously the least literate of the two writers, none of the critics see any significant difference between her and he.

313

7. Although the class was not proud of its academic record, they had good reason to ask who's poison pen had written the editorial castigating them for their ignorance.

8. Between the lamp post and whoever was lying in the gutter, the detective found two cigarettes, neither of which were of the same brand that the suspect smoked.

9. If I was in his shoes, they would be too roomy for me because he is bigger-boned than me.

10. Neither of the two parties or candidates differ appreciably on the fundamental issues, but not one of the party hacks are going to let this cool their enthusiasm.

11. Whenever the news did not sound well, he was likely to curse the newspaper instead of blaming whomever was guilty of the actions that they reported.

12. A stubborn man who despised those kind of compromises, the Governor was torn between signing a popular law who's provisions he did not support and throwing away several thousand votes with a single veto.

13. He argued that even if she was his wife, she would have no right to object to him going out with the boys once in a while.

14. I am the kind of person who am always insisting that one can never have an excuse for hurting somebody else, no matter what your motivation may be.

15. After a thorough review of grammar, each of the students were willing to concede that the bulk of the errors they made during the year were the result of carelessness rather than ignorance.

11 Punctuation

An ideal punctuation system ... should indicate much more clearly than our own the attitude, the mood, even the tone of voice, of the writer.

Isaac Goldberg

The comma was just a nuisance. If you got the thing as a whole, the comma kept irritating you all along the line.

Gertrude Stein

Punctuation is a delicate art that has defied the best-laid plans of grammarians to convert it into an exact science. In the two centuries since man's first attempts to domesticate the elusive comma in a rule book, he has devised innumerable systems of punctuation, but the best are only rough facsimiles of actual usage. Personal preference still plays a large role. Many authorities feel that the modern tendency toward *open* punctuation is a distinct gain over the cautious *close* punctuation which peppered the pages of our ancestors with commas and semicolons; others are afraid that too strict an economy may plunge the language into chaos. Some writers are fascinated by the power of the comma to convey the most subtle nuances of rhythm and feeling; some treat the comma as a routine signpost whose main virtue is to keep the reader from making a wrong turn; a few (Gertrude Stein, for example) disdain it as an irritating nuisance.

To concede these differences in the theory and practice of experts is not to give the college undergraduate a free ticket to the Confetti School of Punctuation. Students of this popular school handle punctuation marks by the gross. Having scrawled a first draft in blissful disregard of the rule book, they become uneasily aware that they have "not put in enough commas." Whereupon they take a random handful, with an occasional colon or semicolon intermixed, and throw them like confetti at the paper, letting them fall almost where they may. The *almost* means that they may have one or two false principles to misguide them—such as always to toss in one comma before *and* and to enclose *however* with a pair. When the instructor points out that this comma is superfluous and that one downright confusing, they admit humbly that they have "put in too many commas." It is all vaguely quantitative and thoroughly unreasonable.

RULES AND REASONS

Despite the variety in practice, there are reasons for punctuation. Some of the conventions, to be sure, are hard to defend without falling back on tradition. There is probably no good reason, for example, why we should still put a comma between *St. Louis* and *Missouri* when every mature reader knows where the city ends and the state begins. On the other hand, most of the important "rules" have evolved from honest efforts *to make reading easier*.

According to some instructors, punctuation is merely grammar-made-graphic. Others contend that it can be reduced to a table of pauses and stresses like the rests and crescendos in music. Does a period mean "This is the end of a sentence" or "Come to a full stop, please"? Does an exclamation mark mean "You have reached the end of an exclamatory sentence" or "Please register surprise here"? Or both? Such academic questions can be evaded by admitting that experienced writers do much of their punctuating automatically without minding the why and wherefore. The exceptional undergraduate who has read widely and wisely may punctuate well by ear. But for most students, grasping the unmysterious mysteries of commas and semicolons is in direct proportion to their understanding of grammar and sentence structure. It is not very helpful to tell students to "put in commas where the natural pauses come" if they pause naturally in the middle of every strange new polysyllabic word. Moreover, trained readers with keen ears for prose rhythm do not necessarily pause when they see a comma or come to a full stop when confronted by a period; they may speed right through a comma and acknowledge the stop sign by merely tapping lightly on the brake pedal. The schoolchild formula that a comma is a green light, a semicolon an amber light, and a period a red light is too neat to be more than half true. A thorough understanding of a handful of more explicit rules is better for the inexperienced writer.

Remember, however, that the rules here are conventions based on usage and that understanding is not memorizing or unthinking obedience. Understand the reasons behind the rules, and you will begin to feel the distinction between the violations that cause confusion and the sensible deviations that may foretell progress.

THE PERIOD

The period is used

316

1. At the End of a Sentence That Is Neither a Direct Question Nor a Strong Exclamation

This use of the period after a complete sentence need hardly be illustrated.

A period is also used after an incomplete sentence. This one, for example.

2. After Some Abbreviations

A.B.   M.A.   Ph.D.   C.O.D.   Mrs.

But abbreviations for government bureaus, organizations, institutions, and common technical terms, for example, often do without it: FBI, ERA, USC, btu, rpm

3. Sometimes After a Request in the Form of a Question, as in a Business Letter

Will you kindly send a check with your reply. (A question mark here would be considered slightly more formal.)

THE QUESTION MARK

1. A Question Mark Is Used After a Direct Question (Whether Rhetorical or Not) or to Show That a Statement of Fact Is Open to Question

Where were you on the night of March 14, 1979?
That was a close call, wasn't it?
Thomas Dekker's dates are 1570?–1632.

2. A Question Mark Is Not Used After an Indirect Question

INDIRECT QUESTION   I asked why he insisted on dating my girl.
DIRECT QUESTION   I asked: "Why do you insist on dating my girl?"

3. A Question Mark Should Not Be Used in Parentheses to Label Irony or Wit

When it comes to giving out with the French I am the brightest (?) *garçon* in the whole class.

THE EXCLAMATION POINT

The exclamation point (or mark) is used to emphasize an emotion—wonder, surprise, admiration, frustration—or put starch into a command:

317

Oh, what a beautiful morning!

Ah! What a refreshing beverage!

It troubled me that I could speak in the fullness of my own voice only when I was alone on the streets, walking about. There was something unnatural about it; unbearably isolated. I was not like the others! I was not like the others!— Alfred Kazin, *A Walker in the City*

"Blow this joint or I'll drill you!" shouted Lefty.

An exclamation often identifies itself without a label: an *ah* may be openmouthed enough when followed by an unassuming comma. Like the boy in the fable who cried wolf, the effervescent fashion editor or the movie ad can shriek *exclamation* once too often. This sort of shouting punctuation, in which the exclamation point is often accompanied by other artificial aids to emphasis, can quickly bludgeon a mature reader into apathy:

"Do I look like I'd wear mascara with a spikey, sealed-on look? Not me! I want lots and lots of dark lashes that go on *soft* . . . stay on *extra long! I always wear Extra-Long Big Lash Mascara!* Natural Wonder is natural-looking mascara with extra-long wear! The big jumbo brush fattens up my skimpy lashes fast . . . fills in lashes I didn't know I had! Now my lashes look twice as thick . . . and my eyes look twice as *big!*—Revlon ad, *Cosmopolitan*

Of course, the familiar device of exploding a single sentence with exclamation points in duplicate or triplicate (*Zowie!!!*) should be confined to the comic books.

THE COMMA

The comma has five main uses: (1) to separate main clauses; (2) to set off introductory clauses and phrases; (3) to set off nonessential elements; (4) to separate parts of a series; (5) to avoid ambiguity. It also has numerous miscellaneous conventional uses.

1. To Separate Main Clauses

a. A comma is ordinarily used in a compound sentence *before* the coordinating conjunction (*and, but, for, or, nor,* and *yet*):

The radio is a noble machine, but in our time it has been perverted into an instrument for crushing the human spirit.—Russell Baker, "Things Are Tough All Over," *New York Times Magazine*

It is a winter night in the Midwest, and a man is lying alone in a strange room.—James Dickey, *Babel to Byzantium*

b. The comma is often omitted in this construction, especially if the sentence is short:

Scott fought to work but he could only work in snatches—Ernest Hemingway, *A Moveable Feast*

My grandfather's hands were folding and unfolding and his hightop button shoes twiddled in agitation.—John Updike, *The Centaur*

Beware, however, of omitting the comma before *but* and *for* in a compound sentence. The reader is entitled to a warning that the connective is a conjunction introducing a clause, not a preposition introducing a phrase:

> I took part in every sport, but swimming was my favorite. (conjunction)
> I took part in every sport but swimming. (preposition)
> He did not go, for George was already on his way home. (conjunction)
> He did not go for George. (preposition)

c. If the conjunction is omitted from a compound sentence or replaced by a conjunctive adverb or transitional phrase (*however, moreover, nevertheless, therefore, in fact, as a matter of fact, on the other hand,* and so on), the comma is ordinarily replaced by a semicolon:

> John loved Mary, but she loved a non-Greek named Homer.
> John loved Mary; she loved a non-Greek named Homer.
> John loved Mary; however, she loved a non-Greek named Homer.

The comma fault (see p. 82)

The *comma fault*—sometimes called the *comma splice* or *comma blunder*—is *the misuse of a comma in a compound sentence to separate two clauses that are not joined by a coordinating conjunction* (*and, but, for, or, nor,* and *yet*). Here are two typical student examples:

> In the Victorian age a woman was expected to stay in the home, cooking, cleaning, dusting, and looking after the children were her solemn duties.

> The device of separate ballots is being used in some states, however, it is time we decided what officials are to be elected and what ones are to be appointed.

Readers of the first sentence might logically assume that *cooking, cleaning, dusting,* and *looking* are participles modifying *woman,* and that the sentence should end with *children.* When they came to the second verb, *were,* they would naturally be confused. The simple substitution of a semicolon after *home* makes the construction clear:

> In the Victorian age a woman was expected to stay in the home; cooking, cleaning, dusting, and looking after the children were her solemn duties.

The trouble in the second sentence is with the word *however.* An experienced reader, on seeing this squinting connective set off by commas, will naturally regard it as a parenthetical word looking back at a previous sentence, for *however* is commonly used that way as a transition between sentences. Omitting the comma after *however* would help. But a semicolon before *however* makes it immediately clear that this word actually introduces the second independent clause:

The device of separate ballots is being used in some states; however, it is time we decided what officials are to be elected and what ones are to be appointed.

Notice the same difference in these illustrations:

CLEAR The circus is coming to town. I am not excited, however, about educated pachyderms. (Here *however* is a transitional word linking the second sentence with the first and, like many other interrupters—see pp. 322–324—is set off by commas.)

CLEAR The circus is coming to town. I am not excited; however, I shall probably go. (Here *however* introduces the second coordinate clause of a compound sentence.)

COMMA FAULT The circus is coming to town. I am not excited, however, I shall probably go. (Although *however* introduces a new clause, it is punctuated as if it were a transitional word linking the first and second sentences.)

If you habitually commit the comma fault before a conjunctive adverb, you should ask yourself whether you need a lesson in puctuation or in style. Is your writing doughy from too many conjunctive adverbs? It could be leavened by substituting *but* for *however* and *nevertheless; and* for *moreover* and *furthermore*. Are there too many artificial compound sentences in which the clauses are not genuinely coordinate—that is, of equal importance? Some of them could be replaced by complex sentences (see p. 84).

Experienced writers often deviate from the strict letter of the comma fault law, especially in a short balanced construction where the relation between the clauses is close in *both thought and structure*. Such *contact clauses* can be spliced with a comma without danger of ambiguity:

Asians squat when they sit, Westerners sit upright in chairs.—Malcolm X, *The Autobiography of Malcolm X*

He is close-lipped, he watches his words.—Walker Gibson, *Tough, Sweet & Stuffy*

I was awed by the system, I believed in it, I respected its force.—Alfred Kazin, *A Walker in the City*

This discussion of the comma fault can be summarized as follows:

When two independent clauses in a compound sentence are not joined by a coordinating conjunction (and, but, for, or, nor, *and* yet), *do not use a comma between them unless they are brief and balanced. When in doubt, play safe and use a semicolon.*

EXERCISE A

In accordance with the first rule for the comma, make all necessary changes in the following sentences and give a reason for each. If you leave a sentence unchanged, explain why.

1. This is not to say that my father is frugal, whenever it is possible to please a member of his family, he eagerly responds.

2. Over half the freshmen never took calculus, consequently they are lost in the college course.

3. Maurice argued heatedly that it was his duty to absent himself from the polls for a vote for either candidate would merely perpetuate current evils.

4. He had lived in the limelight spending his money lavishly, he died in obscurity begging for a handout.

5. The President's speeches are not without stylistic devices, in fact some could be called ornate.

6. She was quick to agree that television in general was an intellectual wasteland and a waste of time but she occasionally tuned in on a program that almost atoned for all the sins of the medium.

7. He would creep into the room and sit for hours by the window but never look at the world outside.

8. She is a young woman who has had an extensive exposure to life through travel with her father, however, she is completely unaware of the corruption of society.

9. The rains came down, the game was postponed for two hours, the final inning was played in darkness.

10. Everyone in the sorority came to the party but Phoebe was a reluctant guest.

2. To Set Off Introductory Clauses and Phrases

a. A comma is commonly used to set off an introductory (dependent) clause or phrase preceding the main clause:

When the song had been dropped in New Haven, I was not sorry to see it go.—Alan J. Lerner, *The Street Where I Live* (introductory clause)

In a fundamentalist Islamic society, stability is provided by allegiance to the Koran and to the king as head of the tribe.—Adam Smith, "Maybe I Am Easily Scared," *Atlantic* (introductory phrase)

This comma is essential to avoid confusion when it is not clear where the introductory element ends; it is welcome when the introductory expression is long:

CONFUSING A short while after I visited the school and decided Peddie was the place for me. (Without the comma following *after*, the reader might be misled into assuming that a subordinate clause ends with *school*.)

CONFUSING The planes having passed over George lay in the ditch cursing his luck. (Without the comma after *over*, the phrase would probably be read: The planes having passed over George.)

CLEAR In the years that followed, Sarah devoted herself to domestic concerns—James L. Clifford, *Young Sam Johnson*. (Without the comma, the reader might be confused momentarily by "the years that followed Sarah.")

CLEAR To illustrate the principle and technique to be used in developing equivalent circuits, suppose that a given nonlinear circuit element has the current-voltage characteristic shown in figure (1.2a).—Thomas I. Martin, Jr. *Electronic Circuits* (long introductory phrase)

b. After a short introductory clause or phrase, where there is no danger of ambiguity, the comma may be omitted:

When we drew out of the station the elderly woman opposite me glanced up at the ventilation window.—John Fowles, *Daniel Martin* (short introductory clause)

Within a few days Ramona was saying that this was an ordinary affair.— Saul Bellow, *Herzog* (short introductory phrase)

3. To Set Off Nonessential Elements

The term *nonessential* is a general adjective applied here to words or groups of words which interrupt the flow of the sentence or are not closely related to its central thought. The list includes nonrestrictive modifiers, transitional words and phrases, mild interjections, words in direct address, interrupters in dialogue, and other interrupters. If one of these elements comes in mid-sentence. it is set off with *two* commas.

a. Nonrestrictive vs. restrictive modifiers

A nonrestrictive modifier (clause, phrase, or word) is set off by commas; a restrictive modifier is not:

NONRESTRICTIVE   John B. Throckmorton III, *who does not understand the principles of punctuation*, will not recognize the nonrestrictive clause in this sentence.

RESTRICTIVE   A student *who understands the principles of punctuation* will recognize the restrictive clause in this sentence.

The commas in the first sentence can be said to designate the two places where most people would pause in speaking it. No such pauses would occur before and after the restrictive clause in the second sentence. But you should also see that the two kinds of clauses play different roles in the meaning of the two sentences. In the first sentence the subject has already been restricted on being named (there is presumably only one John B. Throckmorton III), and the clause that follows merely supplies additional information. It can restrict him no further, it is nonrestrictive. In the second sentence the clause *who understands the principles of punctuation* is needed to restrict the general subject *a student* to a special kind of student. Take another pair of examples:

NONRESTRICTIVE   He ran toward Wilbur, *who had observed the flight*.
RESTRICTIVE   A college professor is not usually a man *with more than one car*.

Observe that the nonrestrictive clause in the first sentence can be deleted without appreciably altering the meaning (*He ran toward Wilbur*). Removal of the restrictive phrase in the second completely changes the writer's point (*A college professor is not usually a man*). In other words, a nonrestrictive modifier is *nonessential*; a restrictive modifier is *essential*. A student may see the difference more clearly by applying these less technical terms.

To put it another way, a restrictive modifier limits the scope of the word it modifies. The name *Wilbur* already identifies a specific person and is therefore not further limited by the nonrestrictive clause that follows. On the other hand, *man* must be specifically limited to a particular group of men (those with more than one car) by the restrictive phrase that modifies it.

Often the choice of punctuation involves a choice of radically different meanings:

NONRESTRICTIVE   Women, who can't keep secrets, should never be told about their husbands' business affairs.
RESTRICTIVE   Women who can't keep secrets should never be told about their husbands' business affairs.

The same sentence, but two commas make the difference between woman-hating and simple prudence.

An appositive (see p. 286) can also be classed as restrictive or nonrestrictive:

NONRESTRICTIVE   Joe Louis, *the fabulous brown bomber*, had passed his peak.
NONRESTRICTIVE   Dr. James Bohan, lecturer in logic and epistemology, is more sedate now.—Herbert Livesey, *The Professors*
RESTRICTIVE   Charles *the First* was executed in 1649.
RESTRICTIVE   The fact *that punctuation cannot cure a sick sentence* is overlooked by some students.

Do not settle for a single comma when the construction demands two. Remember always that *when a clause or phrase comes in midsentence the choice is between two commas and none*.

b. Other nonessential elements

TRANSITIONAL EXPRESSIONS   The doctor said, *however*, that the patient would recover. *As a matter of fact*, he predicted that Sam would be back at work on Monday. The fever, *nevertheless*, continued unabated. *Also* strange new symptoms appeared. (As in the last sentence, the punctuation is often omitted if the expression does not appreciably interrupt the flow.)
MILD INTERJECTIONS   *Well*, let me try just once. *Oh*, I don't think I need your help. *Why*, it's really easy.
WORDS IN DIRECT ADDRESS   *Gentlemen*, you come along with me. *George*, you stay here. As for you, *Joe*, suit yourself.
INTERRUPTERS IN DIALOGUE   "After all," *he said bitterly*, "we can't achieve peace if we assume that war is inevitable."

323

OTHER INTERRUPTERS This is not, *if I understand the gentleman's argument,* the most logical defense of his position.

Undergraduates are, *on the whole,* eager to be taught how to write but slow to learn.

Capital punishment is, *in my opinion,* morally wrong.—Karl Menninger, *A Psychiatrist's World*

EXERCISE B

In accordance with the rule for restrictive and nonrestrictive modifiers, make all necessary changes in the following sentences and give a reason for each. If you leave a sentence unchanged, explain why.

1. Most companies, which hire young scientists, insist that they be able to write clearly.

2. Charles, the Second, who reigned in England from 1660 to 1685, had a notorious liaison with an actress called Nell Gwynn.

3. Any man who hopes to marry a woman, who will get his breakfast every day of his life, is in for bitter disillusionment.

4. Professor Rowbottom maintained that a student who writes for the college newspaper should not use freedom of the press as an excuse for misrepresenting facts that are common knowledge on the campus.

5. The Darwin who wrote *The Loves of the Plants* was the grandfather of the Darwin who wrote *The Origin of Species*.

6. Teen-agers who have no understanding of the value of money should not be given their own checking accounts.

7. In other words, photosynthesis which is one of the most important means of accumulating free energy available in nature has emerged from a symbiotic arrangement.—Sergius Morgulis, Introduction to Oparin's *The Origin of Life*

8. It was one of those strange, unhomogenized gatherings, at which nobody knew anybody else or cared if the person, standing next to him, was a celebrity or a nonentity.

9. My father goes back to the time when a man who wore his hair long, was usually suspected of playing the violin.

10. In all countries the serious threat to scientists who have once touched the fringes of secret subjects is that they are then caught in something from which they can never escape again.—J. Bronowski, "The Real Responsibilities of the Scientist," *Bulletin of the Atomic Scientists*

4. To Separate Parts of a Series

a. Commas are used to set off words, phrases, and clauses in a series (When the parts of a series are long, semicolons are often used—see p. 328):

The room was dark, damp, and dreary. (words)

Lincoln was not the first to speak of government of the people, by the people, and for the people. (phrases)

A speeding car swerved around another, ricocheted against a concrete wall, turned completely around in the road, righted itself miraculously, and sped on.—Caskie Stinnett, "Heels on Wheels," *Atlantic* (clauses)

b. Although the traditional formula retains the comma before *and* in a series, some writers (or editors) do without it:

His themes are mostly the Nashville perennials of hootch, heartbreak and hallelujah.—"Country's Platinum Outlaw," *Time*

Some people argue that the omission of the comma before a conjunction suggests a closer relation between the last two items than between other parts of the series. Obviously the comma should be omitted if the final pair is as inseparable as *ham and eggs* or *Gilbert and Sullivan*. In other contexts, it is better to use the comma regularly to avoid this sort of confusion: "an apartment with three rooms, kitchen, bath with shower and garage."

c. When more than one conjunction connects the parts of a series, commas are usually omitted before conjunctions:

Before the dawn of progressive education, pupils in the elementary schools concentrated on reading and writing and 'rithmetic.

From time to time they made up packages to Jefferson, antelope skins and skeletons, plants and roots, wolf skeletons, deer-horns, weasel skins and buffalo robes, a foxskin, bows and arrows and painted Indian robes and pottery.—Van Wyck Brooks, *The World of Washington Irving*

d. Like other words in a series, coordinate adjectives are usually set off by commas:

COORDINATE She wore a *long, sheer, glittering* gown.
NOT COORDINATE The man in the *gray flannel* suit married a *little rich* girl.

In the first example *long, sheer,* and *glittering* receive equal emphasis as modifiers of *gown*. They could be separated by *and* and arranged in any order without appreciably altering the meaning of the sentence. In the second sentence the adjectives do not receive equal emphasis: *gray* modifies *flannel*, and *flannel* modifies *suit*; the stress in the second phrase is obviously on *rich*. To separate these adjectives by *and* or change the order would significantly alter the meaning. Thus the difference between a *smelly, old pipe* (coordinate adjectives) and a *smelly old pipe* (not coordinate) is one of emphasis: in the first the emphasis is equally distributed between odor and age; in the second it is largely on the odor.

325

5. To Avoid Ambiguity

Regardless of the other rules, use a comma whenever it is necessary to avoid even passing ambiguity:

CONFUSING Inside the horses were eagerly awaiting the big day. (We are taken inside the horses.)
CLEAR Inside, the horses were eagerly awaiting the big day.

CONFUSING He told the student to come now and again the following week. (To come now and again?)
CLEAR He told the student to come now, and again the following week.

Beware, however, of depending too heavily on commas to improve an ambiguous sentence. A clumsily mortised joint cannot be saved with one or two tacks.

6. Some Miscellaneous Uses

a. The comma is often used before a coordinating conjunction in a compound predicate:

Mr. Horowitz nodded, and jumped up from the bench. He looked at the ceiling, and then pushed the piano a few inches farther into the center of the orchestra.—"The Talk of the Town," *New Yorker*

b. Commas are also used conventionally in the following ways:

1. To separate day and year in dates:

December 7, 1941, was a day of infamy. (the second comma is often omitted)

Both commas are omitted when no day is given:

December 1941 is a month to remember.

If you put the month second, omit the comma after it: 7 December 1941.

2. To separate places in addresses:

Ottumwa, Iowa   Easton, Pennsylvania

3. To separate names from titles or degrees:

John D. Rockefeller, Jr.   George Lyman Kittredge, A.B.
Alexander Throttlebottom, Vice President

4. To set off direct quotations, especially in dialogue:

She said, "I was best at netball," breaking in on his thoughts.—Graham Greene, *The Heart of the Matter*

When short quotations are closely woven into the sentence, the commas are usually omitted:

Henry David Thoreau called Cape Cod "the bared and bended arm of Massachusetts" and walked over it in search of "solitude sweet to me as a flower."—Kenny Moore, "Even in a Crowd He Runs Alone," *Sports Illustrated*

5. In numbers of four or more digits (separating groups of three):

456,789   999,999,999   1,256 (or 1256)

Phone numbers, social security numbers, and years in dates are among the many exceptions to this rule.

6. After the salutation in friendly letters:

Dear Damon,

And after the complimentary close in all letters:

Sincerely yours,
Pythias

THE SEMICOLON

There are two common uses of the semicolon, both of them already mentioned in the discussion of the comma:

1. Between Main Clauses

a. A semicolon is used to separate main clauses in a compound sentence when the conjunction is omitted or replaced by a conjunctive adverb (see pp. 301, 320):

As a dictionary maker Mr. Partridge is unrivalled in his liveliness and terseness; as a grammarian and a critic of language, he does not always make so good a showing.—Edmund Wilson, *The Bit Between My Teeth* (the "omitted conjuction" is *but*)

To use the body as a means of expressing the anguish of the human soul is no longer a possible enterprise; we do not know how to represent the body and do not believe in the existence of the soul.—Kenneth Clark, *The Romantic Rebellion* (the semicolon can be considered as replacing *for*)

He pretended to be a law-abiding citizen; nevertheless, he consistently drove on the highway at seventy-five miles an hour. (the conjunctive adverb *nevertheless* replaces *but*)

Notice that the semicolon indicates a closer connection between clauses than a period between separate sentences.

b. A semicolon is used in a compound or compound-complex sentence before the coordinating conjunction (*and, but, for, or, nor,* and *yet*) when the clauses are long or the writer wishes to emphasize the pause between them:

327

Reading the *Autobiography* of John Stuart Mill at the age of fifteen while in the editorial office of the old New York *Sun* led me to the discovery of Socrates; and this, in turn, formed my early resolution to try to become a philosopher.—Mortimer Adler, *Philosopher at Large*

The replacement of soap by detergents has made us cleaner than we were; but it has made the environment more foul.—Barry Commoner, *The Closing Circle*

This use of the semicolon is especially important when the clauses are heavily punctuated internally:

Though he could usually distinguish fish, flesh, and fowl, his taste buds were, to put it charitably, underdeveloped; and he often annoyed his gourmet friends by ordering ham and eggs in a fancy restaurant.

Avoid the common habit of using a semicolon to separate a main clause from a subordinate clause or phrase:

UNACCEPTABLE She could not be sure that English was a proper major for a pre-med; although she found the reading fascinating.
IMPROVED Although she found the reading fascinating, she could not be sure that English was a proper major for a pre-med.

2. Between Parts of a Series

A semicolon is used to separate parts of a series, especially when the parts are long and contain commas within them:

In any nonviolent campaign there are four basic steps: collection of the facts to determine whether injustices exist; negotiation; self-purification; and direct action.—Martin Luther King, Jr., "Letter from Birmingham Jail," *Why We Can't Wait*

In the afternoons the programme was: Mondays and Fridays, tilting and horsemanship; Tuesdays, hawking; Wednesdays, fencing; Thursdays, archery; Saturdays, the theory of chivalry, with proper measures to be blown on all occasions, terminology of the chase and hunting etiquette.—T. H. White, *The Once and Future King*

She gave the following reasons for liking the course: she was fascinated by the subject, the teacher, and the reading assignments; she enjoyed the field trips, which gave her welcome opportunities to get away from the campus; and her fellow students, most of them serious seniors heading for medical school, shared her enthusiasm.

THE COLON

A single rule summarizes all the important uses of the colon: A colon is used to introduce something that immediately follows. The material introduced may be of several kinds:

1. A Series of Clauses, Phrases, or Words

He used the following arguments: that big-time football did more harm than good to the players; that it did not support the rest of the athletic program; and that it was intended primarily to appease the alumni, entertain the trustees, and provide a spectacle for the general public.

For the earliest men, life was an incessant battle: against the hostile Pleistocene environment, against other mammals for food, against their own kind for a sheltering cave, a water hole, a hunting range, a mate.—John Fischer, "Substitutes for Violence," *Harper's*

Eventually the whales, as though to divide the sea's food resources among them, became separated into three groups: the plankton-eaters, the fish-eaters, and the squid-eaters.—Rachel Carson, *The Sea around Us*

As the last two illustrations show, such formal expressions as *the following, as follows,* and *namely* can be avoided in introducing a series; the colon carries the meaning without them.

2. An Illustration or Explanation

Among the incidental oddities of our queer times is a question often discussed: is it possible for modern man to write tragedy?—Herbert J. Muller, *The Spirit of Tragedy*

Smackenfelt's sanity hung by a single thread: the belief that he was Edwin Booth.—Peter De Vries, *Forever Panting*

A ghetto can be improved in one way only: out of existence.—James Baldwin, *Nobody Knows My Name*

3. A Quotation, Often Long or Rather Formal

There is a certain American magazine which sends out slips for its contributors' guidance, stating: "Humor, tragedy and pathos are acceptable, but not stories that are morbid or that leave the reader uncomfortable."—Elizabeth Drew, *The Modern Novel* (longer quotations are usually indented in a separate paragraph—see p. 235).

4. The Body of a Business Letter

Dear Sir:
We have received your order for four jumbo self-lathering windshield wipers.

Except in beginning a business letter or introducing a quotation of one or more complete sentences, a colon may be followed by either a small letter or a capital. The capital is more common when a complete sentence follows the colon. It is superfluous to supplement the colon with a dash (:—).

329

EXERCISE C

Without changing the wording of the following passages, correct the punctuation in accordance with the conventional uses of the semicolon and colon:

1. She had three reasons, however, for deciding to stay out of college for a year; a lack of funds to pay the tuition, which had been getting higher every semester, a desire to have some experience in the outside world, preferably a job in industry, and a decline of interest in all her courses except Cost Accounting.

2. Borzoi was what is known in the sports world as a *walk-on*, he had not received a scholarship, he had not even been asked to try out for the team.

3. No literary experience is more rewarding than reading Shakespeare, however, it takes patient study to appreciate the nuances of his language and the subtle music of his poetry.

4. Referring in his *Memoirs* to his dismissal of General MacArthur, President Truman wrote; "If there is one basic element in our Constitution, it is civilian control of the military."

5. Mabel was keenly interested in a legal career, in fact, she once dreamt of playing Portia in *The Merchant of Venice*; although she had never revealed any interest in dramatics.

6. Christianity satisfies suddenly and perfectly man's ancestral instinct for being the right way up; satisfies it supremely in this; that by its creed joy becomes something gigantic and sadness something special and small.—G. K. Chesterton, *Autobiography*

QUOTATION MARKS

(See pp. 234–236)

Right and Wrong Uses

1. Quotation marks are used to enclose words quoted directly from either speech or writing

"I was thinking about the children," says Erica, who is not aware of having sighed aloud. "I'm not sure we should have let them go alone." . . .
"They're not alone," he says impatiently. "They're with three thousand other people."
"That's what bothers me. Among three thousand people there's sure to be some bad characters."
"Don't worry about it. Most of them are kids. Or students."
"What difference does that make?"—Alison Lurie, *The War Between the Tates*

In one of his distinguished speeches Judge Learned Hand argues for an education that develops "an open mind, enriched by reading and the arts." He goes on to say that a man cannot acquire political wisdom without a "bowing acquaintance" with the humanities, by which he means history, literature, philosophy, the plastic arts, and music. "For these are fitted to admonish us how tentative and provisional are our attainments, intellectual and moral; and how often the deepest convictions of one generation are the rejects of the next."

If a quotation is longer than four lines of typing, it should be set off from the text, indented, single-spaced, and *without* quotation marks (see p. 235).

2. Quotation marks are usually omitted from short familiar quotations

Because of strict controls on fireworks, the rockets' red glare and the bombs bursting in air are now confined to one public display on the Fourth of July.

Once, several years back, I thought perhaps I had left my heart in San Francisco, somewhere in the vicinity of Telegraph Hill.—Jane Howard, *A Different Woman*

3. Quotation marks are not used around an indirect quotation

DIRECT QUOTATION   He said: "I don't go to the movies more than twice a year."
INDIRECT QUOTATION   He said that he didn't go to the movies more than twice a year.

4. Quotation marks enclose titles of works that do not appear as whole volumes, including essays, short stories, poems, and chapters and other sections of books.

Titles of magazines, newspapers, and whole volumes are italicized (underlined). See pp. 336–337 and throughout Chapter 9.

Theodore Roethke's poem "The Shape of the Fire" is included in *The Lost Son*.

Virginia Woolf's essay "The Art of Biography" was published in the *Atlantic Monthly*.

When a title appears by itself on a title page or at the top of page 1, neither quotation marks nor italics are used unless you have a quotation or title within the title.

5. Quotation marks are also used (a) to distinguish words-as-words; (b) to call attention to irony; and (c) to label unfamiliar terms or slang

a. Some people would like to abandon the word "race" altogether and substitute a more neutral term like "ethnic group."—Marston Bates, *The Prevalence of People* (without quotation marks the reader might be puzzled by the "word race")

b. First is the widespread illusion that education is something that goes on in the classroom, something that comes by way of a "course" that a professor "gives" and a student "takes."—Henry Steele Commager, "Is Ivy Necessary?" *Saturday Review* (quotation marks here are the equivalent of a mildly ironic *so-called* and make that overworked word unnecessary

c. The domain of the electrician, or "juicer," has its own peculiar vocabulary in which lighting experts are called "gaffers" and installations are made by "riggers" with the aid of assistants dubbed "carbon monkeys."—William Fadiman, "Lingua California Spoken Here," *Saturday Review*

In the third illustration the writer is using quotation marks legitimately to label shoptalk unfamiliar to the general reader. But this device should be used sparingly. Modern American writers seldom segregate slang in apologetic quotes. Contemporary usage can be pretty well summarized in this blunt rule of thumb: *If an expression belongs, admit it without quotation marks; if it doesn't, leave it out.*

Beware especially of the common habit of spreading quotation marks around indiscriminately like measles, enclosing not only slang but respectable colloquial idioms, trite expressions, and commonplace metaphors:

Applying the principles of research he took 150 executives "apart." . . . And in his fascinating book *How to Develop Your Executive Ability*, he shows what makes them "tick." (The quotation marks are used around *apart* and *tick* presumably because the words are not to be taken literally, but any reader knows that the executives have not swallowed watches and are not being drawn and quartered.)

At this point I find that like the proverbial "sore thumb" it is standing out again. (Here the student has already apologized unnecessarily for borrowing from proverbial wisdom without adding excuse to apology by using quotation marks.)

6. Single quotation marks are used for material quoted within quotations

Virginia Woolf's novel *To the Lighthouse* opens brightly: " 'Yes, of course, if it's fine tomorrow,' said Mrs. Ramsey. 'But you'll have to be up with the lark.' "—Gertrude Himmelfarb, *Victorian Minds*

Position of Quotation Marks

It has already been said that both the comma and the colon are used to introduce quotations and that interrupters in quotations are usually set off by commas. Most style books prescribe the following order when quotation marks are combined with other punctuation:

Put quotation marks

1. Always outside the comma and period

"I die," he said, "worshipping God, loving my friends, without hatred of my enemies and detesting superstition."—George R. Havens, *The Age of Ideas*

This practice of going in and burning the Pathan villages and then retreating was called the policy of "butcher and bolt."—Walter Wallbank, *India in the New Era*

Notice that this order is followed even when the quoted matter is only a short part of the sentence.

2. Always inside the semicolon and colon

He lived in what he optimistically called "luxury"; he died in real poverty.

There was only one reason why he was not "good college material": he was too lazy to study.

3. Outside or inside the question mark and exclamation point, depending on the context

a. If only the quoted matter is a question or exclamation, put the quotation marks outside:

He said, "Where are you going, my pretty maid?"
She shouted, "None of your fool business!"

b. If the entire sentence is a question or exclamation, put the quotation marks inside unless the quoted matter is also a question or exclamation:

What do you mean by saying, "I won't do that"?
What a story from a man who still says, "I am innocent"!
Did you ask this young woman, "Where are you going?"

Notice that only one question mark or exclamation point is used.

THE DASH (On the typewriter, two hyphens)

The dash is a strong comma usually employed to convey an abrupt break in the sentence. It may be used

1. To Break Off an Unfinished Sentence

Then he shook his head and said heavily, "No, not everybody, but—" He paused, dissatisfied with explanation.—Randall Jarrell, *Pictures from an Institution*

2. To Prepare the Reader for a Climax or an Anticlimax

All through the forties the more enlightened kept pointing out that by closing libraries, parks, art galleries, museums, and zoological gardens you drove the proletariat to the source of pleasure which was not legislated against the gin mill and the beer shop!—John W. Dodds, *The Age of Paradox*

As for my experience with articles by experts in anthropology and sociology, it has led me to conclude that the requirement, in my ideal university, of having the papers in every department passed by a professor of English might result in revolutionizing these subjects—if indeed the second of them survived at all.—Edmund Wilson, *A Piece of My Mind*

3. To Introduce a Series (Where More Formal Writing Would Have a Colon)

This is true of all the dissenting pioneers—Isadora Duncan, Ruth St. Denis, Mary Wigman, Martha Graham, Doris Humphrey, Sybil Shearer, Pearl Lang, Anna Sokolow, and the author.—Agnes DeMille, "Creating a Dance," *Atlantic*

All the King's Scholars attended the great church regularly, and part of their curriculum was to turn in a detailed report of the sermon—the smaller boys in English, the older ones in Latin prose and the most advanced in Latin verse.—Marchette Chute, *Two Gentle Men*

4. To Gather Up the Parts of an Extended Subject, Often a Series

The constant barrage of pollution news, the incessant forecasts of energy depletion, the daily announcement of discoveries that things once thought harmless cause stroke, cancer, heart attack, kidney failure, blindness, liver atrophy, defective births, idiocy—all this is the daily American routine, and there is much more.—Russell Baker, "Things Are Tough All Over," *New York Times Magazine*

False relaxation, genial improvisation, a belief in good intentions, youthfulness, verve—a new sentimentality threatens the revolution at birth.—Elizabeth Hardwick, "Notes on the New Theater," *New York Review of Books*

5. To Set Off—Two Dashes—an Interrupter—a Clause, Phrase, or Single Word—When Commas Would Not Convey the Desired Emphasis or Abruptness

What Mary Tyler Moore can do—and it's nothing to be embarrassed about—is act.—"Once in Love with Mary," *Time*

Theoretically—and secretly, of course—I was all for the Burmese and all against their oppressors, the British.—George Orwell, "Shooting an Elephant"

He sat there saying nothing, with his ferocious face and his basilisk eye, which he turned on me—reprovingly—from time to time.—Alistair Cooke, *Six Men* (notice how, in this illustration, segregating the word *reprovingly* tends to emphasize it instead of sidetracking it as an incidental comment)

The dash is also used as an all-purpose gadget by people dashing off letters and notes in too much of a hurry to punctuate precisely. Such promiscuous use of the dash can become an irritating nuisance when it occurs in writing more serious than chitchat between pen pals.

334

PARENTHESES

Parentheses (curves) are used

1. To Enclose Parenthetical Matter

Like two dashes, parentheses normally imply a stronger interruption than commas. Although some writers use two dashes and parentheses interchangeably, dashes often emphasize the interrupter, whereas curves tend to isolate it as an aside (see p. 334).

It was a special trick, and, until you learned it (usually from another Ford owner, but sometimes by a period of appalling experimentation) you might as well have been winding up an awning. The trick was to leave the ignition switch off, proceed to the animal's head, pull the choke (which was a little wire protruding through the radiator), and give the crank two or three nonchalant upward lifts.—E. B. White, "Farewell My Lovely!" *The Second Tree from the Corner*

If the matter in parentheses is a complete and separate sentence, a period (question mark, or exclamation point) is supplied inside the second curve; if the parenthetical element interrupts another sentence, both capital and end-punctuation may be omitted:

Its fins are the size and weight of a pretty large dining-table, and its flukes would make an excellent pair of wings for a fighter aircraft. (They are perfectly streamlined, and, as I am sure their toughness and quality exceed that of Duralumin, I commend them to aircraft designers.)—R. B. Robertson, *Of Whales and Men*

In the early years of his career, Nureyev tended to be temperamental. But now, a new Rudolf (he hates to be called Rudy) has emerged.—Sally Quinn, "Not Only Is He Beautiful, But He Can Dance Too," *Washington Post*

2. To Enclose Dates; and Numbers or Letters Introducing Parts of a Series

In the year which is traditionally set as the end of the Romantic Period (1832), three important events occurred: (1) the death of England's robust story-teller Sir Walter Scott; (2) the death of the great German sage Goethe; and (3) the first Reform Bill, which extended the franchise to thousands of new voters.

SQUARE BRACKETS

Square brackets are used when you want to insert a comment of your own inside a quotation (see p. 235):

What he actually wrote was: "These arguments [referring presumably to the

335

assertions in the *Times*] are entirely irrevelant [sic] to the present question."

Here *sic* means: *Thus* it was in my source; don't blame me for the misspelling.

DOTS (ELLIPSIS POINTS)

Dots are used

1. To Indicate an Omission (or Ellipsis) in a Quotation

The first quotation given in the *Dictionary of Americanisms* published by Chicago University is from a letter of Jefferson's of 1797: "The parties here in debate continually charged each other ... with being governed by an attachment to this or that of the belligerent nations, rather than the dictates of reason and pure Americanism."—Edmund Wilson, *A Piece of My Mind*

The standard number is three dots (periods on the typewriter separated from each other and from the text by single spaces) in addition to other punctuation. This means four dots at the end of a sentence. To indicate an extended ellipsis in prose or the omission of one or more lines of verse, use a series of spaced dots from margin to margin.

2. To Indicate a Hesitation or Interruption in a Passage of Dialogue

"Why where ..." Mary began, for there was nobody in the kitchen.
"Must be in the living room," her father said, and took her arm.—James Agee, *A Death in the Family*

3. To Break Off an Unfinished Statement or Suggest an Indefinite Series

Meanings themselves are a dime a dozen. In literature humankind becomes abstract when we begin to dislike it. And ...
Interruption by a deep reader: Yes, yes, we know all that.—Saul Bellow, *Plain Style*

UNDERLINING (ITALICIZING)

Underlining means to a printer: Set this in italics. It is used:

1. To Distinguish Titles of Magazines, Newspapers, and Whole Volumes (see p. 331)

When Ellen in *The Male Animal* observes that Tommy has had several articles in *Harper's* and the *Atlantic Monthly*, and Joe replies that the *Reader's Digest* is a great little magazine, Tommy quietly asks, "Do you like bouillon cubes?"

Of Dickens' two historical novels, many people remember *A Tale of Two Cities*, but few are familiar with *Barnaby Rudge*.

A title should not be italicized when it appears alone on a title page or at the top of the first page of a work.

The article *the* of a periodical title and the name of a city in the title of a newspaper are often not italicized even if part of the masthead: the *New York Times* or sometimes the New York *Times* instead of *The New York Times*.

2. To Distinguish Words Themselves from The Things to Which They Refer

If one speaks of the tendency toward homogeneity in modern culture, one is necessarily implicated in the semantic difficulties of the word *culture*.—Lionel Trilling, *Beyond Culture*

Quotation marks may also be used for this purpose. Whatever convention you follow, be consistent.

3. To Mark Foreign Words and Phrases That Are Not Naturalized into English

This disability no doubt makes them tend, when they assume the pince-nez of the *juge d'instruction* and open Dossier D, to lean more towards drama than reality.—D. B. Wyndham Lewis, *The Hooded Hawk* (here pince-nez and dossier are treated as assimilated English words—a good dictionary makes such distinctions)

4. Occasionally to Denote Emphasis

Most leading histories of literature are either histories of civilization or collections of critical essays. One type is not a history of *art*; the other, not a *history* of art.—René Wellek and Austin Warren, *Theory of Literature*

If we are condemned to a complex social existence, as it seems we are, then the trick is to ensure that *we* make use of *it*, rather than let *it* make use of *us*.—Desmond Morris, *The Human Zoo*

But chronic underlining, like exclamation pointing, quickly defeats its own purpose. Notice how the young Queen Victoria's breathless italics make everything in plain roman type seem strangely trivial:

A great event and a great compliment *his* visit certainly is, and the people *here* are extremely flattered at it. He is certainly a *very striking* man; still very handsome. His profile is *beautiful*, and his manners *most* dignified and graceful; extremely civil—quite alarmingly so, as he is so full of attentions and *politeness*. But the expression of the *eyes* is *formidable*, and unlike anything I ever saw before.

Other matters sometimes discussed as punctuation—the apostrophe, capitalization, and the hyphen—are considered in the chapter on Spelling.

A LAST WORD

So much for the conventions of punctuation. Building on this foundation, you can learn to use punctuation marks with a skill that goes far beyond these simple principles. According to Fowler, for example, the difference between "The master beat the scholar with a strap" and "The master beat the scholar, with a strap" is the gulf between matter-of-factness and indignation. Punctuation, in short, can be more than a slavish salaaming to mechanical rules, a rigid system under which a student accepts bondage to escape ambiguity. It is an important part of the writer's obligation to cooperate with the reader. It can also be a subtle index to style and tone, a significant aspect of the writer's art.

EXERCISE D (General Review)

In accordance with the conventions explained in this chapter, make all necessary changes in the punctuation of the following passages and give a specific reason for each.

1. There are undergraduates, who believe, that if they can just struggle through college without learning to spell or punctuate, they will graduate to a secretary who will do it all for them.

2. Although I had shown no interest in sociology before coming to college had not read any of the standard works or even as a matter of fact heard of them I am now planning to major in it.

3. On June 4 1978 in Ashtabula Ohio I had an automobile accident that has given me an entirely different attitude toward driving, in fact, the experience made it doubtful for a while that I would ever drive again.

4. Selma Robinson, who had wasted too much time reading articles by "experts" with titles like *The Dropout Problem—a National Disgrace* in magazines such as Cosmopolitan and Redbook was now devoting hours to worrying about whether she was going to "make the grade" or "flunk out" of college.

5. The distressing outflow of American dollars, the persistence of unemployment which brought distress to millions, the burgeoning national debt, and the problem of how to control wasteful government· spending, all these dilemmas were bringing headaches to the economists in Washington.

6. Dear Mr. Ohm;
We are sorry that the Jiffy Static Selector is no longer manufactured by our firm, we have however referred your order to the Miracle Electronics Corporation of Brook-

lyn and they we are sure will give it their immediate attention. If we can be of any further help to you in building your hi-fi set please let us know.

Sincerely yours

Herman Sherman Vice President
Special Electric Company

7. He insisted that nobody who had not lived through the crisis could possibly understand the reasons that had motivated the Governor to act as he did.

8. Of the many reasons for the failure of the plan the following were most often cited; the failure of many citizens, including a large number who are normally in favor of redevelopment, to go to the polls, the general belief that the project would raise taxes by at least three mills, and the propaganda disseminated by many private entrepreneurs, some of whom were apparently more interested in their own pocketbooks than in the obliteration of slums.

9. Instead of saying, "How do you feel today Joe?" he said "that he wanted an explanation of my inexcusable behavior of the night before."

10. After a successful operation for cataract his eyes seemed to be as good as new, in fact, he was reading more than ever to make up for the time he had lost.

11. Inside the school was in a state of chaos the clutter of overturned furniture torn papers and pulverized chalk was unbelievable.

12. The scientific education of the typical literary man distressed C. P. Snow who once wrote indignantly: "So the great edifice of modern physics goes up, and the majority of the cleverest people in the western world (he was speaking particularly as the result of his experience at social gatherings of Englishmen) have about as much insight into it as their neolithic ancestors would have had.

13. "Is it conceivable," Masterson asked, "that only two of the men, whom I used to regard as my close friends, are willing to accompany me on this mission"?

14. He had asked everyone but Hutchins and Zorg were the only two who were willing to accompany him.

15. It does not necessarily follow that a Sunday newspaper which carries colored comics is any worse than one that does not, however, it is a fact that in two of the best papers the New York Times and the London Observer comics are notable by their absence.

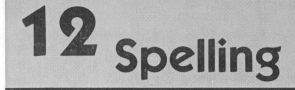

12 Spelling

If the question is one of spelling, you can
depend on the dictionary absolutely.
Paul Roberts

I hold that a word is something more than
the noise it makes; it is also the way it looks
on the page.
T. S. Eliot

GOOD AND BAD SPELLERS

Students who can't spell by the time they get to college are often full of
excuses. Some bitterly reproach the eccentricities of the language.
Some blame their unfortunate heritage. "My father couldn't spell
either, and neither could my grandfather. Nobody in my family can
spell." One gets a ludicrous picture of thousands of six-year-olds spelling *cat c-a-t-t* and *dog d-o-g-e* on the very first day in the first grade.
Others, with more justification, blame a misguided school system that
tried to teach them to spell long words by taking a running jump into
the middle instead of breaking them up logically into syllables. Still
others, even closer to the truth, admit that they can't spell because they
don't read. But many of them have cheerfully diagnosed their own cases
as both rare and hopeless.

It is doubtful that any college misspeller of normal intelligence is a
hopeless case. Some, to be sure, need special clinical help, either physical or psychological. A student who tells the instructor, "All I see when I
look at a page of print is some tall thin letters and some short fat ones,"
cannot be helped merely by studying a spelling book. But most poor
spellers are the victims of nothing more mysterious than carelessness
and indifference. With a little help and a lot of self-discipline, they can
become good spellers.

What is a good speller? According to the tradition of the old-
fashioned American spelling bee, good spellers are freckled geniuses of

340

twelve who through a combination of punishing drill, phonetic intuition, and sheer luck, can rattle off the spelling of hundreds of words that they never use, including the ultimate demon that wins the cup—an exotic, eccentric montrosity such as *syzygy*. According to the philosophy of this chapter, a good speller is a human being with enough sense to learn and apply the few useful spelling rules, to memorize a few hundred common words that don't follow useful rules, and to make regular use of a dictionary.

Good spelling is a mechanical virtue at best, far less important in good writing than organization, sentence structure, diction, or even punctuation. Most college English instructors would rather have a student who can write and can't spell than one who can spell and can't write. But the world at large closely associates spelling ability with intelligence and education. An executive will shamelessly dictate the most meaningless gobbledygook to a secretary and hit the ceiling when the secretary types it with an extra *c* in *recommendation*. Nor will anything convince the executive that the brand-new college graduate who ends a letter of application "Hopping to hear from you soon" may possibly be guilty of nothing more monstrous than an unfortunate typographical error. A good speller may not deserve any loving cups, but a bad speller goes through life with a handicap. In a college-educated man or woman, society takes good spelling for granted.

Whether your spelling is good, bad, or indifferent, you should be able to improve it by carefully studying the suggestions, rules, and lists in this chapter.

READING ALOUD

Read your first draft aloud slowly. There is little relation in English between correct spelling and careful pronunciation. Good spelling is largely based on eye-memory. If you don't know how to spell a word, it will probably do no good to linger lovingly over the syllables, pronouncing it in the most fastidious manner. But in slow oral reading the eye is less likely to overlook misspellings resulting from hasty writing or typing. Transposing letters and adding or omitting entire syllables are often errors of indolence, not ignorance. A thorough oral reading would probably have caught the following student slips:

Britian for *Britain*	*motony* for *monotony*
competion for *competition*	*pratical* for *practical*
convient for *convenient*	*proganda* for *propaganda*
critize for *criticize*	*realtion* for *relation*
extracurcular for *extracurricular*	*rember* for *remember*
graudate for *graduate*	*typlify* for *typify*
mechism for *mechanism*	*villian* for *villain*

341

USING THE DICTIONARY

When reading over your first draft, circle all doubtful words. When you have finished, look them all up in a dictionary and copy them carefully letter for letter. (Many careless students look a word up, close the dictionary, and calmly misspell it again.) Don't guess. Don't ask your roommate.

At first, if you are a very poor speller, you may have to count nearly every word you write as doubtful. After a few weeks of reasonable effort, you should know whether you are more likely to misspell short words or long words, whether you have trouble with doubling consonants or with *ie* vs. *ei*, whether you are addicted to omitting syllables indiscriminately or have a special affection for ignoring *ed* in the past tense of weak verbs. But whatever your personal idiosyncrasies, you should view the following with particular suspicion:

1. All words ending in *ance* or *ence*, *ant* or *ent*, *able* or *ible*. Such words are annoyingly common in English. They follow no useful rule, and some English instructors have to look them up regularly.
2. All words with *neutral vowels.* For example, the pronunciation of *defin(i)tely, hypocr(i)sy, and rep(e)tition* gives no clue to the choice of the vowels in parentheses. An ingenious student may spell them correctly by analogy with *definition, hypocritical,* and *repetitive,* but poor spellers are likely to come up with something like *definately, hypocracy* (by a false analogy with *democracy*), and *repitition* unless they get into the habit of looking the words up.
3. All possessives and contractions—because the omission of apostrophes is one of the most unnecessary oversights in undergraduate writing (see pp. 347–348).
4. All words that are pronounced or spelled like other words (see pp. 350–353).
5. All words that you rarely use or see in print.
6. All recent arrivals in your vocabulary.

When you come across a new word in a textbook or look up a strange one in a dictionary, learn a double lesson by examining its spelling at the same time that you familiarize yourself with its meaning. It is ridiculous to stay long in a course in biology without learning the difference between *species* and *specie*, or linger in a class in literature without learning to spell *heroes, villain, playwright* (not *playwrite*), *tragedy, metaphor,* and *rhythm.* The same logic goes for spelling proper names, a problem that some college students approach with sublime indifference. When 300 freshman examinations on *Othello* contain twenty-seven different misspellings of *Desdemona*—including such combinations and permutations as *Desmonia, Desmondia, Dexdenomia, Desdomnia, Demonia, Desdoma,* and *Desmando*—it is high time students took the spelling of proper names more seriously.

342

By reading the explanatory notes in the front of your dictionary, you can learn its methods of designating which of two or more spellings of a word is preferred. The distinction is sometimes between American and British English, sometimes between a long, older form and a short, newer form. With some words the short form (*tho* for *though*, *thru* for *through*) is distinctly informal; with others (*alright*), it may be listed as questionable usage.

SPELLING CONVENTIONS

Five Useful Rules

Learn and apply the following spelling rules:

1. IE vs. EI

I before *e*	(believe, piece, relieve, siege)
Except after *c*	(conceive, deceive, perceive, receive)
Or when sounded like *a*	(eight, freight, reign, sleigh)
As in *neighbor* or *weigh*.	

The common exceptions are *either, neither, leisure, seize,* and *weird*.

2. Doubling

In words of one syllable and in accented final syllables, double a single consonant after a single vowel when adding a suffix beginning with a vowel:

brag doubles the single consonant *g* after the single vowel *a* before adding a suffix beginning with a vowel, *ed* or *ing*: bragged, bragging.

net doubles the single consonant *t* after the single vowel *e* before adding a suffix beginning with a vowel, *ed* or *ing*: netted, netting.

occur doubles the single consonant *r* after the single vowel *u* before a suffix beginning with a vowel, *ence, ed, ing*: occurrence, occurred, occurring.

On the other hand, if a word is *not* accented on the final syllable, the general tendency in American English is not to double: *benefited, totaled, traveling*.

This complete rule may be too complex for handy use by misspellers with a poor ear for accents. The following simpler rule will apply to most one-syllable words, except those ending in *l* and *r*: *Double the consonant, shorten the vowel*. Note the difference in these examples:

Double consonant following short vowel (ă, ĕ, ĭ, ŏ, ŭ)	*Single consonant following long vowel* (ā, ē, ī, ō, ū)
He *tăpped* on the table.	The trainer *tāped* my ankle with adhesive.

343

I was slow in *lĕtting* him in.	Good revision requires *delēting*.
The day was *bĭtter* cold.	The dog was not a barker but a *bīter*.
She was always *mŏpping* the floor.	He was *mōping* all week after falling out of love.
The Coast Guard *cŭtter* sank.	Kittens are *cūter* than cats.

3. Final silent E

Drop final silent *e* before a suffix beginning with a vowel; keep it before a suffix beginning with a consonant:

hate	drops the *e* before *ed* and *ing*:	hated, hating
	keeps it before *ful*:	hateful
state	drops the *e* before *ed* and *ing*:	stated, stating
	keeps it before *ment, ly*:	statement, stately
complete	drops the *e* before *ed, ion, ing*:	completed, completion, completing
	keeps it before *ly, ness*:	completely, completeness

The common exceptions to this rule are *argument, awful, duly, truly,* and *ninth;* and words in *ce* and *ge,* where the *e* is kept before *a* and *o: irreplaceable, noticeable, courageous, manageable.* With some words (*hatable, hateable; movable, moveable*), usage is divided.

4. Final Y

When a word ends in *y* after a consonant, change the *y* to *i* before all suffixes except *ing*:

try	tries, tried	trying
rely	reliable, reliance, relied	relying
happy	happiness, happiest, happily	
pity	pitiful, pitied, pitiless	pitying

But keep the *y* after a vowel:

employ, relay	employable, relayed	employer,	employed,	employment

Common exceptions are *laid, paid,* and *said.*

5. Final AL and LY

When an adjective ends in *al,* form the adverb by adding *ly:*

accidental	accidentally
incidental	incidentally
musical	musically
practical	practically

344

Adjectives ending in *ic* usually add *ally* to form the adverb:

automatic	automatically	but *not* publically
basic	basically	
drastic	drastically	
chronic	chronically	
frantic	frantically (or franticly)	
specific	specifically	

The natural tendency to hurry through the *ally* in pronouncing some of these words results in such misspellings as *accidently* and *incidently*, and foretells the time when we shall probably drop the extra syllable throughout the group.

Helping the Memory

Learn to use the aids to memory called *mnemonic devices*. Handy gimmicks in all kinds of studying, they can be especially useful in spelling. With a little ingenuity, you can freely devise your own. One student, reluctant to learn even four lines of doggerel about *i* before *e*, thinks of *Celia*. Another calls the *police*. A third recalls the common exceptions (*either, neither, leisure, seize, weird*) by repeating a sentence in which each word begins with the key initial letter: "*E*very *n*ovice *l*oves *s*uch *w*ords." Another remembers that a princi*pal* is a *pal*, a princip*le* a ru*le*. Still another remembers that *lose* loses an *o*. The field is wide open.

Capitals

Capitals are used for

1. The personal pronoun I and the first words of sentences, quotations, and lines of traditional poetry

I shouted at him: "Quote the passage exactly! It goes:
Water, water, everywhere,
And all the boards did shrink;
Water, water, everywhere,
Nor any drop to drink."

Fragmentary quotations are not capitalized:

He did not speak of "unconditional surrender."

Some modern poets have abandoned the convention of capitalizing the first word of every line. In quoting, follow carefully the author's own punctuation.

2. Persons, titles, and personification

John Hancock, Eliza Doolittle

Titles, when used before names of individuals or referring to them specifically:

President Carter, Senator Blathers, Mother Machree
She found the President in.

Specific titles of some high offices:

the Vice President of the United States, the Queen of England, the Secretary of Commerce

Otherwise, when individuals are not referred to specifically, use small letters:

It is not easy to be a president of a great nation or the mother of nine.

Personification:

Do not let Conscience make you a coward. Tennyson referred to Nature as "red in tooth and claw."

3. References to deities and sacred texts

God, Allah, Isis, the Bible, the Torah, the Koran

4. Calendar words: days, months, holidays and holy days

This year *Labor Day* comes on *Monday, September 4, Yom Kippur* on *Thursday, September 21.*

But not usually seasons of the year:

spring, summer, fall, winter

5. Geographical words: cities, countries, lakes, rivers, languages, people, races, regions, and so on

In the *United States* many people of *Oriental* extraction live in the *Northwest* and speak *Chinese* or *Japanese* as well as *English.*

Duluth is on *Lake Superior, London* is on the *Thames.*

But not the points of the compass:

He went *west.*

6. Specific courses in school or college, but not subjects in general unless they are languages

She took *History 31* and *Economics 12* because of her interest in *history, government,* and *economics.* She was required to take *French.*

7. Important words in titles of books, articles, poems, plays, movies, TV shows, musical compositions, and so on   (*this usually includes the first and last words and all others except articles, conjunctions, and prepositions*)

The Decline and Fall of the Roman Empire
"Student Politics in a Democratic Society"

"Ode to the Confederate Dead"
Cat on a Hot Tin Roof
Gone with the Wind
As the World Turns
Afternoon of a Faun

8. Names of clubs and other institutions

Kiwanis, Phi Beta Kappa, National Organization for Women (NOW), Alcoholics Anonymous (AA), Sierra Club

This summary of general practice is incomplete. An experienced writer may capitalize for stylistic reasons—emphasis, for example—in the absence of any specific convention. But there has been a marked tendency in recent writing to reduce capitals to a minimum. Students are more likely to over- than undercapitalize.

The Apostrophe

Use the apostrophe in accordance with the following rules:

1. To denote possession

Unless a word ends in *s*, form the possessive of both singular and plural by adding *'s*

a man's man	men's shorts
Mary's book	women's dresses
someone's hat	children's day
anybody's coat	people's faith

If a singular noun ends in *s*, add either *'s* or the apostrophe only, depending on the pronunciation:

the bass's singing	Venus' or Venus's son
Charles' or Charles's reign	Xerxes' wrath

If a plural noun ends in *s*, add the apostrophe only:

the Joneses' standard of living	the boys' coats
the horses' stable	the girls' behavior

2. To indicate the omissions in contractions

aren't	o'clock (literally *of the clock*)
isn't	It's a great life
doesn't	who's who and what's what

3. To form the plural of letters, figures, and words-as-words

Italicize and add *'s* (which is not italicized):

He knew neither his *p*'s and *q*'s nor his *abc*'s.

He was always rolling his *7*'s and *11*'s.
She used too many *and*'s and *so*'s in her sentences.

Plurals of dates (not italicized) occur both with and without the apostrophe:

the 1920's or the 1920s
the 'twenties or the twenties

Do not use an apostrophe in non-possessive plurals:

WRONG Officer's wishing checks for payday's please notify the disbursing office at least two day's before payday's.

Do not use the apostrophe to form the possessive of personal pronouns *(his, hers, its, our, yours, their)* or the relative or interrogative pronoun *whose* (see pp. 288–289). Distinguish carefully between

It's a nice day. (contraction) and The dog lost *its* head. (possessive)
Who's afraid? (contraction) and *Whose* book is that? (possessive)

The Hyphen

Use the hyphen in accordance with the following principles:

1. To divide a word at the end of a line

Words are divided by syllables. A *one-syllable* word should never be divided, *even if it ends in* ed. (WRONG: *fish*-ed, *crown*-ed.) *Syllable* divisions can usually be determined by careful pronunciation. Double consonants are almost invariably split (*nap-ping, af-fection, mil-lion*). When in doubt, consult the dictionary. With a little foresight and discreet use of the margin release, any typist can avoid dividing a word after a single letter (*e-rupt*) or giving a hyphenated word a compound fracture (*red-head-ed*).

2. To separate compound numbers and fractions

The hyphen is regularly used in all compound numbers from *twenty-one* to *ninety-nine*. It is commonly employed in fractions used as *adjectives* but not in fractions used as nouns or when either the numerator or the denominator is hyphenated.

seventy-seven   twenty-seven   two hundred (and) forty-three
a two-thirds majority   two thirds of the people

3. To separate prefixes from roots if two vowels or a small letter and a capital will otherwise run together

pre-existent   re-election   semi-independent   un-American

A *diaeresis* is occasionally still used over the second vowel: *preëmi-*

nent, reëxamine. In some common compounds, the modern tendency is to let readers make the separation in their own minds: *cooperate, coordinate.*

4. To separate prefixes from roots if the unhyphenated word has a different meaning

re-count (to *count again*) vs. recount (to *tell*)
re-sort (to *sort again*) vs. resort (to *go* or *apply to*)
re-collect (to *collect again*) vs. recollect (to *remember*)

5. To combine words functioning as a compound adjective before a noun

well-known authorities	up-to-the-minute record
hard-working student	door-to-door canvasser
end-over-end kick	X-ray pictures (verb *X-ray*, noun *X ray*)
coast-to-coast flight	pay-as-you-go taxes
wall-to-wall carpet	would-be gentleman
110-volt line	consumer-oriented economy

But omit the hyphen when the expression follows the noun (the authority was *well known*; the record was *up to the minute*); or when one of the words is an adverb ending in *ly* (a *beautifully played shot*).

It is vain to compose or remember rules to cover the thousands of possible compounds in English. For example, the prefix *non* and the suffix *like* are usually not separated with a hyphen (*nonabsorbent, nonabstainer, nonacid, lifelike, birdlike, childlike*) but the prefix *self* is usually followed by a hyphen (*self-control, self-knowledge, self-service*). Some compounds are traveling from two words to one word via the hyphen route, and even the lexicographers have trouble deciding how fast each is moving and what territory it has reached.

6. To combine the parts of a compound which are separated by a conjunction

He wore air- and waterproof clothes.
Fairy stories are full of two- and three-headed giants.
Students are more likely to over- than underhyphenate.

There is only one sure way out of any hyphen dilemma: *When in doubt, use a dictionary.*

Abbreviations and Clipped Words

Some abbreviations are acceptable on any level of writing. Examples:

1. *Mr., Mrs., Ms., Dr.,* and the like before proper names.
2. *Jr., Sr., M.D., Ph.D.,* and the like after proper names.
3. *A.D.* and *B.C., a.m.* and *p.m., No.* and *$* when used with dates and figures.

4. Well-known organizations or agencies: *ASPCA, ERA, NAACP.* Less familiar names should be spelled out the first time: *National Association for Mental Health (NAMH).*

Abbreviations are especially common in technical writing, where the reader is expected to understand them: *AC, DC, Btu, cm, rpm, H₂S.* They are expected in footnotes and bibliography (see Chapter 9).

But in the text of most nontechnical writing, however informal, use abbreviations sparingly. General readers want to read words, not shorthand symbols; they prefer *Street* to *St., chapter* to *chap.* or *ch., Charles* to *Chas., Wisconsin* to *Wis., for example* to *e.g., that is* to *i.e., and* to *&,* and so forth (which they prefer to *etc.*).

The choice between the "clipped" and full forms of a word depends on the level of language. Such shortenings as *dorm* for *dormitory, exam* for *examination, lab* for *laboratory, prof* for *professor,* and *psycho* for *psychopathic* might belong in an informal narrative but would strike a jarring note in a formal essay.

Numbers

Though usage varies widely, this is a useful general rule:

Except in technical writing and in a few special instances, such as dates, hours, addresses, and volumes and pages (in bibliography and footnotes), spell out all numbers if you can do it in one or two words

forty	137
twenty-three	$7.98
8 a.m. (*but* eight o'clock)	1,248

If you can't avoid beginning a sentence with a number, spell it out; if a passage contains one number that can't be spelled out, use figures consistently throughout the passage.

SPELLING LISTS

Study the following lists of commonly misspelled words.

1. Words Often Confused (Homonyms)

Words are often confused because of similarity in spelling or pronunciation. Even good spellers have trouble with these *homonyms* until they understand the differences in meaning. The starred words are explained in the Glossary of Usage; the others should be carefully checked in a dictionary. In studying, try to associate each word, not with the one above or below it, but with similar words that may not be in this book. For example, associate *isle* with *island, alley* with *valley, ascent* with *descent, breath* with *death, climactic* with *climax* (not *climate*).

* accept
* except

* adapt
* adopt

  advice
  advise

* affect
* effect

  aisle
  isle

  alley, alleys
  ally, allies

* allusion
* illusion

* already
* all ready

  altar
  alter

* altogether
* all together

  alumna,
    alumnae
  alumnus,
    alumni

  angel
  angle

  ascent
  assent

* aural
* oral

  bare
  bear

  baring
  barring
  bearing

  berth
  birth

* born
* borne

  bough
  bow

  breath
  breathe

  bridal
  bridle

  Britain
  Briton

  buy
  by

  canvas
  canvass

* capital
* capitol

  Calvary
  cavalry

* censor
* censure
* censer

* cite
* sight
* site

  climactic
  climatic

  clothes
  cloths

  coarse
  course

  complement
  compliment

  conscience
  conscious

* council
* counsel
* consul

  corps
  corpse

  costume
  custom

* credible
* creditable
* credulous

  dairy
  diary

  decent
  descent
  dissent

  desert
  dessert

  device
  devise

  die, dying
  dye, dyeing

  dining
  dinning

  discussed
  disgust

  dual
  duel

  elegy
  eulogy

  elicit
  illicit

* emigrate
* immigrate

* eminent
* imminent

  emphasis
  emphasize

  fair
  fare

  faze
  phase

  flair
  flare

  formally
  formerly

351

forth, forty
fourth,
  fourteen

gambit
gamut

genteel
gentile
gentle

hear
here

heard
herd

hoard
horde

holly
holy
wholly

human
humane

idle
idol

incidence
incidents

* ingenious
* ingenuous

* instance
* instant

its
it's

later
* latter

* lead (verb
    present)
* lead (metal)
* led (verb
    past)

lessen
lesson

loath
loathe

* loose (adj.)
* loose, loosing
    (verb)
* lose. losing

mantel
mantle

marital
martial

metal
mettle

* moral
* morale

naval
navel

nineteen
ninety
ninth

ordinance
ordnance

passed
past

peace
piece

* persecute
* prosecute

personal
personnel

perspective
prospective

plain
plane, planed
plan, planned

populace
populous

pore
pour

* precede,
    preceding
* proceed,
    proceeding
* procedure

precedence
precedents

prescribe
proscribe

presence
presents

* principal
* principle

profit
prophet

* prophecy
* prophesy

quiet
* quite

rain
reign
rein

respectably
* respectfully
* respectively

right
rite
write

road
rode
rowed

role
roll

seams
seems

shone
shown

sole
soul

speak
speech

* specie
* species

stationary
stationery

statue
stature
statute

steal
steel

straight
strait

suit
suite

tale
tail

* than
then

* there
* their
* they're

therefor
therefore

threw
through

* till
* until
* 'til

* to
* too
two

unkempt
unkept

venal
venial

waist
waste

weak
week

weather
whether

which
witch

who's
whose

woman
women

your
you're

2. Other Commonly Misspelled Words

The numbers in parentheses designate words that follow the rules on pp. 343–345.

absence
absorption
accelerate
acceptable
accessible
(5) accidentally
accommodate
(4) accompanying
accomplish
accumulate
accustom
(3) achievement
acknowledgment
   or acknowledgement
acquaintance
acquire
(2) acquitted
across
(5) additionally
address
adequate
adolescence

aggravate
aggressive
agreement
alcohol
all right
allege
almost
already
although
always
amateur
among
amount
analysis
analyze or
   analyse
annual
answer
(1) apiece
apologize
apology
apparatus

apparent
appearance
appreciate
approach
appropriate
arctic
(3) arguing
argument
(3) arising
arithmetic
around
arouse
(3) arrangement
article
artillery
assistant
association
(3) athletics
attacked
attendance
audience
auxiliary

awful
awkward

bachelor
background
balance
balloon
banana
barbarous
battalion
(4) beautiful
(3) becoming
before
beggar
(2) beginning
(1) believe
beneficial
(2) benefited
biscuit
boundary
brilliant
Britain
bureau
burglar
bus
(4) business

calendar
candidate
career
(3) careless
carriage
category
(1) ceiling
cemetery
certain
(3) changeable
chauffeur
choice
choose
chosen
college
(3) collegiate
colonel
colossal
column
comedy
(3) coming
commission
(2) committed

(2) committee
(3) comparatively
comparison
(2) compelled
competent
competition
(3) completely
concede
(1, 3) conceivable
(1) conceive
concrete
condemn
(2) conferred
confidently
congratulate
conqueror
conscientious
consciousness
consensus
consistent
continuously
(2) controlled
convenient
corner
counterfeit
courteous
(4) cries
criticism
criticize or
    criticise
curiosity
curriculum
cylinder

dealt
debater
(1) deceive
decide
decision
defendant
definite
(3) definitely
(3) definition
democracy
dependent
describe
description
(3) desirable
despair
desperate

destroy
develop
development
different
dilapidated
diminution
disagree
disappearance
disappoint
disastrous
discipline
discussion
dissatisfaction
dissension
dissipation
divide
divine
doctor
dormitory
drunkenness
duly

(4) easily
ecstasy
efficient
eighth
eligible
eliminate
embarrass
(3) encouraging
enemy
engineer
enthusiastic
(3) entirely
environment
equipment
(2) equipped
equivalent
erroneous
(5) especially
etc.
evidently
exaggerate
excellent
exhausted
exhilarate
existence
expense
experience
(3) extremely

familiar
fascinate
February
fiery
(5) finally
(5) financially
foreign
forward
(4) fraternities
freshman
(adj.)
friend
(5) fundamentally

gauge or gage
(5) generally
ghost
goddess
government
(3) governor
grammar
(1) grievance
(1, 3) grievous
group
guarantee
guard
(3) guidance

(1) handkerchief
(4) happiness
harass
height
heroes
hindrance
(2) hoping
huge
humorous
hurriedly
(4) hurrying
hypocrisy

image
(3) imaginary
(3) imagination
(3) immediately
(3) immensely
impossible
impromptu
(5) incidentally
incredible

independent
indispensable
inevitable
(3) infinitely
instead
intellectual
intelligent
(5) intentionally
interest
intramural
irrelevant
irresistible

judgment or
judgement

khaki
know
knowledge

laboratory
laborer
laid
legitimate
leisure
library
lightning
(3) likable
or likeable
(3) likely
(3, 4) loneliness
(3, 4) loveliness
lying

maintenance
manual
manufacturer
(4) marriage
mathematics
mattress
meant
medicine
medieval
or mediaeval
Mediter-
ranean
(3) merely
metaphor
millionaire
miniature

minute
(1) mischievous
misspelled
monotonous
mortgage
murmur
mysterious

(5) naturally
necessary
neither
nickel
(1) niece
(3) noticeable
nowadays

oblige
obstacle
occasion
(5) occasionally
(2) occurred
(2) occurrence
off
omission
(2) omitted
omniscient
opinion
opportunity
optimist
(5) originally

paid
pamphlet
parallel
paralysis
parliament
particularly
pastime
(2) peaceable
(1) perceive
perform
perhaps
permanent
permissible
(3) perseverance
perspiration
persuade
pertain
(5) physically
picknicking

355

playwright
poisonous
politician
portray
possess
possession
possibly
(5) practically
predominant
preference
(2) preferred
prejudice
preparation
prevalent
prisoner
privilege
probably
professor
prominent
pronunciation
propaganda
proportion
prove
psychology
purpose
pursue
(3) pursuing
pursuit

quantity
(2) quizzes

rarefy
(5) really
recede
(1) receipt
(1) receive
recipe
recognize
recollect
recommend
refer
(2) reference
(2) referred
(2) referring
regard
(1) relieve
religious
remembrance
renown(ed)

repetition
representative
resemblance
reservoir
resistance
restaurant
rhythm
ridiculous
roommate

sacrifice
(3) sacrilegious
(3) safety
schedule
secretary
seize
sentence
separate
sergeant
(3) severely
shepherd
(2) shining
(1) shriek
(1) siege
significant
similar
simultaneous
(3) sincerely
skis
smooth
sophomore
source
(5) specifically
specimen
sponsor
(2) stopping
strenuous
stretch
strictly
stubborn-
ness
(4) studying
succeed
successful
succumb
sufficient
superintend-
ent
supersede
(4) supplies

supposed
(3) surely
surprise
syllable
symmetry
sympathize

teammate
temperament
temperature
tendency
therefore
thorough
thought
through
together
toward
tragedy
(4) tries
truly
twelfth
typical
tyrannical
tyranny

unanimous
undoubtedly
unnecessary
(3) used
(3) using
(5) usually

vacuum
(3) valuable
vegetable
vengeance
view
village
villain

(2) warring
Wednesday
weird
welfare
withheld
(2) writing
(2) written

yours

Finally, if you are a chronic misspeller, *keep your own list.* Many words listed in this chapter you never misspell. Some of your favorites are missing. The best list for you is tailor-made by the only expert who has struggled continually with your spelling problem since the first grade: yourself. Delete from the foregoing list all the words that cause you no trouble. Copy the rest into a large notebook reserved for spelling. Add others that you misspell on themes and examinations; carefully copy the correct spelling from the dictionary and, if possible, add a note explaining the source of any common error. Put a black mark beside a word every time you misspell it. Make a separate card for each of the words you misspell most often, and study your way through the pack at regular intervals. This is old-fashioned discipline, but it is the only kind for students who can't spell by the time they get to college.

A Glossary of Usage

The following glossary is an alphabetical guide to many of the common errors and problems in English usage. If you do not find an item here, consult the general index to see if it is considered elsewhere in the text. You will find more detailed help in the dictionaries of usage listed on page 221.

Some entries in the glossary clearly distinguish "correct" usage from "incorrect"; some represent "divided usage," where more than one expression is acceptable; others involve levels of usage (see pp. 15–20). Because many expressions are labeled "colloquial," consider the implications of this passage from Chapter 5:

A *colloquialism* is a word or phrase more common in speech than in writing. In an age when informal writing closely reflects natural conversation, it is neither possible nor advisable to restrict colloquialisms to the spoken language. . . . Generally speaking, colloquial expressions are out of place in formal writing, including undergraduate critical essays, and should be used with discretion on the informal level. There is a rough proportion between the frequency of colloquialisms and the informality of style and tone.

a, an *A* is used before consonant sounds (*a* hotel, *a* union, *a* one dollar bill). *An* is used before vowel sounds, including silent *h* (*an* opening, *an* hour, *an* honorary degree). The use of *an* where *h* is pronounced in an unaccented first syllable is less common in America than in England (*an* historical novel, *an* hysterical patient).

above The use of *above* to refer to a point previously made (the *above*, the *above* argument, the *above*-mentioned facts) is widely condemned as Commercialese or Legalese. The same is true of *aforementioned* and *aforesaid*. If the reference is clear, natural substitutes are *this*, *these*, or *therefore*.

accept, except *Accept* is a verb meaning *receive*. *Except* is a preposition meaning *excluding* or *but*, or a verb meaning *exclude, omit*. (The fraternity *accepted* everyone *except* George into the group. It was easy to see why they *excepted* him.)

adapt, adopt *Adapt* means *adjust*. (She *adapted* to the new environment.) *Adopt* means *accept* or *take possession*. (The senate *adopted* the resolution by an overwhelming vote. The parents had *adopted* the child.)

affect, effect *Affect* is a verb meaning *influence* or *pretend*. (Her attitude *affected* me deeply, but I *affected* indifference.) *Effect* is a verb meaning *bring about* or a noun meaning *result*. (The weather *effected* a change in his disposition; the *effect* was disastrous.) Remember that, except as a technical term in psychology, *affect* is never a noun.

aforementioned, aforesaid *See* **above.**

aggravate In formal English *aggravate* means *increase an evil* or *make worse*. (Exposure to the sun *aggravated* his wound.) The word is widely condemned when used as a loose synonym for *annoy, disgust, displease, irritate, madden, offend,* or *provoke*.

agree to, with One *agrees to* a plan and *with* a person. (The only members who *agreed to* the president's proposal were those who always *agreed with* him.)

ain't Except in written dialogue, there is no need to use *ain't* seriously as a contraction of *is not, are not, has not,* or *have not*. Though it has its defenders as a contraction for *am I not, ain't* is generally regarded as nonstandard. *Aren't I (Are I not)* is indefensible.

all, all of The preposition *of* is necessary before pronouns (*all of* me, *all of* it) and before people's names (*all of* Shakespeare). In other contexts it can usually be dropped as redundant (She ate *all* the crumpets and drank *all* the wine).

all-around, all-round *See* **around.**

all ready *See* **already.**

all right *See* **alright.**

all together *See* **altogether.**

allusion, illusion, delusion An *allusion* is a *passing reference*, usually indirect (see p. 138). An *illusion* is a *misconception* that may be either pleasant or harmful. The word *delusion* may refer to anything from a strong *illusion* to a deep-seated misconception requiring psychiatric treatment. (The *allusion* in my speech was to the common *illusion* that every patient who suffers from *delusions* of grandeur thinks he is Napoleon.)

almost *See* **most.**

alot, a lot The article should be separated from the noun (*a lot* of nonsense). *Allot*—one word, two *l*'s—is a verb meaning *apportion* or *distribute*. *See* **lot, lots.**

already, all ready The single word *already* is an adverb meaning *previously*. *All ready* is a phrase meaning *completely ready* or signifying that every member of a group is ready. (He had *already* had his swim before we were *all ready* to set out for the lake.)

alright, all right Regardless of any analogy with *already, all right* is the standard spelling.

although, though Although the first is more formal, many writers choose whichever sounds better in context. Neither should be used in place of *however* at the beginning of a sentence (see p. 78).

altogether, all together The single word is an adverb meaning *entirely. All together* is an adjective phrase meaning *united*. (He was *altogether* wrong in assuming that the politicians were *all together* in their beliefs.)

amid, amidst, among, amongst All are generally acceptable, but the *-st* forms are more common in Great Britain.

among *See* **amid, between.**

amoral, immoral *Amoral* means *unrelated to moral standards*, neither moral nor immoral. (He argued that, because Art is *amoral*, his works should not be judged according to moral conventions.) *Immoral* means *contrary to moral standards*. (It is *immoral* to cheat on examinations.)

amount, number *Amount* refers to things in bulk or in the aggregate, *number* to things that can be counted separately. (*Correct:* a large *amount* of ink, a large *number* of bottles. *Incorrect:* a large *amount* of bottles.) Compare *less, fewer.*

and/or Legalese. (The students were pursuing love *and/or* knowledge.) The nonlegal writer should say *love and knowledge, love or knowledge,* or *love, knowledge, or both.*

anyone, any one Distinguish between *anyone* meaning *anybody* and *any one* person singled out of a group. The same logic applies to *everyone* and *someone*. (*Everyone* is going with *someone*; *every one* of the men plans to go with *some one* of the women.) *No one* is two words. For number see p. 306.

any place *Any place* (sometimes spelled *anyplace*), *every place* (*everyplace*), *no place,* and *some place* (*someplace*) are all colloquial when used instead of *anywhere, everywhere, nowhere,* and *somewhere*. (*Colloquial:* He was going *no place* fast. *Formal:* He was going *nowhere* fast.)

anyways, anywheres, everywheres, nowheres, somewheres Colloquial. The acceptable written forms have no *-s*. Distinguish between "I don't like you *anyway*" and "*Any way* I go I get lost."

anywheres *See* **anyways.**

appraise, apprise *Appraise* and, less often, *apprise* (*apprize*) can both mean *put a value on. Apprise* (*apprize*) also means *inform*. (When the realtor *appraised*—or *apprised*—the house, he did not *apprise* the tenants of his estimate.)

apt, liable, likely Carefully distinguished in formal English. *Apt* means *quick to learn* or *inclined to*. (An *apt* student of languages, he is *apt* to do well in Russian.) *Liable* implies exposure to danger, risk, or punishment (*liable* to fall downstairs, *liable* to fine or imprisonment). *Likely* merely suggests probability. (It is *likely* to rain tomorrow.)

around Colloquial in place of *about*. (*Around* six o'clock he made *around* five dollars.) Most careful writers prefer *about*. A versatile athlete may be either *all-around* or *all-round*.

as Often ambiguous when meaning *because, for, since,* or *while*. (*Ambiguous: As* i was looking out the window, I noticed that, *as* it was snowing, my neighbor was putting on chains. *Clear: While* I was looking out the window, I noticed that, *because* it was snowing, my neighbor was putting on chains.) *See* **like, as.**

as regards *See* **regard.**

as to Acceptable in the sense of *in regard to, about, of*. (*As to* her qualifications, I cannot speak with authority.) Redundant before *whether*. (I do not know [*as to*] whether he is coming.)

aural See **verbal**.

average, median Strictly speaking, an *average* is obtained by dividing a total by the number of items. The *average* of 2, 4, 5, 9, 11, 18, and 21 is 10 (70 divided by 7). A *median* (in statistics) is the middle number—or the average of two middle numbers—in a sequence (9 in the previous example). As a synonym for *common, ordinary,* or *typical, average* is an inaccurate colloquialism (the *average* unmarried woman, my *average* day).

awhile, a while The single word *awhile* is an adverb meaning *for a short time*. When the noun *while* occurs in a prepositional phrase, it is separated from *a*. (He stood *awhile* in thought, but only for *a while*.)

because See **reason is because**.

being as, being that Unacceptable: *Being as (that)* she was sick, she couldn't get away. Substitute *because*.

beside, besides Careful writers distinguish between *beside*, meaning *at the side of*, and *besides*, meaning *in addition to*. (They were sitting *beside* the pool. *Besides* the swimmers, many vacationers were sunning in deck chairs.) *Besides* also means *furthermore*. (*Besides*, some were tossing beach balls.)

between, among Some careful writers still limit *between* (literally *by twain*) to two objects and *among* to more than two. (*Between* you and me, experts differ *among* themselves.) But *between* is common with more than two, especially if each is individually related to the others. (*Between* pity and guilt and fear I began to feel there was another me trapped in my skull.—James Baldwin, *Notes of a Native Son*) Harder to defend is the use of *between* with *each* and *every* (*Between* every hedgerow was a field of clover). *Between you and I* (*he, she*) is incorrect. Use *me* (*him, her*). See pp. 288–289.

bimonthly, biweekly Because each of these words has two contradictory meanings in general use, a careful writer will use such explicit phrases as *every two months, twice a month, every two weeks,* or *twice a week*. (*Semimonthly* and *semiweekly* always mean *twice a month* and *twice a week*.)

born, borne *Born* is used for *given birth to* except after *have* or before *by*. (Lincoln was *born* in a log cabin. Nancy Hanks had *borne* a great man. Edward VII was *borne* by Queen Victoria.) For other means of the verb *bear, borne* is the past participle. (He was *borne* aloft by his excited teammates. I had *borne* his insolence too long.)

but that, but what Replace these redundancies with the single word *that*. (I have no doubt [*but*] *that* he is right.)

can, may In formal English *can* (*be able*) and *may* (referring to probability, possibility, or permission) are still distinguished. (You *may* stay at the party if you *can* avoid my mother.) Colloquially *can* is frequently used to give or request permission. (You *can* go if you want to. *Can* I come with you?)

cannot, can not Although *cannot* is more common, *can not* is equally acceptable and puts more emphasis on the *not*.

can't hardly, scarcely, can't help but See **double negative**.

capital, capitol The *capitol* is a building. In all other contexts (*capital* ship, gains, letter, punishment; *capital* as a sum of money or the ornamentation of a column in architecture) the spelling is with *-al*.

censor, censure, censer *Censor* is a noun standing for a person who examines books, plays, and so forth to suppress objectionable matter; or a verb denoting the act of censorship. *Censure* is a noun meaning *an expression of* *disapproval*; or a verb meaning *condemn*. (The city *censor censored* the movie by cutting out half the plot. The action was met with *censure* by the producers, who *censured* his ignorance of art.) A *censer* is a container for burning incense.

center around A colloquialism often condemned for bad logic. Many writers prefer *center in, on,* or *upon. Centre* is the British spelling.

childish, childlike *Childish* refers to the unpleasant or immature behavior of children or to the infantile activities of adults. *Childlike* connotes the pleasant qualities. (With an air of *childlike* innocence the Dean said: "This college is no place for *childish* students.")

cite, sight, site *Cite* is a verb meaning *quote* or *refer to*. (She *cited* a passage to prove her point.) It can also mean *summon*, as before a court, or *mention*, as in awarding an honor. (He was *cited* for criminal contempt only a week after being *cited* for bravery.) *Sight* is a verb meaning *observe* or *aim* or a noun meaning a *view* or an *aid to aiming*. (He *sighted* a flamingo as he *sighted* along his rifle. It was a beautiful *sight* in his *sights*.) *Site* is a noun meaning a *location* (the *site* of the excavations at Troy).

compare, contrast *Compare* can mean either *liken* (The relatives *compared* the baby to her mother) or *set together to reveal both likenesses and differences* (The students were asked to *compare* Shakespeare with Milton). The preposition *to* is more common in the first sense, *with* in the second.

consensus General or harmonious agreement. The word should not be confused with *census*, a count. (The *consensus* of the community was that the council should require a new *census* of property owners.) *Consensus of opinion* is often condemned as redundant.

considerable Colloquial as a noun (He lost *considerable*) and as an adjective meaning *many* (*Considerable* people attended the game).

contact The verb is overworked Commercialese. Try a more precise expression: *cable, phone, talk to, write.*

continual, continuous *Continual* means *often repeated*; *continuous* means *uninterrupted*. (She made *continual* visits to the river to watch its *continuous* flow.)

contrast *See* **compare.**

could of *See* **of.**

council, counsel, consul A *council* is a group of people (a city *council*, a *council* of war). A member of a *council* is a *councilman* or *councilwoman*. Counsel is a noun meaning *advice* or *one who gives it* or a verb meaning *advise*. (To avoid being deceived by bad *counsel*, they hired legal *counsel* to *counsel* them.) An adviser in a law office, school, or camp is a *counselor* (*counsellor*). A *consul* represents the government abroad.

couple Strictly used, the noun means *two things or persons united* (a married *couple*, a *couple* on the dance floor). In the sense of *approximately two* it is a loose colloquialism. (Give me a *couple* of bucks until Saturday.) Do not omit the *of*.

credible, creditable, credulous *Credible* means *believable*. (His tale was too *credible* to be doubted.) *Creditable* means *worthy of praise or reward*. (Her performance on the piano was *creditable*.) *Credulous* means *quick to believe, gullible*. (*Credulous* children believe in Santa Claus.)

criterion, criteria *Criterion* is singular, *criteria* plural. Compare *phenomenon, phenomena.*

curriculum, curricula *Curriculum* is singular, *curricula* (*informal: cur-*

riculums) is plural. The adjective is *curricular,* as in *extra-curricular* activities.

cute In the sense of *appealing* (What a *cute* puppy!), this is an overworked colloquialism.

data In origin *data* is plural, but the singular *datum* is now rare. *Data* as a singular noun (*This data is* conclusive) is common, even in some formal scientific writing. But it is safer to keep the Latin plural (*These data are* conclusive).

delusion See **allusion.**

different from, than Although *different from* is more widely acceptable in formal American English, *different than* is common in reputable writing and often less redundant. Contrast *"different than* I had expected" with *"different from* what I had expected."

discreet, discrete *Discreet* means *tactful* or *prudent. Discrete* means *separate* or *distinct.* (Too *discreet* to offend her listeners, she carefully explained the *discrete* origins of the three groups.)

disinterested, uninterested Disinterested means *impartial, neutral, unbiased. Uninterested* means *lacking in interest, indifferent.* (A baseball umpire must be *disinterested* if he wants to be fair, but he can't afford to be *uninterested* in the rules of the game.)

double negative Although double and even triple negatives were once reputable, it is now unacceptable to say "I can't do nothing right" instead of "I can't do anything right." With adverbs that are negative by implication (*can't hardly, can't scarcely*) the same convention applies. (*Correct:* I *can hardly* do it.) *Can't help but* (She *can't help but* succeed) is widely accepted; but many people insist on the gerund (She *can't help succeeding*).

due to Despite its widespread use, some people argue that *due to* should not begin a sentence or introduce an adverbial phrase. (*Questionable: Due to* trouble with mathematics he failed. He failed *due to* trouble with mathematics. *Acceptable:* Because of trouble with mathematics he failed. His failure was *due to* trouble with mathematics.) In the last example, *due* is an adjective modifying *failure.* See **fact that.**

effect See **affect.**

either, neither Strictly speaking, these words should refer to *one of two.* (He did not like the play of *either* team in the game.) For number see p. 306.

emigrate, immigrate *Emigrate* (nouns *emigrant, emigration*) means to *migrate out* of a country; *immigrate* (*immigrant, immigration*) means to *migrate in.* (The Pilgrims *emigrated* from England and *immigrated* to America.)

eminent, imminent *Eminent* means *outstanding, imminent about to happen.* (Her book made her an *eminent* scholar when her death was *imminent.*)

enormity, enormousness *Enormity* should be reserved for something *monstrous* or *outrageous* (the *enormity* of the terrorists' bombing). *Enormousness* refers to great physical size.

enthuse A natural "back formation" from *enthusiasm*—like *donate* (from *donation*) or *reminisce* (from *reminiscence*). But objections to *enthuse* are still widespread. (*Questionable:* He *enthused* (was *enthused*) over the Red Sox victory. *Acceptable:* He was enthusiastic.)

equally as Redundant. The adverb alone serves *equally* well.

etc. An abbreviation of *etcetera,* meaning *and other things.* Often a lazy escape from the problem of selecting details in a series, leaving the reader wondering what the "other things" could possibly be. If you must suggest that the series is interminable, replace the abbreviation with an expression such as *and so forth. Such as . . . etc.* (or *and so forth*) is redundant, for *such as* indicates that you are making a selection (*such as* oats, peas, beans, and barley). *And etc.* (literally *and and other things*) and the misspelling *ect.* reveal ignorance of Latin.

everywheres *See* **anyways.**

except *See* **accept.**

fabulous *The Arabian Nights* ia a *fabulous* book, but when the word is used indiscriminately to express enthusiastic approval (What a *fabulous* party!), it conveys no specific meaning. The same is true of other overworked counter-words, including *fantastic, great, lovely, marvelous, terrific, tremendous*, and *wonderful* (see pp. 133–134).

fact that Expressions containing these words can nearly always be improved by weeding. Use *because* instead of *because of the fact that* or *due to the fact that*; use *although* (or *though*) in place of *in spite of the fact that*. Often *that* is the one word necessary: The obvious point is [the fact] *that* wordiness weakens writing.

factor A favorite with victims of gobbledygook. Unless *factor* has a specific technical meaning, as in biology or mathematics, replace it with a more appropriate word (*aspect, cause, circumstance, element, phase*).

famed, famous, noted, notorious Both *famed* and *noted* are Journalese for *famous*, a word that should be reserved for the widely known, not lavished on the merely fashionable. *Notorious* means *widely known but not in good repute.* (John Wilkes Booth, a *notorious* assassin, shot Lincoln, a *famous* president.)

fantastic. *See* **fabulous.**

farther, further According to a formal distinction, now widely ignored, *farther* refers to physical distance, *further* to degree or quantity. (The man *farther* down the road went *further* in his protest.) The adjective meaning *more* or *additional* is *further* (a *further* point in the discussion).

fewer *See* **less.**

finalize *See* **-ize.**

fine Colloquial in the sense of *well* (The tomatoes are coming up *fine* this year.) (see pp. 133–134).

firstly the *-ly* serves only to make the adverb *first* two unnecessary letters longer. The same is true of *secondly, thirdly, thusly*, and so forthly. Often, especially in technical prose, the adverbs can be replaced by Arabic numerals in parentheses (see p. 335).

flaunt, flout Flaunt means *display conspicuously*, *flout* means *mock* or *scoff at*. (By *flaunting* his slovenly clothes he *flouted* his clean-cut associates.)

foot, feet When used after a number before a noun, *foot* is the proper plural (a four-*foot* fence, a seven-*foot* basketball player). Before an adjective or adverb *foot* is colloquial (five *foot* two inches tall, six *foot* away).

former, latter The *former* is the first of a pair; the *latter* is the second. Do not use them with more than two or with one of a pair in the absence of the other. (*Wrong:* Of her three sons—Tom, Dick, and Harry—the *latter* is the best looking. I do not like people who are always talking about themselves. The *latter* bore me.) Even when properly used *former* and *latter* can send the reader searching for their antecedents. Depending on the context, it is better to use *first, second* or *last* or a pronoun or repeat the noun.

364

freshman, freshmen The adjective is *freshman* (the *freshman* class). *Freshmen* is the plural of the noun (a thousand *freshmen*).

further *See* **farther.**

get, got, gotten *Get* is an overworked verb that is typically either colloquial or slang. *Have got* in the sense of *have* (I *have* [*got*] five dollars) is redundant. In American English both *got* and *gotten* are acceptable as past participles meaning *obtained* (She had *got*—or *gotten*—a new Cadillac.).

good, well *Well* is either an adverb (He played *well*) or an adjective (He felt *well*). *Good* is an adjective. (His playing was *good*. He felt *good*.) The difference between *feeling well* and *feeling good* is one of meaning, not grammar: *well* suggests only that a person does not feel ill or unhappy; *good* carries a more positive connotation of health or happiness. See pp. 302–303.

graduate *She graduated from college* is the standard idiom. *Was graduated* is more formal. *She graduated college* is nonstandard.

great *See* **fabulous.**

had better, best Both *had better* and *had best* are acceptable in formal and informal writing. (You *had better* do it.) *You better do it* is colloquial.

had have, of If I *had have* (or *had of*) *known* is nonstandard. (*Standard: If I had known*).

had ought, hadn't ought Awkward and redundant. Use *ought* alone or *should*. (You *ought* to do it. You *shouldn't* do it.)

hardly *See* **double negative.**

have got *See* **get.**

heighth A variant of *height* by analogy with *length, width, depth*. Now avoided by educated people.

herself, himself *See* **self.**

hopefully A vogue word often used ambiguously (*Ambiguous:* I am *hopefully* going to take my examinations next year. *Clear:* I hope to take my examinations next year. *Or:* Hoping to pass, I am going to take my examinations next year).

however It is acceptable to write, "*However,* I do not agree with him" or "*However* convincing he is, I do not agree with him." In the first instance the writer may prefer to replace *however* with *but* or to set it off with commas in mid-sentence (I do not, *however,* agree with him). Do not put a comma before *however* when it introduces a second main clause. (*Comma fault:* I do not agree with him, *however,* I defend his right to protest.) See pp. 319–320.

illusion *See* **allusion.**

immigrate *See* **emigrate.**

imminent *See* **eminent.**

immoral *See* **amoral.**

imply, infer One person *implies* something in speech, writing, or manner; another *infers* something from it (Although she meant to *imply* that I was right, I *inferred* the opposite from her remarks).

in, into According to strict formal usage, *in* refers to a *state of rest* or to *motion within; into* indicates *motion toward* or *direction* (They were either standing or swimming *in* the lake when he dove *into* the water). In "He was *into* rock music," *into* is a colloquial vogue word.

in regard(s) *See* **regard.**

individual, person, party Careful writers use *individual* to distinguish a person from the group (the rights of the *individual* in a democratic society) or to stress a person's distinctive qualities (In a family of conformists, she stands out as an *individual*). Indiscriminate use of *individual* as a synonym for *person* dilutes its individuality. The widespread use of *person* for the suffix *man* (*chairperson, congressperson, spokesperson, brakeperson*) offends many, who point out that *man* has traditionally stood for both sexes and that the innovations are awkward. *Party* is Legalese (*party* of the first part) or Commercialese (Did I connect you with your *party?*).

infer *See* **imply.**

ingenious, ingenuous *Ingenious* means *clever;* *ingenuous* means *naive* or *innocent.* (Although he was the *ingenious* inventor of the phonograph, Edison was strangely *ingenuous* about grand opera.)

inside of When *inside* is a preposition, *of* is superfluous (*inside* [*of*] the house).

instance, instant An *instance* is an example, as in *for instance;* an *instant* is a *moment.* (Here is an *instance* of how he tends to make up his mind in an *instant.*)

into *See* **in.**

irregardless Nonstandard. Say *regardless.*

irregular verbs Some irregular verbs are listed in separate entries: *born, borne; get, got, gotten; lay, lie; lead, led; leave, let; raise, rise; set, sit.* Here is a selected list of others that often cause trouble. Where usage is divided, acceptable alternate forms appear in parentheses.

PRESENT INFINITIVE	PAST TENSE	PAST PARTICIPLE
awake	awoke (awaked)	awoke (awaked, awoken)
beat	beat	beaten (beat)
begin	began	begun
bid (command)	bade (bid)	bidden (bid, bade)
blow	blew	blown
break	broke	broken
bring	brought	brought
broadcast	broadcast (broadcasted)	broadcast (broadcasted)
burst	burst	burst
choose	chose	chosen
clothe	clothed (clad)	clothed (clad)
deal	dealt	dealt
dig	dug	dug
dive	dived (dove)	dived
draw	drew	drawn
drink	drank	drunk (drank)
drive	drove	driven
fit	fitted (fit)	fitted (fit)
forget	forgot	forgotten (forgot)
forecast	forecast (forecasted)	forecast (forecasted)
freeze	froze	frozen
hang	hung (hanged-executed)	hung (hanged-executed)
hide	hid	hidden (hid)
lend	lent	lent

PRESENT INFINITIVE	PAST TENSE	PAST PARTICIPLE
quit	quit (quitted)	quit (quitted)
ride	rode	ridden
ring	rang	rung
seek	sought	sought
sew	sewed	sewed (sewn)
shaved	shaved	shaved (shaven)
shine	shone (shined)	shone (shined)
show	showed	shown (showed)
shrink	shrank (shrunk)	shrunk (shrunken)
sing	sang	sung
sow	sowed	sown (sowed)
speed	sped (speeded)	sped (speeded)
spring	sprang (sprung)	sprung
steal	stole	stolen
strike	struck	struck (stricken)
swim	swam	swum
swing	swung	swung
throw	threw	thrown
tread	trod (treaded)	trodden (trod)
wake	waked (woke)	waked (woken, woke)
wear	wore	worn
write	wrote	written

is when, is where   Do not use a noun clause beginning with *when* or *where* after the verb *to be*. (*Inaccurate:* Chauvinism *is when* patriotism is carried too far. Onomatopoeia *is where* the sound of words suggests the sense. *Accurate:* Chauvinism is patriotism carried too far. Onomatopoeia is the use of words whose sound suggests the sense.)

-ize   Beware of random coining of unnecessary verbs ending in *-ize* (*concretize, prioritize, randomize*). See p. 135. Especially common are *finalize* and *utilize*. Does *finalize* mean *put an end to* or *put in final form*? *Utilize* can nearly always be replaced by *use*. Both are Commercialese.

kind of, sort of   Widely used in speech where written English would normally use *rather* or *somewhat*. (*Colloquial:* They were *kind of* annoyed. He looked at me *sort of* queerly.) Acceptable in written English when followed by a noun (a *kind of* cheese, a *sort of* intellectual). Avoid *kind of a* and *sort of a*.

latter   See **former.**

lay, lie   *Lie* is an intransitive verb meaning *recline*. (I *lie*—am *lying*—down now. I *lay* down yesterday. I have *lain* down before.) *Lay* is usually a transitive verb meaning *place*. (I *lay*—am *laying*—the book down. I *laid* the book down yesterday. I have *laid* the book down there before.) The commonest errors are using the present participle and past tense of *lay* for those of *lie*. (*Wrong:* The football player was *laying* on the field. He *laid* there unconscious. *Right:* The football player was *lying* on the field. He *lay* there unconscious.) Compare *raise, rise* and *set, sit*.

lead, led   When *lead* rhymes with *bread*, it is a noun meaning a *metal*. Do not confuse it with *led*, the past tense or past participle of the verb *to lead*. (*Correct:* The child *led* the *lead* soldiers as they had never been *led* before.)

leave, let   Generally speaking, *leave* means *abandon, depart, desert; let* means *allow, permit*. (Don't go away and *leave* me; *let* me go with you.) Careful writers distinguish between "*let* me alone" (don't bother me) and "*leave* me alone" (depart hence). Only *let* should be followed by an infinitive. (*Nonstandard: Leave* George *do* it.)

led *See* **lead.**

lend *See* **loan.**

less, fewer In formal English *less* refers to amount, degree, quantity or value; *fewer* refers to number. (*Less* silverware, *fewer* knives and forks; *less* trouble, *fewer* difficulties; *less* traffic, *fewer* cars.) Compare *amount, number.*

let *See* **leave.**

liable *See* **apt.**

lie *See* **lay.**

lighted, lit. Either may be used as the past tense or past participle of *light.* (Her face *lighted*—or *lit*—up. The house was *lighted*—or *lit*—with candles.)

like, as In formal and in most informal writing, a strict distinction is kept between *like,* a preposition, and *as* (or *as if*), a conjunction. (He walks *like* me, but he doesn't run *as* I run. He runs *as if* he were imitating a crab.) When it means *in the role of, as* may be a preposition. (She struggled *as* the family breadwinner.)

likely *See* **apt.**

lit *See* **lighted.**

literally The *literal* sense of a word is its primary or actual meaning. The figurative colloquial use of *literally* sacrifices accuracy to an attempt at emphasis. (*Colloquial:* She was *literally* crushed [actually pulverized] by his refusal. *Formal:* She was crushed by his refusal.)

loan, lend Despite some objections, *loan* is widely accepted in the United States as a verb meaning *lend.* (Would you *loan*—or *lend*—me ten dollars until Saturday?)

loose, lose *Loose* can be either an adjective meaning *free from restraint* or a verb meaning *set free.* (The ropes were *loose* because someone had *loosed* them.) *Lose* is a verb meaning *suffer loss.* (Heads I win, tails you *lose.*) *Aid to memory: lose* loses an *o.*

lot, lots *Colloquial in the sense of many, much, a large amount.* (In speech *lots* of people use these words *a lot.*) See **alot, a lot.**

lovely *See* **fabulous.**

luxuriant, luxurious *Luxuriant* means *abundant, exuberant* (the *luxuriant* growth of the tropics). *Luxurious* refers to man-made luxury (the *luxurious* homes of the movie stars).

majority, plurality In counting votes, a *majority* means *more than half* the total cast; a *plurality* means *more than the next highest candidate.* As a synonym for *most* (the *majority* of the students), *majority* is an awkward colloquialism, especially objectionable when counting is impossible (the *majority* of the effort).

marvelous *See* **fabulous.**

may *See* **can.**

medium, media In many contexts, the plural can be either *mediums* or *media.* Spiritualists are *mediums. Media* is the common plural in scientific writing and in reference to advertising or communication. Do not use it in the singular. (*Wrong:* The mass *media is* often blamed for violent crime.)

might of *See* **of.**

moral, morale *Moral,* noun or adjective, refers to right conduct. *Morale* is a noun meaning *attitude, mental outlook, spirit* (The *moral* of the story is that the coach's *moral* lessons improved the team's *morale.*).

most Colloquial as a substitute for *almost, nearly* (He came *most* every day to see me.)

myself *See* **self.**

neither *See* **either.**
no one *See* **anyone.**
no place *See* **any place.**
noted, notorious *See* **famed.**
nowheres *See* **anyways.**
number *See* **amount.**

of Do not use *of* instead of *have* in *could have, might have, should have* and so forth.

off of Redundant. *Write:* She jumped *off*—or *from*—the train.

oral *See* **verbal.**

ought *See* **had ought.**

outside of Colloquial in the sense of *besides, except* (No one was invited *outside of* her.). In the sense of *beyond*, the *of* is redundant. *Write:* His house was *outside* the city.

pair The formal plural is *pairs*, but *pair* is acceptable after a number in informal writing.

party *See* **individual.**

persecute, prosecute *Persecute* means *harass* or *oppress; prosecute* means *bring to trial* (Despite the evidence that the child's parents had *persecuted* him since infancy, they were never legally *prosecuted*).

person *See* **individual.**

phenomenon, phenomena The singular is *phenomenon*. In its philosophical and scientific uses the plural is *phenomena*. Compare *criterion, criteria*.

plan on, plan to Although some authorities insist on *plan to* (He *planned to* go), *plan on* is widely accepted (He *planned on* going).

playwrite A misspelling of *playwright*. *Wright* means *worker*, as in *shipwright, wheelwright*.

plenty The adjective should be followed by *of* (She has *plenty of* money). Colloquial when used as an adverb (My father was *plenty* angry).

plurality *See* **majority.**

precede, proceed, procedure *Precede* means *go before; proceed* means *go ahead*. (Do not *precede* your partner when you *proceed* down the aisle.) Note the spelling of *procedure*.

predominant, predominate In general usage, *predominant* is the adjective, *predominate* the verb (My *predominant* impression is of a man who wants to *predominate* over others).

prejudice Students who omit the *d* from *supposed* and *used* often make the same mistake with *prejudiced*. (Wrong: she was *prejudice* against careless spelling.) *Prejudice* is not a past participle.

preposition at the end of a sentence The old rule (A preposition is a bad word to end a sentence *with*) is not based on modern usage. Whether you write, "She was the one I talked *to*" or—more formally—"to whom I talked," is a matter of choice. Be careful not to combine both constructions: She was the one *to* whom I talked *to*.

presently Widely used to mean either *at present* or *in a short while*. To avoid ambiguity it is better to use those expressions or simply *now* or *soon*.

pretty Colloquial as an adverb meaning *considerably, moderately, rather* (*pretty* dark in here). Often redundant ([*pretty*] nearly finished).

principal, principle As an adjective, *principal* means *chief* (the *principal* point involved). As a noun it means either *chief* (the *principal* of a school) or a sum of money (interest on a *principal* of ten thousand). *Principle* is always a noun meaning a *rule, law,* or basic truth (Appropriateness is an important *principle* of composition). *Aid to memory:* Both *principle* and *rule* end in *-le*.

proceed, procedure *See* **precede.**

prophecy, prophesy *Prophecy* is the noun; *prophesy* (not *prophesize*) is the verb. (Because her *prophecy* did not come true, she vowed never to *prophesy* again.)

prosecute *See* **persecute.**

proved, proven As the past participle, either is acceptable in American English (The case was *proved*—or *proven*).

provided, providing As a conjunction, *provided* is preferable because *providing* is often ambiguous. (*Clear: Provided* [that] it doesn't rain, he will go. *Ambiguous:* He will put up the money *providing* [that] his conditions are met.)

quite In formal English *quite* means *completely* (*quite* the opposite) or *really* (*quite* an experience). In its loose colloquial sense it means *rather, somewhat, to a considerable extent* (a *quite* common usage).

quote(s) The uses of *quote* as a noun meaning *quotation* and of *quotes* instead of *quotation marks* are both colloquial shortcuts. (*Colloquial:* The *quote* from Bellow should be enclosed in *quotes*.) In formal writing *quote* should be used only as a verb (He *quoted* a passage from Updike).

raise, rise *Raise* (*raised, raised*) is a transitive verb (She *raised* the window.). *Rise* (*rose, risen*) is an intransitive verb (He rose from his seat).

rarely ever, seldom ever If you mean *rarely* or *seldom*, the *ever* is redundant. If you mean *rarely (seldom) if ever*, it is more accurate to say so.

real As an adverb meaning *very* or *really* (She looked *real* happy), *real* is colloquial.

reason is because Since *because* means *for the reason that*, the expression is redundant. (*Redundant:* The *reason is because* fluoride prevents cavities. *Improved:* The *reason is that* fluoride prevents cavities.)

reckon Dialectal (mostly Southern) in the sense of *think* or *suppose* (I *reckon* I'll stay home tomorrow).

regard, regards, respect *As regards, in regard to, with regard to, regarding,* and *with respect to* proliferate in Commercialese and are often redundant. (*Redundant: In regard to* required courses, the curriculum has too many. *Improved:* The curriculum has too many required courses.) *In regards to, with regards to,* and *irregardless* are nonstandard.

respective(ly) Although sometimes useful in clarifying relationships, these overworked words are often redundant. (*Redundant:* After the concert the students returned to their [*respective*] dormitories. Do not confuse *respectively* with *respectfully (full of respect).*

rise *See* **raise.**

round *See* **around.**

same *Same* is common in conversation as a pronoun (Make mine the *same*). In writing it usually has a legal or commercial flavor, especially if *the* is omitted (He sent a package and she received *same*).

seldom ever   *See* **rarely ever.**

self   In formal English, *himself, myself,* and so forth are either reflexive pronouns (He hurt *himself*) or intensive pronouns (I'll marry her *myself*). Their use in place of personal pronouns (She and *myself* are going) is colloquial.

sensual, sensuous   *Sensual,* usually unfavorable, means *carnal, voluptuous, preoccupied with bodily pleasures. Sensuous,* usually favorable, refers to the five senses. (Fanny Hill was a *sensual* woman. Spenser and Keats wrote *sensuous* poetry.)

set, sit   *Set (set, set)* is usually a transitive verb meaning *to cause to sit* (He *set* the table on the floor). *Sit (sat, sat)* is usually an intransitive verb meaning *to be seated* (He *sat* on the floor). In special contexts *sit* may be transitive, *set* intransitive. (She *sat* the baby in the highchair. She *sits* her horse well. A hen, the sun, concrete, and jelly may all *set.).*

shall, will   Here are the traditional rules: To express simple future, use *shall* in the first person, *will* in the second and third. (I *shall* go, but he *will* stay home.) To express determination or a command, reverse the process. (I *will* not go, and you *shall* not make me!) In asking a question, use the same word you expect in the answer. (*Shall* you go with me? *Answer: I shall.*). These rules don't conform to usage and never did. The tendency among reputable writers is for all forms to level to *will* for simple future. (I *will* go, but he *will* stay home.) Shall is now common in the first person to express determination. (We *shall* not flag or fail.—Winston Churchill.) *Will* is the natural form for the second person in asking a question. (*Will* you go with me?)

should of   *See* **of.**

sight   *See* **cite.**

sit   *See* **set.**

site   *See* **cite.**

so, so that   The trouble with the "so habit" is not only the monotony of repeating one sentence pattern too often but the resulting neglect of the more emphatic periodic sentence with the main clause last. Compare "I was bored, *so* I went home." with "Because I was bored, I went home." The omission of *that* in *so that* is a colloquial shortcut (I came early *so* [*that*] I could see you). As an intensive (*so* round, *so* firm, *so* fully packed), *so* is weak from overwork.

some place   *See* **any place.**

someone   *See* **anyone.**

somewheres   *See* **anyways.**

sort of   *See* **kind of.**

specie, species   *Specie* means *coined money* and has no plural form. *Species,* meaning *kind* or *class,* has the same form for both singular and plural. (A piggy bank is a *species* of animal that eats *specie.* There are other *species* of animals.)

split infinitive   Any blanket condemnation of the split infinitive ignores the facts of usage. The question of whether to split or not to split depends on considerations of meaning, smoothness, rhythm, and emphasis. "He failed entirely *to comprehend* it" (unsplit) is ambiguous. "He failed *to* entirely *comprehend* it" (split) is clear. If a split infinitive is awkward, the sentence should be rewritten, especially if the wedge consists of more than one word ("We do want *to,* at this triumphant time, *thank* all those who supported us throughout the campaign." That would be a smoother sentence with "at this triumphant time" at the beginning and the infinitive unsplit).

such, such as   As an intensive followed only by a noun (I never saw *such* a day), *such* is colloquial. Do not follow *such as* with *etc. See* **etc.**

371

suppose, supposed   Do not omit the *d* from the past participle. (*Wrong:* He was *suppose* to go to class).

sure, surely   The use of *sure* as an adverb instead of *surely* is colloquial (He *sure* looked good in there today).

terrific   *See* **fabulous.**

than   Whether the pronoun after *than* is nominative or objective depends on the meaning. Strictly speaking, "He has known better poets *than* me" means "better than I am." "He has known better poets *than* I" means "better than I have." To avoid misunderstanding, it is better to include the verbs. See *different from, than.*

that, which   See p. 287. Beware of the superfluous *that* (He argued *that*, after passing the examination, [*that*] he deserved course credit).

there, their, they're   Distinguish them carefully. *There* is usually an adverb meaning *in that place* (She is sitting *there*); or an introductory expletive (*There* were three men in the boat). *Their* is a possessive pronoun (*their* country, *their* dinner). *They're* is a contraction of *they are* (*They're* going to Florida tomorrow).

this   The use of *this* in place of the article is common in oral story-telling (The movie is about *this* old fisherman who hooks *this* young mermaid). The idiom has no standing in written English.

though   *See* **although.**

thusly   Write the word *thus. See* **firstly.**

till, until, 'til   Take your choice between *till* and *until,* depending on the rhythm. *'Til* is a folksy, pseudopoetic shortcut like *o'* in *bit o' heaven.*

to, too   Spell them correctly. *To* is a preposition that commonly expresses *motion or direction toward* (He moved *to* Peoria). *Too* is an adverb meaning *in addition* (The children are going *too*) or *excessively* (*too* hot in the summer). Do not use *too* as an adverbial conjunction in place of *also* or *besides* (*Too,* she had problems at home). Avoid *too* as a synonym for *very* (She did not work *too* hard).

toward, towards   *Toward* is the more common preposition in the United States, *towards* in Britain. Take your choice.

tremendous   *See* **fabulous.**

try and, to   In formal writing, *try to* is preferred (I shall *try to* come.). *Try and* is a time-honored colloquialism (*Try and* stop me).

type   The use of the noun *type* immediately before another noun (What *type* woman is she?) is colloquial. The standard written expression includes the preposition (What *type* of woman?). Hyphenated compounds should be reserved for advertising (*Scotch-type* liquor). Often *type* is deadwood: How does a motherly *type* of woman differ from a motherly woman?

uninterested   *See* **disinterested.**

unique   In its strict literal sense, *unique* (Latin *unus, one*) means *unequaled,* the *only one* of its kind (Every person's fingerprints are *unique*). Avoid its indiscriminate use as a counterword meaning *outstanding, rare, unusual.* In formal writing there is no such expression as *more unique, less unique, most unique,* or *very unique.* See p. 302.

until   *See* **till.**

usage, use   Usage refers to *established custom* or *tradition* (American English *usage,* the *usages* of the past half century). *Use* (the noun) means merely *the act of employing* (the *use* of a hammer to drive a nail). Often *use* is redundant (He was a victim of [the *use* of] alcohol). Don't omit the *d* from the past tense or past participle of *use*. (*Wrong:* I *use* to go to the movies more often.)

utilize *See* **-ize.**

verbal, oral According to their Latin origins, *verbal* (*verbum, word*) means *in words; oral* (*os, oris, mouth*) means *spoken*. Although a *verbal* agreement or order is widely understood as spoken—especially in legal and military language—the distinction is worth keeping. (*Aural* refers to the ear or sense of hearing.)

very A *very* common word that gets *very* tiresome when it is used *very* much in a vain effort at emphasis. See p. 133.

way, ways When it means *away* or *condition, way* is colloquial (*Way* over in Japan, he was in a bad *way*). *Ways* is colloquial for *way* (He was a long *ways* from home).

well *See* **good.**

when, where *See* **is when.**

which, that *See* **that** and p. 287.

while Overworked colloquially as a substitute for *and, but, though,* and *whereas.* It is used more accurately in expressions of time. *Colloquial:* She is going away, *while* he is staying home. *While* I don't know her, I hope she has a good time. *More accurate:* She is going away, *but* he is staying home. *Although (though)* I don't know her, I hope she has a good time. He will mind the cats *while* she sees the sights.

-wise A common suffix in a number of well-established words (*clockwise, likewise, otherwise*). But when wise-words are coined unwisely, the result can be both clumsy and redundant. (*Poetry-wise* he was a good writer. *Stature-wise* Napoleon was short. *Improved:* He was a good poet. Napoleon was short.)

with regard(s) to *See* **regard.**

wonderful *See* **fabulous.**

would have (of) *Dialectal:* If I *would have* known that, I never *would have* come. *Standard English:* If I *had* known that, I never *would have* come. *Would of* is a common misspelling of *would have.*

A Glossary of Grammatical and Rhetorical Terms

This glossary is meant for both reference and review. It includes nearly all the "technical terms" considered—usually at greater length—elsewhere in the book. Some definitions are repeated word-for-word, but the illustrations are different. All terms in **boldface** are explained either within the entry or elsewhere in this glossary.

absolute   An **adjective** or **adverb** that cannot logically have a **comparative** or **superlative degree.** Strictly speaking, nothing can be *more* or *most unique* or be done *more* or *most perfectly.*

absolute phrase   A **phrase** independent grammatically of any other part of the sentence. *Example: The game being ended,* they crowded to the exits. Unlike a **dangling** or **misplaced modifier,** an absolute phrase is not regarded as faulty usage.

abstract noun   A **noun** expressing a concept that cannot be directly perceived by the senses: *ambition, democracy, honor, patriotism, sincerity.* Contrast with **concrete noun.**

accusative case   *See* **case.**

acronym   A word, often pronounceable, formed from the first letters of the words of a phrase. *NOW* (National Organization for Women); *radar* (radio detecting and ranging); *snafu* (situation normal all fouled up).

active voice   *See* **voice.**

adjective   A word used to modify (describe, limit, or qualify) a **noun** or **pronoun:** The *new* house was *expensive,* but she was *wealthy.* (*New* and *expensive* modify *house; wealthy* modifies *she.*)

adjective clause   A **clause** that functions as an **adjective:** The book *that lay on the table* had a blue cover.

adjective phrase A **phrase** that functions as an **adjective:** The book *on the table* had a blue cover.

adverb A word used to modify (describe, limit, or qualify) a **verb, adjective,** or other **adverb:** she spoke *softly* because she was *unusually* shy. Her words came out *very slowly*. (*Softly* modifies *spoke; unusually* modifies *shy; very* modifies *slowly*, which modifies *came*.)

adverbial clause A **clause** that functions as an **adverb:** *When she came to dinner*, she brought a bottle of wine.

adverbial conjunction *See* **conjunctive adverb.**

adverbial phrase A **phrase** that functions as an **adverb:** *After dinner*, they went to the movies.

agreement Matching **subjects** with **verbs, pronouns** with **antecedents,** and **demonstrative adjectives** with **nouns.** Errors in agreement: Their favorite *cousins was* coming. *Each* of the girls *were* ecstatic. *These kind* of meetings were exciting.

alliteration The repetition of an initial sound, usually a consonant, in two or more words of a group: He *t*ells a *t*ale of *t*error about a *r*ascal's *r*ighteous *wr*ath. More generally effective in poetry than in prose.

analogy A rhetorical device developing or implying a resemblance between two things that are similar in some respects: for example, between licensing handguns and licensing cars. Though all analogies are "false" from the standpoint of strict logic, a "tight analogy," where the resemblance is close, can be effective in **description, exposition,** or **argument.**

antecedent The word or word group to which a **pronoun** refers: *George* arrived without saying that he was coming. (*George* is the antecedent of the pronoun *he*.) *See* **reference of pronouns.**

anticlimax An abrupt falling off that works "against the climax" at the end of a phrase, sentence, paragraph, or entire composition: for God, for country, and for Yale. Anticlimax may take the reader from the important to the trivial and replace the expected with the unexpected. It may be intentionally ironic or unintentionally ludicrous.

antonym A word of opposite, or nearly opposite, meaning to another. *Hot* is an antonym of *cold; antonym* is the antonym of **synonym.**

appositive A **noun** or **phrase,** usually set off in commas, that repeats the meaning of (is in **apposition** with) a grammatical element immediately preceding: The price of gasoline, *a precious commodity*, is a cause of great concern.

archaic *Antiquated, old-fashioned.* A dictionary label for words or meanings no longer in use (**current**) except in special contexts: *affright (terrify); poesy; wouldst.* Words or meanings that have dropped completely out of the language are labeled **obsolete.**

argumentation (argument) The process by which a writer or speaker tries to persuade the reader or listener to accept a certain position on a debatable topic. *Argumentation* is distinguished from: **description,** writing that pictures a place, person, or object; **exposition** (explanation); and **narration (narrative),** story-telling. In practice, these four "modes" of composition often overlap.

argumentum ad hominem "Argument against the man." A **fallacy** in logic especially common in political discussion, by which a writer or speaker ignores the issues to attack an opponent personally.

article *A* and *an* are **indefinite articles,** *the* is the **definite article.** They are traditionally regarded as **adjectives.**

375

assonance Partial rhyme, consisting of the repetition of vowel sounds in stressed syllables with different consonant sounds: She made the same cake. An effective device in poetry, often annoying in prose.

auxiliary verb A "helping **verb**" used with another verb or with a **verbal** to express **number, person, mood, voice,** or **tense:** I *can* go with you if you *are* going. I *do* want to see if the house *has been* finished.

begging the question The **fallacy** of assuming the truth of something that remains to be proved. A familiar kind of question-begging is **circular reasoning.** *Example:* Censorship should be strictly enforced in school libraries because of the presence of books that need to be censored.

bibliography An alphabetical list of articles, books, or other sources on any subject: specifically the sources actually consulted for a particular research project.

blend (portmanteau word) A word coined by combining parts of other words: *brunch (breakfast* and *lunch); gasohol (gas* and *alcohol); smog (smoke* and *fog).*

case A pattern of changes (**inflections**) showing the relation of **pronouns** and **nouns** to the other parts of a sentence. Pronouns change form to indicate whether they are **subjects** (**subjective** or **nominative case**); *he, she, who,* etc., **objects** (**objective** or **accusative:** *him, her, whom,* etc.), or **possessive** (**possessive** or **genitive case:** *his, her, whose, its,* etc.). The possessive of nouns is formed with an apostrophe.

cause and effect A method of developing a paragraph or an extended argument by showing the relation between a result and its origin, or between a conclusion and the reasons behind it.

charged (loaded) words Words that carry a heavy load of **connotation,** whether favorable or unfavorable, as distinct from more strictly **denotative neutral** words: *crazy (vs. eccentric); jellyfish (vs. weak-willed person); jock (vs. athlete); ravishing (vs. attractive).*

circular reasoning *See* **begging the question.**

circumlocution A roundabout expression, a common species of wordiness: [*There is*] nobody in the world [*who*] is perfect.

clause A group of related words containing a **finite verb** and forming part of a (1) **compound** or (2) **complex sentence:** (1) *He had an invitation,* but *he never came.* (2) *Although he was expected* (**dependent clause**), *nobody missed him* (**independent clause**).

cliché A trite (hackneyed) expression, often a **figure of speech** or familiar quotation, worn out from overuse: *swift as lightning; tight as a drum; icy stare; Christmas comes but once a year; love makes the world go round.*

coherence The connection ("sticking together") of the parts of a composition to produce a logical sequence. For example, the sentences of a paragraph are made coherent by using **transitions,** either expressed or implied.

coinage (neologism) A recently invented word or expression: *chickenburger; meltdown; petrodollars.*

collective noun A **noun** that denotes a group of persons or things: *collection, flock, committee, group, series, class.* Though **singular** in form, a collective noun may be either singular or **plural** in **number,** depending on the context.

colloquialism A word or phrase more common in speech than in writing;

376

conversational: a *pretty* penny; he is a little *shrimp;* she *hasn't got* it. Some dictionaries use the label *informal.*

comma fault (comma splice)   The misuse of a comma between **independent clauses** in a **compound sentence:** My father used to be completely intolerant of the music our group played, now he has learned to tolerate everything but the volume. *Acceptable revisions:* Replace the comma with a semicolon or insert *but* after the comma.

Commercialese   *See* **gobbledygook.**

common noun   A **noun** that names any member of a class of persons, places, or things: *child, dancer, optimist, city, country, computer, happiness.* Contrast with **proper noun.**

comparative degree   *See* **comparison.**

comparison   The grammatical system by which the changing forms of **adjectives** and **adverbs** express **positive degree** (*happy, happily*), **comparative degree** (*happier, more happy, more happily*), and **superlative degree** (*happiest, most happy, most happily*). *See* **false comparisons.**

complement   A **subject (subjective) complement** follows a **linking verb** or a **passive transitive verb** and renames or modifies the **subject.** It may be a **predicate nominative** (**predicate noun** or **pronoun**) or a **predicate adjective.** *Examples:* She was a *friend* of his (predicate noun). He looked *happy* in her presence (predicate adjective). An **object (objective) complement** renames or modifies a **direct object:** She considered him an *intellectual.* He called her *beautiful.*

complete sentence   *See* **sentence.**

complex sentence   A sentence with one **independent clause** and one or more **dependent clauses:** *She stammered* (independent) *whenever she rose to speak* (dependent)

compound predicate   Two or more **verbs**—with or without **modifiers**—sharing a single **subject:** Summer *came and went once more.*

compound sentence   A sentence with two or more **coordinate clauses** but no **dependent clause:** *The winds blew fiercely,* but *the tree weathered the blast.*

compound-complex sentence   A sentence with two or more **independent clauses** and one or more **dependent clauses:** *When the accident was reported in the press* (dependent), *many people fled the area* (independent), but *others sought refuge behind locked doors* (independent).

compound subject   A **subject** formed with two or more elements joined by *and* and normally taking a **plural verb:** *Alcohol and gasoline* do not mix.

concrete noun   A noun naming something that can be seen, heard, touched, smelled, or tasted: *desk, gurgle, velvet, incense, hamburger.* Contrast with **abstract noun.**

conjugation   *See* **inflection.**

conjunction   A word that connects (1) words, (2) **phrases,** or (3) **clauses:** (1) death *and* taxes; (2) in the city *or* in the country; (3) *Although* she applied, she was not hired.

conjunctive adverb (adverbial conjunction)   An **adverb** that connects **independent clauses** (after a semicolon) or separate sentences (after a period): They signed the peace treaty; *however,* important problems were unsolved. *Therefore,* many people were pessimistic.

connective   A word, such as a **conjunction** or **preposition,** that connects words, **phrases, clauses,** or **sentences.**

connotation   The overtones of a word or **phrase:** what it suggests by association as distinguished from its **denotation,** the basic, literal meaning. For example, *pooch denotes* a dog, but it *connotes* a small mongrel without social pretensions. In heraldry, *sinister denotes* the left side of a coat of arms; in mystery stories, it *connotes* darkness, evil, underhanded plotting.

contact clauses In a **compound sentence,** brief, balanced **coordinate clauses** linked by a comma in the absence of a **coordinating conjunction:** She lived in poverty, she died in luxury. *See* **comma fault.**

context The parts of a composition that immediately surround a particular word or passage and determine its meaning and appropriateness.

coordinate clauses **Independent clauses** of equal rank joined by a **coordinating conjunction** (*and, but, for, or, nor, yet*): *She took the lift to the top of the mountain,* but *she did not ski down the other side.* Contrast with **subordinate clause.**

coordinating conjunction A **conjunction** that connects grammatical elements of equal rank: for example, *and, but, for, or nor,* and *yet* joining **coordinate clauses** in a **compound sentence.** *See* **correlative conjunction.**

coordination Joining grammatical elements of equal rank: for example, **coordinate clauses** joined by a **coordinating conjunction.** Common sentence errors include **false coordination,** in which elements are unnaturally joined, and **excessive coordination,** in which all clauses are made equal (joined by *and, but,* or *so*), emphasizing everything—and nothing.

correlative conjunctions **Coordinating conjunctions** used in pairs in a parallel construction: *both . . . and, either . . . or, neither . . . nor, not only . . . but also. Examples: Both* Donald *and* his brother stayed home. *Neither* was pleased by the invitation *nor* excited by the prospect of boredom. *See* **parallelism.**

counterword A word frequently used in everyday language without reference to its precise meaning. Counterwords often express undiscriminating approval (*fabulous, marvelous*) or disapproval (*awful, terrible*).

dangling modifier (infinitive, gerund, participle, elliptical clause) *See* **misrelated modifier.**

declarative sentence A sentence that makes a statement: The sky is blue today. Distinguished from an **interrogative sentence** (Will it rain tomorrow?), an **exclamatory sentence** (What a sunny day!), or an **imperative sentence** (Keep off the grass).

declension *See* **inflection.**

deduction In logic, the process of deriving (deducing) a conclusion from one or more statements called **premises.** *See* **induction** and **syllogism.**

definite article. *See* **article.**

degree *See* **comparison.**

demonstrative adjective, demonstrative pronoun Words that serve to point out or demonstrate. Though they have the same forms, a **demonstrative adjective** functions as a **modifier,** normally agreeing with its **noun** in **number:** *This* kind of cheese appeals to *those* people. Demonstrative pronouns: *These* are cheaper, but *that* tastes better.

denotation *See* **connotation.**

dependent (subordinate) clause A **clause** that cannot stand alone but is subordinated to an **independent clause** in the same sentence: *Whenever he wanted to relax,* he headed for the swimming pool.

description *See* **argumentation.**

378

dialectal Belonging to a **dialect,** a variety of language peculiar to a region or social group: *all* (The potatoes are *all* [gone]); *arter* (*after*); *hootenanny* (gadget).

diction The choice and use of words; specifically in speech, the enunciation.

direct address A word or phrase, usually set off by commas, identifying the audience to whom a remark is directed: Jump in, *Mary,* and go for a ride. Farewell, *cruel world.*

direct discourse Quoting the exact words of a speaker or writer: He asked, "Where are you going?" The example is both a **direct quotation** and a **direct question.** Distinguish this example from **indirect discourse,** where the writer **paraphrases** the words without quotation marks in order to fit them into an **indirect question** in an **indirect quotation:** He asked me where I was going.

direct object A person, place, or thing directly affected by the action of a **transitive verb:** The mouse ate the *cheese.* The boy caught *him* in a trap.

direct question *See* **interrogative pronoun.**

division A method of organizing and developing a paragraph or whole composition by separating it into parts.

doublespeak A kind of **gobbledygook** (or **jargon**), typically cluttered with **euphemisms,** intended to confuse or mislead the reader or listener.

ellipsis The use of three spaced dots plus end punctuation to indicate words omitted from a quotation: "Birds of a feather. . . ."

elliptical construction A construction in which certain words are understood but not expressed. Acceptable **elliptical clause:** *When* [*you are*] *crossing the street,* look both ways. **Dangling elliptical clause** (unacceptable): *When crossing the street,* a car killed him.

emphasis The use of a number of devices—such as **isolation, position, repetition,** and **proportion**—to stress what is important in a sentence, **paragraph,** or entire composition.

endnote *See* **footnote.**

equivocation In logic, the **fallacy** of changing the meaning of a repeated word or phrase: Because he is a *liberal* in politics, he believes in *liberal* education.

essay A short composition (literally a "try") on a single topic, usually presenting the writer's own viewpoint. An essay may be formal or informal, impersonal or personal, and may involve one or more of the common "modes" of composition: **exposition, description, narration** (but not fiction), and **argumentation.**

etymology The historical development of a word, going back to its earliest origins; also, the systematic study of word derivations. The etymology of *holocaust* is the Greek words *holos* (*whole*) and *kaustos* (*burnt*).

euphemism The substitution of a presumably inoffensive word for one that might give offense: *indisposed* for *sick; remains* for *corpse; unusual* for *retarded.*

euphony The pleasing (euphonious) sound of a succession of well-chosen words, as distinct from jarring (dissonant, cacophonous) sounds.

evading the issue *See* **ignoring the question.**

exaggeration *See* **hyperbole.**

excessive coordination *See* **coordination.**

exclamatory sentence *See* **declarative sentence.**

expletive   A word that anticipates the **subject** without affecting the **number** of the verb: *It* is a spring day and *there* are buds on the trees. (*Day* and *buds* are the delayed subjects.)

exposition   *See* **argumentation.**

fallacy   A violation of logical reasoning, not an error in fact. *See,* for example, **argumentum ad hominem, begging the question, equivocation, false dilemma, faulty assumption, non sequitur, statistical fallacy.**

false comparisons   Violations of **parallelism:** either (1) an **incomplete comparison** or (2) a comparison with **incomparable terms:** (1) *Incomplete:* I told Peter more than Pamela. *Revised:* I told Peter more than I told Pamela. *Or:* more than Pamela did. (2) *Incomparable:* Herman is funnier than anybody in the family. *Revised:* anybody else in the family.

false coordination   *See* **coordination.**

false dilemma   In logic, the **fallacy** of basing an argument on only two alternatives when others are possible: We must either give athletic scholarships or abandon intercollegiate football.

faulty assumption   The **fallacy** of basing an argument on one or more suppositions that are not necessarily true. For example, a writer arguing against equal rights for women begins with the assumption that women cannot compete with men in the business world.

figurative language   The use of **figures of speech,** as distinct from **literal** expressions, to make writing more clear or lively. Common figures of speech are **metaphor, simile, analogy, assonance, hyperbole, irony,** and **personification.**

fine writing   A term applied ironically to the false notes struck by writers who struggle too hard to be vivid or eloquent or "poetic."

finite verb   A **verb** limited to a specific **person** and **number,** as distinguished from a **verbal:** Finite verbs: I *sing* (first person **singular**); they *listen* (third person **plural**).

flat writing   Writing that is prosaic, pedestrian, dull, monotonous, utterly lacking in flavor.

footnote   A note at the bottom of a page or the end of a paper (**endnote**) citing indebtedness to a source or adding a brief comment, or both.

formal usage   A variety of language appropriate when the occasion calls for a dignified or exact treatment of a serious subject. It is common in scholarly books, research papers, technical reports, essays in criticism, textbooks, legal briefs, business letters, and addresses for such ceremonial occasions as commencements and inaugurations. Formal writing avoids colloquialisms and slang and tends to use technical or learned terms, many of them abstract, carefully contrived sentences, and strict traditional grammar. *See* **levels of usage.**

fragment   *See* **sentence.**

fused sentence   *See* **run-on sentence.**

future perfect tense   The **verb** form expressing action completed at a specific time in the future: By the end of the semester she *will have finished* her course requirements.

future tense   The **verb** form expressing action still to come: He *will go* with me, and nobody *will stop* him.

gender   In English, the classification for identifying sex and its absence in **pronouns** and occasionally in **nouns:** *he* (masculine), *she* (feminine), *it* (neuter), *actor, actress, host, hostess,* and so forth.

380

genitive case *See* **case.**

gerund A **verbal** with the same form as the **present participle** (ending in -*ing*) but used as a **noun:** Her experience reinforced her *understanding* that *seeing* is *believing*. A typical **gerund phrase** has a gerund, its **object,** and one or more **modifiers:** I did not like *her treating me with such indifference.*

gobbledygook (jargon) An epidemic disease infecting writing and speech. Among its symptoms are involved sentence structure, unnecessary repetition, **circumlocutions,** and a gobbledygook vocabulary cluttered with abstractions and pseudotechnical terms. The varieties of gobbledygook include the jargon of business (**Commercialese**), bureaucracy (**Officialese**), the law (**Legalese**), and education (**Pedagese**).

grammar The formal features of a language, including **inflection** (the changes to indicate **case, number, gender, degree,** and so forth) and **syntax** (the order of words in a phrase or sentence). "Correct grammar" is determined by socially acceptable **usage** among educated people.

historical present The use of the **present tense** to give immediacy to past events: It *is* November 22, 1963. John F. Kennedy *waves* at the crowds lining the streets of Dallas.

hyperbole **Exaggeration** or **overstatement** to emphasize a point, get a laugh, or sell a product: She had a smile you could have poured on a pancake.

idiom A common expression that has grown naturally in the language without necessarily conforming to logic or the usual grammatical patterns. *Examples* He *dressed* her *down.* She was *fed up.* The word *idiom* also stands for the general way of speaking or writing that is peculiar to a language. Hence an **unidiomatic** expression violates the **idiom** of English.

ignoring the question (evading the issue) In logic, the **fallacy** of straying, intentionally or not, from the point under discussion. Common examples are the **argumentum ad hominem** and the **false dilemma.**

imperative mood The **verb** form used for commands: *Go* away and *stop* teasing me.

imperative sentence *See* **declarative sentence.**

incomplete sentence *See* **sentence.**

indefinite article *See* **article.**

indefinite pronoun A **pronoun** that does not specify the person or thing to which it refers: *any, anybody, everybody, everyone, nobody, some, somebody* and so forth.

indention (indentation) Setting the first line of a paragraph or extended quotation in from the left margin (using five spaces on the typewriter).

independent (main, principal) clause A **clause** that can stand alone as a **complete sentence,** in contrast with a **dependent** (or **subordinate**) **clause:** After the dance was over (dependent), *they went to a discotheque* (independent).

indicative mood The **verb** form used to make a statement or ask a question: He *is living* for today. Who *will pay* for his funeral tomorrow?

indirect discourse, indirect question, indirect quotation *See* **direct discourse.**

indirect object A person, place, or thing indirectly affected by the action of a **transitive verb.** It precedes the **direct object:** Einstein left the *world* (indirect object) an awesome *legacy* (direct object).

indirect question *See* **interrogative pronoun.**

induction (inductive reasoning)   The logical process of reasoning from particular evidence (data, examples, statements) to a general conclusion. Thus a detective who has seen tracks in the snow leading to the smashed door of a house in which a safe is open and empty might reach the inductive conclusion that an intruder has committed a burglary. Contrast **deduction.**

infinitive   The root form of the **verb,** often preceded by *to*; a verbal that can function as a **noun,** an **adjective,** an **adverb,** or as part of a **finite verb.** *Examples: To be* is not always the question (noun). That is the place *to visit* (adjective). *To find* it, you need a map (adverb). You can *lose* your way without one (part of a finite verb). A typical **infinitive phrase** has an **object** and one or more **modifiers:** He asked the pitcher *to throw the ball more slowly.*

inflection   The changes in word forms to indicate **case, number, gender, tense, degree,** and so forth. The inflectional patterns of **nouns** are called **declensions;** of verbs, **conjugations;** of **adjectives** and **adverbs, comparison.**

informal usage   A variety of language common among educated Americans—in friendly letters and many business letters, newspaper columns, magazine articles, books, talks, and undergraduate essays, depending on the assignment. The vocabulary includes many **colloquialisms** and occasional **slang.** In some dictionaries, *informal* is a **label** for *colloquial.*

intensive pronoun   A word with the same form as a **reflexive pronoun** but used for emphasis: I agree with you *myself,* but she *herself* disagrees.

interjection   An exclamation, an expression of emotion unrelated grammatically to the rest of the sentence: *ah, oh, ouch, wow.*

interrogative pronoun   A **pronoun** that introduces a **direct** or **indirect question:** *who, which what, whoever, whichever, whatever. Who* are you (direct)? I don't know *who* you are (indirect).

interrogative sentence   *See* **declarative sentence.**

intransitive verb   A **verb** that does not require a **direct object** to complete its meaning: He *sleeps* as soon as he *lies* down.

inversion   Switching the normal order in a sentence to achieve emphasis or variety: Exhausted she was after the race. Never again would she enter a marathon.

irony   A **figure of speech** in which the speaker or writer asserts the opposite of the intended meaning: My roommate's talent for missing classes marks him as a paragon of intellectual curiosity. The contrast between statement and intent creates a tone of ridicule characteristic of **satire.** Effective irony should not be confused with **sarcasm,** which has a sneering tone.

irregular verb   A **verb** that does not form its **past tense** and **past participle** by adding *-ed* or *-d* to the **infinitive:** *lie (lay, lain); rise (rose, risen); sit (sat, sat).* See the Glossary of Usage.

isolation   The device of setting off one or more short, wiry sentences from more elaborate constructions to achieve **emphasis** in a paragraph.

jargon   *See* **gobbledygook.** The word also applies to the restricted vocabulary of a special activity or group: the *jargon* of rock music.

Journalese   The **jargon** common in newspapers and newscasts; notable for headline shortcuts (*grill* for *question, rap* for *criticize, oust* for *dismiss*) and exaggeration (*crisis* for *problem, clash* for *disagreement*).

label   An italicized designation in a dictionary to restrict the use of a word in accordance with subject (**subject label**), time (**temporal label**), place (**regional**

label), and **level of usage (status label).** Common status labels are **nonstandard, colloquial (informal),** and **slang.** *See also* **archaic** and **localism.**

Legalese *See* **gobbledygook.**

levels of usage Varieties of language depending on the writer's education, subject, and purpose, the reader's expectations, and the requirements of a particular assignment or occasion. The general levels discussed in this book are **formal** (*fatigued*), **informal** (*tired*), and **nonstandard** (*blowed*). Levels of usage are distinguished not only by **diction** but by **grammar, sentence structure,** punctuation, and such intangibles as **rhythm.**

linguistics The science of language, with special reference to the actual structure of speech.

linking verb A **verb** that connects the subject with a (1) **predicate noun** or (2) **pronoun** or (3) **predicate adjective:** (1) I *am* the law. (2) This *is* it. (3) Why *feel* unhappy?

literal language Words that carry the ordinary or primary meaning, as distinguished from **figurative language:** He *picked a lemon* from the tree vs. He *picked a lemon* in the garden of love.

loaded words *See* **charged words.**

localism A word or phrase characteristic of a particular locality: *mesa* (*plateau*, Southwest); *spa* (*soda fountain*, New England); *wash* (*dried-up stream*, West).

loose sentence *See* **periodic sentence.**

main clause *See* **independent clause.**

major premise *See* **syllogism.**

malapropism An error in **diction** based on the confusion of one word with another having a similar sound but a far different meaning. The term memorializes Mrs. Malaprop, who blundered through Sheridan's *The Rivals* spouting boners like *allegory* for *alligator* and *pineapple* for *pinnacle.*

metaphor A **figure of speech** involving an implied comparison (her *speech* was *music*), as distinguished from a **simile,** an explicit comparison using *like* or *as* (her *speech* was *like music*). Many **clichés** are trite or dead metaphors. A typical **mixed metaphor** is a collision of (1) two or more metaphors or (2) **figurative (metaphorical)** and **literal** meanings: (1) In making *strange bedfellows*, warfare does not play *second fiddle* to politics. (2) In his *salad days* he went in for *fancy dressing.*

meter A pattern of regular **rhythm,** common in poetry but rare in prose.

minor premise *See* **syllogism.**

misrelated modifier A **modifer** that does not clearly relate to the intended term elsewhere in the sentence. A **dangling modifier (participle, infinitive, gerund,** or **elliptical clause)** usually has nothing in the sentence that it can logically modify: *Being very hungry*, the fish was delicious (dangling participle). A **misplaced modifier** can be corrected by merely changing its position in the sentence. *Faulty:* We watched the soaring gulls *lolling on the sand. Corrected: Lolling on the sand*, we watched the soaring gulls.

mixed metaphor *See* **metaphor.**

modifier A word, **phrase,** or **clause** that describes, limits, or qualifies another element in the sentence: a *green* hat. She ate *with chopsticks.* The storm came *when the weatherman had predicted.*

mood The pattern of **verb** forms by which writers and speakers indicate

383

their attitudes toward what they are saying. See **imperative mood, indicative mood, subjunctive mood.**

narration (narrative) *See* **argumentation.**

neologism *See* **coinage.**

neutral words *See* **charged words.**

nominative case *See* **case.**

nonrestrictive modifier A **modifier** that does not identify (or restrict) the word it modifies and can be deleted without changing the essential meaning of the sentence. It is set off with one or two commas. **Nonrestrictive clause:** Jane Fonda, *who plays the role of the TV reporter,* has serious political convictions off screen. Contrast **restrictive modifier.**

non sequitur A conclusion that does not follow from the **premises** or evidence presented. *Example:* Within a year after Mayor Monahan took office, the cost of living rose 13 percent. Obviously he is to blame. The example represents a common kind of non sequitur called **post hoc, ergo propter hoc**—"after this, therefore because of this."

nonstandard usage A variety of language that is little touched by formal education: He played *good; in regards* to usage; *them* people; *youse.* A word labeled "nonstandard" should be avoided in polite speech and serious writing except when recording the language of others.

noun The name of a person, place, or thing: *Mona* went to the *city* to buy a new *dress.*

noun clause, noun phrase Groups of words that function as **nouns. Noun clauses:** *That he would succeed* was obvious (**subject** of *was*). I knew *what she had in mind* (**object** of *knew*). **Noun phrases:** *To eat a whole lobster* requires patience (**infinitive phrase, subject** of *requires*). She prefers *eating lobster salad* (**gerund phrase, object** of *prefers*).

number The category or form that distinguishes one (**singular**) from more than one (**plural**): *He is* going (singular **pronoun** and **verb**). *They* enjoyed *themselves* (plural pronouns).

object The name for the person, place, or thing that (1) is directly or indirectly affected by the action of a **transitive verb** or (2) follows a **preposition** to complete a **phrase:** (1) He opened the *book.* (2) She was in a *daze.*

objective case *See* **case.**

object (objective) complement *See* **complement.**

obsolete *See* **archaic.**

Officialese *See* **gobbledygook.**

onomatopoeia The use of word and phrases imitating sounds: *bang; chirp; clank;* the *murmuring* of *innumerable* bees; the *pitter-patter* of raindrops.

ornate style A manner of writing marked by long, carefully balanced sentences, calculated **rhythm,** and abundance of **metaphors** and other **figures of speech.** Distinguished from **plain style.**

outline A plan for organizing a composition, distinguishing main points from subordinate points with the help of numerals, letters, and appropriate **indentions.** The headings in a **topic outline** are restricted to single words or phrases; a **sentence outline** is composed entirely of **complete sentences.**

overlapping synonyms *See* **synonym.**

overstatement *See* **hyperbole.**

overweight construction An unnecessarily heavy construction that can be reduced by converting a **clause** to a **phrase,** or a **phrase** to a single word: *Wordy:* The man *who was wearing the red jacket* muttered *in a hoarse vo ce. Improved:* The man *in the red jacket* muttered *hoarsely.*

paradox A statement that may be true even though it seems contradictory.

paragraph A unit of organization composed of one or more sentences, the first of which is indented from the left margin. A well-developed paragraph has **unity,** often represented by a **topic sentence; coherence,** with the help of **transitions; emphasis;** and **completeness.**

parallelism The repetition of corresponding grammatical structures in a symmetrical pattern. Parallelism may be *required,* as with **correlative conjunctions:** She was not only *a celebrity in her home town* but also *a citizen of the world.* Or parallelism may be *optional* to achieve emphasis: *Many are called,* but *few are chosen.* Violations of parallelism include: (1) **shifted constructions** and (2) careless use of **correlatives:** (1) He was *trustworthy, loyal, helpful, friendly,* and *he always behaved courteously* (shift from one-word **adjectives** to a **clause**). (2) Not only *was she a celebrity in her home town* but also *a citizen of the world.*

paraphrase A rewording of a passage without relying on the exact language of the original. *See* **direct discourse.**

participial phrase *See* **participle.**

participle A **verbal** that functions as (1) an **adjective,** (2) part of a **finite verb,** or (3) in an **absolute phrase:** (1) a *running* brook. (2) I am *going* home. (3) The play *having ended,* the audience cheered. Nos. 1 and 2 are **present participles;** No. 3 is a **past participle.**

parts of speech In traditional grammar: **verb noun, pronoun, adjective, adverb, preposition, conjunction, interjection.**

passive voice *See* **voice.**

past participle *See* **participle, principal parts.**

past perfect tense The **verb** form expressing the "past before the past": He *had been* (**past perfect**) there for a week before his wife *arrived* (**past tense**).

past tense The **verb** form expressing an action completed in the past. She *arrived* yesterday.

Pedagese *See* **gobbledygook.**

period fault *See* **sentence.**

periodic sentence A sentence in which the writer puts the **main clause** last or postpones the main point until the end: When I first visited Waikiki Beach, *I was unprepared for what I saw.* A **loose sentence,** by contrast, puts the main clause first: *I was unprepared for what I saw* when I first visited Waikiki Beach.

person The pattern of changing forms of **pronouns** and corresponding **verbs** to indicate whether someone is speaking, spoken to, or spoken about: *I (we) try* (first person); *you try* (second person); *he (she) tries, they try* (third person).

personal pronoun A type of **pronoun** that changes its form to indicate **person:** *I, we, you, he, she, it, they,* and so forth.

personification A **figure of speech** in which a writer ascribes gender and other human traits to a thing or an abstract idea: His paragraphs were *anemic,* lacking the *lifeblood* of specific detail. Some **clichés** represent "pseudopoetic personification": *Old Man Winter.*

phrase Any group of two or more grammatically related words without a **subject** and **finite verb,** acting in a sentence as a single **part of speech:** The

385

swimmer jumped *into the water* and swam *with powerful strokes*. A phrase may be classified according to form (**prepositional, infinitive, participial, gerund, verb**) or function (**noun, verb, adjective, adverb**).

plagiarism   Taking words, ideas, opinions, theories, or facts from somebody else without properly acknowledging the debt; a form of dishonesty.

plain style   A manner of writing marked by the use of everyday language in conversational sentence patterns and the absence of **metaphors,** calculated repetition, insistent **rhythm,** and other **rhetorical devices.** *See* **ornate style.**

plural   *See* **number.**

point of view   The angle from which a writer presents material, an especially important consideration in **narrative.** Where is the narrator located in time and space? What feelings or attitudes does the writer intend to present? Through whom is the story told—a limited outside observer ("author observant"), a character involved ("author participant"), or an all-seeing authority ("author omniscient")? Should the writer be impersonal or personal? What **person** should be used—first, second, or third?

portmanteau word   *See* **blend.**

positive degree   *See* **comparison.**

possessive case   *See* **case.**

post hoc, ergo propter hoc   *See* **non sequitur.**

predicate   The part of the sentence or **clause** that includes the **verb** with (or without) **objects, complements,** and **modifiers:** The lazy dog *ignored the leap of the quick brown fox.*

predicate adjective   *See* **complement, linking verb.**

predicate noun (nominative)   *See* **complement, linking verb.**

prefix   *See* **root.**

premise   *See* **syllogism.**

preposition   A word that connects a **noun** or **pronoun,** its **object,** with some other word in the sentence and shows the relation between them: She ran *to* her room and threw herself *onto* her unmade bed. A **prepositional phrase** (*to her room, onto her unmade bed*) contains a preposition and its object and often one or more **modifiers.**

prepositional phrase   *See* **preposition.**

present participle   *See* **participle, principal parts.**

present perfect tense   The **verb** form expressing past time continuing to the present: I *have worked* here since last Friday.

present tense   The **verb** form that commonly expresses the time now: Today *is* Friday. It may also express future time (I *go* home next week), past time (the **historical present**), or a statement that is presumably true at any time (All cows *eat* grass).

primer prose   The monotonous repetition of **simple sentences** with no attempt at **coordination** or **subordination.**

principal clause   *See* **independent clause.**

principal parts   A series of **verb** forms from which the other forms are derived: **present infinitive; past tense (first person singular);** and **past participle** (*go, went, gone; lay, laid, laid; lie, lay, lain; swim, swam, swum*). Some grammarians include the **present participle** (*going, laying, lying, swimming*).

pronominal adjective   A word that resembles a **pronoun** but functions as an **adjective:** *That* professor enjoys *those* students. *See* **demonstrative adjective.**

pronoun   A word used in place of a **noun:** *He* spoke to *her himself*. The eight classes in English are: **personal pronouns, relative pronouns, interrogative pro-**

nouns, **indefinite pronouns, demonstrative pronouns, reflexive pronouns, intensive pronouns,** and **reciprocal pronouns.**

proper noun   The name of a particular person (George Eastman), place (Rochester), or thing (Kodak). Usually capitalized. Contrast with **common noun.**

proportion   Organizing a composition so that the length of each part conforms to its relative importance; an aspect of **emphasis.**

reciprocal pronouns   **Pronouns** expressing a mutual relationship: The children loved *each other.* Why did they kick *one another's* shins?

redundancy   Unnecessary repetition of words or meaning.

reference of pronouns   The relation of **pronouns** to their **antecedents:** I checked my battery to make sure *it* would survive the trip. (The pronoun *it* refers to the **noun** *battery.*) Four kind of **faulty reference** are called *no reference, remote reference, wrong reference,* and *squinting reference.*

reflexive pronoun   A **pronoun** that usually serves as the **direct** or **indirect object** of a **transitive verb** or the object of a **preposition** and refers to the **subject:** I kicked *myself.* He gave *himself* another helping.

regional label   *See* **label.**

regular verb   A **verb** that forms its **past tense** and **past participle** by adding *-ed* or *-d* to the **infinitive:** *help, helped, helped; tame, tamed, tamed.* Contrast **irregular verb.**

relative pronoun   A **pronoun** introducing a **subordinate clause** that relates back to an **antecedent:** Miriam did not know the man *who* was going. (The antecedent of *who* is *man.*) He read the book *that* she lent him. I heard the orchestra, *which* delighted me. (The antecedents are *book* and *orchestra.*)

restrictive modifier   A **modifier** that identifies (or restricts) the word it modifies and cannot be deleted without changing the essential meaning of the sentence. It is *not* set off by commas. **Restrictive clause:** A student *who dislikes mathematics* should not go in for engineering. Contrast **nonrestrictive modifier.**

rhetoric   In its favorable sense, the art of using language effectively, or a book devoted to that art. The **noun** and the **adjective (rhetorical)** are also used to condemn writing or speech that is artificial, insincere, or bombastic.

rhetorical question   A question asked for effect without expecting an answer.

rhyme (rime)   Two or more words with identical terminal sounds: *face, grace; loon, moon; honey, money; financial, substantial.* In prose, rhyme is usually a distraction.

rhythm   The flow of sounds in a series of words, with special reference to their accents. *See* **meter.**

root   In **grammar,** the base or stem of a word, to which **prefixes** are added (before) and **suffixes** (after). In *rechargeable,* the *root* is *charge,* the prefix is *re- (again),* and the suffix is *-able (capable).*

run-on sentence (fused sentence)   The error of running two sentences together with no punctuation to separate them: The man ran out of the bank Officer Hogan caught up with him on the corner. (A period or semicolon should come after *bank.*)

sarcasm   *See* **irony.**

satire   A form of literary ridicule in which the **tone** may range from playful to savage and the common method is **irony.** Even playful satire may imply one or more moral lessons.

semantics The systematic study of the meanings of words and their historical change.

sentence A **complete sentence** must contain a **subject** and a **finite verb,** and every **dependent clause** must be supported by an **independent clause:** *I finished* the book, *though it bored me.* A typical **incomplete sentence (fragment, period fault)** has either a **verbal** instead of a finite verb or an unsupported dependent clause: *Finishing* the book. *Though it bored me.* In some contexts, incomplete sentences are acceptable.

sentence outline *See* **outline.**

shifted construction An inconsistent switch from one grammatical element to another within the sentence. *Examples:* shifts in **subject, voice, tense,** and the **number** or **person** of **pronouns.** A shift such as the following is a violation of **parallelism:** If you go shopping, the car should be taken (instead of "you should take the car").

simile *See* **metaphor.**

simple sentence A sentence with no **coordinate** or **subordinate clauses:** The horse ate the oats.

slang A popular, free-wheeling vocabulary more common in speech than in writing. *Examples: bug (to annoy); marbles (wits); mooch (scrounge); in the doghouse (in trouble); cash in your chips (die).* For reasons discussed on pp. 123–125, a word (or meaning) labeled *slang* in the dictionary should be avoided entirely in **formal** writing and used sparingly on the **informal level.**

split infinitive An **infinitive** in which a **modifier,** often a single **adverb,** separates *to* from the root form of the **verb:** *To gladly teach* is *to gladly learn.* See Glossary of Usage.

standard English The speech and writing, both **formal** and **informal,** that is most widely used and approved by educated English-speaking people. Contrast **nonstandard.**

statistical fallacy Invalid reasoning based on inaccurate, inadequate, or misinterpreted numerical data.

status label *See* **label.**

style The way in which thought is expressed in language. *Style* may refer to the manner peculiar to an individual writer or speaker or to characteristics common to many. *See* **ornate style** and **plain style.**

subject A word or group of words about which something is said or asked in the **predicate:** *Henry* likes music. Do *you* care for it? His *skill* in playing the piano is impressive. (In the last sentence, *skill* is the **simple subject;** *his skill in playing the piano*—simple subject and **modifiers**—is the **complete subject.**)

subject (subjective) complement *See* **complement.**

subjective case *See* **case.**

subjunctive mood The **verb** form used to express (1) wishes, (2) doubt, or (3) condition contrary to fact; and (4) in *that* **clauses** after such verbs as *demand, recommend, require,* and *urge:* (1) I wish I *were* a singer. (2) She wondered if she *were* losing her grip. (3) If I *were* a singer, I would try opera. (4) I demand that you *be* here.

subordinate clause *See* **dependent clause.**

subordinating conjunction A **conjunction** that connects a **dependent clause** with an **independent clause:** *Whenever* he sat down at the piano, people laughed. *Although* he played well, he was expected to clown.

substantive A **noun, pronoun,** or any word or group of words functioning as a noun.

388

suffix *See* **root.**

superlative degree *See* **comparison.**

syllogism A form of **deductive reasoning** consisting of a **major premise,** a **minor premise,** and a **conclusion:** All snakes are reptiles (major premise); my pet is a snake (minor premise); therefore, my pet is a reptile (conclusion).

synonym A word with nearly the same meaning as another. *Infrequent, scarce, uncommon,* and *unusual* are all synonyms for *rare.* **Overlapping synonyms** (life, *liberty,* and *freedom*) are a common kind of wordiness. *See* **antonym.**

syntax *See* **grammar.**

temporal label *See* **label.**

tense The pattern of **verb** forms for expressing differences in time: **present tense, past tense, future tense,** and so forth.

thesis The main point or idea in a composition, particularly in **argumentation** and **exposition.** A thesis may be either implied or explicitly proposed in a **thesis statement.** A thesis is also an extensive research paper written in pursuit of an academic degree.

tone The writer's attitude toward the material as reflected in the **style.** The tone may also reflect the writer's attitude toward the reader. Good writing may be **ironic, sarcastic,** savage, complacent, nostalgic, straightforward—the variety of possible tones is endless.

topic The limited subject of a composition after the writer has staked out a specific claim in a broad subject area. The word *topic* may also apply to the unifying point of a **paragraph,** as in a **topic sentence,** or to any point in the organization of a paper, as in a **topic outline.**

topic outline *See* **outline.**

topic sentence A sentence, often at the beginning, that summarizes the unifying point in a **paragraph.**

transitions The links that provide **coherence** by connecting the sentences in a **paragraph** or the paragraphs in the composition as a whole. Transitions may be directly expressed (*however, moreover, therefore, for example. on the other hand*), or they may be implied by using **pronouns,** repetition, and **synonyms.**

transitive verb A **verb** that requires a **direct object** to complete its meaning: He *cleaned* the house while she *practiced* law.

understatement Achieving **irony** or **emphasis** with language more restrained than the reader might normally expect: Warfare is not one of the more humane outdoor sports of mankind. *See* **hyperbole.**

unity The quality of "oneness" achieved by focusing on a single point in a sentence, **paragraph,** or whole composition. Unity in a paragraph is often expressed in a **topic sentence;** the unifying idea of a whole composition may be summarized in a **thesis statement.**

upside-down subordination A sentence in which the main idea is put in a **subordinate clause** or **phrase:** He was living in San Francisco *when his house burned down.* Probably more logical (depending on the writer's intended emphasis): *When he was living in San Francisco,* his house burned down.

usage The way in which language is customarily used in speaking and writing. "Correct usage" reflects the socially acceptable practice of educated people. **Divided usage** means that there is no generally preferred choice between two or more expressions.

verb   A word used to express (1) action, (2) state, or (3) being: (1) The cat *drank* the milk. (2) The cat *appeared* content. (3) The cat *was* Siamese.

verb phrase   Two or more words forming a **verb:** The work *is finished.* We *have triumphed.*

verbal   A **verb** form that does the work of a **noun, adjective,** or **adverb** but does not carry the entire verb load in a **sentence.** The three verbals are **infinitive, participle,** and **gerund.** Verbals are not, like **finite verbs,** limited by **person** and **number.**

vogue word   An expression that is highly fashionable at a particular time but seldom survives as a useful addition to the language: I *could care less* (meaning *couldn't*); *hang-up; put-down; name of the game; you know?*

voice   The **verb** form indicating whether the **subject** acts **(active voice)** or is acted upon **(passive voice):** The treaty *ended* the war (active). The war *was ended* by the treaty (passive). Excessive use of the passive voice makes writing wordy.

Index

a, an, 282, 358
abbreviations: in footnotes and
    bibliography, 242–243;
    punctuation, 317; spelling,
    349–350; in the theme as a whole,
    350
above, 358
absolute (adjective and adverb), 302,
    374
absolute phrase, 89, 298, 374
abstract and concrete words,
    141–145, 197–198, 284, 374, 377
accept, except, 359
accusative case, *see* objective case
acknowledging indebtedness, 7; *see
    also* bibliography, footnotes
acronyms, 374
active vocabulary, 110–111
active voice, 100, 294, 390
adapt, adopt, 359
additions, 42
addresses, punctuation of, 326
adjectives: absolute, 302; clauses,
    312, 374; comparison, 301–302;
    contrasted with adverbs, 300;
    coordinate, punctuation of, 325;
    defined, 282, 374; demonstrative,
    305, 378; forms, 301; infinitives,

298; participles, 298; phrases,
    311–312, 375; position, 87;
    predicate, 302–303, 377, 383;
    pronominal, 300, 386
adjectivitis, 173–174
Adler, Mortimer J., 61–62, 328
adverbial conjunctions, *see*
    conjunctive adverbs
adverbs: assertion and concession,
    301; clauses, 311–312, 375;
    comparison, 301–302;
    conjunctive, 301, 327, 377;
    contrasted with adjectives, 300;
    defined, 282, 375; forms, 301;
    infinitives, 297–298; phrases,
    311–312, 375; position, 87–88;
    spelling, 344–345
affect, effect, 116, 359
aforementioned, aforesaid, 359
Agee, James, 336
aggravate, 359
Agle, Janet, 38
agree to, with, 359
agreement, 304–310, 375
ain't, 122, 359
Alice in Wonderland, 152
all, all of, 359
all-around, all-round, 359

all ready, 359
all right, 359
all together, altogether, 360
Allen, Frederick Lewis, 185
alliteration, 153–154, 375
Allport, Gordon W., 45
allusion, illusion, delusion, 359
allusions, 138
al, ly, final (spelling), 344–345
almost, 369; position of, 90
along with, agreement with, 305
alot, a lot, 359
already, all ready, 359
alright, all right, 359
also: position of, 90; punctuation
  with, 323
although, though, 359
altogether, all together, 360
ambiguity, punctuation to avoid, 326
American Heritage Dictionary and
  New College Edition, 112
amid, amidst, among, amongst, 360
Amis, Kingsley, 291
among, between, 361
amoral, immoral, 360
amount, number, 360
analogy: arguing from, 209–211;
  defined, 375
and: beginning a sentence with, 54;
  as coordinating conjunction, 304;
  punctuation with, 318–319,
  327–328
Anderson, Sherwood, 95–96
and/or, 360
anecdote for beginning, 38
anemic paragraphing, 56
Angell, Roger, 57–58
Anglo-Saxon words, 140
annotating, *see* footnotes
answers, incomplete sentences in, 80
antecedent of pronoun: agreement,
  307; defined, 375; reference,
  290–291
anticlimax, 375; punctuation of,
  333–334
antonyms, 114, 375
any, agreement with, 306
anybody, anyone, agreement with,
  306
anyone, any one, 360
any place, 360

anyways, anywheres, everywheres,
  nowheres, somewheres, 360
apology, 36
apostrophe, 347–348
apposition, appositive, 286, 375;
  punctuation of, 323
appraise, apprise, 360
appropriateness: of figures of speech,
  159–160; of style, 167–168; in the
  theme as a whole, 13–20; of tone,
  183; of words, 163
apt, liable, likely, 360
archaic words, 121, 375
argumentation (argument), 375; *see*
  also clear and cloudy thinking
argumentum ad hominem, 199, 375
Aristotle, 35, 158
Arnold, Matthew, 168
around, 360
articles (grammar), 282, 375
articles: in bibliography, 228–229;
  in footnotes, 239–241
as, 360
as a matter of fact, punctuation with,
  319
as, like, 368
as regards, 370
as to, 360
as well as, agreement with, 305
assonance, 153, 376
assumptions, faulty, 202–203, 380
atlases and gazetteers, 225
Auchincloss, Louis, 162
aural, 373
authorities: acknowledging
  indebtedness to, 7; discriminating
  among, 206–207; misinterpreting,
  207–208; *see also* bibliography,
  footnotes
autobiographical narrative, 32–33
auxiliary verbs, 293, 295, 376
average, median, 361
awful, 133–134, 378
awhile, a while, 361
awkwardness, 12

bad, badly, 302–303
Bagehot, Walter, 74
Baker, Carlos, 131
Baker, Russell, 165, 318, 334
balance, 155; *see also* parallelism

Baldwin, James, 37, 45, 58–59, 329, 361
Barnett, Lincoln, 153
Barzun, Jacques, 64–65, 144, 309–310
Bate, Walter Jackson, 22
Bates, Marston, 17–18, 331
because, reason is, 370
Becker, Carl L., 62–64, 105–106
begging the question, 203, 376
beginnings, 35–39, 44–45
being as, being that, 361
Bellow, Saul, 322, 336
Bennett, Arnold, 28–29, 52
Beringer, R., 80
beside, besides, 361
Bethell, Tom, 310
between, among, 361
bibliography: defined, 376; final, 243–244; preliminary, 226–229; specimen, 275–277
Bierce, Ambrose, 9, 74, 196
bimonthly, biweekly, 361
biographical references, 222
blank verse, 169–170
blends, 135, 376
Bolitho, William, 159
Bonney, Margaret K., 156
booksellers' guides, 226
Boorstin, Daniel, 60
born, borne, 361
both . . . and, 92–93
Boulding, Kenneth, 214
brackets, 235, 335–336
Bradley, John Hodgdon, 66
Brinton, Crane, 25
broad reference, 291
Bronowski, J., 138, 324
Brooks, Van Wyck, 325
Brown, Barbara, 81
Brown, John Mason, 166
Brown, Margery Finn, 104
Brown, Rollo Walter, 207
Bryan, William Jennings, 208
Buchan, John, 138
Buffon, Comte Georges de, 166
Bullitt, W. C., 214
Bülow, Baron Friedrich Wilhelm von, 198
Burgess, Gelett, 134
Burnett, George F., 188

Burrows, Millar, 15
business jargon (Commercialese), 176, 381
business letters, punctuation of, 327, 329
but: beginning a sentence with, 54; as coordinating conjunction, 304; punctuation with, 318–319, 327–328
but that, but what, 361

Caldwell, Erskine, 39
calendar words, capitalizing, 346
Campbell, Oscar James, 196, 309
can, may, 361
Canby, Henry Seidel, 159
Canby, Vincent, 162
cannot, can not, 361
can't hardly, scarcely, can't help but, 363
capital, capitol, 361
capital letters, 345–347
card catalogue, 219–220
caret, 42
Carlyle, Thomas, 211
Carroll, Lewis, 135
Carson, Rachel, 128, 187, 329
case: defined, 376; of nouns, 285; of pronouns, 288–290, 307
case, 99
Catlin, George, 20
Catton, Bruce, 79
cause and effect: defined, 376; in developing paragraphs, 64–65; in logical argument, 208–209
censor, censure, censer, 361–362
center around, 117, 362
character, 99
charged words, 147–151, 203, 376
Cheever, John, 45
Chesterton, G. K., 214, 330
childish, childlike, 362
Chomsky, Noam, 37–38
choosing a subject: for research, 218–219; for short themes, 30–33
Church, Joseph, 164, 292
Churchill, Winston, 170–173, 371
Chute, Marchette, 334
Ciardi, John, 74
circular reasoning, 203, 376
circumlocutions, 99, 175, 376

cite, sight, site, 362
citing authorities, 206–208; *see also* footnotes
clarity, 8–9
Clark, Kenneth, 327
clauses: coordinate and subordinate, 83–84, 312; defined, 312, 376; dependent and independent, 83–84, 312; elliptical, 89, 312, 379; introductory, punctuation of, 321–322; kinds, 312; main, punctuation of, 318–320, 327–328; nonrestrictive and restrictive, punctuation of, 322–323; series, punctuation of, 324–325, 329
clear and cloudy thinking: arguing from analogy, 209–211, 375; arriving at conclusions, 208–209; begging the question, 203, 376; citing authorities, 206–208; deduction vs. induction, 200–202, 378, 382; definition, 197–199; errors in deductive argument, 202–203; fallacies, defined, 196, 380; faulty assumptions, 202–203, 380; finding the facts, 204–205; ignoring the question, 199–200, 381; interpreting statistics, 205–206; opinion vs. prejudice, 196–197; problems of inductive argument, 204–211
clichés, 6, 39–40, 136–139, 158–159, 376; punctuation of, 138
Clifford, James L., 321
climax, punctuation of, 333–334
clipped forms, 349–350
clubs, capitalizing, 347
cobblestone rhetoric, 153, 176
Cohen, Felix S., 152, 204
coherence: defined, 376; in the paragraph, 53–54; in the theme as a whole, 47, 69
coinages, 134–135; with *-ize* (367) and *-wise* (373)
Colby, Frank Moore, 157–158
collective nouns, 284, 376; agreement with, 307
colloquialisms, 17, 122–123, 376–377

colon, 328–329
combination of methods in developing paragraphs, 65
commas: to avoid ambiguity, 326; after introductory elements, 321–322; between main clauses, 318–320; miscellaneous uses, 326–327; between parts of a series, 324–325; to set off nonessential elements, 322–324; with quotation marks, 332–333
comma fault (splice), 82, 319–320, 377
Commager, Henry Steele, 331–332
Commercialese, 176, 381
common nouns, 284, 377
Commoner, Barry, 64–65, 328
comparative degree, 301–302, 377
compare, contrast, 362
comparison and contrast in developing paragraphs, 62–64
comparison of adjectives and adverbs, 301–302, 377
comparisons, faulty, 93, 380
complement, 77; object(ive) and subject(ive), 286, 377
complete sentences, 77–78, 388
completeness: in the paragraph, 54–56; in the theme as a whole, 47–48, 69
complex sentence, 84, 377
complimentary close, punctuation of, 327
compound adjectives (spelling), 349
compound predicate, 77, 377
compound-complex sentence, 84, 377; punctuation of, 327–328
compound numbers and fractions (spelling), 348
compound sentence, 83, 377; punctuation of, 318–320, 327–328
compound subject, 77, 305, 377
compound words (spelling), 349
conclusions: in argument, 208–209; *see also* endings
concrete and abstract words, 141–145, 197–198, 284, 374, 377
conditional clauses, 296
conjugation, 382
conjunctions: defined, 282, 377;

conjunctions—*continued*
kinds, 303–304; punctuation with coordinating, 82, 318–319, 327–328; for transitions, 53–54
conjunctive adverbs, 301, 304, 377; punctuation with, 319–320; for transitions, 53–54
connectives, 282, 377; careless use of, 86
Connolly, Cyril, 111, 168
connotation, 127–128, 148–151, 377–378
Conrad, Joseph, 40
consensus, 362
considerable, 362
consistency: of level of usage, 20, 125; of number, 309; of point of view, 20; of sentence elements, 91–93; of tenses, 295–296; of tone, 183; *see also* clear and cloudy thinking, mixed metaphors
contact, 362
contact clauses, 320, 378
content, 5–6
context: defined, 378; ignoring, 207–208; importance of, 80–81, 163; learning the meaning of words from, 113
continual, continuous, 362
contractions, 122, spelling, 347
contrast, compare, 362
Cooke, Alistair, 109, 334
Coon, Carleton S., 38
Cooper, James Fenimore, 164
coordinate adjectives, punctuation with, 325
coordinate clauses, 83–86, 312, 378; punctuation of, 83, 318–320, 327–328
coordinating conjunctions, 304, 378; punctuation with, 318–319, 327–328
coordination in the sentence, 82–86, 378
corrections, 42
correctness, 10–12; in pronunciation, 115
correlative conjunctions, 304, 378; careless use of, 378
could of, 369

council, counsel, consul, 362
counterwords, 133–134, 378
couple, 362
courses, capitalizing, 346
credible, creditable, credulous, 362
criterion, criteria, 362
Cummings, E. E., 12
curious, 113–114
Curme, George O., 76
curriculum, curricula, 362–363
curves, 335
cute, 363

dangling modifiers, 88–89, 378
Darling, Edward, 204
Darwin, Charles, 208
dash, 329, 333–334
data, 363
dates: punctuation of, 326, 335; spelling of plurals, 348
declarative sentence, 77, 378
declension: defined, 382; of nouns, 285; of pronouns, 288–290
deduction, 200–203, 378
definite article, 282, 375
definition: of abstract words, 144–145; in beginning, 36; and clear thinking, 197–199; in developing paragraphs, 60–61; in dictionaries, 114, 119–126
degree (comparison), 303–304, 377
degrees, punctuation of, 326
deities, capitalizing, 346
deletions, 42
DeLillo, Don, 55
delusion, 359
De Mille, Agnes, 334
demonstrative adjectives, 305, 378
demonstrative pronouns, 287, 305, 378
Denney, Reuel, 37
denotation, 127–128, 148–151, 377–378
dependent clauses, 77–78, 83–86, 312, 378; punctuation of, 321–322
De Quincey, Thomas, 94
derivation (etymology), 114, 117–118, 379

description: defined, 375; incomplete sentences in, 80; specimen paragraphs, 57–58

details in developing paragraphs, 57–58

developing paragraphs, ways of, 56–65

De Vries, Peter, 26, 329

Dewey, John, 281

diaeresis, 348–349

dialectal words, 121, 379

dialogue: incomplete sentences in, 80; paragraphing of, 55; punctuation of, 323, 326, 330, 336

Dickens, Charles, 204, 206

Dickey, James, 91, 318

diction, 379, see words

dictionaries: choosing, 111–112; definitions, 36, 114, 119–126; denotation and connotation, 127–128; etymology, 114, 117–118; grammar and idioms, 116–117; kinds, 112, 221–222; labels and levels, 120–126; limitations, 129; looking up a word, 112–114; pronunciation, 114; spelling, 114, 342–343; synonyms and antonyms, 114

Didion, Joan, 57–58, 279

different from, than, 363

Dillard, Annie, 152

direct address, 286, 379; punctuation of, 323

direct discourse, 235, 379

direct object, 285, 293, 379

direct question, 379; punctuation of, 317

direct quotation, 379; punctuation of, 235–236, 326; see also dialogue

direct statement as a beginning, 37

directive phrases, 53–54

discreet, discrete, 363

discussion questions on examinations, 56

dishonesty, 7; see also plagiarism

disinterested, uninterested, 363

disunity, see unity

divided usage, 305, 358

division: in developing paragraphs, 61–62, 379; of words by syllables, 348

Dobrée, Bonamy, 167–168

Dodds, John W., 333

dots (ellipsis points), 235, 336, 379

double negative, 363

doublespeak, 147, 379

doubling final consonants, 343–344

dramatic incident as beginning, 39

Drew, Elizabeth, 329

Drucker, Peter F., 56

Duerr, Alvan E., 210–211

due to, 363

e, final silent (spelling), 344

each, agreement with, 306

each other, one another, 287

Earnest, Ernest, 207

economy, see wordiness

editorial we, 13–14

Edman, Irwin, 309

effect, affect, 116, 359

ei vs. ie (spelling), 343

Eiseley, Loren, 91, 162, 193

either: agreement with, 306; spelling, 343; usage, 363

either . . . or, agreement with, 305; parallelism, 92

either-or reasoning (false dilemma), 200, 380

elegant variation, 68

Eliot, T. S., 26, 183, 340

ellipsis, 235, 336, 379

elliptical clauses, 89, 379

Emerson, Ralph Waldo, 74

emigrate, immigrate, 363

eminent, imminent, 363

emphasis: defined, 379; in the paragraph, 56; by punctuation, 337; in the sentence, 80, 102–'06 in the theme as a whole, 48–49, 69

encyclopedias, 222–225; articles in bibliography and footnotes, 229, 240–241

endings, 39–40

endnotes, see footnotes

endorsing papers, 42, 245–246

enormity, enormousness, 363

enthuse, 363
equally as, 363
equivocation, 198–199, 379
essay questions on examinations, 56
etc., 350, 363–364
etymology, 114, 117–118, 379
euphemisms, 146–147, 379
euphony, 152–156, 379
evading the issue, 199–200, 381
Evans, Bergen, 204
even, position of, 90
every, everybody, everyone, agreement with, 306
everywheres, 360
evidence, evaluating, 208–209
exaggeration, 183–184, 381
examination answers, 56
except, accept, 359
excessive coordination, 85, 378
exclamation point, 317–318, 333
exclamations as incomplete sentences, 80
exclamatory sentence, 77, 378
exercises: clear and cloudy thinking, 211–216; getting under way, 44–45; good writing and correct English, 22–25; grammar, 284, 290, 292–293, 296, 299, 300, 303, 310, 313–314; organizing and developing, 70–75; punctuation, 320–321, 324, 330, 338–339; sentences, 79, 81, 82, 86–87, 90–91, 94, 97–98, 101, 106–109; spelling (lists), 350–357; style and tone, 186–195; What's in a word?, 111, 116, 117, 118, 120, 121, 126, 128, 129–130; words in action, 132–133, 135, 139, 145–146, 147, 151, 156, 161, 163–165
expletive, 308, 380
exposition, 375

fabulous, 133–134, 364, 378
fact that, 99, 364
factor, 364
facts: importance of, 5–6; vs. folklore and judgments, 204–205
Fadiman, William, 332

fallacies, 380; *see also* clear and cloudy thinking
false coordination, 84–85, 378
false dilemma, 200, 380
famed, famous, noted, notorious, 364
familiar quotations: as clichés, 136–138; punctuation, 331; reference books, 224
familiar tone, 14, 183
fantastic, 364
farther, further, 364
Faulkner, William, 151–152
faulty assumptions, 202–203, 380
faulty comparisons, 93, 380
faulty reference, 290–292, 387
feet, foot, 364
feminine, *see* gender
Ferguson, Otis, 154
Ferril, Thomas Hornsby, 186
fewer, less, 368
field, 99
figurative language (figures of speech), 156–161, 380
figures, *see* numbers, statistics
final *al, ly*, consonants, *e*, and *y* (spelling) 343–345
final draft, 42–43
finalize, 135, 367
fine, 134, 364
fine writing, 173–174, 380
finite verb, 77, 380
first draft, 33–35
firstly, 301, 364
Fischer, John, 329
flat writing, 172–173, 380
flaunt, flout, 364
Flesch, Rudolf, 96
folklore vs. facts, 204
Follett, Wilson, 279
foot, feet, 364
footnotes, 237–243, 269–273, 380
for: as coordinating conjunction, 304; punctuation with, 318–319, 327–328
foreign words and phrases, punctuation of, 337
form and content, 46
formal usage, 15–17, 380
former, latter, 364

Forster, E. M., 3, 37, 104
Fowler, H. W., 123, 139, 146, 221, 338
Fowles, John, 322
fractions, spelling of, 348
fragments, 78, 388
Frankel, Charles, 16−17, 94
free writing, 29−30
freshman, freshmen, 365
Freud, Sigmund, 214
friendly letters, punctuation of, 327, 329
Frost, Robert, 76, 152, 214
Funk and Wagnalls Standard College Dictionary, 112
further, farther, 364
fused sentence, 82, 387
future perfect tense, 295, 380
future tense, 295, 380

Galbraith, John Kenneth, 74, 101, 181−182, 307
Galsworthy, John 74
Gardner, John W., 38, 192
Garfield, James A., 74
gender: defined, 380; of nouns, 285; of pronouns, 286
generalizations, 201−202, 208−209
genitive case, *see* possessive case
genteelisms, 146
geographical words, capitalizing, 346
gerunds: dangling, 88; defined, 381; phrases, 311, 381; subject of, 298−299; uses, 298
get, got, gotten, 365
Gibson, Walker, 138, 320
Gilbert, W. S., 209
Glazer, Nathan, 37
glossaries. of grammatical and rhetorical terms, 374−390; of usage, 358−373
gobbledygook (jargon), 174−178, 381
Goldberg, Isaac, 315
Goldsmith, Oliver, 140
good, well, 302−303, 365
goon, the, 185
graduate, 365
grammar: adjectives and adverbs, 282, 300−303; agreement, 304−310; conjunctions, 282,

303−304; defined, 381; dictionary, 114, 116−117; importance of terms, 280−281; interjections, 282; nouns, 281, 284−286; parts of speech, 281−283; phrases and clauses, 311−312; prepositions, 282; pronouns, 281, 286−292; reference, 290−292; verbals, 297−299; verbs, 281, 293−296
grammatical terms, 374−390
Graves, Robert, 96
great, 133, 364
Greene, Graham, 103, 326
Gregg, Marjorie, 153
Gregory, Dick, 81
Gunther, John, 159
Guthrie, Tyrone, 299

hackneyed expressions, *see* clichés
had better, best, 365
had have, of, 365
had ought, hadn't ought, 365
Hadas, Moses, 103
Halle, Louis J., 307
Halper, Albert, 142
Hand, Learned, 187
hardly, 363
Hardwick, Elizabeth, 334
Hardy, Thomas, 101−102
have got, 365
Havens, George R., 332
Hazlitt, William, 163, 191
Heckscher, August, 305
Heggen, Thomas, 70, 307
heighth, 365
Hellman, Lillian, 105
Hemingway, Ernest, 5−6, 168−170, 319
Herring, Hubert, 141
herself, himself, 371
Hertzberg, Hendrik, 70
Himmelfarb, Gertrude, 310, 332
Hirsch, E. D., Jr., 46
historical present, 295, 381
Hodge, Alan, 96
Holmes, Oliver Wendell, 74, 177−178
homonyms, 350−353
honesty, 7
Hope, Anthony, 8

hopefully, 365
Horace, 140
Horgan, Paul, 103
Howard, Jane, 162, 331
Howe, Irving, 104
however, punctuation with, 319–320;
    usage, 365
Hoyle, Fred, 37
humor, 184–185
Humphreys, R. F., 80
Huxley, Aldous, 54, 74–75, 159
Huxley, Thomas Henry, 134,
    150–151, 167, 201, 210–211
hyperbole, 183–184, 381
hyphen, 333, 348–349
hypothesis, 201–202

I, 14
iambic pentameter, 155, 169–170
identical rhyme, 153
idioms, 116–117, 381
ie vs. *ei* (spelling), 343
ignoring the context, 207–208
ignoring the question, 199–200, 381
illiterate usage, 122
illusion, allusion, delusion, 359
illustration: in definition, 144–145;
    in developing paragraphs, 58–59;
    punctuation of, 329
illustrative anecdote as beginning,
    38–39
immigrate, emigrate, 363
imminent, eminent, 363
immoral, amoral, 360
imperative mood, 294, 381
imperative sentence, 77, 378
imply, infer, 365
in addition to, agreement with, 305
in fact, punctuation with, 319
in, into, 365
in regard(s), 370
inappropriateness, *see*
    appropriateness
inchworm transitions, 68
incoherence, *see* coherence
incomparable terms, 93
incomplete comparisons, 93
incomplete sentences, 78–81, 388
inconsistency, *see* consistency
indefinite articles, 282, 375

indefinite pronouns, 287, 381;
    agreement with, 306–307
indention (indentation): defined,
    381; of paragraphs, 49; of
    quotations, 235, 331
independent clauses, 77–78, 312,
    381; punctuation of, 82, 319–320,
    327
indexes, periodical, 220–221
indicative mood, 294, 381
indirect discourse, 235, 379
indirect object, 285, 381
indirect question, 379, 382;
    punctuation of, 317
indirect quotation, 379; punctuation
    of, 331
individual, person, party, 366
induction (inductive reasoning), 150,
    200–202, 204–211, 382
infer, imply, 365
infinite predication, 100
infinitives: dangling, 88; in
    incomplete sentences, 77; phrases
    311–312, 382; split, 90, 371, 388;
    uses, 297–298, 382
inflection, 382
inflectional endings, 116
informal usage, 17–18, 122–123, 382
ingenious, ingenuous, 366
inside of, 366
insincerity, 8
instance, instant, 366
intensive pronouns, 287, 382
interjections, 282, 382; punctuation
    with, 323
interrogative pronouns, 287, 382
interrogative sentence, 77, 378
interrupters, punctuation of,
    322–324, 334
into, in, 365
intransitive verbs, 293, 382
introductory elements, punctuation
    of, 321–322
inversion, 103, 382
irony, 182, 382; punctuation of,
    331–332
irregardless, 122, 366
irregular verbs, 300, 382; list of,
    366–367
is when, is where, 367

isolation, 48, 102–103, 382
it as an expletive, 308, 380
It is I, me, she, etc., 13, 288–289
italics, 336–337
its, it's, 288, 348
-ize, 12, 135, 176, 367

jargon (gobbledygook), 174–178, 381
Jarrell, Randall, 333
Jespersen, Otto, 12
jigger, the, 185–186
Johnson, Samuel, 111, 119, 129–130, 140, 145, 191
Joubert, Joseph, 131
journal, keeping a, 27–29
Journalese, 176, 382
Joyce, James, 12
judgments vs. facts, 204–205

Kael, Pauline, 123
Kandel, Bethany, 164–165
Kant, Immanuel, 94
Kazin, Alfred, 318, 320
Keats, John, 37, 135, 138, 216
Kennan, George, 80
Kerr, Walter, 55
Kilpatrick, James J., 137
kind of, sort of, 367
King, Martin Luther, Jr., 189, 328
Kinsey Report, 205
Knowles, John, 157–158
Krutch, Joseph Wood, 209–210
Kwitney, Jonathan, 37

labels, dictionary, 120–126, 382–383
Lardner, Ring, 134
Lask, Thomas, 91
Latin words, 140
latter, former, 364
lay, lie, 367
Le Carré, John, 162
Leacock, Stephen, 8, 34
lead, led, 367
leave, let, 367–368
led, lead, 367
Legalese, 176, 381
lend, loan, 368
length: of paragraphs, 54–56; of sentences, 94–97; of words, 140–141

Lerner, Alan J., 321
less, fewer, 368
let, leave, 367–368
letter writing, punctuation of, 327, 329
letters of the alphabet: punctuation of, 335; spelling plurals of, 347–348
levels of usage, 15–20, 120, 122–126, 383
Lewis, C. Day, 164
Lewis, C. S., 192–193
Lewis, D. B. Wyndham, 337
liable, apt, likely, 360
library research paper: bibliography, 226–229, 243–244, 275–277; card catalogue, 219–220; choosing and limiting a subject, 218–219; definition of research, 217–218; discriminating among sources, 229–231; finding material, 219–226; footnotes and endnotes, 237–243; note-taking, 231; outlines, 231–233, 247; quotation and paraphrase, 234–237; reference works, 220–226; specimen paper, 245–277; writing the paper, 233–237
lie, lay, 367
light tone, 185–186
lighted, lit, 368
like, as 368
likely, apt, liable, 360
limiting a subject: for research, 218–219; for short themes, 31–33
Lincoln, Abraham, 91–92, 211
Lindbergh, Anne Morrow, 109
linguistics, 383
linking verbs, 286, 293, 383
Lipton, Lawrence, 134
listing, 55
lit, lighted, 368
literal language, 383
literally, 368
literary definition, 60
Livesey, Herbert, 323
loaded words, 147–151, 203, 376
loan, lend, 368
localisms, 121, 123, 383
logic, *see* clear and cloudy thinking
long sentences, 94–97

long words, 140–141
loose, lose, 368
loose sentences, 104, 385
lot, lots, 368
loud, loudly, 301
lovely, 133, 364
Lowell, Robert, 154
Lucas, F. L., 3, 45, 123
Lurie, Alison, 163
luxuriant, luxurious, 368
Lynes, Russell B., 24, 123, 161, 307

Macdonald, Dwight, 135, 307
magazines, *see* periodical indexes, titles
Mailer, Norman, 60, 91
main clauses, *see* independent clauses
main point, choosing a, 34
major premise, 201, 389
majority, plurality, 368
Malamud, Bernard, 80
malapropisms, 131–132, 383
Malcolm X, 320
manuscript, 42–43
Mannes, Marya, 195
March, Robert H., 62–64
margins, 42
Markel, Lester, 192
Markowitz, Charles, 162
"Martians and Mass Hysteria" (specimen research paper), 246–277
Martin, Thomas I., Jr., 321–322
marvelous, 133, 364, 378
masculine, *see* gender
Maugham, W. Somerset, 109, 126, 181–182
Maverick, Maury, 174
may, can, 361
McCarthy, Mary, 149
McClelland, David C. K., 70
McGinley, Phyllis, 103
medium, media, 368
Mencken, H. L., 38, 44, 74, 151
Menzel, Donald H., 144–145
Meredith, George, 37
merely, position of, 90
Messinger, Karl, 324
metaphor, 156–161, 383
meter, 154–155, 169–170, 383

Michener, James, 81
might of, 369
Milburn, George, 23
Miller, Arthur, 100
Miller, Henry, 81
Milstein, Gilbert, 113
minor premise, 201, 389
misplaced modifiers, 89–90, 383
misrelated modifiers, 88–90, 383
mixed metaphors, 160–161, 383
MLA Handbook, 226, 237
mnemonics in spelling, 345
modifiers: dangling, 88–89; defined, 282, 383; misplaced, 89–90; nonrestrictive and restrictive, 322–323; position of, 87–88; squinting, 89
Montagu, Ashley, 204
mood, 294, 383–384
Moore, Kenny, 327
moral, morale, 368
moreover, punctuation with, 319
Morgan, Elaine, 44
Morgulis, Sergius, 324
Morley, Christopher, 54
Morris, Desmond, 327
Morrison, Donald R., 190
Morton, Charles, 141
most, 369
Muller, Herbert J., 71, 329
Mumford, Lewis, 194
Murray, K. M. Elizabeth, 108
Murry, J. Middleton, 166–167, 173
Myers, Henry Alonzo, 24
myself, 371

Nabokov, Vladimir, 76, 134
name-calling, 203
narration (narrative), 375
naturalness, 20–21, 139
nature, 99
neither: agreement with, 306; spelling, 343; usage, 363
neither . . . nor: agreement with, 305; parallelism, 92
neologisms, *see* coinages
neuter, *see* gender
neutral words, 147–151, 376
nevertheless, punctuation with, 319
New English Dictionary, 112, 221

no one, 306, 360
no place, 360
no reference, 291
nobody, no one, agreement with, 306
nominative case, *see* subjective case
nonce words, 135
none, agreement with, 306–307
nonessential elements, punctuation
  of, 322–324
nonrestrictive modifiers: defined,
  384; punctuation of, 322–323; *that*
  and *which,* 287, 372
non sequitur, 209, 384
nonstandard usage, 18–19, 122, 384
nonstop sentences, 97
nor: agreement with, 305; beginning
  a sentence with, 54; as
  coordinating conjunction, 304;
  position with *neither,* 92;
  punctuation with, 318–319,
  327–328
not only . . . but also, 92–93
noted, notorious, famed, famous, 364
notes, rough for first draft, 33–34
note-taking, 231
nouns: case, 285; clauses, 312, 384;
  collective, agreement with, 307,
  376; defined, 281, 384; direct
  address, 286; gender, 285; gerunds,
  298–299; infinitives, 297; kinds,
  284; number, 285; phrases, 311,
  384; uses, 285–286
nowheres, 360
number, amount, 360
numbering: footnotes, 237; pages, 42;
  short paragraphs, 55
numbers: punctuation of, 327, 335;
  spelling, 347–348, 350

object, 285, 384
objective case, 288–290, 376
object(ive) complement, 286, 377
obsolete words, 121, 375
of, 369
off of, 369
Officialese, 176, 381
Ogilvy, David, 164
O'Hara, John, 24–25
omissions: in contractions, 347; in
  manuscript, 42; in quotations
  (ellipsis), 235, 336

on the other hand, punctuation with,
  319
one, 309
one another, each other, 287
one of those who, agreement with,
  307
one-word, one-meaning fallacy, 119
only, position of, 90
onomatopoeia, 154, 384
opinion vs. prejudice, 196–197
or: agreement with, 305; beginning a
  sentence with, 54; as coordinating
  conjunction, 304; position with
  either, 92; punctuation with,
  318–319, 327–328
oral, verbal, 373
order, 47
organization, 9, 45–75
origin of words, *see* etymology
originality, 6–7; *see also* clichés
ornate style, 168–172, 384
Orwell, George, 8, 108, 131, 146–147,
  158–159, 164, 334
Osmond, Humphrey, 134
Otto, Max C., 60–61
ought, 365
outlines, 34, 231–233, 247, 384
outside of, 369
overlapping synonyms, 98–99, 389
overstatement, 183–184, 381
overweight construction, 100,
  384–385
Oxford English Dictionary, 112, 221

pair, 369
Papanek, John, 123
paradox, 385
paragraphing: anemia, 56;
  coherence, 53–54; completeness,
  54–56; defined, 385; dialogue, 55;
  emphasis, 56; length, 54–56;
  listing, 55; purposes, 49–50;
  repetition, 65–68; topic sentence,
  50–52; transitions, 53–54; unity,
  50–53; ways of developing, 56–65
parallelism: defined, 385; in the
  paragraph, 54; in the sentence,
  91–93, 102, 105–106
paraphrase, 234–237, 385
parentheses, 42, 317, 335
Parker, William Riley, 217

participles: dangling, 88; in incomplete sentences, 77; phrases, 311, 385; uses, 298, 385
Partridge, Eric, 123
parts of speech, 161, 281–283, 385
party, individual, person, 366
passive voice, 99–100, 294, 390
past perfect tense, 295–296, 385
past tense, 295, 385
Pater, Walter, 191–192
Pedagese, 176, 381
parenthetical expressions, punctuation of, 322–324
period, 316, 332–333
period fault, 78, 388
periodic sentences, 104, 385
periodical indexes, 220 221
periodical titles: in bibliography, 228–229; in footnotes, 239–240; punctuation of, 336–337
Perkins, Maxwell, 37
Perry, Ralph Barton, 203
persecute, prosecute, 369
person, individual, party, 366
personal pronouns: agreement, 305–307, 309; case, 288–289; defined, 286, 385; spelling, 348
person, 13–14, 288, 293, 305, 307, 309, 385
personal tone, 183
personification, 137, 345–346, 385
persons, capitalizing, 345–346
phenomenon, phenomena, 369
phrases: dangling, 88–89; defined, 311, 385–386; introductory, punctuation of, 321–322; kinds, 311–312; misplaced, 89–90; nonrestrictive and restrictive, punctuation of, 322–333; series, punctuation of, 324–325, 329
Pirsig, Robert, 80
places, punctuation of, 326
plagiarism, 7, 218, 386
plain style, 168–172, 386
plan on, plan to, 369
playwrite, 369
plural, 287, 347–348, 384
plurality, majority, 368
poetry: capitals in, 345; quoting, 234–235
point of view, 13–14, 183, 386

Pope, Alexander, 138
portmanteau words, 135, 376
position: for emphasis, 49, 102–104, of modifiers, 87–88; of quotation marks, 332–333
positive degree, 301, 377
possessive case: defined, 376; with gerunds, 298–299; of nouns, 285; of pronouns, 288–289; spelling, 347–348
post hoc, ergo propter hoc, 209, 384
precede, proceed, procedure, 369
predicate, 77, 386; adjective, 302–303, 377, 383; noun (nominative), 293, 297, 377, 383
predominant, predominate, 369
predication, reducing, 100
prefixes: 111, 387; spelling, 348–349
prejudice vs. opinion, 196–197
prejudice, 369
premises, 201, 389
prepositions: defined, 282, 386; at the end of a sentence, 369; object of, 288–290; phrase, 311, 386
present perfect tense, 295–296, 386
present tense, 295, 386
presently, 369
pretty, 370
pre-writing, 26–30
Price, Reynolds, 95–96
primer prose, 84, 96–97, 386
principal, principle, 370
principal clauses, *see* independent clauses
principal parts: 299–300; of irregular verbs, 366–367
proceed, procedure, precede, 369
Prokosch, Frederic, 150–151
pronominal adjectives, 300, 386
pronouns: agreement, 305–310; to avoid repetition, 68; case, 288–290, 307; defined, 281, 386–387; gender, 286; kinds, 286–287; reference, 290–292, 387; spelling, 348; for transitions, 53–54
pronunciation: 114–115; and spelling, 341
proper nouns, 284, 387
prophecy, prophesy, 370
proportion, 49, 387

prosecute, persecute, 369
proved, proven, 370
proverbs, overworked, 136–137
provided, providing, 370
punctuation: close and open, 315;
  colon, 328–329· comma, 318–327;
  comma fault, 82, 319–320; dash,
  333–334; dots (ellipsis points),
  336, exclamation point, 317;
  overpunctuating, 315–316;
  parentheses, 335–336; period,
  316–317; question mark, 317;
  quotation marks, 330–333,
  reasons, 316; semicolon, 327–328;
  square brackets, 335–336; and
  tone, 186; underlining (italics),
  335–336
purpose, 15, 34

question mark, 317, 333
questions: in beginnings, 37–38
  direct and indirect, 317, 379, 382;
  as incomplete sentences, 80;
  rhetorical, 38, 317, 387
quick, quickly, 301
Quiller-Couch, Sir Arthur, 20, 174
Quinn, Sally, 335
quite, 370
quotation marks, 234–236; position
  of, 332–333; right and wrong uses
  of, 330–333
quotations: in beginnings, 38;
  capitalizing, 345; as clichés,
  136–138; interpolated comments
  in, 335–336; omissions in, 336;
  punctuating, 235, 326–327,
  329–333; reference books, 224; in
  research papers, 234–236
quote(s), 370

raise, rise, 370
Random House College Dictionary,
  112
*Random House Dictionary of the
  English Language,* 112
rarely ever, seldom ever, 370
rationalizing, 197
Read, Herbert, 46, 155
reader, the, 14
reading aloud, 41, 67, 340
real, 370

reason is because, 370
reasoning, *see* clear and cloudy
  thinking
reciprocal pronouns, 282, 387
reckon, 370
recognition vocabulary, 110–111
reducing predication, 100
redundancy, *see* wordiness
reference of pronouns, 290–292, 387
reference works: atlases and
  gazetteers, 225; biographical, 222;
  booksellers' guides, 226;
  dictionaries, 221–222;
  encyclopedias and others,
  222–226; general use, 41;
  periodical indexes, 220–221;
  yearbooks, 225
references: in bibliography,
  226–229, 243–244, 275–277, 376;
  in footnotes, 237–243, 269–273,
  380
reflexive pronouns, 287, 387
regard, regards, respect, 370
regional words, 121, 382–383
regular verbs, 300, 387
relative pronouns: case, 288–290;
  defined, 286–287, 387; spelling,
  289, 348; *who* and *whom,* 289–290
remote reference, 291, 387
repetition: device and vice, 65–68;
  for emphasis, 49, 102, 105; and
  gobbledygook, 175; of same
  thought in different words, 98–99;
  for transitions, 53–54; *see also*
  wordiness
report writing, *see* library research
  paper
research paper, *see* library research
  paper
respective(ly), 370
restrictive modifiers: defined, 387;
  punctuation of, 322–323; *that* and
  which, 287
Reston, James, 310
revision, 40–41
rhetoric, 387
rhetorical questions, 38, 317, 387
rhetorical terms, 374–390
rhyme, 153, 387
rhythm, 154–155, 387
Riesman, David, 37

rise, raise, 370
Roberts, Paul, 340
Robertson, R. B., 335
Robinson, Henry Morton, 203
Robinson, James Harvey ˀ17
Roethke, Theodore 110
Rogers, Will, 12
Roget's Thesaurus, 68 126, 222
roots, 11, 387
round, around, 360
Rovere, Richard, 133
rules for correct writing, 10–12
Ruml, Beardsley, 190
run, meanings of, 119–120
run-on (fused) sentence 82 387

Safire, William, 44
Salinger, J. D., 13
salutation in letters, punctuation of,
 327
same, 370
sarcasm, 382
satire, 382, 387
Sayles, John, 37
Schulberg, Budd, 108–109
Sears, Paul B., 208
seldom ever, 370
selecting a subject: for research,
 218–219; for short themes, 30–33
self, 371
semantics, 110, 388; *see also* words
semicolon, 319–320, 324, 327–329,
 333
sensual, sensuous, 371
sentence fragment, 78, 388
sentence outline, 222–233, 384
sentences: complete and incomplete,
 77–81, 388; coordination and
 subordination, 82–86; defined,
 76–78, 388; economy, 98–100;
 emphasis, 102–106; fragment, 78,
 388; kinds, 77, 83–84; length,
 94–97; loose and periodic, 104;
 modifiers, 77, 87–90; parallelism,
 102, 105–106; run-on (fused), 82;
 summary, 107; variety, 101–102
sequence of tenses, 295–296
series, punctuation of, 324–325,
 328–329, 334
set, sit, 371
Sevareid, Eric, 23, 80

Shakespeare, William, 12, 138, 145,
 148, 216
shall, will, 371
Shaw, Bernard, 74, 166–167
Sheridan, Richard Brinsley, 26, 131
shifted constructions, 92, 296, 309,
 388
shoptalk, 124, 332
short paragraphs, 55–56
short sentences, 94–97, 103
short words, 140–141
should of, 369
Siamese twin sentences, 53, 84–85
sic, 243, 336
sight, cite, site, 362
silent *e* (spelling), 344
Sillitoe, Alan, 154
simile, 156–160, 383
Simon, Kate, 193–194
simple sentence, 82–83, 388
sincerity, 8
single quotation marks, 332
sit, set, 371
site, cite, sight, 362
slang: 122–125, 388; punctuation of,
 331–332
slow, slowly, 301
Smith, Adam, 321
Smith, Red, 134
Snow, C. P., 213
so, so that, 371
soft, softly, 301
Solberg, Carl, 51
some place, 360
somebody, someone, agreement with,
 306
someone, spelling of, 360
somewheres, 360
sort of, 367
sound of words, 152–156, 379
sources, *see* reference works
Spacespeak, 176
specie, species, 371
specific writing, 9, 57–58, 69
speech and writing, 20–21
spelling: abbreviations, 349–350;
 apostrophe, 347–348; capitals,
 345–347; conventions, 343–350;
 dictionary, 114, 342–343; good
 and bad spellers, 340; hyphen,
 348–349; importance, 341;

spelling—*continued*
lists, 350—357; mnemonics, 345; numbers, 350; pronunciation, 341; reading aloud, 341; rules, five useful, 343—345
split infinitive, 90, 371, 388
square brackets, 235, 335—336
squinting modifiers, 89
squinting reference, 291, 387
staking out a claim, 31—33
standard English, 18, 388
statistical fallacy, 205—206, 388
statistics, interpreting, 205—206
status labels, 382—383
Stebbing, L. Susan, 139
Steffens, Lincoln, 66
Stein, Gertrude, 12, 147—148, 315
Stein, Leo, 164
Steiner, George, 110
Stephen, James, 7
Stinnett, Caskie, 325
Strachey, Lytton, 33, 51—52
Strunk, William, Jr., 105
style: 166—178; defined, 166—168, 388; flat writing and fine writing, 172—174; gobbledygook (jargon), 174—178; plain and ornate, 168—172, 384, 386
subconscious, using the, 33
subject: defined, 388; of a gerund, 298—299; of a sentence, 77—78, 285
subject of a composition: announcing, 37; research papers, 218—219; selecting and limiting, 30—33
subjective case, 288—289, 376
subject(ive) complement, 286, 377
subjunctive mood, 294, 388
subordinate clauses, *see* dependent clauses
subordinating conjunctions, 77—78, 304, 388
subordination in the sentence, 82—86
substandard usage, 19, 122
substantives, 281, 388; *see also* nouns, pronouns
such, such as, 371
suffixes, 111, 387
Sullivan, Frank, 238
superlative degree, 301—302, 377
suppose, supposed, 372

sure, surely, 372
Swift, Jonathan, 129, 182, 190—191
Sykes, Christopher, 25
syllable division, 348
syllogism, 201, 389
synechdoche, 160
synonyms: and antonyms, 114, 126; to avoid repetition, 68; defined, 114, 126, 389; overlapping, 98 -99 389; for transitions, 53—54

taking notes, 231
temporal labels, 382
tenses, 295—296, 389
term paper, *see* library research paper
terms, grammatical and rhetorical, 374—390
terrible, 133—134, 378
terrific, 133—134, 364
than, 372
that, which, 287, 372
there is, was, are, were, 99, 380; agreement with, 308
there, their, they're, 372
therefore, punctuation with, 319
thesauruses, 68, 126, 222
these kind, those kind, 308
thesis, 32, 34, 389
thesis statement, 32, 389
thinking, *see* clear and cloudy thinking
this, 372
Thomas, Dylan, 152
Thomas, Lewis, 65—66, 195, 310
Thompson, Lawrance, 307
Thoreau, Henry David, 14, 197
though, 359
Thurber, James, 105, 134, 148, 154, 184—185
thusly, 372
tight, tightly, 301
till, until, 'til, 372
"Time and the Machine," 74—75
title page, 245—246
titles: capitalizing, 346—347; choosing, 43; position of, 42; punctuation of, 331, 336—337
titles and degrees, capitalizing, 345—346

Tobias, Sheila, 55
to, too, 372
together with, agreement with, 305
tone: defined, 178–179, 389; examples, 179–182; hints, 182–186
topic, 32–33, 389
topic outline, 232–233, 384
topic sentence, 32, 50–53, 389
toward, towards, 372
Toynbee, Arnold, 16–17
transitions: defined, 389; incomplete sentences for, 80; between paragraphs, 69; within the paragraph, 53–54; punctuation of, 323; short paragraphs for, 55
transitive verbs, 293, 389
tremendous, 333, 364
Trilling, Lionel, 337
triteness, *see* clichés
truisms, 35–36, 39–40
try and, to, 372
Tuchman, Barbara, 104, 109, 188
Turner, R., 134
Twain, Mark, 13, 22–23, 132, 134, 184
type, 372
typing, 42
typographical errors, 11

underlining, 336–337
understatement, 185, 389
unfinished sentences, punctuation of, 333, 336
uninterested, disinterested, 363
unique, 302, 372
unity: defined, 389; in the paragraph, 50–53; in the theme as a whole, 47, 68–69
until, till, 'til, 372
Updike, John, 108, 319
upside-down subordination, 85, 389
usage: defined, 389; dictionaries, 221; glossary of, 358–373; levels of, 15–20, 120, 122–126, 383
usage, use, 372–373
Ustinov, Peter, 109, 162
utilize, 367

vagueness, 8–9
variety in sentence structure, 101–102

verbal, oral, 373
verbals, 77, 297–299, 390
verbs: agreement, 305–309; defined, 281, 390; finite, 77, 297, 380; kinds, 293; mood, 294; phrases, 311, 390; principal parts, 299–300, 386; tenses, 295–296; voice, 294
very, 373
Victoria, Queen, 337
vocabulary: building, 110–111; gobbledygook, 175–178; *see also* words
vogue words, 133, 390
voice, 99–100, 294, 390
Voltaire, François Marie Arouet de, 197
Von Bülow, Baron Friedrich Wilhelm, 198
vulgar usage, 19, 122

Walker, Alice, 38, 71
Wallbank, Walter, 333
Warren, Austin, 337
Washington, George, 207–208
Waugh, Evelyn, 164
way, ways, 373
we, 13–14
Webster's New Collegiate Dictionary, 112
Webster's New Dictionary of Synonyms, 126
Webster's New World Dictionary, 112
Webster's Third New International Dictionary, 112, 221
Weldon, T. D., 164
well, good, 302–303, 365
Wellek, René, 337
when, where, 367
which, that, 287, 372
while, 373
White, E. B., 13, 27, 65, 105, 148, 188–189, 194, 335
White, T. H., 328
Whitehead, Alfred North, 196
Whitehorn, Katharine, 214
who, whom, 289–290
whose, who's, 289, 348
Whyte, William H., Jr., 23–24
will, shall, 371
Wilson, Edmund, 327, 334, 336

-*wise*, 12, 373
with, agreement with, 305
with regard(s) to, 370
Wolfe, Thomas, 37, 168–170
wonderful, 133, 364
Woolf, Virginia, 28–29, 101–102
word order, inverted, 103, 382
wordiness: and gobbledygook, 175;
  in the paragraph, 67–68; in the
  sentence, 98–100; in the theme as
  a whole, 9–10
words: archaic and obsolete, 121,
  375; charged and neutral,
  147–151, 376; clichés, 136–139,
  376; coinages, 134–135, 376;
  colloquialisms, 122–123,
  376–377; concrete and abstract,
  141–145, 374, 377; counterwords,
  133–134, 378; definitions,
  119–126; denotation and
  connotation, 127–128, 148,
  377–378; dictionary use, 110–129;
  etymology, 117–118, 379;
  euphemisms, 146–147, 379; fresh
  and tired, 133–139; grammar and
  idioms, 116–117, 381; labels,

120–126, 382–383; levels of usage,
  122–126; 382–383; local and
  dialectal, 121, 379, 385; long and
  short, 140–141; malapropisms,
  131, 383; nonstandard, 122, 384;
  pronunciation, 115; right and
  wrong, 131–132; simile and
  metaphor, 156–161, 383; slang,
  123–125, 388; sound, 152–156;
  synonyms and antonyms, 114, 375,
  389; vocabulary building,
  110–114; vogue words, 133
words-as-words, punctuation and
  spelling of, 331–332, 337, 347–348
would have (of), 373
Wright, Nathan, Jr., 156
Wright, Richard, 35
writing and speech, 20–21
wrong reference, 291, 387
wrong, wrongly, 301

y, final (spelling), 344
yearbooks, 225
yet, punctuation with, 318–319,
  327–328
you, 309–310

Notes

Notes

A QUICK QUESTIONNAIRE FOR THE WRITER

1. Have you chosen a subject you can handle and limited it to a clearly defined topic? (30–33)
2. Does your beginning get the reader off to a good start? (35–39)
3. Do you have at least one main point or thesis? (34)
4. Does your paper follow an orderly plan? (34)
5. Is each paragraph unified around a single point? (50–53)
6. Do you progress by smooth, logical transitions between sentences and paragraphs? (47, 53–54)
7. Are your paragraphs well-developed? (56–65)
8. Have you used specific details or illustrations, avoiding unsupported generalities? (9, 57- 59)
9. Have you eliminated all wordiness, including unnecessary repetition? (65–68, 98–100)
10. Do the parts all fit into a whole composition? (68–69)
11. Are your sentences monotonously alike in length and structure? Or have you aimed at variety and emphasis? (84, 101–106)
12. Have you used your dictionary regularly to check on any meaning or spelling in doubt? (110–130)
13. Is your language appropriate and consistently sustained on the same level? (13–20, 122–126)
14. Have you chosen your words carefully, considering both denotation and connotation? (127–128, 148)
15. Have you eliminated all overworked expressions and confused or inappropriate figures of speech? (133–139, 156–161)
16. Wherever possible, have you preferred concrete to abstract words? (141–145)
17. Is anything in the paper ambiguous, vague, or misleading? (8–9)
18. Have you said simple things simply without settling for flat writing? (172–173)
19. Have you eliminated all passages of fine writing and gobbledygook? (173–178)
20. Is your tone appropriate and consistent? (183)
21. Are your opinions based on accurate facts and logical reasoning? (5–6, 196–216)
22. Have you clearly distinguished quotation from paraphrase and properly acknowledged all indebtedness? (7, 234–244)
23. Did you revise your first draft thoroughly before making the final copy? (40–41)
24. Did you read the final copy aloud, neatly correcting all mechanical errors, including typos? (42–43)
25. Does the ending follow logically from the beginning and the middle, or have you tacked one on or merely stopped when you ran out of gas? (39–40)